THE ULTIMATE EU TEST BOOK

Assessment Centre 2021

Working for the EU:
How to Get In

By Johannes de Berlaymont

€17
Local prices may vary

ISBN: 9781999959531

'I think you should stress one positive particularity of working in the institutions; nobody works here by accident. Given the whole competitive selectiveness of the system – no matter which way you get in – there are hardly any of the indifferent, random colleagues one encounters in other organisations. Most colleagues worked really hard to get in. That changes the dynamics. People want to be here.'

A quote from one of the many EU officials who contributed their insights to the book

This is *the* book for anyone wanting to know about the opportunities a career in the EU public administration can provide – and the many different ways to 'get in'. It is also highly relevant to those already with temporary positions or internships who want to move their careers forward. Among the many topics covered are:

- The wide range of positions in the EU institutions and agencies, in Brussels, Luxembourg and worldwide
- The types, advantages and disadvantages of permanent and temporary posts
- How temporary posts can become stepping stones to permanent or very long-term jobs
- The critical difference between being selected and being recruited – and how recruitment really works
- The little-known alternatives to passing an open competition
- The value of *stages* and other types of traineeships
- The crucial importance of building your networks
- Why and how you should think strategically, keeping as many options open as possible

Johannes de Berlaymont is the nom de plume of a widely experienced former EU insider.

For the latest information about all our books visit

www.johnharperpublishing.co.uk

www.eu-testbook.com

€35
Local prices may vary

ISBN: 9780993454936

WITH ACCOMPANYING FREE-TO-USE ONLINE TOOLKIT

The Ultimate EU Career Development Book

By Jan De Sutter

This book shows you how to evaluate and improve your personal performance in the EU core competencies, for job satisfaction and career advancement.

It is designed for all EU staff at all levels, permanent, temporary or contract and is supported by a free online toolkit. The main focus of the book is an in-depth exploration of the EU core competencies:

- analysis and problem solving
- communicating
- delivering quality and results
- learning and development
- prioritising and organising
- resilience
- working with others
- leadership

Coach, trainer and former EU official Jan De Sutter draws on the best ideas and practice in current management thinking and applies them to the specific context of EU institutions. He explains how the competencies fit into the overall EU system for staff selection, appraisal and promotion and the book is amply illustrated with practical examples.

THE ULTIMATE EU TEST BOOK
ASSESSMENT CENTRE 2021

András Baneth and Jan De Sutter

JOHN HARPER PUBLISHING

The Ultimate EU Test Book Assessment Centre 2021

ISBN 978-1-8380898-2-5

Published by John Harper Publishing
27 Palace Gates Road
London N22 7BW, United Kingdom.
www.johnharperpublishing.co.uk
Sales and distribution: Turpin Distribution Services Ltd.

First edition May 2015
Revised impression January 2016
2018 Edition February 2018
2019 Edition November 2018
2020 Edition March 2020
2021 Edition February 2021

Typeset mainly in 9 & 10/11pt Palatino
Printed and Bound in the UK by Severn

TABLE OF CONTENTS

ABOUT THE AUTHORS

ANDRÁS BANETH, an SHL-certified assessor, is a trainer, consultant and partner at Arboreus EU Training. His bestselling Ultimate EU Test Book has helped thousands of candidates prepare for EPSO competitions since 2005. András has a wide knowledge of EU policies, institutions and communication, his career having included seven years' experience at the European Commission and the European Court of Justice, where his roles included coordinating briefings for Commission President Barroso and serving as member of the cabinet of Commissioner Kovács. He holds an M.A. in law and political sciences and the degree of Master of European Public Administration from the College of Europe, Bruges, Belgium. He is always open to invitations to speak about EU careers, strategic communication or public affairs. His personal website is available at www.baneth.eu and his direct e-mail is andras@baneth.eu

JAN DE SUTTER, after a career in IT, defence systems and people management, joined the European Economic and Social Committee in 2000, where he was Head of Unit of the budget and finance department. While at the EESC Jan served on EPSO Selection Boards and was president of a Selection Board for IT specialists. Since 2013 Jan has worked as an independent entrepreneur and coach, focusing on personalised coaching and preparation for the EPSO Assessment Centre. He works in close collaboration with Arboreus (eutraining.eu), the market leader in the area of online EU training. Having managed teams for over 30 years in a wide range of environments and disciplines, and with his knowledge of how EPSO Selection Boards operate, Jan knows exactly what assessors look for in a candidate and how Assessment Centres really work. He is happy to share his knowledge and experience in this book – and in person through individual face-to-face coaching or classroom training. Jan's full biography can be found on LinkedIn at https://be.linkedin.com/in/jan-desutter

The authors would like to thank Lenke Szasz, Ticiana Tucci, Ben Williams and Anna Schmidt for their contribution of ideas and content to the creation of this book.

ABOUT THE ULTIMATE EU TEST BOOK SERIES

This Assessment Centre edition is part of a wider series – "The Ultimate EU Test Book" – published to help candidates in their preparation for European Personnel Selection Office (EPSO) competitions, the gateway for recruitment into the EU institutions.

The series covers the entire competition process, from filling out the application form, the talent screener, the computer-based testing of numerical, verbal and abstract reasoning, up to the Assessment Centre. It includes three separate editions specifically designed for Administrator and Assistant competitions and the Assessment Centre phase. The series also goes beyond the competitions, providing advice for those who succeed in becoming EPSO laureates in The Ultimate EU Career Development Book, covering self-development as an EU official. The books can in addition be seen in an even wider context, as they are mirrored by online, face-to-face, and classroom training provided by Arboreus EU Training. Books and training can complement each other, offering a comprehensive EPSO preparation environment.

For full details of the series, please visit www.johnharperpublishing.co.uk

FOREWORD

Welcome to the 2021 edition of The Ultimate EU Test Book Assessment Centre.

2020 was a year of exceptional challenges for the EU personnel selection system thanks to the Covid-19 outbreak, and these challenges are continuing into 2021. Inevitably the Assessment Centre phase, with its reliance on bringing individuals together from all over Europe for testing in group situations in close proximity, was particularly affected.

From 6 March 2020 onwards EPSO had to suspend all Assessment Centre activities at its premises in Brussels and Luxembourg. EPSO initially planned to resume the Assessment Centres from mid-September 2020. However, given the situation towards the end of the summer, it was still not possible to organise tests with candidates physically gathered together on EPSO premises.

To conclude open competitions within a reasonable period, EPSO decided to organise remote online testing for the Assessment Centre tests. Remote online testing allows candidates to sit the tests at home or in the office without needing to travel to an EPSO testing centre. The testing takes place via online videoconferencing.

Some candidates in some competitions had already taken their Assessment Centre tests before 6 March 2020. However, to ensure equal treatment, all candidates must take the same tests and the group exercise cannot be conducted remotely in a satisfactory way. Therefore all candidates (including those who had already taken part in a group exercise) were required to take another newly-created test, the situational competency based interview (SCBI).

It took some time for EPSO to organise the remote testing, and there was a long period of confusion on the SCBI, but finally, in December the remote Assessment Centre tests for the specialist Law and Finance competition took lace, including the new SCBI. Further open competitions were announced as resuming at the start of 2021.

For this 2021 edition, we have accordingly added the changes to the Assessment Centre testing methods currently in place because of the Covid-19 pandemic. We highlight what to expect – and how to behave – in a remote testing environment. There is also a completely new chapter, covering the previously unknown SCBI. The information we provide is based on official EPSO publications, in combination with our experience in the Assessment Centre process and the feedback we have received from candidates who have already faced the SCBI.

The future is unclear. Will EPSO revert back fully, once the pandemic has subsided, to testing with physical presence? Will the group exercise come back, or will it be replaced permanently by the SCBI? How will EPSO respond to the rather critical report that was issued by the Court of

Auditors in 2020? We don't know. That is why this edition retains full coverage of the testing methods used with physical candidate presence, as this could resume at any time in 2021.

Finally, we would like to express our special thanks to Lenke Szasz, EU Training Marketing Manager, and Ticiana Tucci, EU Training Assessment Centre Coach, for helping us get our heads around the methodological and practical challenges created by the Covid-19 outbreak. Without them we could not have written this special edition of the book.

András Baneth and Jan De Sutter

February 2021

1. The EPSO Assessment Centre

This chapter gives an overview of how an Assessment Centre is conducted in "normal" times. As of early 2021, however, times are far from normal and we also highlight the variations currently in operation as remote testing is used.

Introduction

The European Personnel Selection Office (EPSO) is responsible for selecting staff to work for the institutions and agencies of the European Union. It is important to note that EPSO is NOT involved in *recruiting* EU staff; it is only involved in the *selection* process, resulting in a **reserve list** of successful candidates. Each institution recruits its staff from among the pool of successful candidates – the reserve lists provided by EPSO. For the full picture on how EPSO works, watch the video at https://vimeo.com/104704292.

EPSO is one of the largest selection centres in the world. Today, EPSO processes on average 50,000 applications a year for approximately 1,500 places. Testing is carried out in 24 languages – this is unique in the selection world.

The Management Board of EPSO, comprising the heads of administration of the institutions and agencies, decides exactly which competitions EPSO is to organise and how many candidates should figure on the reserve lists. These decisions are based on the estimated future needs of the recruiting bodies.

Once it is decided to organise an open competition it is published in the Official Journal of the European Union by means of a **Notice of Competition** laying out the admission criteria, the selection procedure, and the number of successful candidates sought (i.e. the size of the reserve list). Candidates can then apply for this competition by filling out an application form in a personal EPSO online portal.

Each open competition has its own **Selection Board**, responsible for selecting candidates at each stage and for drawing up the final list of successful candidates, the reserve list. Each Selection Board is made up of officials from the EU institutions and EPSO ensures that all Selection Boards adhere strictly to the internal procedures, in compliance with the EU Staff Regulations.

The number of candidates that apply for any given competition is unpredictable, but it is usually many times bigger than the reserve list aimed at. The main challenge for EPSO is therefore to select the "best possible" candidates from the list of admitted candidates. In practice, this process is organised as a "funnel" in which the number of candidates still in the running is gradually reduced during the successive stages of the selection process.

The Classic Generalist Selection Procedure

Figure 1.1 depicts the selection process for an AD5 "generalist" competition. Because AD5 is the entry level for administrators (ADs) and no prior professional experience is required, this (traditionally yearly) competition is now also called the "graduate" competition. It has usually been the biggest competition of the year, attracting more than 20,000 candidates. As can be seen from Figure 1.1, there are three stages to this competition: the pre-selection stage, the intermediate stage, and the Assessment Centre.

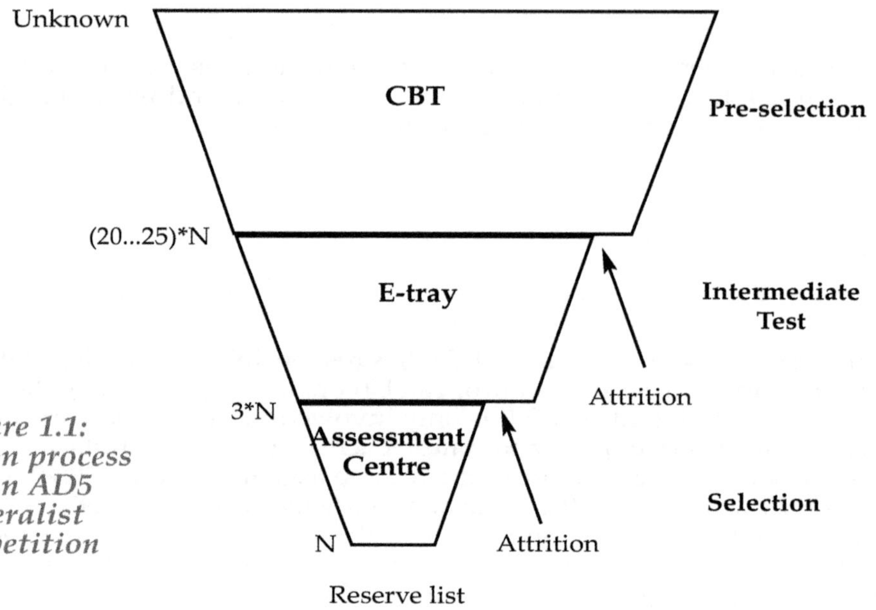

Figure 1.1: selection process for an AD5 generalist competition

At the **pre-selection stage** the large number of candidates is initially reduced to some 20 or 25 times the number of successful candidates sought (N). This is done by means of computer-based tests (CBTs) comparing the candidates' numerical, verbal and abstract reasoning skills. Only those candidates who obtain a pass mark for these tests, and end up with the highest scores for the CBTs, are invited to the next stage. The objective value of these CBTs is debatable, but it is a very pragmatic approach to reduce the number of candidates to more manageable quantities for the following stages. CBTs have the enormous logistical advantage that they can be run remotely, so that candidates don't have to travel to Brussels to take their tests. Also, these tests are typically taken in the mother tongue of the candidates (Language 1 in EPSO jargon).

In 2015, EPSO introduced an **intermediate stage** in the selection procedures for AD5 generalists (and AD5 auditors), involving an e-tray.

This intermediate stage was brought in to avoid the automatic elimination of otherwise potentially valuable candidates who happened to have a slightly lower – but still very good – score in the CBTs. In addition, it had happened in the past that a Selection Board could not manage to make up a complete reserve list because there were not enough candidates passing the Assessment Centre stage. To avoid the latter problem the intermediate stage needed to be a kind of "pre-Assessment Centre" focusing already on the "general competencies" measured by the Assessment Centre rather than the "general intelligence" measured by the CBTs. Because of the significant number of candidates involved this stage also needed to be computer-based and the e-tray (or in-tray) exercise was adopted as the best solution to this problem.

The e-tray is a kind of situational judgement test focusing on some of the general competencies that will be further assessed during the Assessment Centre. It is important to note that the scores obtained in the e-tray are taken into account for the final scoring, so – in fact – the e-tray is effectively part of the assessment. At the end of the intermediate stage around 3 times the number of candidates intended for the reserve list get an invitation for the Assessment Centre.

The Selection Procedure for specialists

In the period from 2010, when the current EPSO testing regime was introduced, to around 2015 most candidates were taking generalist competitions. In more recent years, however, specialist competitions have come to predominate and these work differently in some important respects.

One important difference is that in specialist competitions a so-called **talent screener** is used to eliminate a proportion of candidates before any tests are administered at all. This is very different to generalist competitions when anyone who meets the basic criteria can go on to take the pre-selection tests.

Another important difference is that the verbal, numerical and reasoning tests may be carried out as part of the Assessment Centre, rather than as a preliminary stage. Whether or not this happens depends on how many are left after the talent screener and is decided case by case, but in general the fewer the remaining candidates the more likely it is that the tests will be administered at the Assessment Centre.

The third difference is that specialist skills will loom large in the assessment process and, as well as other Assessment Centre tests, there is an **interview in the field** (meaning the field of the competition).

The talent screener and the interview in the field are covered in detail in Chapter 10. Candidates in specialist competitions will still face assessment of their "core competencies", as discussed below, and have more generic tests, but their specialist skills, and how they demonstrate these, will loom large in the overall assessment.

As there are variations from one specialist competition to another, it is vital to familiarise yourself with the rules applying to your competition. The Notice of Competition will always tell you what will be tested and using which tests and how the marks will be allocated. This is essential guidance for your preparation.

Notes:

What the Assessment Centre is

The Assessment Centre, or AC for short, is the final testing phase in the EPSO selection procedure. It is an advanced approach to evaluating pre-defined competencies by observing participants' behaviour. The term Assessment Centre, as well as being a phase in the selection process also describes a physical location, normally in Brussels, although certain AC tests may be undertaken in the candidates' Member States.

During the Covid pandemic EPSO has introduced online testing because of the difficulty in getting candidates to travel to Brussels from all over Europe and then participate in exercises together.

Whereas the so-called "pre-selection" or "admission tests" stage in EPSO competitions usually involves the elimination of the great majority of candidates, typically one out of three of those who reach the Assessment Centre stage will go on to become laureates and eventually take up an EU job. Each and every person, therefore, who makes it to the Assessment Centre, is being seriously and conscientiously evaluated for his or her potential in terms of the contribution they can make to the EU institutions.

In essence, an Assessment Centre consists of asking candidates to complete a varied set of exercises that are designed to simulate different aspects of a role and work environment. A team of assessors who make judgements on the candidates' performance observes candidates by watching their behaviour during the AC in terms of what "good" and "poor" performance looks like. Candidates are observed by a number of assessors (typically four) throughout the event, to minimise the likelihood of any bias on the part of assessors.

Assessment Centres are one of the most fair, objective and effective ways of identifying high-potential candidates who will fit in with a role and an organisation's culture. Research shows them to be far more predictive of future job performance than individual tasks, such as a job interview. This is because a number of different assessors get to see the candidates perform over a relatively long period of time and have the chance to see how they *actually* behave in a variety of situations (rather than what they might *say* they do in an interview).

The EPSO Assessment Centres (excluding the case study exercise, usually done separately – see below) typically last one day. (Exceptionally, for specialist roles, EPSO may have one-and-a-half day ACs given the number of tests they are required to sit.) EPSO usually runs the Assessment Centre with six candidates and four assessors who assess them during the day, though it is important to underline that observation is limited to the exercises, and coffee breaks or other informal situations are never considered. Given the large number of candidates, EPSO runs multiple streams on the same day.

As a candidate, you should bear in mind two important points. Firstly, it is hard to "fake" a good performance at an Assessment Centre. Trying to act in a manner contrary to your natural style over an eight-hour period and across multiple exercises can be mentally taxing and may actually cause your performance to suffer. If the behaviours you are trying to convey do not come at all naturally, you will be found out. Secondly, it is contrary to both your and EPSO's interests to find yourself in a role for which you are neither behaviourally nor motivationally suited. As well as underperforming, you are likely to experience greater levels of stress and job dissatisfaction if you are placed in a role that you are not well suited to have.

By going to the event, well-prepared, with your eyes open and having planned how you can show off your strengths to their maximum advantage, you will give yourself the best possible chance for success, not to mention that the assessment tasks will not take you by surprise if you are fully aware of what to expect.

Skills vs. Knowledge

The most significant element in the current selection system is the shift from the old pre-2010 knowledge-based testing to an emphasis on competencies. This means that multiple choice tests and essays focused on memorising "EU knowledge" facts and figures are a thing of the past. However, a knowledge of how the EU works and EU terminology can certainly help in some of the tests.

EPSO has instead created a "**competency framework**" against which all candidates are now evaluated, with a set of seven **general competencies** (eight for Administrators) that are relevant to all roles to some extent. These are also known as "core competencies".

The general competencies are described in more detail in Chapter 2, but are summarized by EPSO as follows:

- **Analysis and problem solving** – Identifies the critical facts in complex issues and develops creative and practical solutions
- **Communicating** – Communicates clearly and precisely both orally and in writing
- **Delivering quality and results** – Takes personal responsibility and initiative for delivering work to a high standard of quality within set procedures
- **Learning and development** – Develops and improves personal skills and knowledge of the organisation and its environment
- **Prioritising and organising** – Prioritises the most important tasks, works flexibly and organises own workload efficiently
- **Resilience** – Remains effective under a heavy workload, handles organisational frustrations positively and adapts to a changing work environment
- **Working with others** – Works co-operatively with others in teams and across organisational boundaries and respects differences between people
- **Leadership** – Manages, develops and motivates people to achieve results (Note: this is only for Administrator grades, and the word "manages" does not imply any management experience)

It is important to note that all the above **general competencies have the same weight**, meaning that they each account for the same number of points in your total score (usually 10 per competency, so it is 10 points each and 70 in total for Assistant (AST) competitions, and 10

Notes:

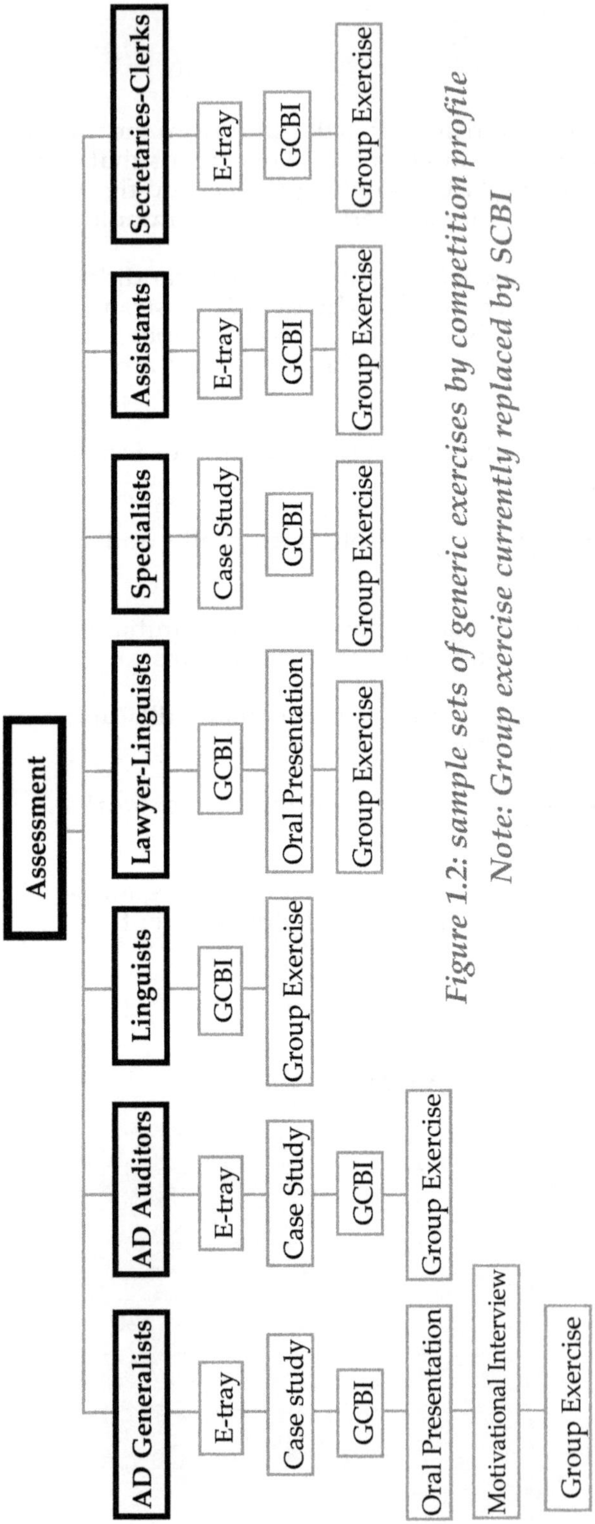

Figure 1.2: sample sets of generic exercises by competition profile
Note: Group exercise currently replaced by SCBI

points each and 80 in total for Administrator (AD) competitions.

Candidates are tested not only for their general competencies but also for their **specific (or "field") competencies**. These specific competencies consist of the applied knowledge and skills needed to satisfy the immediate requirements in the field of the specific job profile for the competition at hand. For specialists, the field competencies will have a greater weight than the general competencies, in line with the concept of selecting candidates who can be "operational from day one", amounting to 100 points in total. In broad terms, the more "generalist" the roles being selected for, the more the weight that is put on the general competencies.

Exercises and Tests

Both general competencies and specific competencies are at the base of a set of exercises and tests which go beyond the immediate in order to assess the candidate's all-round abilities and therefore their potential for a long-term career in the European public service. Figure 1.2 on page 6 shows typical sets of exercises to be taken by various profiles that are selected in EPSO competitions.

The core generic exercises are:

- The case study
- The group exercise
- The general competency-based interview, GCBI
- The oral presentation
- The e-tray (or in-tray) exercise
- The motivational interview
- In response to the Covid pandemic the group exercise has been suspended and replaced by a situational competency-

based interview (SCBI). It is not known at this stage whether this will be retained or is a temporary expedient. It is covered in detail in a new chapter (chapter 10). In the matrices in the following pages you may find therefore that in your competition the group exercise has been replaced by an SCBI.

These exercises are "generic" in the sense that they test personal behaviours and qualities in ways which are relevant to the wide range of roles that candidates may be called on to undertake in the course of their career.

Not all the exercises are undertaken for all profiles, as EPSO does not use exercises which are not relevant to the job profile in the specific competition. Thus, for example, Assistants are not required to give an oral presentation, as their job roles will not require them to give presentations. The competency-based structured interview is common to all profiles.

For more specialised roles, such as macroeconomists, nuclear scientists or public health experts, the competition will involve other tests focusing on specialised knowledge.

Linguists (including lawyer-linguists), depending on the competition, may have their computer-based reasoning tests (i.e. verbal, numerical and abstract reasoning tests – the tests taken by most candidates at the admission phase) as part of the Assessment Centre phase, though these may be administered at centres in the Member States. At the Assessment Centre their general competencies will be measured by a structured interview, group exercise and oral presentation. For Linguists their specific competencies (i.e. in translating or interpreting) not surprisingly weigh more heavily in the final mark than their general competencies, but there will still be a minimum pass mark required in the general competencies.

As noted above, for **specialists**, the computer-based pre-selection reasoning tests may also be moved into the Assessment Centre stage, depending on the number of applicants. Moreover, specialists need to go through an online pre-screening questionnaire, called a talent screener. The purpose of this is to identify their work experience and qualifications in the given field that can help the Selection Board (for which see below) evaluate specialist candidates' suitability and eligibility for the post. (Even though these are declared on "word of honour", they will be checked by bringing supporting documents, to the Assessment Centre and the specific "field" interview also checks many of the elements that the candidate has declared.)

Specialist knowledge is tested in the assessment phase by specific tests, an interview in the field, and/or with a case study. This latter is closely related to the exam profile and the sub-profile or domain that the candidate chose at the time of application.

More is said about each of these exercises in the relevant chapters of this book.

Notes:

The Assessment Matrix

As part of the Assessment Centre design, the competencies are "mapped" to each of the Assessment Centre exercises, depending upon where they would be best

Competency	Tests	
Analysis and problem solving	Oral Presentation	E-tray
Communicating	Oral Presentation	Case Study
Delivering quality and results	Case Study	E-tray
Learning and development	Group Exercise	General Competency Based Interview
Prioritising and organising	Case Study	E-tray
Resilience	Oral Presentation	General Competency Based Interview
Working with others	Group Exercise	E-tray
Leadership	Group Exercise	General Competency Based Interview

Table 1.1: an AD5 generalist matrix

Competency	Tests	
Analysis and problem solving	Case Study	Group exercise
Communicating	Case Study	General Competency Based Interview
Delivering quality and results	Case Study	General Competency Based Interview
Learning and development	Group Exercise	General Competency Based Interview
Prioritising and organising	Case Study	Group exercise
Resilience	Group Exercise	General Competency Based Interview
Working with others	Group Exercise	General Competency Based Interview
Specific Competencies	Specific Competency Based Interview	

Table 1.2: an AST3 matrix

Competency	Tests	
Analysis and problem solving	E-tray	
Communicating	General Competency Based Interview	
Delivering quality and results	E-tray	
Learning and development	General Competency Based Interview	
Prioritising and organising	E-tray	
Resilience	General Competency Based Interview	
Working with others	General Competency Based Interview	
Specific Competencies	Microsoft Office Skills test	Drafting Skills Test

Table 1.3: an AST-SC matrix

observed. EPSO specifies that each of the competencies is observed at least twice over the course of the event. This is in fact considered industry best practice, as it prevents someone's rating being overly affected by a particularly bad or good performance in just one exercise. Moreover, given that there are usually four assessors for each group, different exercises are observed by different assessors, further improving the unbiased nature of the assessment.

Competency	Tests	
Analysis and problem solving	Case Study	Group Exercise
Communicating	Case Study	General Competency Based Interview
Delivering quality and results	Case Study	General Competency Based Interview
Learning and development	Group Exercise	General Competency Based Interview
Prioritising and organising	Case Study	Group Exercise
Resilience	Group Exercise	General Competency Based Interview
Working with others	Group Exercise	General Competency Based Interview
Leadership	Group Exercise	General General Based Interview
Specific Competencies	Field Interview	

Table 1.4: an AD7 Specialist matrix

Table 1.1 is the **2019 AD5 generalists graduate competition** matrix (EPSO/AD/373/19). In this example, you can see the prominent role of the e-tray exercise, despite the fact that this exercise was taken before the actual Assessment Centre. Furthermore, the communicating competency was assessed during the case study (written communication) and the oral presentation. In comparison with the previous AD5 competitions the general competency based interview was only used to assess 3 competencies, as opposed to 5 in the pre-2015 competitions (the 2016 AD5 competition was cancelled!)

In Table 1.2 you will find an assessment matrix used for a competition for **Assistants at AST3 level** for jobs in finance and human resources (EPSO/AST/139/16). Notable differences from the AD matrix in Table 1.1 are that there is no oral presentation and the communicating competency is assessed during the general competency based interview, as well as in the case study.

In Table 1.3, by way of contrast, you will find the matrix for a competition for **secretaries/clerks** in support roles at the lower **AST-SC** (SC = secretarial) level (EPSO/AST-SC/06/17). Note that the tests are rather different to those used for the AST3 competition: in particular, there is no case study or group exercise, but instead there is a Microsoft Office skills test and a drafting skills test to assess particularly spelling, syntax and grammar (these two last tests representing 30% of the marks). The variation between the two matrices reflects the expected differences in the actual daily content of the jobs being selected for.

A further example is given in Table 1.4, this time for a typical **AD7 specialist** competition. Unlike for the AD5 graduate generalist competition, this one (like the AST3 in Table 1.2) has an interview in the field of the competition testing specific competencies. Most specialist competitions have no oral presentation. However, during the general competency based interview, candidates will be

Notes:

assessed for 6 competencies: five with questions and one (communicating) by observation during the interview.

Please note that these examples are for illustration purposes only and the exact matrix for your competition might be different. You should always check the Notice of Competition (NoC) or the invitation letter to the Assessment Centre for any information provided on this topic.

In order to give you a better idea of what these tests look like EPSO provides a number of example tests on its website: https://epso.europa.eu/how-to-apply/sample-tests_en

Once the Assessment Centre is underway, assessors will make copious notes on everything you say and do during each exercise to collect "evidence" that can later be mapped to the various competencies that are being tested. Afterwards, and based on the evidence they have gathered, they will rate you on each competency that has been linked to each particular exercise on the matrix, using a prescribed performance scale.◉ Following an Assessment Centre the assessors will meet to discuss the results for each candidate and reach a group consensus about each candidate's ratings for each competency.

Assessment Centre for Middle Management Positions

From time to time the institutions organise competitions for what in the EU institutions are termed middle management positions (Head of Unit). Even though the same principles in regard to general competencies apply, for these competitions the focus is placed on the competencies that are generally expected in such positions in the EU institutions. Usually, the Assessment Centre for these competitions is outsourced to an external service provider, specialised in the selection and recruitment of middle and senior management staff. Even though the final selection is done by EPSO, the jury takes the results of this externalised assessment into account.

The profile of the competencies for middle management is as follows:

Information Management

Establish pertinent links between various data in order to integrate these data in a synthetic and coherent way. Generate alternatives and translate these – along with the synthesis – into adequate and convincing conclusions.

Task Management

Business management: develop and implement processes and structures covering multiple domains of activity. Establish budgets and manage these in a realistic and logical manner. Introduce and implement change, test new methods with the objective of improvement.

Steering: evaluate and manage people, resources, budgets and time. Follow-up and adaptation of plans as required.

People Management

Motivation: recognise and value other people for their contribution, adapt leadership style and confine responsibilities and tasks to the adequate people in order to optimise their functioning.

Direction: induce appropriate behaviour by giving clear instructions and follow-up, and by adjusting the performance to the objectives and available resources.

Interpersonal Management

Influencing: reach objectives by making a good impression, making their ideas accepted, using convincing arguments, establishing win-win relations, and giving pertinent answers.

Personal Management

React to frustrations, obstacles and opposition while keeping focus on the results, staying calm, controlling one's own emotions, and reacting constructively to criticism.

In more general terms, if you are taking part in such a competition the assessors will be looking for your leadership skills. A good leader delegates. Work cannot be done by you alone. You must divide up the work between the others and ensure proper follow-up and quality control of the delivery.

You may wish to read about the so-called "situational leadership" approach: it provides that each subordinate or employee must be treated according to two main factors, namely their level of knowledge of the issue at hand and their level of willingness to act. The four combinations (willing/unwilling, knows/does not know) demand the adoption of very different management approaches.

A good leader uses the strengths of others. You must identify the strengths of the individuals in your group (which may be a challenging task given that you have no prior knowledge of your group's members) and use them in appropriate ways.

A good leader takes an overview. Do not get too involved in actioning things. It's better to monitor what's going on and then suggest changes at a later stage if required.

The procedure for the assessment could consist of:

- A general competency based interview
- Simulation exercises
  - Management exercise
  - Analysis and presentation
- A personality questionnaire
- An abstract reasoning test
- A group exercise

The competency-based structured interview for managers is much like the one described in Chapter 5 of this book.

The management exercise is in two parts: an interactive session with a member of your team (a role played by one of the assessors) and a written report to your hierarchy.

The analysis and presentation exercise is an oral exercise during which you have to formulate, present and defend your proposals and points-of-view on a given file.

The personality questionnaire is

Notes:

....

....

....

....

....

intended to form a clearer opinion on your self-evaluation with respect to the competency profile.

The abstract reasoning test is intended to assess your intrinsic intellectual potential, and your capacity to adapt to new situations and acquire new skills.

You may be asked to chair a meeting or act as leader of your group. Once again there will be a set task but this time you will be expected to be in charge and to lead the others to success.

Internal Competitions

One important result of the 2013 Staff Regulation negotiations has been that that the EU institutions now regularly organise "internal" competitions to give better career prospects for their contractual and temporary staff.

The most recent internal competition of the Commission was organised in 2019 (published November 2018). This was a massive internal competition as no less than 411 positions were to be filled. Three parts of this competition were open to Contract Agents, Temporary Agents and Officials: AST/SC2, AST2 and AD6. Five were open to Temporary Agents and Officials only: AST4, AD7, AD8, AD10 and AD12.

Other recent internal competitions were organised by the Committee of the Regions and the European Parliament, and the Council started one in 2019.

Even though the institutions have the freedom to organise these internal competitions using their own selection criteria they are bound by the Staff Regulations, so they have to rely on the principles and ideas that govern the "open" competitions as organised by EPSO. This also means that the tools and techniques as described in this book fully apply.

Waiting for the Assessment Centre

As you are reading this book, it is quite possible that you have already succeeded in the admission phase, and passed the pre-selection tests with flying colours. You are well aware that competition for positions in the EU institutions is intense and only a small number of candidates have made it this far. You have come a considerable way towards being selected.

You will be informed via your EPSO account of the results you obtained in the admission tests and whether you are amongst the candidates admitted to the next phase of the competition. The Selection Board has examined your application forms, submitted electronically on the EPSO portal. This examination has been carried out in descending order of points in order to establish the list of candidates who obtained the highest aggregate marks in the admission tests (relative scoring), and obtained a pass mark in each test (objective scoring), and who satisfy the general and specific conditions listed in the Notice of Competition. Only the candidates on this list will be admitted to the Assessment Centre.

The number of candidates invited varies from competition to competition, but the Notice of Competition typically requires it to be around 2.5 or 3 times the number of candidates who can be placed on the final reserve list of laureates eligible for recruitment.

A candidate's experience

I received the first results of my CBT tests early July. I had taken these tests in May and the competition had been published in the Official Journal in February. However, these first results initially didn't help me out that much, as I still didn't know if I had made the cut. The letter only stated that I would be notified if my results were amongst the highest scores, meaning that I would be admitted to the next phase. So, my initial joy of finding out that I had passed the CBT was quickly tempered down again as I very soon realised that I still wasn't any closer to achieving my goal...

On the first of September, I was finally informed that my scores were amongst the highest and that I would be invited to the AC centre shortly. This letter also informed me that the AC would start in October and that it would be a whole day.

Finally, by mid-September I received my invitation letter for the AC which was going to take place in the beginning of December. So, again, another 2 months of anxiety. The good news about this, however, was that I could prepare thoroughly for my day at the Assessment Centre.

The complete procedure for admission to the competition is explained under chapter V of the Notice of Competition.

The Assessment Centre phase (in normal times) will commonly be split into two parts over two non-consecutive days. The case study will take place on one day, in test centres around the individual Member States. The rest of the Assessment Centre will be held in Brussels. You will have to attend both parts, on both days. Exceptionally and only for lawyer-linguists, there is an Assessment Centre in Luxembourg too. For specialists, the Assessment Centre day can actually spread over a day and half as opposed to a single day, given the fact that in most cases they will need to take computer-based psychometric tests also (just like the ones that most others have already done in the pre-selection phase).

With the invitation letter for the case study you will be informed of the exact date and location where the exercise will take place. You should verify and if necessary modify within the allowed deadline the city where you will sit the case study. The case study will be computer-based and will need to be delivered in your second language (see "Language Rules" on page 23).

To facilitate the organisation of these tests, EPSO will already have assigned a language 2 keyboard to you, it will be provided at the test centre on the day of the case study. Please verify and if necessary change the type of keyboard you want to use as the French and English keyboards are significantly different and this can have a major impact on your typing speed and accuracy.

Notes:

You will not be required to book your case study appointment. You will be automatically booked to the location you have chosen. You will receive a booking confirmation by email with the address, date and time. Make sure to check how to get to the venue and plan your trip accordingly as if you arrive a few minutes late, you can lose valuable time which can severely impact your performance.

Sometime later you will receive the invitation for the second part, that is, the Assessment Centre day, which usually takes place in Brussels. The exercises to be taken as well as the language(s) to be used for these exercises will be marked in the invitation letter.

You are not allowed to alter the date that you have been allocated. However, in exceptional circumstances only (serious illness, pregnancy or disability) and by applying by email to the secretariat, EPSO may allow you to change the date of your appointment, but only within the available testing period.

Regarding documents to bring, you will be asked to print out a copy of your on-line application form, sign it, and bring it to the Assessment Centre, together with the supporting documents, proving that you fulfill the general and specific conditions as laid down in the Notice of Competition, as well as a recent ID with photograph.

A recent development in this respect is that you are now asked to put the supporting documents on a USB stick to be handed in upon arrival for your Assessment Centre. Modern times.

Venue and Costs

The case study exam will take place in test centres across the EU member states. The oral part of the Assessment Centre will be held in Brussels. Exceptionally and only for lawyer-linguists, there is an Assessment Centre in Luxembourg too.

The address of EPSO is Avenue de Cortenbergh, 25 in B-1049 Brussels (Belgium). This is about 100 metres away from the Schuman roundabout, which is the heart of the Brussels "EU area" and easily accessible by public transportation. For your personal travel advice check www.stib.be/horaires. The closest station is Schuman Railway station.

EPSO does not have any parking facilities for candidates. However, a few spaces are available for disabled candidates so please ensure that you inform EPSO in advance should you wish to reserve one of these.

Access to the EPSO building may be difficult during the EU summits (which take place in the same neighbourhood) or when public transportation services are on strike. EPSO will inform you of these situations in advance, through their portal but best is to allow enough time to get there even if there is an unforeseen hurdle.

EPSO building in Brussels and its position in the EU quarter on p.15

Candidates who need to travel there are reimbursed for their travel costs and also given a daily subsistence allowance for hotel and food costs in some circumstances (see FAQs in Annex 9). The specific rules are always communicated in advance either as early as in the Notice of Competition or later to those who actually make it through to the assessment phase. The underlying principle is that nobody should suffer any disadvantage in attending the competitions due to budgetary issues.

Please note that no contribution will be paid for participation in tests forming part of the Assessment Centre (e.g. the case study) which are organised in the candidate's Member State (country of residence). If your place of residence is outside the EU you will have to complete and sign two electronic forms ("Legal entities" and "Financial identification") and send them with a copy of your identity card or passport to EPSO. It is the address that appears in your EPSO account that will be used to calculate the financial contribution.

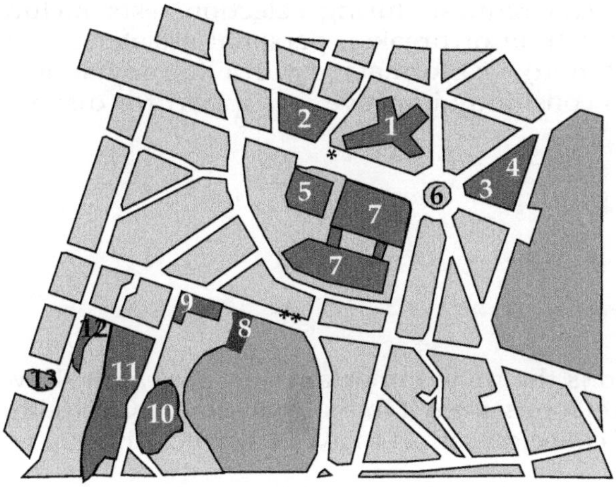

1 – Berlaymont (European Commission)
2 – Charlemagne (European Commission)
3 – European External Action Service
4 – European Personnel Selection Office
5 – Europa Building (European Council / Council of the European Union)
6 – Schuman roundabout (rond-point Schuman)
7 – Justus Lipsius (Council of the European Union)
8 – House of European History
9 – Jacques Delors (European Economic and Social Committee / Committee of the Regions)
10 – Paul-Henri Spaak (European Parliament)
11 – Altiero Spinelli (European Parliament)
12 – Parlamentarium
13 – Place du Luxembourg
* – Rue de la Loi
**– Rue Belliard

Provision for candidates with disabilities

EPSO makes "reasonable accommodations" for candidates with disabilities. Information about this is provided on the EPSO website, in the application form and in each individual Notice of Competition (for open competitions) or call of expression of interest (for CAST selections).

EPSO has developed promotional materials to explain how candidates can request special adjustments in selection tests.

- There is video on how to request special adjustments in the selection tests, at: https://epso.europa.eu/content/join-our-network-disability-organisations_en

Notes:

- A step-by-step flyer is available on:

https://epso.europa.eu/sites/epso/files/documents/special-adjustment-leaflet.pdf

- The flyer is also available in an accessible version at:

https://epso.europa.eu/sites/epso/files/documents/accessibleformat-stepbystepguide.docx

- The flyer can be printed out in Braille upon request at:

EPSO-ACCESSIBILITY@ec.europa.eu

Possible special arrangements candidates can request during selection tests include adjustments to time and location (e.g. extra time or breaks), personal assistance (e.g. reading assistant or sign language interpretation), text formats (e.g. Braille), adjustments to equipment, and others. EPSO's aim is to constantly improve its support for disabled candidates.

Dress Code

The first impression you make on a person is the most important one. Research shows that most of the initial perception is based on looks, even if in the Assessment Centre this is slightly less relevant given the assessors' conscious effort to avoid any positive or negative bias on this score.

At the same time, the first impression any person makes is going to be based on how they look and what they are wearing: the dress code. That is why it is important to dress professionally, whether it is during your day at the Assessment Centre or for the job interview once you are on the reserve list.

So what is the appropriate dress code? You want that first impression to be not just a good one but a great one. There are a few simple rules you can follow to do it right.

Dress as if you already have the job

Remember that the assessors are EU officials as well, so try to dress like them. This will be something like "smart casual" with the emphasis on "smart". If you are a man, probably the safest course of action is to wear a suit and a tie. Pick out a darker colour – like dark grey or marine blue – for the suit and a tie that adds a colourful, but sophisticated, accent. Women's clothes should best have some tailoring with a definite shape at the shoulders, but making sure there isn't too much skin revealed.

Everything you wear should be in perfect condition

If you look scruffy the assumption will be that the same is true of your thinking. If you are unaware of how you look you may lack self-awareness, and self-awareness is essential for any job. If you had to travel to come to Brussels you will probably arrive a day before, and stay in a hotel or with friends, which is a better option than going to the Assessment Centre or interview straight from a long flight or tiring trip.

Dress for authority and status

You will want to suggest self-awareness, self-confidence and natural authority. Choose "high status" rather than "low status" as your theme. This means immaculate grooming, quality clothes in good condition, contemporary and elegant. Well-manicured hands, smart shoes that are well polished will add up to this.

One last message about "smell control": be careful. If you are a smoker you may not be aware that others, non-smokers, can smell you from a distance. Anti-smokers can see this as an argument to dismiss you right away. On the other hand, don't overdo it with after-shave or perfume. Fragrance is highly personal and other people may not like your taste.

A Day at the Assessment Centre (in normal times)

You will be invited to be there early in the morning, between 08:00 and 09:00, and the first thing you will have to do is register at the reception desk. For some competitions EPSO doesn't invite everybody at the same time; they sometimes ask candidates to be there half an hour or so before their first exercise of the day. As the jury proceeds sequentially (i.e. one candidate after the other) for the structured interviews there is no need for everybody to be there at the same time in the morning, but the EPSO administration may decide otherwise.

Arrive on time and unaccompanied. Friends or relatives will not be allowed to wait in the building, or to contact you while you are sitting the tests. If you arrive late, you will not get any additional time to complete the exercises. You might also be excluded from participating at all, especially if you miss one of the exercises entirely.

You will receive all material necessary for the various exercises on the spot.

A locker will be provided for your luggage and other personal belongings. You should leave your mobile phone and other electronic devices in this during the exercises.

A waiting room will be provided for your breaks, with vending machines for drinks and snacks, so keeping your wallet or coins with you is a good idea.

During the AC exercises, it is strictly forbidden to use your mobile phone or any kind of electronic device with or without memory (laptops, computer, dictionary or calculator etc.), encyclopaedias, reference books, newspapers, magazines, personal notes or pens, etc., correcting fluid, or similar correction material (which, given that virtually all tests are now computer-based, would not be useful anyway).

During the day, it is strictly forbidden to disturb the other candidates and the assessors. The AC is a non-smoking environment.

Please note that no lunch will be provided. However, you can have lunch outside the AC premises during the lunch break.

Candidates are invited in groups of 6, though occasionally some candidates may fail to show up and in the case there will be fewer in your group than normal. For every group there will be 4 assessors taking care of the candidates for the whole day. Below is a typical overall schedule for an AD5 specialist competition; please note that the schedule of your specific competition may be different.

You will notice from Table 1.5 that **each candidate is seen by two pairs of asses-**

Notes:

		Assessor 1 Assessor 2	Assessor 3 Assessor4
08:20–09:00	Welcome	All	
09:00–09:50	Competency based interview	Candidate 1	Candidate 4
10:00–10:50	Competency based interview	Candidate 2	Candidate 5
11:00–11:50	Competency based interview	Candidate 3	Candidate 6
12:00–13:30	Lunch	All	
13:30–14:20	Field Interview	Candidate 4	Candidate 1
14:30–15:20	Field Interview	Candidate 5	Candidate 2
15:30–16.20	Field Interview	Candidate 6	Candidate 3
16:30–17:35	Group exercise	All	

Table 1.5: a typical AD5 Specialist day at the AC

sors. This is to avoid what is known as the "halo-effect" (a cognitive bias in which an observer's overall positive impression of a person influences the observer's feelings and thoughts about that person's actual character or properties).

You will have plenty of time in between the exercises. Use this to relax and, more importantly to socialise with the other candidates of your group. This can also prove very useful for the group exercise because if you manage to get an initial impression of each team member's communication style, social skills, extroversion or introversion, it will greatly help to adapt your interaction with them in the actual exam.

Once registered you will be picked up by a competition assistant, who will accompany you to the floor where your Assessment Centre will take place. You will get a private locker where you can store your luggage and other personal belongings. As you get the key to this locker you will have access to your items anytime you want, but, as mentioned above, don't forget that it is not allowed to bring electronic gadgets into the rooms where the exercises take place. At that point you will also have to hand in the documents you were required to bring with you (photocopies of your diplomas, proof of previous

A Selection Board president's point of view

The most stressful moment of the day is between 08:30 and 09:00. You are never sure that all the assessors are going to show up for that day, and there's always a risk that you will have to jump in for an assessor who was delayed in traffic, taken ill, or having an important activity to attend to at the office. When all goes well, the team starts working at 09:00 and then the president can take on his routine activities like supervising the interviews, preparing replies to disgruntled candidates, discussing the planning of the coming days, etc. I truly believe we are lucky with the very professional – and loyal – staff of the EPSO administration. These people move mountains to get everything running smoothly. Thank you for that!

A candidate's experience

Here came my day in the EPSO AC. I will definitely remember it as one of the most stressful days in my life so far. I had the interview at 11:00 and ended the day with the group exercise at 16:45, in between having the oral presentation and numerous interesting discussions with the other candidates there. I reached the floor where my structured interview was supposed to take place 10 min before, extremely nervous and feeling like I have no memories whatsoever of any past behaviour that I can come up with. Luckily, the feeling was a false one and I managed to remember my preparation and give mostly good answers to the questions asked. It seemed like a never-ending interview, although there were only 3-4 questions per competency and sometimes some follow-up questions from the assessors. The 2 people in the committee showed no emotion and gave no feedback to my answers, they were just taking notes on what I was saying. The most difficult part seemed to me to remember to breathe, detach and not rush in when giving the answers. There were also some questions to which I didn't have a "perfect" answer, but I tried to offer some alternatives and illustrate that particular competency through a different example.

employment, a photo of yourself, etc.). The assistant will then give you some general instructions about your day in the AC.

Most probably, the first exercise you will have to do is the **general competency based interview**, which is the subject of Chapter 5. This is sometimes referred to as the "structured interview" but in fact the interview in the field, which is now part of many competitions, is also a structured interview (see Chapter 8).

You may have to wait a couple of minutes in front of the door where the interview takes place. Don't knock on the door; one of the assessors will invite you in when they are ready for you.

After the GCBI you are free to go for what remains of the morning. You can stay on the same floor and have a coffee with the other candidates who are there, or leave the building to clear your mind for the rest of the day. Your badge will not give you any access to the other floors of the building as these are off-limits for the candidates.

After lunch the exercises continue. You may have an **oral presentation**, an **interview in the field**, or an **e-tray exercise**, depending on the competition you are taking. Specialists may have to do some particular exercises and/or verbal, numerical or abstract reasoning tests.

Usually, the last exercise of the day is the **group exercise**. This means that you will probably be tired – but you should definitely not let your shoulders or your spirits drop at this point.

This schedule is only indicative and you must of course consult the Notice of Competition and other information provided by EPSO to know exactly what

Notes:

....

....

....

....

....

your day at the AC will look like. But the mere fact of knowing what to expect will hopefully make you feel more comfortable and more able to focus on your performance.

EPSO has produced a little video, which you can find on *https://www.youtube.com/watch?v=T6nVuwr31wQ*. This gives a very realistic impression of what a day at the Assessment Centre is like. You are advised to watch this video carefully as it will help you to feel more at ease on "D-day". Please note that in this video the "actors" are not real candidates, but members and staff of EPSO. Candidates will never be filmed for privacy reasons.

Remote online testing

In the face of the Covid-19 pandemic and to enable it to conclude existing competitions within a reasonable period, as well as start new ones, EPSO is now carrying out online testing – remotely – for the Assessment Centre tests. Remote online testing allows candidates to sit the tests at home, in the office, or in an EPSO accredited test centre throughout Europe and worldwide. The testing takes place via online videoconferencing, using Skype for Business, now Microsoft Teams.

As a candidate you will receive instructions stating that:

- All tests will be done remotely.
- A connectivity trial will be organised approximately one to two weeks prior to your first appointment.
- You will receive an email invitation for each test, including for the connectivity trial call.
- The general competency-based interview (GCBI) and the field related interview (FRI) will take place on the same day, but in two separate sessions (which due to organisational reasons might not be consecutive).
- The situational competency-based interview (SCBI), which replaces the group exercise, will be organised at a different date.
- For the connectivity trial and the actual test sessions, you must make sure you are ready to connect 10 minutes prior to your actual appointment.
- You must have an identification document with your photograph (ID card or passport) at hand for each test session, including for the connectivity trial.

It is obviously vital that you read carefully and follow any instructions EPSO sends about the arrangements for these tests. You should email EPSO as soon as possible if you wish to request an alternative date (only within the available testing period and in exceptional circumstances) or if you wish to withdraw from the competition.

For the actual tests there will be a preparatory introduction consisting of a briefing about the rules. The interviewers will check that there is nobody in the room. Then you will have to show your ID. They then explain how long the test will last and that if the connection is lost for more than 10 minutes you will be contacted to reschedule.

In the case of an SCBI there will be just one interviewer, but he or she will state that two members of the Selection Board will be listening but not asking questions, and that the president of the Selection Board also sometimes joins (but also won't be asking questions). Finally, they ask if you have read the assignment.

Points to Watch in Online Testing

In order to take your online tests in the best possible conditions, there are some points that require special attention: framing, backgrounds, lighting, and sound quality.

Framing

Framing refers to where you are positioned in the shot in relation to your camera. To avoid unflattering angles, and to keep everything in proportion and have your eyes looking up, position your camera parallel to the ground and at eye level by elevating it using a stack of books, boxes or a stand to get it to sit at the right height. It is best not to sit too close to the webcam or lean in too much otherwise the lens will distort certain areas of your face.

Eye contact is different in a video meeting. In-person, you would look directly at someone's eyes. In a video meeting, you maintain eye contact by looking into the camera. If you can't help looking at someone's face on the screen instead of the camera, it helps to move the video window to the part of the screen nearest to the camera. So, at least you're looking at approximately the right place when you're looking at their face.

Backgrounds

Backgrounds can be highly distracting. Remove clutter from behind and around you. Before starting the event, let everyone in your household know to stay out of your space and place a "Do not disturb!" sign on your door to avoid any "BBC interview" (https://youtu.be/Mh4f9AYRCZY) situations.

Your background should be nice, neat and professional. You may wish to have on your bookshelf books or documents enhancing your credibility. This can send a subconscious message to the assessors about your motivation and interest in the topic being discussed.

Lighting

Never sit with your back to a window or have a bright light directly behind you. You will be backlit, meaning the interviewer and assessors will only see a blacked-out silhouette of you and nothing else. To be well lit, make sure you always face towards a big, bright, yet soft light source. Using a lamp may produce "catch lights" (eye reflections), which will indicate that your light source is in the right place. Catch lights can also have the positive effect of giving a lot of life to your image.

Notes:

....

....

....

....

....

Sound quality

As strange as this may seem, when you sound better, you look better. The goal here is to transmit your voice with a nearness and a warmth that commands attention at the other end.

Be conscious of the environment you are in. You don't want to be in a room with lots of echo, background noise or ambient noise. Remind others in your household to be quiet for the duration of your session.

Use a wired headset that comes with a microphone to ensure your voice will not have an echo or hollow sound to it. In addition, to get even better sound conduct the talk in a quiet and preferably well-furnished space to keep echoes and background noise to the absolute minimum.

When pausing, make sure you don't stay silent for too long, otherwise the interviewers might wonder if your audio has cut out or if your internet connection is erratic.

Professional studio

If you are in Brussels and want to present yourself in the best possible way, making sure there is no disruption by screaming kids, or that nosy colleagues or construction noise don't spoil your remote tests, you can come to Ambiorix Centre's professional studio on exam day. There is secure internet, great lighting, high-quality audio, pre-exam soothing words and encouragement.

Ambiorix Centre has the technical stuff covered, so all you need to focus on is doing your very best!

Ambiorix Centre is located at Ambiorix Square, 7 in Brussels, at only a five-minute's walk from the Schuman roundabout, in the European quarter. For pricing and further details please contact https://ambiorixcenter.eu/get-in-touch

Waiting for the Results and the Competency Passport

You should be aware that the "in-person" part of the Assessment Centre (that is, once the computer-based case study is completed) is spread over multiple weeks, even months for the bigger competitions. The Selection Board can only establish the reserve list after all the candidates have been through the complete AC. On top of that, the case studies also have to be assessed and scored. However, this is done by a group of other people (the "markers") and as the case study is usually before the in-person part, this can be done in parallel.

Besides the calculation of the aggregate scores, the Selection Board also has to establish the "competency passport" for all the candidates who participated in the Assessment Centre (not just the ones that will end up on the reserve list). This is a tedious job as they have to come up with a coherent justification of the detailed scores for every competency. Clearly, this justification is based on the observations they made during the AC, but as every competency is assessed through different exercises, these observations may contradict. In order to be of any value, the comments must stick to the (average) score and assessors' overall perception of how a candidate did in the AC.

For the candidates that are to be put on the reserve list, a final verification of the admission criteria, based on the supporting documents provided during their day at the AC, has to be performed. Given the huge disparity in education systems within the EU, this is not always straightforward. While the European Commission has a lot of experience in establishing the equivalence of degrees, diplomas and certificates, this still takes some time.

All this explains why it can take so long between your day at the AC and the moment that you are informed of the results. Results are sent to you in the form of a letter (via your EPSO account), which will also contain your competency passport.

The competency passport consists of the following elements:

- A general description of the competency framework, common to all EU institutions
- An overview – in a chart – of the candidate's strengths and weaknesses
- The main findings per competency
- A general conclusion

Examples of competency passports can be found in Annex 8.

EPSO will make the competency passport of the successful candidates – the laureates – available to the human resources (HR) departments of the EU institutions for their recruitment purposes. Candidates who are not on the reserve list can use their competency passport for their individual development.

Who does what in the Assessment Centre?

The Selection Board

Each competition will have an independent jury – or Selection Board – under the supervision of a president.

The **Selection Board** is composed of permanent and non-permanent members. The role of the Selection Board is described in Annex III of the Staff Regulations.

Permanent members are seconded for a period of two years (extendable) from the recruiting institutions. They are – as a team within EPSO – responsible for all selection procedures. They are trained by an external consultant and officially accredited as assessors. As members of a specific Selection Board they assist the president in ensuring a standardised and consistent approach in its procedures. Permanent members participate in the assessment proceedings alongside the non-permanent members of the Board.

Non-permanent members are regular EU officials coming from the recruiting institutions and designated to be a member of a specific Selection Board. They are specialised in the specific fields of knowledge within the competition but have to undertake intensive training in

Notes:

An assessor's point of view

Anyone working in the Assessment Centre has to observe absolute discretion in every aspect of the work. Assessors have to sign a declaration of confidentiality and compliance with the data protection provisions. This declaration specifies amongst others that you will not reveal information about the proceedings to outside persons, that you have to behave impartially, independently and with integrity, and that you will report anything that might compromise these objectives during the proceedings of the Selection Board. Also, any conflict of interest has to be avoided. This means that – as an assessor – you cannot participate in the assessment of a person whom you know, because you have previously worked with that individual, or otherwise. Members of the Selection Board can only be appointed if they certify not having taken up any tasks as a trainer in the preceding twelve months and will abstain from doing so for one year following the end of their mandate as member of the selection board.

the Assessment Centre procedure and all relevant exercises. During the competition, the non-permanent members are only present at EPSO for a few days per week, as they have their other regular duties in their institution of origin.

As a body, the Selection Board is largely independent from EPSO and it enjoys a high degree of autonomy. All the decisions – the composition and content of the exercises, the evaluation grids, the admission of the candidates, and their assessment through to the drawing up of the reserve lists and the individual competency passports – are taken by the Selection Board. EPSO provides administrative and legal support.

For the sake of transparency the names of the Selection Board members are published in the Official Journal. It is however strictly forbidden for the candidates to approach them in any way. Every contact (request for information, appeal, etc.) has to go through EPSO.

Markers

A "marker" is a specialist in the field of the competition. The recruiting institutions, such as the European Parliament, the European Commission or any other EU institution or body, select and provide the markers. Their role is assessing the case studies of the candidates for knowledge in the field and general competencies. Marking is done anony-

A candidate's experience

Don't be put off by people [candidates] who come over as being very confident, or by the fact that they may already be working for one of the Institutions. Don't look at other candidates to compare yourself with. Remember: YOU are being tested. For me personally, I focused on remaining calm and positive and talked to other candidates in a positive way, basically trying to have a general "good vibe" going around. Because tension does mount. Even more as there were long intervals between tests (twice about 2 hours), which of course can really get your nerves running wild. This also means that you are in for a very long day!.

mously (i.e. the marker only sees the candidate's number, not his or her identity). Every case study is marked by two different markers. When the marks are too far apart, a third marking is required. Markers have to undertake special training and respect the written instructions and scoring grids provided by the Selection Board.

The names of the markers are not made available to the candidates, indeed not even to the members of the Selection Board.

Assessment Centre Team

A competition coordinator leads the Assessment Centre team responsible for the coordination and the planning of the competition. The team are all EPSO staff. The competition assistants provide the necessary administrative support and follow-up. They assist the Selection Board and are in charge of the logistics. Even though the assistants do not participate in the actual assessment, you should treat them with the utmost respect – and stay polite – because they are working hard to ensure the smooth operation of your competition.

The Candidates

It is very hard, if not impossible, to describe a "typical" candidate profile given the large number and diverse backgrounds of applicants. However, it is considered that most of the serious applicants have five things in common. They:

- Are interested in EU affairs, committed to European integration and wish to work for a "good cause"
- Have a solid knowledge of at least two foreign languages
- Are flexible and willing to work abroad in a multi-cultural environment
- Have a strong motivation to study for and pass the exams to get into the EU institutions
- Understand and accept that EU institutions are different from the private sector inasmuch as they are a hybrid of a diplomatic corps, an international organisation and a government administration that is based on a hierarchic model

The above qualities will also be looked at by assessors, if only in an indirect way or on an informal level. EU institutions deal with such a wide variety of issues that you can certainly find the job that best suits your interests and personality if your motivation is right.

Notes:

Age

There is no age limit to applying for EU careers and jobs; however, the maximum age is effectively determined by the retirement limits provided by the Staff Regulations of EU officials. A minimum age is not specified either, given the fact that to meet the formal criteria candidates are certain to be at least 18 years old. According to the 2009 European Commission Human Resources Report, the average age of entry for AD5 (entry-level) staff in the Commission is 34 years old, so many candidates at the Assessment Centre will already have acquired work and life skills that can be of benefit in taking the tests.

Whatever your age, you will be required to pass a medical check that will serve as a benchmark for your social security and health insurance file before taking up an EU job. This also serves to ensure that you are physically capable of doing the job you are to be required to perform.

Geographical Balance

It is frequently asked whether the EU institutions apply a quota system for allocating posts to a certain number of officials from each Member State.

Article 27 of the Staff Regulations requires that EU institutions recruit staff from the broadest possible geographical basis. This is essential for each EU institution to adequately reflect the diversity of its constituency, the EU citizens and cultures. However there are significant disparities between the numbers of candidates in EPSO competitions coming from different countries, with proportionately much larger numbers coming from many of the countries of southern and eastern Europe. Inevitably this is reflected in the proportion of candidates from these countries who are successful in the competitions and then go on to be recruited.

With the reform of the Staff Regulations in 2013, the co-legislator introduced a new legal basis for each institution to adopt appropriate measures where a significant imbalance between nationalities of officials, which is not justified by objective criteria, is observed.

As shown by the 2018 report to the European Parliament and Council on Geographical Balance, 10 nationalities of the pre-2004 Member States, excluding the UK (Denmark, Germany, Ireland, France, Luxembourg, the Netherlands, Austria, Portugal, Finland and Sweden) are significantly underrepresented in the junior AD grades.

Also considering the upcoming retirement of staff recruited up to 2004, these 10 under-represented Member States will be progressively more under-represented in the next years.

As for the short term, in order to redress the situation within the next mandate the Commission may adopt measures like:

- Implementing Article 27 of the Staff Regulations in order to proceed with the launch of open competitions by nationality;

- Allowing for recruitment of higher grades for those categories of staff who are more difficult to recruit (experts of under-represented nationalities).

As for the long-term, DG-HR has been working on a comprehensive communication on the attractiveness of the EU institutions as an employer, including measures to address geographical imbalance.

Language Rules

One of the most common sources of confusion regarding EU competitions is the language regime: what is the exact meaning of the so-called "first" and "second" language? In the EU Staff Regulations it is stipulated that you must have knowledge of at least two official EU languages; one at minimum C1 level (thorough knowledge) and the other at minimum B2 level (satisfactory knowledge).

What languages are used in the EU institutions?

The EU currently has 24 official languages. The basic principles underlying its language policy are that EU citizens should be able to contribute to the building of the EU, be informed about what the EU is doing in their name, and have access to EU law in a language they can understand. The EU's very first piece of legislation (Regulation No 1, 1958) lists the official languages and specifies how they are to be used. New languages have been added as new countries have joined the EU. The EU's founding treaty states that EU citizens have the right to communicate with the EU institutions in the official language of their choice, and to receive a reply in the same language. This explains why most official meetings are held with interpretation, and why all official documents have to be translated into these languages. The cost of maintaining this policy represents 1% of the EU budget or around €2.5 per EU citizen.

The so-called "working languages" in the EU institutions are English, French and German. Obviously, for agencies and bodies located in the Member States, the local language will be used for internal proceedings as well.

In the Notice of Competition EPSO refers to these languages as:

- Language 1: language used for the computer-based Multiple-Choice Question tests – the CBTs
- Language 2: language used for the second part of the application form, the e-tray exercise, Assessment Centre and communication between EPSO and the candidates who have submitted a valid application. This must be different from language 1.

In fact the **first language** usually refers to your mother tongue, *as long as it is an official EU language*. The reason why this latter point needs to be specified is because a Latvian candidate, for example, may have Russian as their mother tongue

Notes:

but that cannot be considered as their first language since it is not an official EU language.

In some cases, especially for enlargement-related or Linguist exams, the candidate's citizenship or the given exam's specific language profile automatically determines the required first language. Examples would be competitions for Croatian Administrators and Assistants requiring the first language to be Croatian; or having French as the compulsory first language for translator exams in the French language. In other instances you are free to choose your first language as long as the above rules on citizenship and the official EU language requirements are respected. Thus, for instance, if you have Luxembourgish citizenship, your "first language" may well be French or German as Luxembourgish is not an official EU language.

It is worth noting that "mother tongue" can also mean that if you have a perfect command of a language that you "learned" – and if you are confident that your speaking and writing is close to perfect in that language – you can specify it as your first language.

The **second language** is in fact your first foreign language. However, for Linguist exams (and sometimes for certain Assistant exams) the second language is usually the one for which candidates are sought. For example, if EPSO announces a Linguist exam for Bulgarian translators, the first language is required to be Bulgarian, the second language may be any other EU official language, and there may be a third language (in fact, second foreign language) requirement as well. Note that there is no Bulgarian citizenship requirement here as the goal is the perfect command of a language regardless of which EU citizenship you may have. This is a fundamental rule in the system: the citizenship requirement is decoupled from the language requirements.

Please be aware that the e-tray and the **Assessment Centre exercises testing competencies are in the second language.** Even though there is no formal testing of your command of the second language (Linguists excepted, of course), it goes without saying that the command of your second language will influence your scores for the various exercises (oral and written). It is therefore important at the very outset in applying for a competition that you make the right choice for your second language. By far the greatest number of candidates take the Assessment Centre tests in English but there is no different treatment – or assessment – for candidates who take their Assessment Centre in another second language.

Another crucial piece of advice to bear in mind is that once you know which language you will be assessed in, you should read all preparation materials only in that language. Needless to say, names of EU institutions, abbreviations, programmes and concepts may differ significantly from one language to another, and you certainly do not wish to mix these up.

On 24 September 2015 the European Court of Justice delivered a judgment in Cases T-124/13 Italy vs Commission and T-191/13 Spain vs Commission annulling three Notices of Competition from 2012 and 2013. In essence, those two Member States took the view that the notices were discriminatory and infringed the language regime of the EU laid down by "Regulation No 1" of 1958 and the principle of proportionality. Italy and Spain challenged the requirement imposed on candidates to choose English, French or German not only as the language of communication with EPSO, but also as the second language for the competitions concerned.

As a result of this judgment, it was decided to cancel the 2016 AD5 generalist competition and review the selection procedures in terms of the languages to be used for the tests and the communication with the candidates. For certain competitions EPSO now offers as language 2 the 5 languages most frequently declared by candidates at B2 level or higher in the first part of their application form, while also taking into account the needs of the services:

- For practical and organisational reasons, it is not feasible to offer 24-language testing at all stages of the competition. The methodology of the Assessment Centre in particular requires that candidates work in groups and are assessed by a common Selection Board composed of a limited number of members, to ensure equal treatment.

- Moreover, in order to ensure uniformity when comparing candidates and checking their application forms, EPSO and the Selection Board will work in a limited number of vehicular languages.
- Lastly, the effort and resources for each additional language should be proportionate to the number of supplementary candidates who could apply to the competition should an additional language be offered.

For these reasons, EPSO and the EU institutions agreed that up to a maximum of 5 languages can be offered as language 2.

For these same reasons, it is reasonable to limit the language of communication between candidates who have submitted a valid application and the institutions, including the language in which applications are to be drafted, to the language 2 chosen by each candidate.

In order to include a maximum of applicants having one of the five vehicular languages allowed for above, candidates are invited to declare all official EU languages of which they have knowledge at the minimum required level. EPSO will then consolidate all application forms validated by the first deadline in order to rank the languages declared at B2 level or higher in descending order and compare these with the needs of the services to ensure an appropriate fit. The 5 languages in which the e-tray and the Assessment Centre will take place (language 2) will be determined on this basis by EPSO and communicated shortly after the deadline for registration.

Not surprisingly, the first time this new procedure was applied (EPSO/AD/338/17) the following 5 languages were selected by the most people: English, French, Spanish, Italian, and German (in that order). The AC for this competition was accordingly offered in all those 5 languages. This was repeated for the 2019 AD5 graduate competition.

One last remark about languages. The Staff Regulations stipulate in their Article 45.2:

'Officials shall be required to demonstrate *before their first promotion after recruitment* the ability to work in a third language.'

Good to know when you intend to build a career in the EU institutions…

How to Prepare

Education, experience and self-confidence alone will not be enough to enable you to sweep through the Assessment Centre with flying colours. Preparation is key.

First of all – obviously – read this book carefully as it will provide you with lots

Notes:

of information enabling you to go to the Assessment Centre as a well-informed candidate.

At the end of each chapter you will find a section explaining how you can prepare for the things that have been explained in that chapter. For example, in the next chapter, which is about the competency framework and competencies in particular, we will describe some ways to improve your competencies in a relatively short period. In the chapters about the exercises and tests, we will then give you some very practical advice on how to prepare for these particular tests.

In line with this idea, here are some more general ideas about preparing for the Assessment Centre as a whole.

For the preparation of the case study you can take one or more full-blown case study simulations on the eutraining.eu website. You will get the real "look and feel" of what it's going to be like, and your essay will be assessed – and commented on – by a former member of an actual EPSO Selection Board.

For the oral part of the Assessment Centre you can participate in classroom trainings or get one-on-one coaching or even both. Once again, we gladly refer you to eutraining.eu for more practical information.

Classroom training sessions are usually of a more "general" nature (that is not targeting a specific competition). The big advantage is that you can also learn from the other students by seeing how they do. You also get hands-on practice for the oral presentation and the general competency based interview and a full-blown group exercise, which is arguably the most difficult part of the Assessment Centre.

On the other hand, one-on-one coaching sessions, whether with a professional coach or with a friend or another candidate, are personalised and customised. Particular attention can be paid to your attitude, body language and – more importantly – the answers you intend to give during the competency based interview. Moreover, if this is part of your AC, you can practice an oral presentation as if it were in front of a real jury.

One cannot over-estimate the potential value of preparing in a group for the Assessment Centre, if this is a possibility for you. Try to find like-minded friends and colleagues who are also preparing for your competition, or another competition in the same category (AST, AD, specialist, Linguist…). You could then set up a "study group". A study group is a small group of people who meet regularly to discuss shared fields of study. Each group is unique and draws on the backgrounds and abilities of its members to determine the materials to be covered. The members of a study group share information and experiences, thus learning from each other. Do not consider the other members of your study group as your competitors, but rather as future colleagues: they will help you – and you will help them – to get the job done.

Recently, EUtraining has also introduced so-called "masterclasses", focusing on one particular test in the AC suite: competency based interview, Group exercise and (on request) oral presentation. These half-day classroom trainings provide a very intensive and focused training to a small group (max. 8) of participants and are something in between the general AC classroom training and personal coaching.

Another novelty is the introduction of "middle management coaching". During these personal sessions the candidate is prepared for the specific Assessment Centre that heads of unit- or directors- to be have to take with an external service provider (not EPSO).

On the day of your Assessment Centre, you need to make sure you do all of the little things that help your body and mind to control anxiety. You need to make sure that you're fully rested, with a good night's sleep. Make sure you're properly hydrated and that you've had a full and healthy breakfast. You might want to go jogging or do yoga beforehand, or do something to relieve some of your muscle tension. The less anxious you are, the easier a time you'll have during your day in the Assessment Centre.

Key points to remember

- *The Assessment Centre is the final stage of the EPSO competitions: once you are on the list of invited candidates, the vast majority of other candidates have been eliminated and your chances of success have thus increased dramatically.*
- *EPSO does not recruit EU officials; they only select the most suitable candidates and put them on a reserve list. The EU institutions do the actual recruitment, but they can only recruit people who are on a reserve list.*
- *An assessment is based on competencies, not on knowledge. Competencies are well-defined groupings of behaviours an employee is required to display in the future working environment.*
- *The selection procedure is long and tedious but has proven its worth, both for the future employer and the future employee.*
- *Always read the instructions given by EPSO on your candidate portal very carefully. When in doubt, don't hesitate to ask any question. EPSO has a very efficient user support service.*
- *Preparation is key. You can do it on your own, in a group, or with the help from an experienced trainer or coach.*

Notes:

2. The EPSO Competency Framework

Introduction

The competency framework used by EPSO is the result of a comprehensive job analysis undertaken in 2009 for all entry grades of EU officials across the institutions. All officials recruited at the entry grades between 2004 and 2007 were questioned as were, in parallel, line managers and senior stakeholders. The outcome of the job analysis was the development of the competency framework. The emphasis was on identifying those competencies common to all European institutions and therefore suitable for use in open competitions. As a result, EU institutions are looking for employees who demonstrate the following general competencies, as already described in outline terms in Chapter 1.

- Analysis and Problem Solving
- Communicating
- Delivering Quality and Results
- Learning and Development
- Prioritising and Organising
- Resilience
- Working with Others
- Leadership (only for Administrator grades)

These eight general competencies (see Figure 2.1) are all so-called "soft skills" but limited to those that are generally needed in the administration of the EU institutions. So, for example, "Influencing" or "Customer Orientation" – which are also soft skills – do not figure in the EPSO competency framework because they are not commonly needed by regular EU officials (they would be for sales people, or politicians). This is why we sometimes call the general competencies your "bureaucratic" competencies – as the EU institutions are all bureaucracies (nothing wrong with that, note).

General competencies are not to be confused with intelligence or professional competency, which are an aspect of another dimension of what we are as human beings. This is illustrated in Figure 2.2.

Intelligence is your ability to understand and learn concepts and information. The definition of Intelligence is somewhat controversial amongst psychologists, but by far the most widely used in practical settings is the psychometric approach, trying to capture the complex concept into a single score known as the Intelligence Quotient, or IQ.

The IQ is influenced by environmental and genetic factors, the relative importance of which has been the subject of much research and debate. A person's IQ is derived from the results of standardized tests and is supposed to be stable over time.

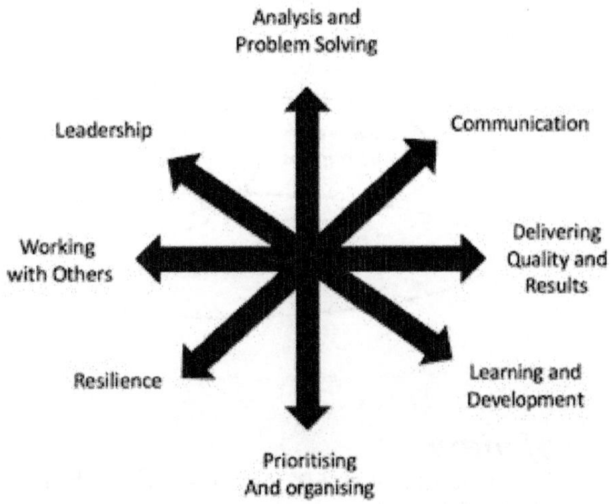

Figure 2.1

In the EPSO process a person's intelligence is tested with the computer based reasoning tests – or CBTs, though the primary purpose of these tests is to "select out" candidates, as opposed to the Assessment Centre whose main goal is to "select in" candidates. For generalists this testing is done during the pre-selection phase, whereas specialists may instead undergo these tests as part of their Assessment Centre depending on the number of candidates. While in both cases a pass mark is required, for generalists the CBTs are extremely important because only the candidates with the highest (aggregate) scores will move on to the next phase.

Professional competencies, referred to in the language of the EPSO competitions as **specific competencies**, are skills, knowledge and attributes that are valued by the other professionals in your profession. You could say "It takes one to know one." When it comes to their professional competencies, only other engineers can properly assess another engineer, or lawyers another lawyer. Professional competencies are usually assessed based on the (formal) education and the (proven) experience in the professional field through an in-depth interview (see Chapter 8). Specialists have to prove that they are capable of applying their specialist knowledge "from day one" once recruited by one of the institutions. That is why the relative weight of their professional competency in their aggregate score is typically higher than their general competencies.

Having the mental capacity (IQ) and professional competency is still no guarantee that you will be a proficient employee; you still need to behave appropriately. A medical doctor surely has the intelligence, and the professional competencies, but when he smokes cigarettes (in public) his behaviour is not what is expected from his patients. A computer programmer can be very intelligent, and proficient at what he is doing, but may lack the social skills to be an effective employee. You can doubtless think of many other examples where these three dimensions need to be sufficiently developed. This is what EPSO is looking for.

Notes:

....

....

....

....

....

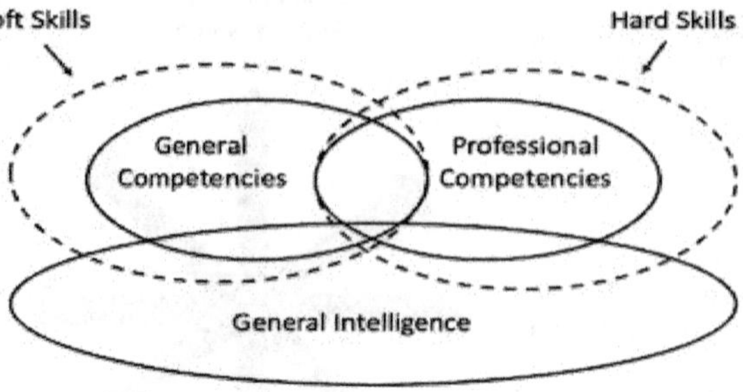

Figure 2.2

An assessor's point of view

The procedure at EPSO makes sure that all candidates have a "level playing field". First of all, we receive a thorough training about what the AC is and clear instructions about how to behave. All candidates are observed by at least four different members of the Board during the various exercises and we have to agree on every score we give. We also have to justify and document our scores, based solely on a "catalogue" of positive and negative indicators. Throughout the AC EPSO keeps statistics on how we behave in terms of scoring and we are indeed encouraged to adapt our behaviour in order to be in line with the other colleagues of the board. Finally, the permanent members, and the president, make sure that the procedures are followed in a uniform way and according to the standards of EPSO.

Perception

The Assessment Centre cannot provide an absolute and 100% accurate measurement of your competencies, even though specific processes and safeguards are built into the assessment process to make a necessarily somewhat subjective evaluation as streamlined and close to objective as possible.

The resulting **competency passport** is a description of how your competencies were perceived during your day at the AC. You could have been overly nervous and performed below your potential for that reason. You could have had an off day, been tired or been in a state of mind from some other cause that hampered your performance. You could have felt more or less comfortable with the topics of the exercises (case study, oral presentation and the group exercise that is currently replaced by the situational competency based interview) in one AC as compared to another. Finally, you could also have been better – or worse – prepared. This, at least partially, explains why your competencies may be assessed differently when participating in multiple ACs.

In addition, for every competition the composition of the Selection Board is different. This means that their perceptions may be different as well, even though everything possible is done to make sure that all the candidates for a given competition are treated (and perceived) in the same way. In case of discrepancy, however, your scores may vary because of your performance's variation relative to the other participants in your competition.

Analysis and Problem Solving

"Identifies the critical facts in complex issues and develops creative and practical solutions."

This competency may be measured in the case study, the group exercise/situational competency based interview (SCBI), the in-tray exercise, the oral presentation, and in some cases in the general competency-based interview (GCBI).

Examples of positive behaviours in a case study or in-tray exercise could include making correct assumptions and analysis of e-mails and data presented in charts (such as instructions from superiors, service offers and quotes for a task that needs to be completed) and poorer behaviour would include taking only a superficial look at issues and missing subtleties such as politically contentious aspects, long-term ramifications of short-term decisions or missing the inherent relations between different groups of information. (For example: a request made by a colleague may need to be cross-checked with official policy, instructions from your superiors and budgetary constraints – therefore you will be expected not to act blindly without taking these factors into account.)

Similar issues are measured in the competency-based interview, e.g. how you managed to overcome a challenge in the workplace or identified the core issue in question by cross- checking facts and instructions.

Communicating

"Communicates clearly and precisely both orally and in writing."

Communication (from Latin "commūnicāre", meaning "to share") is a purposeful activity of exchanging information, and meaning across space and time using various technical or natural means, whichever is available or preferred.

Good communication should be complete, concise, clear, concrete, correct, considerate, and courteous. More specifically, this means that communication should answer basic questions like who, what, when, where; be relevant and not overly verbose (a common mistake in the case study); focus on the receiver and his or her interests (especially in the oral presentation); make sure to include specific facts and figures and active verbs; include examples and visual aids when needed; be tactful and friendly; and be accurate and non-discriminatory. Body language is not to be forgotten either: pacing, posture and fluency are all important factors.

These competencies are likely to be assessed in the oral presentation and the case study. Given the absence of an oral presentation in Assistant exams the competency-based interview is used instead.

Notes:

Better responses would need to convey something of the candidate's passion, conviction and understanding of the "big picture", especially if requested to adopt a role that involved assisting a senior EU official.

As you are taking the Assessment Centre in your language 2, it is clear that a poor command of this language could negatively influence your score for this competency. This underlines the importance of speaking clearly and not too fast, and of writing in a well-structured way, avoiding spelling mistakes and grammatical errors. However, this factor should not be exaggerated. The assessors are used to communicating – both in writing and orally – with non-native speakers, and indeed they may be non-native speakers themselves.

Delivering quality and results

"Takes personal responsibility and initiative for delivering work to a high standard of quality within set procedures."

This competency is usually measured in the case study, e-tray exercise, the competency-based interview or oral presentation.

Positive behaviour would include coming up with realistic ideas and concrete suggestions, while poorer behaviour would mean that abstract or overly ambitious proposals are made. If a candidate, after analysing a Commission initiative, says that the allocated budget should be tripled, it would not reflect on him or her well, as it is probably unrealistic. Ability to work to deadlines and project management skills are at the core of this competency, along with demonstrating that you take responsibility for both the success and the failures of tasks you are given.

Learning and Development

"Develops and improves personal skills and knowledge of the organisation and its environment."

This competency is assessed largely on the basis of what you say about yourself in the competency-based interview, though it may also be measured in the group exercise/SCBI when you proactively try to learn more about other members' positions and views.

A better response would include examples of when you have proactively decided to undertake additional study or training to enhance your employability or skills, such as enrolling in an advanced training course; this might be shown by mentioning the self-development books you have recently read or the public speaking course you signed up for.

In the group exercise/SCBI, a clear demonstration that you can quickly grasp the essence of the simulation task would further improve your scoring on this measure, along with putting good questions to other members of the group to fully understand their arguments.

A poorer candidate response would show little evidence of attempting to proactively improve your knowledge or skills, outside what has been mandated by your studies or employment, or talking negatively of the "burdens" the training your current or previous employer "imposed" on you.

Prioritising and Organising

"Prioritises the most important tasks, works flexibly and organises own workload efficiently."

"Prioritising and organising" is the EPSO terminology for what is often referred to as "time management". Time itself can't be managed, of course. Everyone has the same amount of time in an hour, a day, and a week. Therefore time management simply means you are trying to make the best use of your time. Time management is the act of taking conscious control over the amount of time you spend on specific activities.

At the Assessment Centre this competency is usually measured by the competency-based interview, the group exercise/SCBI, the case study or the in-tray exercise.

In the examples you give during the competency-based interview you have the opportunity to demonstrate to the assessors that you can set goals, effectively schedule your time, and prioritise and choose what to do and what not to do. You can likewise show how you are able to delegate tasks, analyse and review the time you have spent, keep your concentration and focus at work, and motivate yourself.

Because of the large amount of data you are presented with in the case study or in-tray exercises, you actually need to apply these skills in a live setting. You have to identify key priorities – important tasks requiring immediate action (e.g. short deadline items) and manage to complete the exercise in the limited amount of time available.

A less strong performance on this competency would likely be indicated by a haphazard approach to tasks, or tackling them in the exact order they are presented to you rather than by their importance.

Resilience

"Remains effective under a heavy workload, handles organisational frustrations positively and adapts to a changing work environment."

Resilience is defined as an individual's ability to properly adapt to stress and adversity. Individuals demonstrate resilience when they can face difficult experiences and rise above them – or "bounce back" – with ease.

The primary factor in resilience is having positive relationships with other people in one's environment; this is the single most critical means of handling both ordinary and extraordinary levels of stress. Studies show that there are several other factors which develop and sustain a person's resilience, such as the ability to make realistic plans and being capable of taking the steps necessary to follow through on them, a positive self-image

Notes:

and confidence in one's strengths and abilities, and the ability to manage strong impulses and feelings.

In the Assessment Centre, resilience is measured through the group exercise/SCBI, the oral presentation, and the competency-based interview.

In the group exercise, your ability to withstand pressure from other candidates to challenging your views and argue for your case is tested, whereas in the competency-based interview candidates are asked about previous stressful (and often unexpected) experiences they have encountered. It is, therefore, crucial that you try to recall such experiences when preparing for the Assessment Centre so that you will not be left without any ideas when the question is put to you. A good response might be if you described a time when you remained calm and focused when faced with a tight deadline and multiple competing demands (e.g. your boss assigned you two projects where the deadlines seemed unrealistic or your computer broke down right before an imminent deadline was due). A poorer response would be to dwell on the difficulties you had with resolving a project challenge when under pressure without providing an explanation of how the situation was effectively resolved.

In the oral presentation you will be confronted with challenging questions from the assessors, and they will look carefully at how you respond. Are you overwhelmed by panic, or do you withstand the pressure that is put onto you? It is very common that candidates "freeze" or close their arms and legs when questions assessors ask them questions, so it takes conscious effort and self-awareness to avoid these pitfalls.

Working with Others

"Works co-operatively with others in teams and across organisational boundaries and respects differences between people."

This competency is measured by the competency-based interview, the group exercise/SCBI and the in-tray exercise.

Effective behaviours would include fully considering who to consult from among your colleagues as part of a planned project, or understanding whose approval you need to secure before confirming a course of action. (In an EU context, this means you will not only be expected to show a co-operative approach with your fellow candidates, but also to understand the decision-making procedures and consultation mechanisms of the EU institutions; this should then be integrated into your approach.)

Poorer responses would include interrupting or belittling others' points of view in a non-professional way (e.g. by saying "this idea doesn't make any sense") or failing to consider various interests in a situation.

Another important aspect of working with others is your ability (as per the situations you share with the assessors in the competency-based interview or how you demonstrate it in the group exercise) to resolve conflicts with those on the same level of hierarchy (colleagues and co-workers) and those above you (your superiors).

Leadership

"Manages, develops and motivates people to achieve results."

This definition suggests that EPSO seeks two – distinct – capacities: people who are potentially good "managers" and those who are potentially good "leaders".

Leaders lead people. Managers manage tasks. There is a difference.

Managers have subordinates: they have a position of authority vested in them by the organisation. Management is transactional; it operates within the framework of a fixed set of rules. The manager tells the subordinate what to do, and the subordinate does this because they have been promised a reward (a salary, a promotion, or inherent reward for enjoying the work…) for doing so. Managers are paid to get things done (they are subordinates too), often within tight constraints of time and money. Managers are relatively risk-averse and they will seek to avoid conflict where possible.

Leaders have followers, not subordinates. Many leaders do have subordinates, but only because they are also managers. However, when they want to lead they have to give up their formal authority because following (or being led) is a voluntary activity. This does not mean that leaders do not pay attention to tasks – in fact they are often very achievement-focused. What they do realise, however, is the importance of *inspiring* others to work towards their vision instead of directly *telling* them to do so. Leaders are also relatively risk-seeking. They consider it natural to encounter problems and hurdles that must be overcome along the way. They are thus comfortable with risk and will seek routes that others avoid, seeing them as leading to potential opportunities, and will happily break rules in order to get things done.

In real life, of course, these two capacities, of managing and leading, are often combined in one person.

In EPSO, this competency is only assessed for candidates who participate in AD competitions; people who applied for an AST competition are not assessed on this competency.

Why is this competency important? How can it be justified given the fact that for some competitions there is no previous (management) experience required, and the position you will get as a result does not require people management tasks? The reason is that EPSO selects candidates for life-long employment at the EU. Even inexperienced recruits will have to apply their leadership competency, so it is important that people have at least a basic understanding and the proper attitude towards taking initiatives, thinking out of the box and inspiring others to achieve a goal.

Your leadership competency will be tested during the competency-based interview and the group exercise.

During the interview you will be asked to describe situations where you have inspired others to take action, or you were proactive and took the initiative, describ-

Notes:

ing what your approach was and what you did to deliver on this approach in an effective way.

In the group exercise you will be observed in terms of how you behave towards the other participants. It is vital to note that in the group exercise all participants are on an equal footing (you are not allowed to designate a formal chairman), which suggests that behaving as a "leader" will be preferred over the "manager" approach, all the while doing it without being aggressive, overly assertive or dominant in the group.

Specific Competencies

A further dimension to the AC is the assessment in some cases of your "specific competencies" or "specialist/job specific knowledge". As discussed in Chapter 1, this can be a major element in the more specialised competitions.

Your specific competencies can be measured, for example, in the case study – meaning that your answer essay is evaluated both on a matrix of general competencies, as outlined above, and also on the basis of how you apply your knowledge in the field of your competition such as audit, financial assistant, digital forensic expert or other.

This is essentially done by scrutinising your choice of terminology, appropriate categorisation of facts and figures, an evaluation of your understanding of the underlying issue of the file, and other indicators that prove your knowledge. Note, however, that your domain-specific knowledge is never assessed in a *direct* manner, i.e. you will never need to sit a knowledge-based test where you need to recite facts, figures or formulas. The keyword here is *application* of your knowledge, which is always based on a background file.

Many specialist competitions include a second interview (which is different from the competency-based interview) to assess your domain-specific (or "field") knowledge. If there is such an interview in the field, it is almost always based on a talent-screener, i.e. the questionnaire that aims to pre-screen candidates for their suitability for a given role. Even in this interview, however, you will not be asked random specific facts and figures about your field; but it is certainly worth revising this body of knowledge to make sure that you can always demonstrate the right use of terminology and scientific approach to a situation they may challenge you with.

The interview in the field and the talent screener are discussed in Chapter 8.

Competencies, Anchors and Indicators

It should be clear by now that the competencies that are assessed during the AC – including the field-specific competencies – are closely interrelated, and highly overlapping. For example, it is not possible to be an excellent IT project manager if your field-specific IT skills are not complemented by good leadership skills. The general competencies also overlap to a high degree. For example, in order to be a good leader/manager you need to be good at analysing and solving problems, organising and prioritising your own and other people's work, working with others, and – above all – communicating. So, the com-

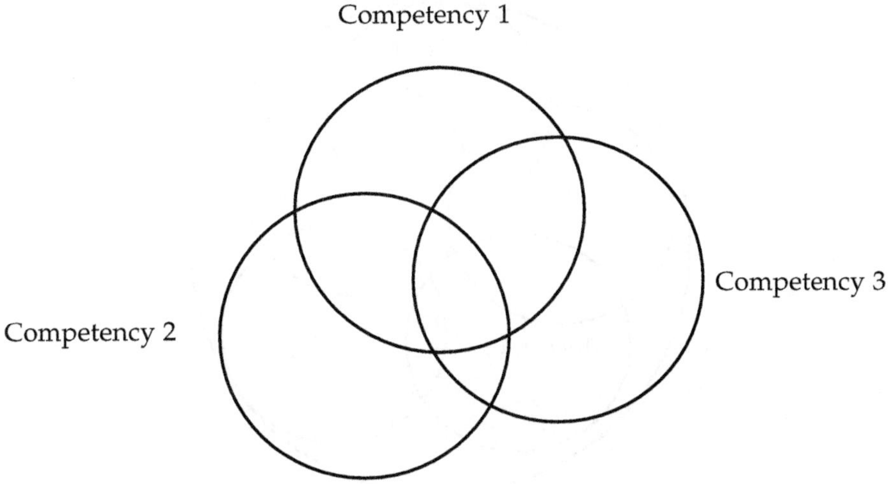

Figure 2.3: competencies are overlapping groups of behaviour

petencies should not be seen as independent "dimensions" but overlapping groups of behaviour, much like in Figure 2.3.

In order to make the assessment process more manageable, EPSO has defined its own competency framework, as described earlier in this chapter. Bear in mind that this is just an artificial – and pragmatic – grouping of the behaviours EPSO want to observe, and not a scientific model based on academic research.

Competencies are further divided into **behavioural anchors**. Behavioural anchors are specific, easy-to-apply examples of behaviours that demonstrate the competency. They are specific examples of a competency level used to help assessors and candidates to understand how to use a competency model; that is why they are also referred to as "defined behaviours".

In EPSO, there are around five anchors for every competency and in every exercise. This actually means that the competencies are not observed comprehensively, since the five anchors do not cover all the possible behaviours related to a given competency. However, the anchors have been chosen in such a way that they will provide the assessors with a very good idea of how you would behave in a real working situation. Once again, there are overlaps between the anchors within a given competency, as depicted in Figure 2.4.

Within every anchor, there are a number of specific associated (observable) behaviours, called **indicators**. These behaviours can be "good", "bad", or somewhere between. In Assessment Centre jargon they are called "positive", "negative", or "neutral" indicators (Figure 2.5).

In practical terms, the assessors have extensive checklists of positive, neutral, and negative indicators (observable behaviours) for every anchor, compe-

Notes:

....

....

....

....

....

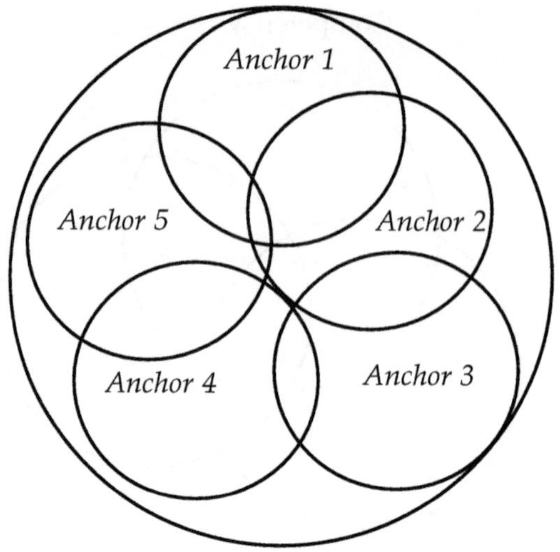

Figure 2.4: anchors

tency, and exercise during which they observe the candidates. These checklists are the foundation of the scoring system, and the observed indicators will be noted down in the file of the candidate, and serve as the basis for the observations that will be reported in the competency passport.

For instance, "team working" would be a behavioural anchor for the Working with Others competency, which is further translated into positive indicators such as "doesn't interrupt the other person".

This means that competencies are interrelated. Certain behaviours (indicators) are the hallmark of a given competency but have a clear relation with some other competencies as well. An example can illustrate this.

One of the anchors for **Resilience** is "Remain effective with high workload and tight deadlines". Some positive indicators (of behaviour) for this are, amongst others:

- Has strategies for coping with large volumes of work
- Sees where corners can be cut to meet tight deadlines
- Copes with a heavy workload over an extended period of time and produces good results
- Takes remedial action when deadlines are in danger of being missed

It is clear that this behaviour is related to some other competencies, such as:

- Analysis and problem solving
- Delivering quality and results
- Prioritising and organising

And to a lesser extent:

- Communicating
- Working with others
- Leadership

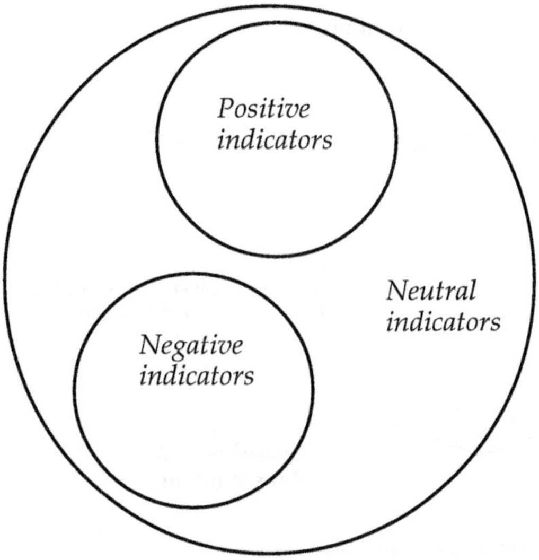

Figure 2.5: indicators

For this reason, competencies should not be seen as separate or isolated entities, but in a wider perspective of the person as whole, much like in Figure 2.6.

This indeed gives a much better view of the overall qualities of that person.

That is why EPSO communicates the results of the Assessment Centre in this "spider's web" format, enriched with a proper explanation of what has been observed, illustrating the strong points, and suggesting areas of improvement. This feedback comes in the competency passport, examples of which may be found in Annex 8 of this book.

How to Prepare

Assessment Centres are all about competencies. Competencies are in turn all about how you behave, so Assessment Centres are all about behaviours. Before giving you any advice on how to improve your competencies, or in other words to improve your behaviours, it is important to introduce the concept of the "comfort zone".

Your comfort zone is any type of behaviour that keeps you at a low anxiety level. Everyday activities that you are used to do won't make you feel anxious and uneasy, so they are part of your comfort zone.

Brené Brown, a research professor at the University of Houston Graduate

Notes:

....

....

....

....

....

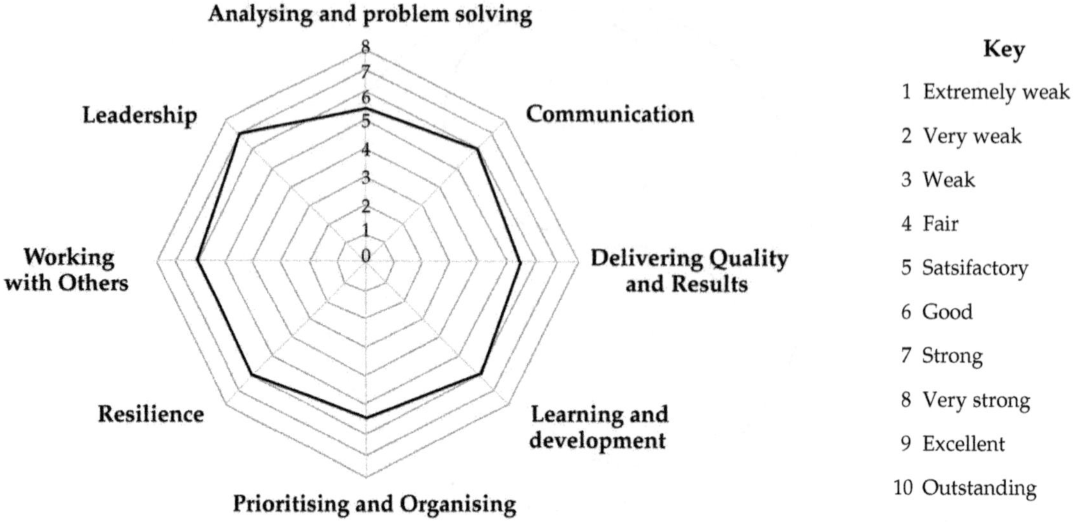

Figure 2.6: "spider's web" view of competencies

College of Social Work, has another definition of the comfort zone in her book *The Gifts of Imperfection*: "Where our uncertainty, scarcity and vulnerability are minimized — where we believe we'll have access to enough love, food, talent, time, admiration. Where we feel we have some control."

Although people often refer to "getting outside your comfort zone" in terms of trying new things, anything that raises your anxiety levels can be counted as being outside that zone.

Anxiety isn't something we are prone to go looking for, but a little bit can be surprisingly beneficial. We often need just a hint of anxiety to push us to get our work done, or to improve our performance.

The comfort zone is often illustrated as in Figure 2.7, where the comfort zone extends into a learning zone, but eventually leads to a panic zone, where anxiety is too high.

A lot of the anxiety that comes from leaving your comfort zone is due to uncomfortable levels of uncertainty. There is a reason that cooking dinner is no big deal when you do it all the time; you know what to expect. Driving a car for the first time or skydiving or starting a new job are all activities that are full of uncertainty, and thus, anxiety.

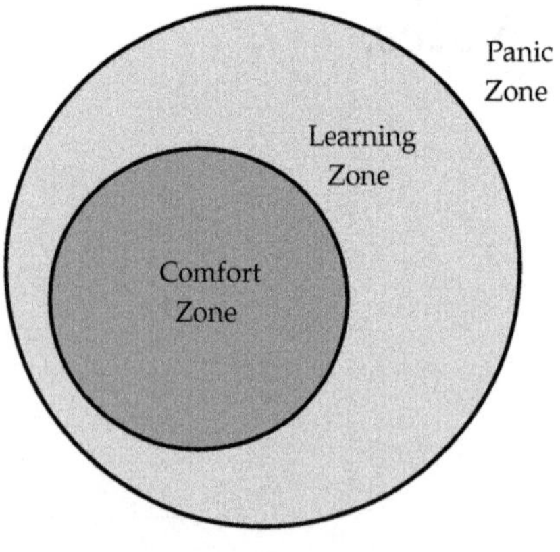

Figure 2.7

Uncertainty can make us respond more strongly to negative experiences. We are more likely to respond negatively to new things, even though we may come to like them over time. Familiarity is comfortable and enjoyable, so it is no real surprise that new things make us put our guard up. From an evolutionary perspective, we see familiar things as more likely to be safe, and so we are more drawn to what we know. Trying new things takes energy, so we are more likely to lean on old habits than take a new risk.

So, should you break out of your comfort zone? Is it actually good for you? The answer is "yes", to some degree.

"We need a place of productive discomfort," says Daniel H. Pink, in his book *Drive: The Surprising Truth about what Motivates us*: "If you are too comfortable, you are not productive. And if you are too uncomfortable, you are not productive either. We can't be too hot or too cold."

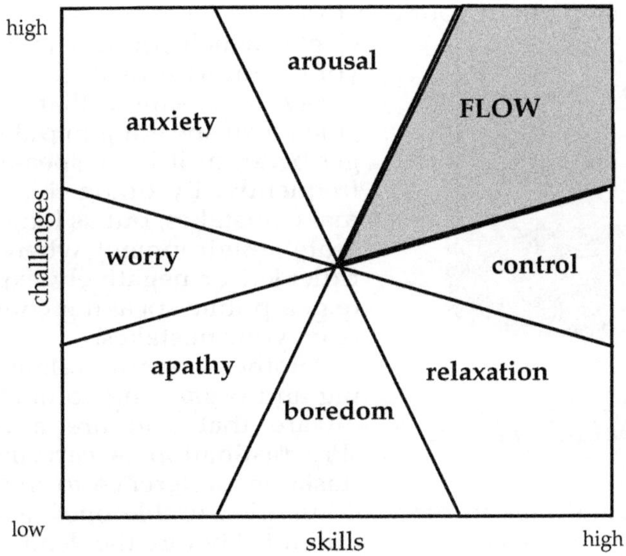

Image source: http://julioterra.com/journal/wp-content/uploads/2010/03/Flow.png

Figure 2.8

Another well-known writer on the subject is the Hungarian-American professor of psychology, Mihály Csíkszentmihályi whose much acclaimed work on "flow" is meant to describe, according to Wikipedia, "the mental state of operation in which a person performing an activity is fully immersed in a feeling of energized focus, full involvement, and enjoyment in the process of the activity. In essence, flow is characterized by complete absorption in what one does" (see Figure 2.8).

The objective is to reach that optimal level so that our skills increase and we become comfortable with that new level of anxiety — then we are in an expanded comfort zone. And ideally, we will get

Notes:

more used to those feelings of "productive discomfort" and won't be too scared to try new things in the future.

When mixed with the feeling of success, some anxiety and self-doubt can lead to personal growth. This is why outdoor adventures like rock climbing or skydiving can be so exciting: they induce anxiety and unease but when completed, they give us a huge feeling of accomplishment and increase our base levels of confidence.

Coming back to the topic of how to prepare for the Assessment Centre, one could say that you should try to step out of your comfort zone for those aspects of the Assessment Centre which you feel anxious about. Leaving your comfort zone is the only way to develop.

Say, for example that you feel uncomfortable when speaking in public: the only way to get better at it is by speaking in public more frequently. By doing this, you will certainly make mistakes, but as long as this is done in a "safe" environment where the risk of being ridiculed or negatively exposed is fairly low (e.g. a public speaking course), you can learn from your mistakes.

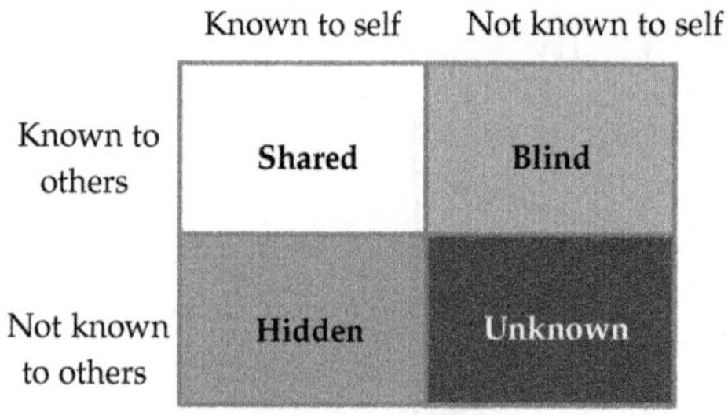

Figure 2.9: the Johari window

Another example relates to your prioritising and organising competency. You may be aware that you are a big procrastinator. Procrastination is carrying out less urgent tasks in preference to more urgent ones, or doing more pleasurable things in place of less pleasurable ones, and thus putting off tasks to a later time, sometimes to the "last minute" before the deadline. Procrastination is negative behaviour in the context of prioritising and organising. To improve this competency you could follow training on time management (there are hundreds of online courses and books you can find on this topic), learn about the principles and adapt your day-to-day behaviour accordingly. By doing this, you will certainly improve your results in the Assessment Centre.

Specific recommendations

It is possible to improve every single competency, but there is no point in trying to improve everything at once and especially not in a short time; this won't work. The best approach is to become aware of your current behaviour and identify your weak points according to the EPSO competency framework. You may need external feedback provided by a professional coach or trainer, an online personality questionnaire (though make sure it's a professional and in-depth one, otherwise the results will do more harm than good) or someone who knows you very well and is willing to discuss it with you in an open and honest manner.

When doing such self-assessment, you may also want to check the concept of the Johari window, which is a concept that summarizes what you and others know or don't know about yourself, as in Figure 2.9.

Once you have a rough idea about your strengths and weaknesses, make a plan to try to improve in those areas where your performance is worst. Have a look at all the "positive indicators" throughout this book, ask yourself the question if you behave in that way, and try to improve your own behaviours accordingly. You can start with this right now.

Another important point is that all the self-development effort you put into your preparation goes beyond EPSO: it is time well invested because it improves your skillset for the future, something you can leverage in any job or position that you may have, whether in the EU institutions or elsewhere.

Self-development is a process that takes time, a lot of time. You may not have that time because your Assessment Centre is already near. Nevertheless, you can improve your performance at the AC by some very targeted training, which will – at the least – remove some of your anxiety, thereby expanding your comfort zone in a very short period of time.

Now take a look at Annex 1. This provides a comprehensive list of anchors for each competency with a detailed description of positive and negative indicators.

And to assess your strengths and weaknesses in the competencies online, use our free online self-assessment tool at https://www.johnharperpublishing.co.uk/the-ultimate-eu-career-development-toolkit/

Key points to remember

- *General competencies are all about observable behaviour in a realistic simulation of your future working environment.*
- *In an AC, competencies are assessed through a variety of exercises and by different people, making sure that the results are not biased by personal opinions.*
- *The scores you obtain are merely a "snapshot" of how you were perceived during the AC. Your scores only have an importance in relation with the scores of the other candidates; they are not absolute.*

Notes:

3. The In-tray (E-tray) Exercise

Introduction

An e-tray exercise is a computer-based simulation of a real work situation and replicates an email inbox which contains information relating to a particular issue. Candidates need to find the best possible solutions within a fixed and limited amount of time. It is a kind of situational judgement test focusing on some of the general competencies that are further assessed by other exercises at the Assessment Centre.

For **Assistant** competitions, this test has been part of the Assessment Centre since 2011.

For **Administrators**, the e-tray was not previously required at any stage of the competition. However, in 2015, EPSO introduced the e-tray as an **intermediate stage** in the selection procedures for AD5 generalists (and AD5 auditors). This intermediate stage was brought in to avoid the automatic rejection of otherwise potentially valuable candidates who happened to have a slightly lower – but still very good – score in the CBTs. It is important to note that the scores obtained in the Administrator e-tray test are taken into account in the final scoring, so in effect for AD5 generalists the e-tray is part of the assessment. Like the other exercises in the Assessment Centre, the e-tray is taken in language 2 of the candidate.

The competencies that are tested by this exercise are analysis and problem solving, delivering quality and results, prioritising and organising, and working with others.

Description and Purpose

In the e-tray exercise you are asked to assume a particular role, for example in a fictitious company or an EU institution. Your task is to decide on priorities and appropriate actions to take.

You will be confronted with 15-20 "scenarios" within a more general context as described in a number of emails. Each scenario has 3 action options and candidates are requested to rank each of the options using the following 5-point scale:

- -	Totally disagree
-	Disagree
+/-	Neutral
+	Agree
++	Totally agree

You are advised to rate each action according to its own merits, as multiple competencies may be tested per question. Therefore the three options are not necessarily alternatives to each other. However, each ranking symbol can only be selected once per question, so the choices will also indicate an order of preference (i.e. best, middle, and worst) among the 3 options.

Time Management

By far the biggest challenge for the e-tray exercise is time management. You get only 40 or 50 minutes to do this exercise – however, the time allowed may vary from competition to competition, so please make sure you know exactly how much time you have when starting the exercise! You can use the clock on your screen, but be aware that timing is absolutely vital in this exercise.

In essence, there are two main tasks to perform: (1) try to understand the general context by reading the information provided in the emails and (2) select the appropriate options for all the situations presented.

Don't underestimate the complexity of this exercise. The amount of information provided in the emails will be huge and it will not be possible to read – and fully understand or remember – everything in the time available. Since there are three options for every scenario you will have to solve between 45 and 60 multiple-choice problems – and in the 2018 AD5 e-tray the time pressure was even higher!

For this reason we would advise you to split up the available time into three blocks, or phases: *discovery, answering, review.*

What in practice does this mean? Imagine that the total available time is T minutes, and the number of scenarios is N (meaning that there are 3xN options to decide upon.) The timing we'd suggest would be as follows:

- Discovery: T – Nx1.5 – 5 minutes
- Answering: Nx1.5 minutes
- Review: 5 minutes

So, for an e-tray of 50 minutes with 20 scenarios, that would mean you should reserve 15 minutes for reading the emails ("discovery"), 30 minutes for answering the scenarios, and 5 minutes to review your answers. Since you use 1.5 minutes per scenario, you have around half a minute to make a choice for every option presented. This may not seem to be a lot, but we'll explain later how you can go about it.

Discovery Phase

As said previously, the purpose of the discovery phase if for you to get a clearer picture of the general situation, and to understand what information is available to you. Do not try to read – or remember – everything in detail, but rather proceed in a "speed reading" mode. (You will find more about speed reading in the chapter on the case study.)

You will have some sheets of paper and a pen, so during the discovery phase you can take some notes – for example, which email contains what information, and when it dates from (the emails are not necessarily in chronological order). You

Notes:

....

....

....

....

....

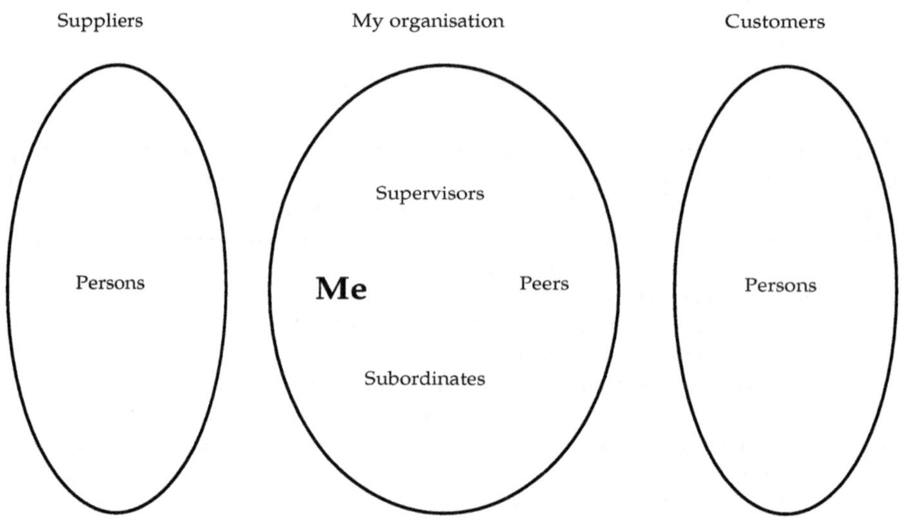

Figure 3.1

could also make a drawing representing the relationships between the various actors, like in Figure 3.1.

Write down the names of all the stakeholders (e.g. individual people, institutions or departments) involved, and draw a simple diagram to show the relationships. Names and positions are typically difficult to remember by heart, so a little drawing might help tremendously.

Answering Phase

It is of the utmost importance that you answer all the questions, so you must mark ALL the options that are presented to you. Why? Because the e-tray exercise is NOT the sort of multiple-choice test which has only one right answer. In fact, there are no "wrong" answers, just very good, good, and not-so-good answers; even if your choice is not the best you can still earn points. *If you leave a choice unanswered you are sure to get no points at all.*

Now how can you go about in making your choices?

They key to this question lies in the condition that "each ranking symbol can only be selected once per question". So you cannot have two options that are "best", "middle" or "worst" for a given scenario. We would therefore advise you to rely mainly on your "gut feeling" and not try to reason too much. In humans, the gut feeling is a well-developed but often underestimated tool, especially for solving problems where there is no single, mathematical solution (too much information, not enough information, contradictory information…). In real life, we use our gut feeling all the time, even for life-changing decisions, so why not do it here, at least as a last resort when time is short?

In practice, you would look at the scenarios as a whole, not at the three options separately, and you will probably immediately have a gut feeling about which would be the "best" – or the "worst" – option in the list. Once you made that choice there are only two to go, and you know that these have to be different from the first choice you made, and from each other.

A good approach would also be to forego the simple "Agree" or "Disagree" choices, and only use "Totally agree", "Neutral" and "Totally disagree". In the worst case this will make you lose one point, but it makes your decision-making much easier.

A candidate's point of view

I was quite afraid of the e-tray exercise as there is not much known about it in advance. Some people told me it was like the situational judgment test, but I found that it was much more like organising and prioritising, in the sense that I had to prioritise information and find the best way forward. The time was quite short so I had to be very efficient, but the computer interface is fairly easy to handle. There are lots of documents, mostly emails, to read through and often they have conflicting information in them so I had to check who's the sender and how important that person or organisation was. I think the most important skills are efficiency and common sense for this exercise, and I think this exercise is not the toughest one in the Assessment Centre after all.

When using this approach, you don't need more than 1.5 minutes to handle a situation, as your better understanding of the context (discovery phase) will surely make your choice an "educated guess".

When in doubt, try this: "How can I – given the situation – make sure that the outcome of my choice is a win-win situation?" After all, the e-tray exercise is about trying to find a good compromise, where every stakeholder's expectation is more or less met, and nobody is left out in the cold.

Review Phase

We would very definitely encourage you not to skip the last five minutes of review, not least because towards the end of the exercise you will have got a better overview of the situation in the exercise, which may help you solve some of the more difficult options.

How to Prepare

Try the sample exercise in this book (Annex 2), just to get a feeling of for how an e-tray works, and then go online to practise further. On eutraining.eu you will find plenty of opportunity to practise, fine-tune your time management and – above all – learn how to employ your gut feeling for this kind of exercise.

Notes:

An assessor's point of view

As assessors, we are not involved in scoring the e-tray exercise as it is computer based, so we get its results automatically from those administering the computer-based tests. The competencies it measures, however, are among those that we evaluate in other exercises, so the scores need to be considered in order to establish an appropriate competency passport. This exercise is probably the most similar to the kind of tasks a candidate will need to do in their job once recruited, so it is a very important one in the Assessment Centre, given that it is so practice-oriented.

Some Tips for the Assessment

- **Full Coverage**: Read through all the correspondence swiftly before doing anything else and only then assess the tasks required and come back to the items that you consider need most of your time.
- **Notes**: You may wish to take notes on the erasable slate given at the Assessment Centre of key pieces of information (names, dates, events, relationships between these etc; the exercise may have hard-to-remember names or similar names to make your task more challenging). Although this might use up some valuable time, it can also help you work more accurately.
- **Clarity**: Make sure you clearly understand what is expected in response to each issue (e.g. a request for a meeting for your director; a problem raised by a colleague in your unit regarding his annual holiday entitlement etc.), according to the instructions.
- **Dates and Deadlines**: Make sure to identify the sending date of the email or the date shown in the signature part, as these may be relevant information to understand the situation. In some cases a relative deadline ("within 30 days") may depend on your understanding of these pieces of information, and this can also have an important impact on your interpretation of the sequence and hierarchy of the facts of the file.
- **Types of Action**: This essentially means deciding on those issues needing immediate or urgent action, those you can delegate, those you can defer (delay), and those you may be able to drop (ignore). If you can successfully identify which action (or inaction) to choose for each, you are halfway done with the exercise, though this will still need to translated into the right multiple-choice option.
- **Priorities**: If something is urgent but not important, choose the option that suggests you deal with it quickly and decisively, or decide if anything actually needs to be done at all.
- **Sender**: Always identify who the message is from because the sender's impor-

tance to the organisation may be a crucial factor. Make sure you act accordingly depending on whether the sender is internal (staff) or external (a citizen, stakeholder, a Member State diplomat, trade union activist or journalist). Try to weigh the information according to the sender's reliability, seniority, whether he or she contradicts another person's communication or the instructions, and the actual content of the message.

- **Deferring**: For tasks that you decide to defer, think about how you would act on them when you have time. Make sure to keep a thorough tracking record of all such items and ensure you do not forget about them under the time pressure. Use the review phase to have a closer look at these.
- **Delegating**: For tasks you can "delegate" (though the exercise is not interactive, this may nevertheless be an option in the multiple-choice options), the background information will normally have references indicating who you can delegate to (e.g. you may see someone is your team's Administrative Assistant from their job title in an email or from an organisation or department structure chart).
- **Solutions**: Remember, there are many shades of good answers in an e-tray: you will need to indicate the most and least suitable choice and there are even two levels within each.
- **Calculations**: Questions will not require you to make exact calculations, but a good sense of proportions, priorities and figures may be required in the exercise.
- **Time Management**: Manage your time so that you deal with everything in your e-tray, but do not rush and miss out key information or act in a way that conflicts with a decision you need to take on the basis of another e-tray item. Try to leave five minutes at the end to double check what you have written before the time is up (but if you are struggling for time, do not rush the task in order to guarantee this).
- **Dates**: As well as keeping track of real time, take note of the dates on which emails were sent to help in your prioritisation decisions and better understanding the context.
- **Relevance**: In all e-tray exercises, more information than is necessary will be provided in order to distract you and test your prioritisation skills. Remember that assessors want you to identify essential key points, rather than over-analyse information and get overwhelmed by detail. At times you will have to make a judgement call based on what information is available and which piece is actually reliable.

Notes:

Key Points to remember

- *Time management is of the utmost importance in this exercise*
- *Try to answer ALL the questions, you can only win points in doing so, not lose*
- *Do not over-analyse the situations, trust your gut feeling*
- *Practise, practise, practise*

4. The Case Study

Introduction

Generally speaking, a case study is a realistic and relevant business problem. Candidates are asked to analyse a problem, interpret data, consider alternatives and produce a written report describing their solutions or recommendations.

In EPSO competitions, the case study takes the form of a computer based written exercise. For a given competition, all the candidates have their case study on the same day, in a test centre of their choice.

You will be given information about an EU-related scenario, presenting you with various questions which you must answer solely on the basis of the materials provided. For this exercise you will need to be familiar with EU issues and the EU institutions, so that you quickly grasp the context of the simulations. The objective of the case study is to assess your general competencies and – for certain competitions – your proficiency in the field.

Not all competitions have a case study. For some AST competitions, for instance, the in-tray exercise may be used to assess much the same competencies, but at a different level (see the AST-SC matrix in Table 1.3; but compare with the AST3 matrix in Table 1.2). Note however that where there is an AST case study, the only real difference between the level of difficulty and an AD case study is the length of the background material. Similarly, Linguist competitions for translators and interpreters are held that do not include a case study.

The case study is not itself eliminatory; the scores you obtain for the various competencies tested will be added to the scores obtained for the other tests aimed at assessing these competencies. Only if you don't obtain the pass mark for any given competency, or the minimum required total score (for all the competencies) will you be eliminated from the competition.

Competencies

The objective of the case study is to assess some of your general competencies and, in certain cases, your ability to become a proficient official in the domain of the competition you are taking. The general competencies likely to be tested are analysis and problem solving, communicating (drafting skills), delivering quality and results, and prioritising and organising.

Analysis and Problem Solving

"Identifies the critical facts in complex issues and develops creative and practical solutions."

Positive Indicators

- Copes well with complexity
- Challenges data (by comparing multiple sources of information)
- Identifies the root cause of issues (by trying look beneath the surface)
- Considers multiple options (and does not say one option is the only one possible)
- Suggests creative solutions
- Makes practical and workable suggestions
- Gathers only relevant information for decision making (keeps a strong focus)

Negative Indicators

- Is confused by complexity
- Accepts data at face value (or uses only one source of information)
- Stays at a superficial level (without understanding the essence)
- Focuses on a single option
- Comes up with conventional ideas (i.e. predictable)
- Makes impractical or not workable suggestions
- Presents irrelevant or too detailed information

Communicating (drafting skills)

"Communicates clearly and precisely both orally and in writing."

Positive Indicators

- Writes clearly and fluently
- Uses proper balance between detail and conciseness
- Writes for the right audience (which is usually indicated in the instructions)
- Captures the attention of the audience (by using good metaphors or examples)
- Conveys key points of arguments (and does not get lost in the details)
- Writes without spelling or grammatical errors

Negative Indicators

- Writes in a way that is difficult to understand
- Is overly detailed or too concise

- Writes for the wrong audience
- Fails to capture the attention of the audience
- Fails to convey the key points of arguments
- Makes many spelling or grammatical errors

Delivering Quality and Results

"Takes personal responsibility and initiative for delivering work to a high standard of quality within set procedures."

Positive Indicators

- Takes responsibility to meet objectives
- Maintains quality at an acceptable level
- Follows guidelines and instructions
- Takes initiative by proposing new solutions
- Accepts challenges and does not ignore them
- Seeks to exceed expectations

Negative Indicators

- Fails to take responsibility
- Allows quality to degrade (the essay is inconsistent in quality)
- Does not follow guidelines and instructions
- Avoids challenges
- Makes only the minimum effort required (too short essay, e.g. less than a page)

Prioritising and Organising

"Prioritises the most important tasks, works flexibly and organises own workload efficiently."

Positive Indicators

- Prioritises tasks appropriately (e.g. if there are issues to address)
- Sets realistic deadlines and milestones (in the essay itself and also in the writing process)
- Monitors progress
- Adapts to changes in plan (if there is new information or instructions)
- Prepares in advance, is proactive

Notes:

Negative Indicators

- Makes incorrect priority judgments (the easy tasks over the important tasks)
- Fails to set realistic deadlines and milestones
- Does not monitor progress
- Fails to adapt to changes in plan
- Fails to prepare in advance, is reactive

The markers will look at all these indicators in your essay and justify their scores by listing the indicators they found. In practice, they have a clear set of instructions – or questions to answer when giving their assessment. This is contained in a "Scoring Guide", a booklet the markers receive along with a training course they have to follow when enlisting for a given competition.

ASSIGNMENT

IMPORTANT NOTICE

This is a fictitious document only produced for the purpose of this exercise. All references to existing states, international organisations, private companies, departments, their representatives etc. should be considered as mere examples. They do not represent any position of these bodies or persons. Participants are therefore advised to rely solely on the information presented in the exercise and not on any prior expertise when responding to questions.

For this exercise you will assume the role of X at Y within the Unit responsible for Z. The documentation you need, is integrated in this booklet. You will find in it a certain number of e-mails, reports, articles and other documents that you will need to analyse and integrate in order to be able to properly deal with the assignment given to you.

It is important that you accept the simulated situation as it is presented to you. Although in a real life situation you would have access to other sources of information and would be able to consult your colleagues, in this exercise you are limited to the information contained in the exercise documents. You are, however, allowed to make logical assumptions where information is missing or incomplete.

You may rearrange the documents in any order you wish and add remarks or make notes as necessary. However, remember that the assessors will base their evaluation exclusively on what you write. Therefore, be sure to write down all the information on which you wish to be evaluated and be sure to explain the reasoning behind your ideas.

The case study aims at assessing the following competencies: Analysis and problem solving, Communicating (drafting skills), Delivering quality & results and Prioritising & Organising.

In addition to the general competencies, it assesses your ability to apply specific knowledge to a particular situation in your domain.

Your concrete task will consist of answering questions concerning the situation described in this exercise:

- **Question 1**
- **Question 2**
- **Question 3**

In total, you have 90 minutes for this case study. Please answer as precisely as you can and write as clearly as possible.

Please note: Today is Friday, 29 June 200X

Last year was 200X-1, next year will be 200X+1

(Source: adapted from EPSO - http://europa.eu/epso/doc/mock_casestudy_en.pdf)

The Assignment

The most important item in the documentation you are given is the assignment. In it you will find instructions about the purpose of the exercise, your role, the time allowed and – most importantly, the questions you are asked to answer. A typical assignment looks like the one on the next page.

Your time will be very limited when it comes to the actual case study at the AC, so it is recommended that you have a good look at this example during your preparation (in other words, right now), and take note of what's in it, so that you don't waste time during the real exercise. All assignments look the same, and **they only really differ in the parts that are put in bold in the example**. Obviously, you have to read – and be aware – of this information during your real exercise.

A frequently heard question is about the topic of the case study: "will the topic be related to the field of the competition?" The answer to this question is not clear cut, but we can give you some idea anyway.

For **generalist competitions** you can expect more or less any topic, but it is a given that the topic will be EU-related, and probably focusing on a recent event or "hot item" in the EU realm. Generalists are expected to have a broad insight and understanding of current (EU) affairs; their knowledge and understanding should go beyond newspaper headlines or bar talk. So, if you have a wide interest in current affairs, and try to understand the context and implications of this or that policy, you should be fine. Even though some topics may seem highly "technical" don't be scared away. The purpose of the case study is not to test your knowledge, but to observe your general competencies.

For **specialist competitions** there are – in fact – two possibilities: either your specific competencies will be assessed during the case study, or they won't.

It is, of course, obvious that in the first case the topic of your case study will be closely related to the field of the competition. The jury will want to see how deep and wide your understanding of the field is, without, however, digging into the theoretical details. The jury is looking for educated and experienced professionals in the field, not for self-declared experts.

In most specialist competitions, however, the case study is not used to assess your competency in the field; instead, that is evaluated though the interview in the field. Since the purpose of these case studies is to assess some of your "general" competencies there is no strict need for the topic to be field-related. However, bear in mind that the jury is mainly composed of specialists in the field of the competition, and that it is the jury that has the final responsibility over the content of all the tests. In many cases it is even a member of the jury who creates the exercises (the so-called "source-person"). Having this in mind, you can therefore expect the topic of your case study to be at least remotely related to the field of the competition.

That being said, do not feel too relieved when you find out that the case study is

Notes:

....

....

....

....

....

about something you know very well. This could be more of a handicap than an advantage. Indeed, in all the assignments it is clearly stated that you are advised to rely solely on the information provided and not on any prior expertise in the field when answering the questions. So, knowing a lot about the topic could lead to a worse performance for the general competencies if you don't follow this rule.

The Structure of Your Essay

You can decide on the structure of your essay right after reading the assignment. In fact, a good structure should always look like this:

INTRODUCTION

TITLE OF YOUR ANSWER TO QUESTION 1

TITLE OF YOUR ANSWER TO QUESTION 2

TITLE OF YOUR ANSWER TO QUESTION 3

CONCLUSIONS

When putting this structure on paper (in the editor) leave some blank lines in between the titles. Don't worry about what you are going to write at this point, you will "fill in the blanks" later on. It is a good idea to write your titles in ALL CAPITAL LETTERS, and even number them, just to make sure that the structure of your text is visible at first glance. You could also leave a blank line between the titles and the actual portions of text, to make the structure even more visible.

Why is this a good structure? Well, because the markers will undoubtedly be looking for the structure, and try to find out if you have answered all the questions. In fact, they will probably go through your essay in a "speed reading" way (at least in a first reading). You can help them with this by using this structure.

The INTRODUCTION and the CONCLUSIONS are there to make your essay complete. Even though not absolutely necessary, it will show the reader that you are delivering a completed work, and that you did not run out of time while writing it. This will be the case if you write a compelling introduction and a well thought out conclusion.

For the "body" of your chapters it is advised to use **bulleted lists** (with – or * symbols) wherever it is possible to do so. This further enhances the visual appearance of your work and makes it very easy for the markers to verify that you have not missed any

A marker's point of view

Even though this is not mandatory it is a good idea to add a header and a footer to your work. These would then typically contain the recipient, a title for the document, the date (header) and a "signature" of the sender (you). Make it look as if you are writing an email – or a memo – about the subject. By doing so, you make it clear that you have understood the context of the exercise.

Never, ever put your (real) name anywhere in the essay. Your work will be marked anonymously (using a "secret" ID). If the document can be linked to a candidate you will be excluded from the competition without further ado.

important information. Do not confuse "lists" with enumerations of incomplete sentences or mere keywords. Try to make concise but grammatically correct and comprehensive sentences. In other words, make your text fluent and readable.

Make your text ready for presentation. Imagine that you will use it as a handout for an oral presentation you will give to the audience.

One last remark on the user interface of the tool you will have to use at EPSO. This is a very simple text editor (a bit comparable to Microsoft Notepad or Mac Notes) and you have very few possibilities to enhance the visual aspect of your work. It is not possible to put words or sentences in **bold**, *italic* or to underline them. You can't even use different fonts or font sizes. The only way to make your text somewhat clearer – or attractive – is the above tools (capitalisation, numbering, lists, blank lines).

The Content of Your Essay

It is clear that the content of what you write is even more important than the structure of your text. The markers are specialists in your field themselves, so you have to demonstrate to them that you have really understood the questions that are asked and that you can come up with acceptable and realistic solutions or recommendations.

A first and important remark can be found in the assignment:

> It is important that you accept the simulated situation as it is presented to you. Although in a real life situation you would have access to other sources of information and would be able to consult your colleagues, in this exercise you are limited to the information contained in the exercise documents. You are, however, allowed to make logical assumptions where information is missing or incomplete.

Does this statement mean that you have to stick absolutely rigorously to what's in the background information provided? Let us give a consultant's answer to this: "it depends".

- **Accept the context**: do not challenge the information as described in the documentation and make sure to stay within this context. So, if your case study is about CO_2 emissions of cars in the EU you should not start talking about greenhouse gases that are emitted by households or industrial activity worldwide. This does not mean, however, that in your solutions or recommendations you cannot suggest anything that puts things in a wider perspective.
- **Accept the data**: the positions of the various stakeholders, and the facts and figures as presented in the background information may not correspond to reality. Even if you know "the truth" you should rely on what's in the documentation to build

Notes:

your arguments. However, when there is information missing or incomplete you can add information of your own. In fact, in doing so, you demonstrate your knowledge in the field.

- **Stay focused on the case study**: do not get sidetracked into talking about the wider outside-world situation unless asked to do so (e.g. if the case study concerns the new mobile phone transmission standards, keep the mention of global telecommunication trends to the minimum).
- **Limited information**: you may not have all the information at hand that you would need; you are usually safe to make reasonable assumptions, but make it clear when you are doing so and where further information would be desirable ("It can reasonably be assumed from the file that…" as opposed to "It is known that…").
- **Focus on the core questions**: it happens frequently that, somewhere in the background documents, somebody asks for something more – or something else – than what is asked for in the assignment. This is a trap! Do NOT answer this as a separate question, but maybe put some hints either in your introduction or in the conclusions.
- **Use the right sources**: sometimes, the background documentation is "enriched" with information coming from less relevant sources. A typical example might be a report that has been published by an interest group or lobbyist. This does not mean that this information is not relevant, but it certainly has to be treated as less important than what is said by "official" sources (institutions, governments, scientists, etc). You may find some interesting ideas for your solutions or recommendations though.
- **Strike a balance between detail and conciseness**: the reader is not interested in the detailed information. Instead, a succinct description makes the reader's life easier, avoiding the need to make that summary themself.
- **Reference facts from the file**: when making a claim or underlining an issue, make sure to rely on and refer to the facts in the background documents (e.g. "Based on the provisions of Article 8 of Directive X, it was not possible for company Y to apply for this grant." or "As seen from the vacancies shown in the organigram of this Directorate, Mr. X could be appointed deputy Head of Unit in December.")
- **Your opinion matters**: as a collaborator who is asked to produce a report for your hierarchy, your opinion matters. It is by bringing your personal assessment of the situation that you show that you have the depth and breadth of knowledge in the field. Especially when your opinion is deviating from well-trodden paths, you should argue it with strong and verifiable evidence, using facts instead of assumptions. If one of the questions refers to "your opinion", make sure you state a position on the issue and don't just recall facts or information. Be cautious, however, about taking a radical view or hurting anyone's sensitivities if you decide to challenge a EU action. Moreover, you are often requested to provide an "executive summary", which is different from a personal analysis. Make sure you understand the type of answer you are asked to provide and adapt your style accordingly.

Try to use **SMART solutions and recommendations**. Nobody is helped by vague statements having no quantifiable elements in terms of outcome or timing. Ideally one can also measure and monitor the progress of time-bound objectives. SMART is a mnemonic for the 5 steps of specific, measurable, achievable, realistic, and time-framed goals. It is a simple tool mostly used by businesses and organisations to go beyond the realm of fuzzy goal setting into an actionable plan for results, but it can also be used for individual goal setting and, in this instance, even in designing your essay for the case study.

- ***Specific*** – Your statements about your goals, i.e. what you are aiming to achieve, should be well defined, specific and focused. For example, "improving European citizens' lives" is anything but specific. In contrast, "increasing employment in the Baltic states by 20% by 2018 compared to 2010 levels" certainly is.
- ***Measurable*** – A goal without a measurable outcome is like a sports competition without a scoreboard or scorekeeper. Monitor progress to know if you're on track. A measurable goal keeps you focused on the targeted results you want to achieve. Saying that "if we pass this legislation, we will cut CO_2 emissions each year" is not measurable, but adding figures to it and methods how this can be measured will fill this gap.
- ***Achievable and Realistic*** – Goals can be stretching but they also have to be grounded in reality. Saying that the EU should aim to double its economic output in 5 years is ambitious, but unfortunately not realistic or achievable.
- ***Time-Framed*** – Goals and objectives just don't get met when there's no time frame tied to the goal-setting process. You have to choose a time frame to accomplish your goal. For example, saying that the legislation must be passed "as soon as possible" is not as good as saying it has to be passed within 3 months.

Encourage compromise: usually, there are different stakeholders with very distinct positions and arguments. Very few "real life" situations are clear and obvious. Don't let yourself be confused by the complexity of the file but try to find a good compromise, a compromise that marries the interests of all stakeholders without jeopardising the "greater interest" of a community, society or humanity as a whole.

When using abbreviations: make sure when using abbreviations or acronyms referenced in the dossier (e.g. CAP for Common Agricultural Policy) that you make clear exactly what they refer to and include a short legend or key to avoid misunderstandings. It is good communication practice to write out abbreviated forms in full the first time you use them, even if the background documentation lists them, since it is your essay that the reader is interested in, not the documents used for the exercise. Of course, use your judgment: if it's entirely obvious, e.g. "EU", it would not need to be spelled out.

The trick about background information: you may find one or two press articles (extracts from newspapers, magazines or news sites) in the documentation. It is a very good idea to have a look at these first. Why? Because

Notes:

(good) journalists are very good at summarising a situation and informing their readers in layman's terms. You may in fact find all the answers to the questions right there. All it takes then is to reformat the information and make it relate directly to the assignment of your case study.

The Length of Your Essay

The length of your essay is an important element used for the assessment of its qualities. Nobody likes to read texts that are too long, especially when they are badly structured. On the other hand, if your essay is too short you might be suspected of having run out of time, resulting in your getting a bad score for prioritising and organising. It is a good strategy to make the life of the markers easy, because after all they are human beings as well, and they have to cope with their own time constraints. And don't forget: they will probably be speed-reading as well.

A marker's point of view

I used to consider a total length of around 1000 words (the equivalent of four pages of A4) to be the perfect length, but I have recently come across a few jewels, very good essays that were much shorter than that. These essays contained all the necessary elements, were very well structured, and written in a fluent and clearly understandable language. I felt compelled to give good scores for all the competencies and realised that the overall length was of little concern. As a result, my recommendation would now be to aim for around 500 words – or two pages of A4 – or preferably a bit more, just to show that you did not run out of time and be potentially penalized for prioritising and organising.

Time Management

You usually have 90 minutes (or one-and-a-half hours). Below are some – indicative – timings you can use for each step.

Step 1. Start by reading the assignment and writing down the structure of your essay (about **5 minutes**). In doing this, bear in mind the key points of what we said in the section on "The Structure of your Essay", above.

Step 2. Go through all the documents in a "diagonal" way and try to find the information which is relevant to the questions that you are being asked. While skimming through the documents you can add this information to the appropriate "chapter" of your text. Use lists with short but complete sentences. There is no problem with literally copying sentences, as long as they convey your ideas. Spend around **30 minutes** on this.

Step 3. Review your text and try to come up with some good recommendations (if

A note on timing

The timings in this section are based on a typical 90-minute exercise. However, in the 2018 AD5 generalist competition the case study only lasted 60 minutes, with 3 competencies being assessed. Conversely, for the AD7 DEVCO competition for 2016, 120 minutes was allocated. Make sure, therefore, to check the details of your competition and adjust your timings and focus for preparation accordingly.

asked for). You may find interesting ideas in the documentation, but it is allowed to be creative and come up with ideas of your own. Ideally, your recommendations should be SMART, as described above. This may take around **30 minutes**.

Step 4. Write an introduction or executive summary that explains to the reader what the context and the content of your essay is (an "abstract"). Be compelling. Limit yourself to around **10 minutes**.

Step 5. Write a conclusion. Repeat in your own words what the general ideas of your essay are. The markers will be "speed-reading" your essay, so make it memorable. Reserve **10 minutes** for this.

Step 6. Review your text to weed out superfluous information, spelling errors and other problems: **5 minutes**. As far as possible try to use words that you are confident of spelling correctly. Choose simpler versions of synonyms – so, for example, use "various" rather than "miscellaneous" if in doubt about its spelling. Again, the computer interface will not have a built-in spell-checker, so you need to ensure proper spelling yourself.

The IT Tool for the Case Study

Since 2019 the case study is delivered on a new platform. The layout of the exercise is a split screen. On the right-hand side you will see the assignment and the text box where you have to write your answer (limited to 32.000 characters). On the left-hand side, you will find the background documents.

The case study platform does not allow for tables, graphs or drawings. It does however allow for a limited set of shortcuts. Please note that you are strongly advised not to use any other shortcuts than the ones given in the tutorial, as

Notes:

....

....

....

....

....

these could lead to accidental deletion of your written work. You are strongly advised to read the tutorial before the actual exam.

Your work will be auto-saved every 30 seconds, as well as when the time elapses at the end of the exam. There is no manual save option in use. Please be aware that each auto-save will permanently overwrite the previous version of your typed text.

You can view a short video on how to navigate through the exam on the EPSO website.

The Role of the Markers

A marker is a specialist in the field of the competition. As such, markers are not members of the Selection Board. They are regular officials (volunteers) provided by the recruiting institutions. Their role is to assess the case studies of the candidates. They mark the case study for knowledge in the field and general competencies.

Imagine that for a given competition there are 1000 candidates, in which case 1000 case studies have to be marked. As every case study has to be marked twice, this adds up to 2000 marked case studies. When the marks given by two markers for an individual case study are too far apart, a third marking is required.

The markers are usually present on the premises where the case study takes place. Markers receive special training in how to mark case studies. Markers also get clear and written instructions on how to do their work. The number of markers and their presence during the exercise depends on the competition.

Once the exercise is finished, markers get a limited amount of time to provide their markings. Usually, this happens in parallel with the rest of the Assessment Centre (which is performed by other people, the members of the Selection Board). Nevertheless, the marking task is on the "critical path" in terms of planning of the whole competition; when the marking is delayed, the whole Assessment Centre is delayed.

The scores given by the markers are simply averaged for the competencies they assessed in your case study. If, for example, one marker gave you a score of 4 for one competency, and the other marker gave you a 6, then your score for that competency in the case study will be 5. This average is then combined (averaged again) with the scores you have received for the other tests.

However, it could happen that the markers don't agree on one or more competencies in your case study. This will be visible by having their marks too wide apart. To come back to the previous example: let's say one marker gave you a 4 and the other an 8. In this case it would be unfair to give you a 6 just like that, without any deliberation. This problem is solved by a "third marker". Usually, it is the president of the competition who plays the role of the third marker. He assesses your work all over again, and decides on the scores you will finally get.

It is our experience that this is a rather exceptional situation; usually the markers more or less agree on the scores, simply because they have to follow the "scoring guide" and if they do this consistently they will come up with similar scores. EPSO has set an objective of less than 10% for the "third marking" in their 2016 Management Plan, and we are confident this objective is being met.

How to Prepare

A full practice case study exercise can be found in Annex 3.

We advise you to make this exercise on paper and without considering the time constraint. This will allow you to get a better feeling of how this exercise works.

Practise "speed reading" and build your EU knowledge

You can do this in advance, and the more you practice the better you will get at it. Do some reading on the EU institutions and the legislative procedures. Places to start could be:

www.europedia.moussis.eu/books/Book_2/2/4/3/?all=1
https://europa.eu/european-union/law_en
www.europarl.europa.eu/aboutparliament/en

Refresh your general knowledge of your field (if applicable)

You may be very specialised in one particular aspect of your domain and have forgotten about some of the underlying bigger concepts.

Keep yourself informed about the EU "hot topics"

The actual case studies are invariably linked to current issues (and often based on real sources), so you can give yourself a head start for the exercise. Possible sources of information are:

europa.eu/rapid
https://euobserver.com
www.euractiv.com
www.voxeurop.eu
www.politico.eu

Improve your drafting skills

Write some more texts and have them verified with free tools like

https://www.online-utility.org
https://www.grammarly.com

Ask a native speaker – preferably a linguist – to review your texts

Make sure you address the right audience.

Carefully read the "Instructions to Candidates"

You will receive these from EPSO with your invitation to the case study exercise.

Notes:

A candidate's point of view

I found the case study simulations on Online EU Training to be very useful as the tool is very similar to the real IT tool that is used by EPSO. I also appreciated very much the "personal" approach of the correction. The "marker" really treated my essay as if they would have done in EPSO with the important difference that I got his feedback, so that I could improve my performance during the real exercise.

Practise online with eutraining.eu

On eutraining.eu you will find a host of case study exercises on a variety of topics. All these exercises have been created by the authors of this book, so you can be sure that they reflect the reality of EPSO competitions. There are two modes to practise: with or without correction. In the mode "without correction" you will get access to a realistic test platform, mimicking the one that is used by EPSO, including the time constraints. When you choose the mode "with correction" you can of course do the exercise as usual but afterwards (within 7 working days) one of eutraining's "markers" will score and comment your work, and send you a report on how you could further improve your performance for the case study. We suggest you do two or three case study practice tests without correction and finalise your practice with one or two exercises with correction.

Key points to remember

- *Do not add any name, signature or distinguishing marks (initials, remarks unrelated to the context, phone numbers, e-mail addresses, etc) anywhere in your essay as this may result in the Selection Board's decision to remove you from the competition.*
- *Read the assignment very carefully, and deduce the structure of your essay from the questions asked in it.*
- *Add "salt and pepper" to your content, making your essay compelling and interesting to read. Think of the markers who have dozens of texts to go through.*
- *Use bullet points, a clear structure and specific examples, referenced to the background materials, making sure your essay flows well.*
- *Try to be creative in your solutions and recommendations. Think "out of the box".*

5. The General Competency Based Interview

For advice on taking this interview online, see pages 21-22

Introduction

The interview to assess your general competencies is referred to in EPSO Notices of Competition as the general competency based interview (GCBI). In the past this was often called the "structured interview". However, many competitions now have an interview in the field, which is also a structured interview, so that term is confusing. The interview in the field is described in detail in chapter 8.

It is worth noting that while the generic competencies are not formally scored during the interview in the field, which is focused on your experience and technical abilities, poor (oral) communication, for example, will inevitably influence the scores for the specific competencies in the in the field interview.

The GCBI is in fact probably going to be the first test of your day at the Assessment Centre in Brussels. Hopefully, you have prepared well, have had a good night's rest and find yourself fighting fit for your big day at the Assessment Centre. You feel in control and look forward to what is ahead with confidence.

Much like the other exercises, what the assessors are interested in is your behaviour under pre-defined circumstances in your working environment. The main difference with the other exercises is that – during the GCBI – they are trying to understand *how* you behaved in the past, by *listening* to "stories" you tell them from your own, personal history.

In the other exercises your behaviour is *observed* "in situ"; in the GCBI in contrast you *tell* the assessors what you did, and how you did it. (This can be somewhat different in the case of specialist competitions, however.)

Your communicating competency may also be observed during the GCBI. There will be no specific questions, but during the exercise you will be observed very carefully, and the assessors will give you a score for this competency, based on what they heard and saw during the interview. We will come back to this point later in this chapter.

What does it mean when we say that the GCBI is a "structured" interview? It means quite simply that **the anchors are pre-defined, and the assessors have to stick to them.** Other than for some follow-up questions, they cannot ask you anything else other than what is on the list of questions in front of them.

It is important to stress that **the GCBI is NOT intended to be like a job interview.** Most job interviews are not structured, nor are they competency based. In a "normal" job interview, the interviewer can ask you any question he wants (within legal boundaries).

An assessor's point of view

A lot of the candidates fear the competency-based interview the most. But there is no reason for that. The assessors are thorough, but they don't want to trick you, or be mean. In fact they even help you to get over your nervousness by first explaining what the interview is about, how it will be conducted and then let you talk about the topic you know best: yourself. The interview is very well structured and all the candidates get to answer the same questions, so there is very little room for subjectivity, or assessors playing games with you.

In a job interview the interviewer seeks to get a general idea of who you are as a person, whether you will fit in the organisation, and whether he likes you or not. Job interviews are therefore much more based on "gut feeling", even though most recruiters claim to be objective. A GCBI, on the other hand, is as close as one can get to a really objective assessment in an interview.

Competencies, Anchors and Questions

During the GCBI a number of competencies will be assessed. Depending on the competition, you will get questions related to 3, 4, or even 5 competencies, and for certain competitions you will also be observed for your (oral) communicating competency. The exact competencies that are to be assessed will be announced in the Notice of Competition, but don't worry, the assessors will explain this to you at the start of the interview as well.

As explained previously, competencies are further divided into "behavioural anchors". A behavioural anchor is a specific example of a competency level used to help assessors and candidates to understand how to use a competency model. Behavioural anchors are specific, easy-to-apply examples of behaviours that demonstrate the competency. For example, for the (oral) communicating competency, the anchors used by EPSO could be:

- Oral communication is clear and precise
- Handles questions confidently
- Simplifies complex subject matters
- Persuades, gets acceptance of their proposals
- Adjusts their style to the audience

In the GCBI, EPSO uses up to five anchors for each competency tested. In fact, there is a question for each anchor. This means that you can expect up to 15, 20, or even 25 questions during your GCBI, which might seem a surprisingly large number for such a short time.

For every anchor (question), the assessors have a "catalogue" of positive and negative indicators they may observe during the exercise. They will have to look for these indicators – and only these – in order to form their opinion. They are not allowed to let other impressions form their judgment.

You will find an overview of the anchors used for the GCBI – and some typical recently asked questions – in Annex 4. This may help you understand what kind of questions you can expect during your GCBI.

Scenario of a GCBI

Your GCBI experience begins as you are waiting in front of the closed door of the interview room. You will know where to go because it will be clearly marked on your personal schedule, the one you received at the start of the day. This is a moment to keep calm. To do so, you can take a couple of deep breaths (don't hyperventilate!) and think of a recent, pleasant experience. Then, imagine yourself sitting in the interview room, in front of the assessors, and calmly but assertively answering all the questions they ask. In this way, you are building up positive energy, something you will need during the actual event.

Do not be tempted to knock on the door, even if the scheduled time has passed. The closed door means that the assessors are not yet ready to see you. They may still be discussing the previous candidate, or simply having a short break, so you should not interrupt them.

Then, the door will open and one of the assessors will invite you in. He or she may or may not offer to shake hands. Adapt your behaviour to how they act and don't try to shake hands unless you're invited to. Say "good morning" to anyone in the room, smile, and wait to be seated until you are asked to do so.

At this point, you will be sitting at a small table, facing your assessors, much like in Figure 5.1.

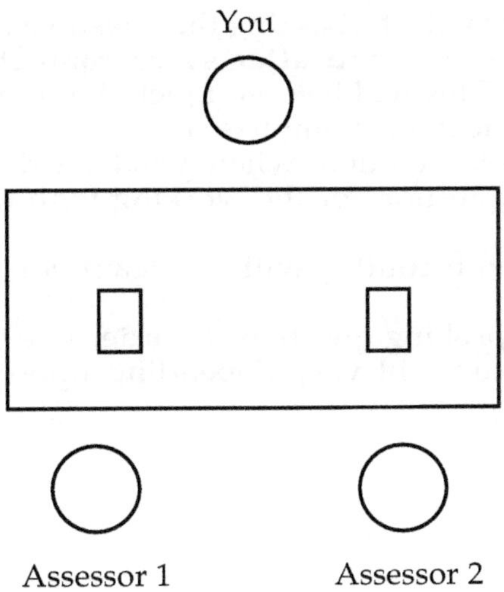

Figure 5.1: in the interview room

The good news is that there will be only two assessors. The purpose of this interview is not to stress you by having a whole panel firing questions at you. It could happen that, during the interview, a third person enters the room. That would most likely be the president of the Selection Board. Don't worry, the president is not there to observe you, but to check on the assessors and verify that they are doing their job following the rules. You can gracefully ignore this person.

Once you are seated, one of the assessors will read out a text. The assessor will explain what the GCBI is about, how long it will take and which competencies they intend to assess. He will also tell you that they will clearly indicate which compe-

Notes:

tency will be next, after every series of questions is completed. You will also be asked to come up with specific examples of situations in your past where you may have had to demonstrate the competency at hand.

You will then be asked to talk for about two minutes about yourself, your educational and professional background, so that they will be able to better understand the examples you give during the rest of the interview.

This procedure may appear a bit strange, but there is a very good reason for it. The fact that you can talk briefly about a topic you know very well (yourself) will automatically reduce your stress level. You could see it as an icebreaker, a gift from the assessors to put you at ease.

Then you can start to tell the story of your (professional) life. We will say more about what you should best say at this stage later in this chapter. For now, all you have to know is that you should try to stick to the time allowed, and even keep it a bit shorter than they suggested.

After you have told the assessors your story, they will start asking the questions. They will proceed in the announced order of competencies, **and after every competency, when switching to the next one, they will say so**. This will help you pick the right stories as your examples, as you will know which indicators to emphasise.

The interviewer will ask you to talk about example situations where you have demonstrated the relevant competency. For example, a question for the working with others competency might be as follows:

"Tell me about a time when you had to deal with conflict within a team you were part of."

The interviewer is then likely to ask follow-up probing questions in order to explore your responses more fully. The exact probes asked will vary depending upon your answer to the starter question. For example:

- "What caused the conflict?"
- "What did you do?"
- "What was the outcome?"
- "With hindsight, what would you do differently?"

Usually, one assessor will ask all the questions (up to 5) for a given competency, while the other will be observing you and taking notes; then they will swap roles for the next series of questions, and so on.

The timing is very strict, and the assessors only have so much time for every competency, so they may regularly interrupt you in the middle of an answer. This is not because they are being rude but because they have to respect the overall duration of the interview. It is vital, therefore, to **go straight to the point in your answers** and keep your message short.

An assessor's point of view

In the competency based interview there is very little room for manoeuvre. Not only is the timing very strict, and the list of questions to be asked fixed, we are only allowed to form our opinion on the basis of observable behaviour. In fact, we have an extensive list of "positive" and "negative" indicators [in other words how the candidate said he or she behaved under given circumstances] and we have to stick to this list. Any other observation that might bias our assessment cannot be taken into consideration. In that way we assure that all candidates are treated in the same way.

Timing

The time allowed for the GCBI is strictly limited, not only because of the schedule of the day (all candidates have to be interviewed before noon) but also because EPSO wants to treat all candidates equally and they don't want to wear you out already by this first exercise, which is pretty intense.

Depending on whether you have 3, 4, or 5 competencies tested, your GCBI will last 30, 40, or 50 minutes. Even if the communicating competency is assessed with the GCBI there will be no extra time for that (mainly because there are no questions for this competency but it is based on observed behaviour).

Say your interview lasts 50 minutes. There will be 25 questions, giving a maximum of 2 minutes per question. However, you have to deduct perhaps one minute for entering the room and listening to the introduction text and another two minutes for your self-introduction. Every question has to be read out and this also takes a few seconds per question. That means that in practice you have quite a bit less than 2 minutes for each answer. This is rather intense and demanding.

Introducing Yourself

When reading a CV we all create some kind of mental image of what a person is like. Based on their gender, age, nationality, education and professional experience, we immediately form an opinion about this person. Looking at the photo that is sometimes attached to the CV may even reinforce this opinion. This is a perfectly normal human reaction.

In order to avoid this phenomenon, the assessors who take your GCBI are not allowed to see your CV, or any other information about you for that matter, before the interview. Otherwise they might be biased in their assessment. **The only thing they know about you is your name**, and they can only guess your nationality and gender based on this piece of information. (The assessors have to know your name beforehand just in case they already know you. Under these circumstances they are obliged to step back from the exercise, and leave the assessment to another colleague because of a conflict of interest.)

All this means that the moment you enter the room is indeed the first time they have ever met you, in any sense of the word. You are a complete stranger. **This moment is crucial**, as you "only have one chance to make a first impression". The way you look, how you are dressed, your posture and body language will immediately have them create a mental image of what you are probably like. This will inevitably influence their assessment – so it is vital to make a good first impression.

Notes:

The secrets of a handshake

Your handshake is a vital part of creating the right first impression; it is the only opportunity where the interviewers actually get to have a physical interaction with you (though not all assessors offer to shake hands). The "ideal" handshake conveys confidence and equality. If you are sitting in a waiting area always stand up as remaining seated looks rude. Wait for the other person to offer their hand; they are on their territory, so they should initiate the handshake. Step towards the person confidently, not too close and not too far away. SMILE! Make direct eye contact and hold it for the whole handshake. A good little trick is try to observe the other person's eye colour during this time, which will inevitably result in you looking deep into the other person's eye for a second or two. Give a brief squeeze, not too gently, not too strong.

After the assessors have read the introductory text you will be asked to tell them about your educational and professional background and motivation for participating in this competition.

Imagine that – during the GCBI – they want to create a picture of what you look like. Metaphorically, as you enter the room, they have only a blank sheet of paper, the canvas on which they will draw your portrait.

During your self-presentation you are providing them with the **outline contours of your portrait (Figure 5.2)**. They need these contours because they have to know where to position your eyes, your nose, and your mouth (in terms of the interview, your professional background, your motivation to work for the EU, your linguistic skills and overall presence). You need to give them a sense of whether they are looking straight at you or at a bit of an angle. With this initial sketch as a starting point they will be able to complete your portrait, based on the extra information they receive from you during the actual interview.

So how should you introduce yourself for this interview?

For one, give them the essential facts about yourself. Tell them where you come from, and your current profession ("Good morning, my name is XYZ and I am Italian. I am a lawyer.") Then start right away with your educational background ("I studied law at the University of Florence, where I got my bachelor degree. In 200X I moved to Rome to continue my studies and to pass the bar exam. Then, I moved to London, and specialised in international law. I graduated cum laude…"). After this you explain about your profes-

Figure 5.2

How to introduce yourself in an online interview

A handshake is a great way for an interviewer to sense your confidence. But online, the interviewer will be looking instead at how you introduce yourself by the way you speak, what you say and your facial expressions. Therefore, when introducing yourself in an online interview, it's important to speak professionally, but also in a friendly manner.

The first step in properly introducing yourself in an online interview is to be on time. To do this, be sure you are familiar with the software beforehand so that you can arrive on the call before the interview starts and so you won't encounter any technical issues.

You may want to wait until the interviewer speaks first. They may speak right away and even address you by name. Then you might just say, "Hello, I'm ready whenever you are." Otherwise, don't be afraid to use a simple greeting and let the interviewer initiate the next step. Do not to plunge into a formal introduction, instead, introduce yourself with a simple phrase like:

- "Good morning" or "Good afternoon"
- "Hello, my name is..."
- "Nice to meet you."
- "Thanks for having me today"

It's not always necessary to say your name, especially if the interviewer says your name first. But, if they don't, then you may want to add it to your initial greeting.

As in every interview, it's important to act natural, and be yourself.

sional career, in chronological order ("At first, I worked as an intern in a renowned international law firm [it's up to you whether or not to give the name]. That was back in 200X, in London. Then I moved to Brussels, to work for…"). Finally, you end up with your current position. Explain how long you have already worked there, what your duties are, some of your main achievements and any other useful details.

If you are already working for an EU institution, for example as a contract agent or Parliamentary assistant, you might wonder if this is a positive or negative factor for the interview. In fact it is neither, and you may want to avoid any misunderstanding or misperception on the part of the assessors by simply saying "I'm currently working for an EU institution in Brussels as a…." as the actual job profile is less important than the competencies and skills it helps you develop.

Telling them about yourself should be done **as far as possible in chronological order**. Remember, you should try to make the assessors' task as easy as possible. Jumping back and forth in time won't help you with that. In addition, you will probably be able to come up with some good examples of what you have done from your recent past. These examples will remain fresh in their minds as the last things you told them.

Notes:

Don't be afraid to give detailed information (dates, places, names, etc.) as this will enhance your credibility and provide the assessors with mental "hooks" to hang your story on later when you tell them about the examples, and you can refer back to these life events at that point.

Clearly, you should not reveal confidential information. However, if you can, do give them some unique or colourful information, catching their attention, and making them remember you until long after the interview. This could be about a fascinating project you ran, an "exotic" assignment you had to carry out in a far-away place, or a little spoken language you learned.

Don't tell them about your feelings ("I was very happy when I was working there because…") or make any self-assessments ("I know I am a good team player…"). They will want to discover this by themselves. You may nevertheless mention a word or two about your motivation to work for the EU, as long as it is not too overwhelming and remains credible.

In 2018 the interviewers started asking candidates about their motivation as part of the self-presentation. You will get some extra time for this. Much like the presentation of your academic and professional background information this part can be very well prepared in advance. Have a look at chapter 9 on the motivational interview to find inspiration.

A specific piece of advice is to "end with an ending" and not just stop speaking. You can say "I'm ready to answer your questions" or close along these lines so it's clear to the assessors that you have nothing else to add and it's their turn.

As this part of the GCBI is already known to you in advance, it is possible and recommended that you practice the introduction. On the other hand, be careful not to come across as artificial or staged, and make sure in preparing that you only write down the key points you want to emphasise at the real interview and not full sentences that you learn by heart. Not only would such pre-scripted texts be hard to recall under stress; if we write down such detailed text, we tend to use more sophisticated words than we would normally use in conversation, and therefore it can easily sound fake.

At the end of the interview the assessors will – ideally – end up with a complete and detailed **portrait of who you are (Figure 5.3)**.

Figure 5.3

How to Pick Your Stories

Have a look at the sample questions in Annex 4: you will notice two key things.

Distant or recent past

The first thing to notice is that most of the questions ask you to describe a situation in your past. Unless specified otherwise, these situations have to be professional in nature. If you have little or no professional experience you will not be able to find many examples. Under these circumstances you can refer to situations happening during your education (university times), semi-professional activities or even your private life **as long as the right competency can be appropriately highlighted**. You will be inclined to give examples from your most recent past, as this is what you remember best, and there is nothing wrong with that. For the sake of variety, however, it is advisable to have at least a couple of examples from your more distant past – though do make sure you are able to remember a sufficient amount of detail in case you are probed further.

Positive stories

The second important thing to be aware of is that what the assessors ultimately want to hear about is **positive behaviour**, even in negative situations or experiences. This will especially be the case in the resilience questions. Here they want to hear how you coped with a negative situation and how you managed to "bounce back" afterwards. An important rule is that "admitting" or talking about a negative experience – such as missing a deadline or not acting in a way that you would have liked to – is perfectly fine and is not considered a weakness, on one condition. You should never stop at describing such failure, otherwise it will backfire, but go on and explain your understanding of why things went wrong, what you learned from it, and ideally, how you managed to avoid repeating your mistake in a later situation, by relying on the conclusions and lessons you had learned as a result of the initial experience. This will turn a negative story into an exemplary one.

Having discussed these two key points, let us now look at some specific issues in picking the right stories.

- Do you have to give a different example for every single question?

Not really, you can "recycle" situations for different questions, especially when dealing with different competencies (or anchors). The competencies are interrelated, and so are the positive indicators. It is absolutely normal to re-use situations but put some different accents in your answer, accents that fit with the competency under scrutiny. This being said, you

Notes:

....

....

....

....

....

should not stick to just a few examples, because otherwise they may get bored (after all, assessors are only human).

- Same story, different narrative

Here is an example: let's say you describe a situation when you had a conflict with a colleague with whom you were assigned to work on a report but she did not deliver her part on time. This situation can be used for the working with others competency, by focusing on the ways in which you tried to sort the problem out co-operatively with her, maintaining good relations while getting the job done. At the same time, this situation can also be used for the resilience competency – but in that case you would focus on how you reacted when you found out that her input was missing, how you handled the stress of not being able to deliver the project on time, and what practical measures you took to find a solution. The very same situation but with a different emphasis added to highlight more relevant elements as per the competency in question.

- How to frame your answers

In the introduction to the GCBI, you are asked to give *specific* examples of situations in your past. Don't start your answers with "yes, this happens to me all the time" or "I am frequently in such a situation". Start right away with the specifics of a situation (who, when, where, what). Many candidates make the mistake of talking about, for example, a long period when they had a heavy workload, or a prolonged period of studying (for the learning and development competency). Don't hesitate to give details when describing the situation; position it in the more general context of your self-description but always pick a very specific element or situation that you focus on. Make the assessors feel as if they were there themselves. Tell a story, but concentrate on a concrete "episode" of that story.

- "I" sentences are key

An essential element for the GCBI is to use "I" sentences. One of the most common mistakes made by candidates is in fact not making enough use of "I" sentences. When you are asked about a situation ("Tell me about a time when you had a conflict with your superior"), the assessors want to hear about *your* role in the situation. Their interest in what your superior, colleague, friend or anyone else did is limited to understanding *your* actions, and they could not care less how Mr Smith looked at you from the other end of the office unless you add how you reacted to it and why that is relevant from the competency's perspective. Hence, make sure to underline your own actions, thoughts, considerations and contribution to the outcome.

An assessor's point of view

Attention is a scarce commodity. It is sometimes difficult for an assessor to focus his or her attention on the Nth candidate in the seemingly endless flow of people coming and going during an AC competition. People tend to get bored when they hear the same story over and over again from candidates with an obvious lack of imagination, or who are simply scared to tell the truth of what really happened. To catch and keep our attention we need our mind to be tickled by fresh, interesting – or even controversial – information, so we love it when a candidate puts some "salt and pepper" – or even a stronger kind of spice on the story they are bringing to us that day.

- Tell them "why"

Another common mistake is when candidates forget to share with the assessors the underlying reason *why* they decided to take a certain line of action, or the reason *why* they tried to convince their superior of their point of view. It's easy to miss this point but you will be rewarded if you keep the "why" in mind. ("Because it's there" was the famous answer given by George Mallory when asked "Why do you want to climb Mount Everest?" – but you can be a bit more forthcoming than that.) The "why" answer clearly reveals your motivation to learn, resolve a conflict, deliver results or have your idea endorsed, which nicely ties into the behavioural competencies the assessors are evaluating.

- Pass on some wisdom

After outlining the story and your contribution to the outcome, you are entitled to share some insights or wisdom with the assessors. For example, you can say "From this experience I learned that...", or "This wasn't a very positive outcome for me but I did realise that..." and finish it with some lessons (just make sure it doesn't sound too much like Yoda from Star Wars). At the same time, your conclusions should not dwell on the specific story you recited but aim for a higher, "conceptual" or "methodology" level with some abstraction, without sounding too clichéd. If you say "People can work surprisingly fast under pressure", this will sound like a cliché, but if you say "I learned that I work surprisingly fast under pressure", this will come across as a life lesson you have learned (and taken to heart) through experience.

- What doesn't seem important to you may be crucial to them

Many candidates have a hard time grasping which pieces of information are important to the assessors and which ones they should skip. A good bit of advice is to add a lot of lively detail when it comes to the "heart" of the issue you are describing so they can easily visualise the situation. For instance, when you talk about doing an MBA in your free time, make sure to provide details about which part of the day you allocated to study, what specific sacrifices you had to make to advance in the studies, how you commuted to college despite not having a car, etc. This gives more credibility to the story and also helps in demonstrating the specific steps you took to achieve your goal.

- EU-related experience

As with every organisation, EU institutions are also keen to see job experience that is related to their own activities, in this case, European affairs. This is of course not to say that someone who has no EU experience would be disadvantaged when applying for a EU competition, but bear in mind that if your experience was not gained inside or in relation to EU institutions, you need to make sure why it is relevant for the profile they are seeking candidates for. This will be regarded positively and can have positive impact on your assessment. Therefore if you have, for instance, project management experience, you can link it to the kind of tasks that are needed in EU institutions even if your experience was gained in a completely different context.

Notes:

The STAR Model

You have on average less than two minutes to formulate your answers, but you are supposed to give all the relevant elements in order to allow the interviewers to probe your response, and to score it for the competency under scrutiny.

A good model to mention here is the STAR model. STAR is the acronym for Situation, Task, Actions, Results. You can usefully apply this whenever you are asked to describe your behaviour in a particular situation, as is the case in the GCBI:

- **Situation** – What was the challenge or situation in which you found yourself?

A common mistake is to provide too much detailed information about the context of the situation, e.g. how many people worked at the company; the educational background of your boss; how you got the job etc., (unless of course these are relevant when describing the essentials of the situation). The context must be kept to the absolute core elements, covering questions such as "who were you in that situation?" (newly hired employee, trainee, team leader, colleague), "what type of organization was it?" (small company,

Application of the STAR model

Competency being tested: RESILIENCE

QUESTION: Have you had a stressful experience with a project? – Give an example and how you dealt with it.

ANSWER

(Situation)

Four years ago I was working as a senior account manager for Company X, an IT consultancy with 80 employees in Brussels. The European Commission had launched a call for tender for renewal of a 5-year, 20 million euro contract which our firm currently held.

(Task)

I was appointed project manager in charge of preparing the tender, with a team of three working to me.

(Situation)

This was a key contract for our company; in fact my boss had made it clear that success – or failure – would have a serious impact on the future of the company, so I really felt the pressure was on me. The problem for me was that I had no previous experience in the EU public sector (my previous customers were all large multinationals) and the deadline was desperately tight; we had only two months to reply and the summer holidays were about to start. So I had to get up to speed on EU procurement double fast.

(Actions)

The first thing I did was put routine work activity on hold or delegate it, and I had to re-schedule my holidays. I had a good team working to me but I quickly realised we had to draft in some extra specialised technical expertise. The directors took some convincing of this, in view of the cost, and I faced a real grilling over it, but finally they accepted my logic. In fact, I don't think we could have got the tender to the right standard without this.

One of the team fell ill at a critical point and I had to burn some midnight oil to plug the gap as there was literally no one else with the skill set to cover the ground at such short notice. However, I got the team to sign up to rigorous progress monitoring, which benefited us all. I knew the deadline and the quality were non-negotiable and I had to answer for the whole team.

(Result)

In the end, we got the tender in on time and the contract was renewed in the face of stiff competition. The holiday was later than planned but I was able to relax. The best moment was when the director who had given me the hardest time when I asked for extra resource came and told me I was getting a promotion. He said I had impressed the directors when I "didn't flinch under fire", but had just calmly and rationally presented the facts of the situation. I've tried to follow this strategy since!

public administration, freelance job), "how did you relate to the others in the situation?" (same hierarchical level, helper or contributor, supplier or other).

- **Task** – What did you have to achieve? What was expected of you?

Here you must also go into the "invisible" part of the situation, where you can describe your feelings and your own motivation to act, other people's expectations of you and whether this was in line with your own thinking – how did you view the task and did you feel determined to complete it or resolve it? (if it was a conflict or pressure situation).

- **Action** – What did you do? How did you do it? How did you respond to the situation?

This is where the "I" sentences become crucial: other people are only important to the extent to which they influenced or affected your behaviour. Assessors want to see what your role was, and therefore you should keep references to what others did to the absolute minimum. Saying that "my boss told me to translate a document because he only spoke some basic French, even though he had studied a year in France when he was doing an Erasmus in Marseille" is time wasted since the description of the Erasmus experience adds nothing to the assessors' understanding of your skills. Instead, you could say that "my boss told me to translate the document into French which I really appreciated as I could use my newly acquired linguistic skills. I felt much appreciated when I got positive feedback afterwards about the quality of my work."

- **Results** – What was the outcome of your actions? What did you achieve? Did you meet your objectives? What did you learn from this experience and have you used this learning since?

Candidates often forget to highlight the outcome of their actions after they finish

Notes:

describing the actions in detail. It is nevertheless vital to take a step back and look at the situation and share some wisdom in hindsight, such as your conclusions and lessons from the situation. For example, you can say "If I look back at this event, it really made me realise that I need to do proper planning beforehand, which is an experience that has served me well in the past 4 years since."

Trained interviewers will immediately recognise this structure when you are using it, and they will be grateful for that because you are making their life a lot easier by doing so. Note that in the example in the box the "Actions" part is pivotal. This is explained by the fact that the assessors can only "observe" your (past) behaviour by what you tell them you did. The other elements are only "circumstantial evidence", and the situation needs to be as concisely explained as possible without too much detail but enough to make it seem realistic and concrete.

We suggest you spend 60% (i.e. a bit more than one minute) of the time available for your answer to explain in detail what you did, the Actions part of your STAR answer. Spend around 20% on the Situation/Task part, and the remaining 20% on Results. In this way you are telling them exactly what they want to hear, nothing more, nothing less. From experience we know that many people tend to spend too much time in describing the *Situation*, because they think that otherwise the audience will not understand fully what they are talking about. Try to suppress that urge, and focus instead on the *Actions*.

The candidate in this example also frequently uses "I" instead of "we". This also makes a lot of sense because – after all – the jury wants to assess his behaviour, and not that of his colleagues or company.

We cannot underline enough the importance of using the STAR model during the GCBI. The STAR model is important for three reasons:

- ***It is easy for you.*** Imagine you get a question for which you don't have an immediate response in mind. You would have to think for 10, 15 seconds, or even longer. Once you have found a situation in your memory you could talk about, the next thing you would have to do is think about how you were going to tell this story. When using the STAR model, as soon as you know what to talk about, you can start talking, just because the Situation/Task is the first part of your STAR story. Actions and Results will follow automatically, as these are the logical next steps in your story.

- ***It is easy for them.*** The assessors are, as a rule, not experienced HR people, or recruiters. However, in order to be on a Selection Board they have had to take a training course. During this training they learn about the STAR model, and they even practise it by conducting mock interviews amongst themselves. So the assessors know the STAR model, and they will "sit back and relax" when they hear you kick off your answer with a nice Situation/Task opening. They will know that they won't have to make an intellectual effort to try to understand your story, and pick those elements they want to hear as "positive indicators" for the competency at hand. By using the STAR model you are making they lives easy.

- ***It is a "best practice" for the communicating competency.*** Using the STAR model, if applicable, is a generally accepted good practice for this kind of interview. As a consequence, your (oral) communication competency will be assessed positively if you use this model.

A similar method is known as the SHARE model. In this instance the acronym stands for Situation, Hindrances, Actions, Results and Evaluation. We suggest, however, that you stick to the STAR model, as this is the model which the EPSO assessors are trained in.

Body Language

It is quite often claimed that only 7% of the impact of our oral communication is attributable to the actual meaning of the words we say, compared with 38% to the tone and speed of our voice, and 55% to our body language. These figures go back to the work of UCLA Professor Albert Mehrabian, as explained in his book *Silent Messages*, originally published in 1971.

However, many trainers and non-verbal communication gurus forget to mention that Mehrabian based his findings on studies that only dealt with the communication of positive and negative emotions via single spoken words. He was trying to understand the mechanisms of feelings of like and dislike. He did not intend this "rule" to apply across the board to all communication, so, unless a communicator is talking about their feelings or attitudes these numbers are not applicable.

Pamela Thorne says something more relevant in her work on "Debunking the Body Language Myth":

- Words are only part of a message, but they are a vital part. We also communicate through body language and tone of voice
- Non-verbals support the words by conveying the speaker's feelings
- When speaking about feelings and attitudes, and there is a mismatch between the words and the body language, we tend to put more trust in the non-verbals
- If we have only words, as in emails, it is possible to misunderstand the emotion behind the words

Consider your body language and tone of voice during the interview: these are among the key aspects interviewers will observe and weigh almost as much as your words.

Keep your arms unfolded and adopt a generally "open" posture. Lean slightly forward in the chair by making sure your arms rest on the table and that your chair is not pulled away from it, which would probably incline you to fold your arms.

Maintain good eye contact with the interviewer (even if they themselves break eye contact to take notes). Smile, nod and repeat back their questions to show you are listening. Be careful of your body language "leaking signals" that you are uncomfortable with a question or subject area: for example, avoid pained expressions when asked a difficult question – look interested, motivated and positive instead.

Your tone of voice is easier to control, especially the pacing (speed), pauses (to add emphasis and allow assessors to catch up with what you are explaining), and volume. Always make sure that you bring down the emphasis at the end of a sentence and you don't "interlink" your sentences by only moderately bringing down your voice before starting a new sentence right away.

Notes:

A good exercise can be a simulation with a friend who, while asking you questions, takes notes on your body language so you can analyse the findings together afterwards. You may also wish to have yourself recorded with a mobile phone or webcam and then try to improve your overall performance; a professional coach can also be of great help.

Some Tips for the Assessment

- **Active listening**: you should listen carefully to what you are being asked; it is perfectly acceptable for you to take a moment to think before responding (you can always say to the interviewer: "If I understand your question correctly, you are asking if [...]. Let me think about that for a moment..." which wins you time to think the issue over).
- **Clarification**: if you are unsure what information a question is aimed at getting from you, ask for clarification: "could you please clarify what you'd like to learn about me here?"
- **Respond to the question**: keep your answers focused (e.g. when asked about your most recent work experience regarding workplace conflicts, do not start by introducing your CV and professional background or how you got your most recent job; keep your focus on the question with only a few words on the overall context). Use the STAR model whenever you can.
- **Confidentiality**: do not disclose confidential information in your responses. It is possible, however, that the *type* of organisation you worked in could be relevant (small, large, public authority or other) as it may have affected the situation and your role in it. Similarly, never disclose the full name of a person with whom you had a conflict or use him or her as an example to describe a situation.
- **Stick to the point**: resist the temptation to describe a situation in unnecessary detail (e.g. "I had a Spanish colleague who had just moved to Latvia where he was travelling in neighbouring countries almost every weekend") unless certain facts are relevant because they affected or explained a certain behaviour you wish to emphasise.
- **Methodology and motivation**: when asked "how did you respond to this situation?", aim to provide an answer that concentrates on the methodology or motivation side ("I understood there was tension between us so I tried to discuss the situation face to face") instead of describing unrelated facts ("I proposed we have lunch in the company canteen as it had just opened on the sixth floor"); when asked "how did you facilitate the teamwork" avoid fact-driven but less relevant answers such as "I heard from the IT department that Microsoft had come out with a great program that ran on Windows 10, so given that we had this operating system, it sounded like a good idea". Instead, focus on your behaviours, solutions, methods, motivation, feelings and ideas. The personal angle and a clear description of your inner thinking are fundamental to demonstrating that you possess a high level of the competency in question.

- **Taking notes**: it is important to allow the assessor or his or her colleague to write down as much information as possible in order to assess your answers afterwards. Watch the note taker's expression or reactions. If they seem to be having trouble keeping up with your answers, you should slow down, pause and allow them to catch up. Conversely, if they have stopped taking notes, or put their pen down, this indicates they are likely to have all the information they need for this competency or you are currently giving them detail that is irrelevant. Pause, and perhaps ask if what you are telling them is useful and relevant. As for note-taking on your part, this is neither recommended and nor is it allowed in most cases, given that you are required to answer right away without any time to take notes yourself.
- **Be honest**: interviewers are trained to probe your responses; if you are embellishing the truth then they may well find this out as you begin to falter under increasingly detailed questioning. This doesn't mean you could not add a bit more "drama" or "colour" to your story, but always make sure you are using a real example and never make up a story. Further, if the event you describe had a negative outcome, you are encouraged to contrast that with a conclusion or lesson you learned or your assessment of the situation in hindsight. As long as you demonstrate awareness of your own actions and what could have been done differently, you demonstrate that your level of competency is sufficient.
- **Trick questions**: you will seldom, if ever, be asked "trick" questions in a professionally run interview.
- **EU jargon**: explain any jargon or acronyms you use. Avoid using slang expressions. For example, if you are sitting a competition for a finance position and you use a technical term, make sure you show that you understand it by explaining its meaning in plain terms; similarly, if you are sitting a specialist competition for e.g. data protection officials, your interviewer may not be an expert in that field even if he or she is an EU official, therefore try to read the interviewer's non-verbal cues regarding their knowledge of the field and adjust your vocabulary accordingly. Similarly, if you talk about previous work and use industry jargon such as "the PHP programmer had a conflict with the Java scripter", make sure you do not overload the interviewer with expressions they may not be familiar with.
- **Stay calm**: even if interviewers are probing your answers or ask many follow-up questions, they are probably just looking for your detailed response; staying calm and professional is the best way to respond to this.
- **Loyalty**: never belittle, directly criticise or give away secrets of any past or present employers – the interviewer will see this as unprofessional and be concerned about you doing the same if you were to leave the role you are applying for. For example, avoid saying something like "I left my last company because it was run by incompetent people".
- **If stuck**: if you find you are completely stuck for an answer and do not have an example to offer, then it is worthwhile trying to make one of your other experiences "fit" the question if at all possible. You may begin by saying "I have never experienced precisely that situation, but let me tell you about a similar situation when..." Even if your response does not help you on this particular competency, it might count as further evidence towards other competencies such as communication or resilience covered by the interview, not to mention your resourcefulness.

How to Prepare

Consider your competencies

As mentioned above, the assessor is going to inform you which competencies are to be covered during the interview. If you have familiarised yourself with the EPSO competencies in advance, then you can ensure that your responses are tailored to the competency under discussion and that you provide relevant answers that help both your assessment and the assessor's job as well. For example, if you are asked a question under the prioritising and organising competency, do not spend a long time describing your teamwork: focus your answers on the planning, prioritising, monitoring and organising type behaviours that you displayed at the time.

Consider your experiences

The GCBI is the only exercise where you can directly influence your assessment and prepare well in advance. It is you who decides what you are going to tell them – and what not – about who you are, and how you behaved. You can control the image the assessors will get of you since you can pick your own stories, not them.

There is nothing wrong with picking the "better" examples of your work experience. We all have good and bad experiences, and you are fully entitled to pick only the good ones for your GCBI.

So, in preparing for the GCBI it is in your interest to think over your entire career or life experience and try to **identify the best possible situations** to fit the questions you will be asked. Have a look at Annex 4, review your CV, check your diary to recall events and meetings you have had in the past year or two, and you will doubtless be able to find good examples that had slipped your mind. Prepare an Excel – or Word – table with five columns. In the first column you write the "anchors". In the second and third columns you write one or two keywords to remind you of the Situation and Task you are going to use. In the fourth column you put a bullet list with at least 5 or 6 keywords describing the Actions, and finally you put one or two keywords in the last column containing the Results.

It's best NOT to write your answers in full text, because you might be inclined to learn them by heart. Don't! Having just the keywords in your mind during the interview, you will be forced to improvise a bit, which will make your story sound more natural and spontaneous. This is a positive indicator for communicating!

Negative Indicators

It is not recommended to learn your examples by heart, though you should indeed collect specific examples and create a "pool" for easier referencing at the interview. Even though the assessors have a fixed questionnaire in front of them, they may change the actual formulation of their questions. They may also ask you follow-up questions, when something in your answer is not fully understood right away. If you learn all your answers by heart you may be caught out by a question that is not put in exactly the same way as in the examples in Annex 4. You will then start panicking, possibly give the wrong answer or otherwise not know what to say.

A far better way is to refresh your memory about your career in terms of the fundamental reasons why you behaved in the way you did. The following exercise will help you with this.

Try to remember your career in terms of how happy and satisfied you were during the various periods, working in different positions for your previous – or current – employers. It is almost certain that there will be periods that you were more at ease than usual. There will also be periods that you were not so happy, or even frustrated. In short, your career will show a pattern much like the one in Figure 5.4.

During the happiest and most satisfied periods of your career you were probably also doing very well professionally. Happy employees tend to give their best. They behave in the way that is expected by their employer, and (past) behaviour is what matters in a GCBI as that is considered to be the best predictor of future performance.

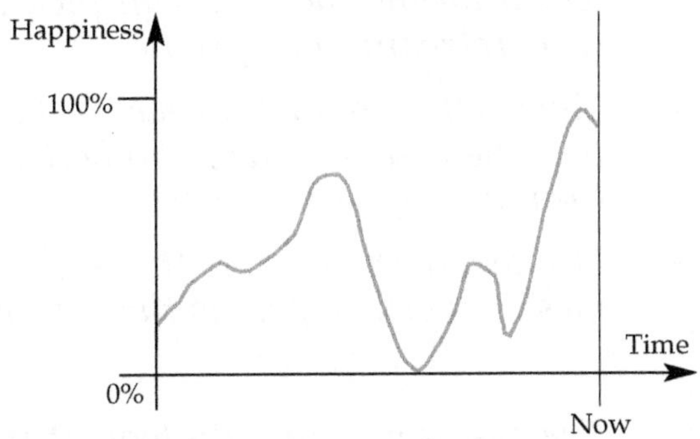

Figure 5.4

Thus, in order to find the "better" examples from your own career, you should look at the periods when you were most satisfied and therefore likely to have been the most productive and effective.

Consider your personal achievements

As described above, the assessors are interested in what you did personally, so make sure this is clear and avoid using collective terms such as "we (made a project plan)" or "the group (came up with the solution)" or "company X launched (an initiative)". Instead, make statements such as "I (suggested we begin with a project plan)". This can be hard if the situation you are describing was genuinely a group process, but you should always be clear about the role you played in helping a group arrive at its decision. At the same time, avoid giving the impression of being an overly confident or egocentric candidate.

Prepare for follow-up questions

Be aware that sometimes an assessor might ask you for a second example once you have already described one situation. This is designed to find out if a candidate only has one "star answer" for a competency. Make sure that you are not caught out by this and have multiple examples in mind.

Notes:

....

....

....

....

....

Key points to remember

- *The GCBI is all about your self-stated behaviour in the past, which means that you can pick your own examples as long as they are true, relevant and specific*

- *Your self-introduction has to be short and to the point, the idea being that the assessors want to better understand the answers you will give them during the interview*
- *Use wherever possible the STAR model to formulate your answers. The most important part is the "Action" part*

- *The assessors can only look at the positive (and negative) indicators in your answers, so make sure these come out in a clear and precise manner*
- *Your behaviour and body language are an important part of the messages you convey*

6. The Oral Presentation

Introduction

Presentation exercises are designed to measure your ability to organise and structure information, to communicate clearly and concisely and to remain resilient under questioning. At the EPSO Assessment Centre, you will be asked to present on a topic in front of (usually two) assessors. It is therefore similar to a public speaking exercise that you may be required to do once recruited, to showcase to your colleagues a certain file you have been working on.

Competencies

Much like in the other exercises of the Assessment Centre a number of your competencies will be assessed.

Most obviously, your (oral) communication skills will be put to test. The positive indicators are:

- Oral communication is clear and precise
- Handles questions confidently
- Simplifies complex subject matters
- Persuades, gets acceptance of their proposals
- Adjusts their style to the audience

On top of this, you will have to prove to the assessors that you are capable of identifying the critical facts in complex issues and developing creative and practical solutions (analysis and problem solving). In other words:

- You cope well with complexity
- You challenge data
- You identify the root cause of issues

- You consider multiple options
- You suggest creative solutions
- You make practical and workable suggestions
- You gather only relevant information for decision making

It may also happen that your "delivering quality and results" competency is assessed during this exercise. Here the assessors will look at the following (positive) indicators, or the lack of them:

- Takes responsibility to meet objectives
- Maintains quality of an acceptable level
- Follows guidelines and instructions
- Takes initiative
- Accepts challenges
- Seeks to exceed expectations

Last but certainly not least your resilience will be tested:

- Remains fully effective under stress
- Adjusts to peaks and troughs in the workload
- Handles failures and interprets setbacks professionally, not personally
- Understands and works constructively with the hierarchy
- Adapts to new ways of working and embraces change

Admittedly, for some of these indicators it is a bit more difficult to "translate" them into real behaviour during the oral presentation, but with a little bit of imagination one can think of something for each and every one of them.

Even though your competencies are being assessed throughout the whole exercise, your focus will need to be different, depending on which part of the exercise you are in.

Competency	Preparation	Presentation	Q&A
Communicating		X	
Analysing and problem solving	X		X
Delivering quality and results	X	X	
Resilience		X	X

Table 6.1: competencies tested in the oral presentation

The Scenario

The oral presentation usually takes place after lunch. This may seem to be trivial information, but one of the most stubborn opponents you can face as a speaker is an audience that has endured a morning full of interviews, escaped to a lunch of heavy food, only to be driven back to their seats to listen to you!

For you, the exercise starts in a separate room where you will get time to analyse a file containing a number of documents with background information. It is important that you **accept the scenario as it is presented to you**. In real life you would have access to other sources and be able to consult your colleagues, but in this exercise you are limited to the information contained in the documents provided. You are, however, allowed to make logical assumptions where information is lacking or incomplete. In the assignment you will read about the setting or – in other words – the role you are about to play when in front of your audience.

You have **30 minutes** to analyse the information, make notes of your most important findings, and prepare a presentation for your audience. As a support to your oral presentation you can prepare a one-page flipchart. Usually, you are only allowed the last five minutes of your preparation time to prepare this flipchart.

At the end of your preparation time you will be invited by the competition assistant to follow him or her to the room where your presentation will take place. You can bring your notes and the flipchart with you but you will be asked to leave the background documentation in the preparation room.

For people who wander around in the Assessment Centre premises early in the afternoon, it is a bizarre sight to see the candidates running behind the assistants, or waiting in front of the presentation room, while carrying their flipchart (size A2) with both hands in front of them. But don't worry; you won't seem ridiculous, because that's how it is supposed to be.

You are then invited into the room by one of the assessors, who will help by taking your flipchart and attaching it to the wall in front of the table they are sitting at.

When you are ready you can then start your presentation. Normally, the assessors won't interrupt you, so you can give your presentation without losing your thread. This will take **10 minutes**.

Once you have indicated that you are done, they will ask you some questions, and you are supposed to answer these as good as you can. The questions-and-answers (Q&A) part of the exercise will last another **10 minutes**.

Time Management

As you saw above, you have 30 minutes of preparation, 10 minutes of presentation and then 10 minutes of Q&A.

Notes:

....

....

....

....

....

You will probably find that the preparation time is too short and, in contrast, the 10 minutes of presentation will feel like an eternity. The Q&A will probably fly by, especially because the speed at which they fire their questions at you will be surprisingly high.

All this, of course, is done on purpose. It is a vital element of the exercise to test your resilience and your prioritising and organising capabilities.

Preparation stage

For the preparation stage your time management could look as follows:

1. Start by reading the assignment and writing down the structure of your flipchart (about 5 minutes). There is more about this in "The content of your Presentation", later in this chapter.
2. Go through all the documents in a "diagonal" way and try to find the information which is relevant to the questions asked. While "skimming" the documents you add this information in the proper "chapter" of your notes, and keywords or icons on the draft flipchart (which is also in your notes as you only get the actual flipchart paper at the end). Spend around 15 minutes on this. There is a vital point to keep in mind: **you will not be allowed to take the background documents with you** to the presentation, only your own notes. Therefore you need to put in your notes all the information you think you will need for the presentation and indeed (as far as you can anticipate the questions) for the Q&A part.
3. Try to think of a good opening statement and a clean and crisp concluding sentence. If possible, rehearse these mentally or out loud. Another 5 minutes.
4. Use the last five minutes to create an abstract and an abridged structure of your presentation on the flipchart. Be careful though: use bullet points and keywords, not complete sentences. If possible – and applicable – use some graphical elements (arrows, boxes, icons…) to enhance the visual appeal of the flipchart, or you may use a mindmap or other elements too if that helps present the structure of your presentation better.

Be ruthless with the content. Inevitably, preparing a presentation will involve your assembling too much information from your background research. Remember what it feels like to listen to a speaker. Too much information and you begin to switch off. Prune your talk to the essentials. You might decide on perhaps no more than three memorable "big ideas" you want your audience to take away with them. And remember: if you have too much information it's also much harder to keep to time. (See more tips on the visual aid below.)

The actual presentation

For the actual presentation you have 10 minutes to fill. Try to stick as close as you can to this, though if you use only 7 or 8 minutes, that's fine. If you go on too long, however, you will not be able to say everything you planned, as the assessors will interrupt you when your time has passed. On the other hand, if you run out of material to talk about before the end of your allotted time, you give them more time to ask questions.

There will be clocks in the room (but these are not necessarily synchronous) so you can watch your timing closely. Ideally, you would have an idea of how long each part of your presentation should last, so you can adjust your pace accordingly. Having an introduction and a conclusion will help – but if you run out of time for the conclusion it is not such a big deal as you should have covered the points already, just without the concluding emphasis. Speaking more slowly (or accelerating) could also help you manage the time effectively. Finally, the occasional repetition of an important idea (using a different wording), or making intermediate conclusions might be useful techniques for managing your time.

With these elements in mind, you would spend the first minute outlining what you will be discussing. The main content section will take a further eight minutes: enough for six to eight main points if you wish. Then comes your conclusion, summarising what you have covered, with your focus on the "big ideas" or main message. When that's finished, thank the assessors for their attention and say you now invite their questions.

A candidate's experience

The oral presentation was probably, along with the case study, my best performance. The domain on which the materials were based on was familiar to me and I had delivered quite a few presentations before. However, the preparation time was extremely short. You can barely skip through the materials and structure your ideas, not to mention that you also have to write something on the flipchart sheet. And then, shockingly, the 10 minutes of presentation are extremely long. So long that I finished a bit before the end of my time... There were numerous questions asked by one of the assessors after the presentation. These were about almost every part of my presentation – about facts contained in the materials, about the viability of my solutions, about resources, opinions and risks. I managed to answer most of them and when I didn't know the answer I offered to re-check the facts and come back with a solution. I kept eye contact and I stayed as relaxed as possible, and I did my best to back up my ideas and opinions.

The Content of Your Presentation

Generally speaking, the first step in preparing a presentation is to determine the essential purpose of the communication. Public presentations tend to have one of three general purposes: to *persuade*, to *inform*, or to *entertain*. The EPSO oral presentation is mostly about informing, to a lesser degree about persuading, and maybe with just a very small amount of entertaining thrown in.

Out of the purpose will come the main ideas to be included in the presentation. These ideas are then organised to include

Notes:

an introduction, a main body, and a summary or conclusion. Or, as the old adage about giving speeches goes, "Say what you're going to say, say it, and then say what you have said." The introduction should grab the assessors' attention and establish the theme of the remainder of the presentation. The main body should concentrate on points of emphasis. The conclusion should restate the key points and summarise the overarching message that is being conveyed.

The assessors will know what's in your file, at least in general terms. As EPSO uses different files with background documentation in the Assessment Centre, they may however lack the more detailed knowledge of your specific file. The assessors are supposed to familiarise themselves with these details during the lunch break but they may have had other things to do.

As such, this is good news and bad news.

The good news is that they will expect a more synthetic overview, which corresponds with their own view on what is important in the background documentation. So, when your analysis corresponds more or less with theirs, you're good.

The bad news is that they may ask you questions to find out what makes today's file different, and this will be in the details – details you may have missed during your analysis of the documentation. Don't worry, there is a workaround and we will explain later how to cope with this.

The content of your presentation should thus focus on a synthetic overview of what's in your documentation, and concentrate only on what is asked for in the assignment (first page).

Do not go into too much detail but stick to a general overview, much as if you were talking to a journalist – or a public audience – when "taken by surprise" with little or no preparation time.

Simplicity

The idea of simplicity is implemented by applying a clear and straightforward structure to your presentation, if possible linear and organised in chronological order. Long sentences, over-sophisticated vocabulary and jargon should be avoided. Complex ideas and concepts should be explained in the simplest way possible, preferably by using metaphors, analogies or real-life examples.

When you convey a message simply, you make life easier for your audience. They don't have to make as much effort to understand what you're saying and you have a much better chance of getting your message across.

Keeping it simple doesn't mean that you are underestimating your own or your audience's level of intelligence, quite the contrary. The best proof of someone's intelligence is the ability to simplify the complex. People who are confident in their knowledge won't hesitate to share it with others in terms that are easily understood. In contrast, people who attempt to talk over people's heads by using overly complex language are typically those who lack a true understanding of the subject themselves and are trying to mask that fact. Albert Einstein once said that "If you can't explain it to a six year old, you don't understand it yourself." Keep this in mind.

Another challenge is "the curse of knowledge", which is the challenge of knowing a topic and jargon so well that it becomes hard to talk about it in simple, non-expert terms. This can become a risk if the topic you are required to speak about happens to be one that you are very familiar with.

Storytelling

People instinctively think about abstract ideas in the form of stories involving people and situations, which is why storytelling is relevant to presentations. For example, character-driven stories with emotional content result in a better understanding of the key points a speaker wishes to make and enable better recall of these points many weeks later. When you want to motivate, persuade, or be remembered, start with a story with a human dimension.

In your presentation, try to think about why anyone should care about what you are proposing. How does it change the world or improve lives? How will people feel when it is complete? These are the components that make information persuasive and memorable. For instance, you might start your presentation by saying "Imagine José Delgado, a Spanish teacher in Alicante. Our proposal today about renewable energy may not seem to directly impact his life, but when he, after working 35 years, retires, he will have saved thousands of euros on his energy bill as a result. Let me explain how."

Remember, the assessors are not your enemy; your enemy is the after-lunch fatigue that makes it hard for them to keep their attention on your message. You must keep them engaged and alert by applying these techniques to the best of your abilities. Your talk must be appetising, adequately salted and spicy with a variety of fascinating facts, insights, and bold opinions that are peppered with a dash of style, passion and humour.

Repetition

We only actually take in part of any message because we are simply not listening all the time. It can therefore be a good idea to build some apparent "over-kill" into your message by repeating the same important points.

People rate statements that have been repeated as more valid or true than things they have heard only once. And when we think something is "more true", we also tend to be more persuaded by it.

Psychological studies clearly suggest that moderate repetition has a positive effect on someone's reception of, and agreement with, a persuasive argument. Low to moderate levels of repetition within a message tend to create greater agreement with the message, along with greater recall. However, too much repetition has an adverse impact and can lead to stronger disagreement with the argument being made.

Ethos, pathos, logos

According to Aristotle, the ancient Greek philosopher, the goal of argumentative speaking is to persuade your audience that your ideas are valid – or more valid than someone else's. He divided the means of persuasion into three categories: *ethos*, *pathos* and *logos*.

Our perception of a speaker's character influences how acceptable or convincing

Notes:

....

....

....

....

....

we find what that person has to say. This projected character is called *ethos*. We are more likely to be persuaded by a person who, we think, has personal warmth, consideration for others, a good mind and erudition.

The influential appeal of *pathos* is a call to the audience's sense of identity, their self-interest, their emotions. Appeals to our sense of identity and self-interest exploit common biases; we naturally bend in the direction of what is advantageous to us, what serves our interests or the interests of any group we believe ourselves a part of. We also naturally find more convincing the speaker or writer who flatters us (especially indirectly) instead of insulting us. Thus skilful speakers create a positive image in their words, an image their actual readers can identify with. In the case of the oral presentation, you can use this appeal to identity by mentioning EU policies, EU institutions, referring to European leaders, and even values that Europeans share such as democracy, human rights, transparency and others – as long as these represent a natural blend with the key message of your presentation and don't come across as too forced.

Finally, we come to the arguments themselves – the explicit reasons the arguer provides to support a position, or *logos*. This can also be a bit personal: mentioning why you appreciate a certain position, or why you can identify with its objectives makes the message less dry or descriptive and turns into a personal conviction that usually resonates much better with the audience.

The Visual Aids

In EPSO competitions, the oral presentation is only used for positions where the leadership competency is also tested. Those having leadership skills are supposed to be able to convince other people. They must look, sound and speak like a leader, not just read out a text from some visual aid or their notes.

One of the biggest mistakes presenters make is to rely too much on their visual aids. Tools like PowerPoint or Prezi encourage them to create slides with nice graphics, animations and too many words. Then, more often than not, they read off their slides word for word to an audience that is not actually listening but instead reading the slides for themselves.

Luckily, for your oral presentation you will not have the temptation of putting on a slide show with PowerPoint. You will only have one sheet – about size A2 – and everything you want to reinforce your message with should be on it – your flipchart.

Your flipchart can be a useful component of your oral presentation, but you should never consider it as your main resource. Your flipchart has to be meaningful, creative, and interesting in order to help you get your message across. It should help to illustrate and strengthen your points and not be a distraction from what you are saying. The key to successful use of visual aids is that they should support the theme of the presentation, especially its structure, but do so without being chaotic, complicated, or even too entertaining.

A good flipchart will make you feel secure and is helpful to the assessors too: they will know where they are and what's to come, so it has to have nicely separated elements, headings or numbers to achieve this effect.

This also applies to the outline you prepare for yourself: **some key concepts, bullet points and reminders are sufficient to help you keep the flow**. Make sure your flipchart is easy to read and that you can quickly find the key information you need there, because when you are standing in front of the assessors, getting "lost" in your notes while trying to retrieve a name or piece of data is the last thing you want to happen. Similarly, make sure the chart or information or bullet points you put on the flipchart have a clear structure: the most important thing is to help the assessors visualise the points you are going to cover. Ensure that you use bold colours that stand out (e.g. not yellow, light blue etc.) and write clearly in a large font. Following this small piece of advice can have an important effect on the success of your presentation.

We can recommend the book *Real Leaders Don't Do PowerPoint* by Christopher Witt, where you will read all about how to speak so people listen. It also worth watching a few TED Talks as, surprisingly, more than half of the 50 most viewed presentations do not use any visual aid whatsoever.

If your interview is online, put what you would have on a flipchart on a single A4 page and keep it handy during the presentation. You can show it if you are asked to and in any case you will have it for your own reference to guide your presentation.

Body Language

You cannot "not" communicate; whatever you do or say, you communicate all the time. Whether you do it in the most optimal way, however, is the question.

Non-verbal elements such as posture, gestures, and facial expressions can be just as important as what you actually say. Some movement may be helpful to hold listeners' attention or to increase emphasis, but constant shifting about or pacing around should be avoided. Likewise, hand and arm gestures can be used to point, describe, or emphasise, but these too should be varied, carefully timed, and adapted to the audience. Finally, good speakers make frequent eye contact with their audience; they let their facial expressions show their interest in the ideas they are presenting, and never turn their back to the audience. Again, it is worth watching and analysing TED Talks as they tend to have professional speakers from whom you can learn a lot of techniques.

An important note, however, is that **we don't recommend challenging the assessors or asking them questions** in order to bring them into the presentation. While these are valid and often applied techniques of trainers and speakers, the oral presentation is about you only and the assessors are there to evaluate you, not to participate as a mock audience.

Even if you do not feel confident, try to look as if you are – keep a good upright posture, don't speak too quickly, look up as much as you can at each member of the panel, and smile occasionally. Less experienced presenters have a tendency to speed up as they talk, especially as the end of their allotted time approaches: try to speak clearly and at a measured pace. If you feel yourself start to rush, pause and get yourself back on track.

If you feel comfortable with this, it can be a good idea to shift your position very occasionally to the other side of the flipchart, which helps keep attention.

Notes:

Never turn your back on the assessors even when you point at the flipchart, and try not to stand in front of it either. Remember, though you may be nervous or feel exposed, **during the presentation you are in control**. You are the leader, and your "followers", in this case the assessors, need to be inspired – at least until the Q&A begins.

If you are doing your presentation online, keep your body movements to a minimum and also try to keep your hands within the viewing window.

An assessor's point of view

Our first candidate for today's oral presentation was really problematic. In fact, I felt sorry for him because I could feel that he knew what he was talking about, but the way he presented it was really bad. Things already turned bad when he entered the room. He looked really frightened, I could see his hands trembling, he didn't look us in the eyes and barely said hello. A beaten dog couldn't have looked worse. Then, when we saw his flipchart, things got even worse. It was a real mess: too much information, small print, no structure. In short, a nightmare.

The thing is that we hadn't had the time to have a closer look at today's version of the background documentation since we had a long conversation about one of the candidates we saw in the morning, so we were eager to hear a fresh story. Unfortunately, this person did not meet our expectations. While talking, he did almost everything wrong. Mumbling in a monotonous voice, his arms glued to his body, avoiding eye contact and turning his back to the audience while reading almost literally word for word from the flipchart. Because of that, we were compelled to look at his flipchart all the time, but as this was so messy and difficult to read, we didn't understand a word of what he wanted to say. No wonder that my colleague and I agreed to give him a bad score on all accounts.

If you are a French speaker, we advise you to read the book *Prendre la parole en public* by Bernard Blein; it contains a wealth of very practical ideas. The book *Made to Stick*, by Chip and Dan Heath, also has many great ideas about how to make presentations, and communication in general, impactful and memorable.

The Q&A Phase

The oral presentation is a **role-play exercise throughout, even during the Q&A phase**. You are supposed to be delivering a presentation to your colleagues, or your Head of Unit, and act as if you were doing so. In this context, your audience may ask you questions, even if they are fully aware of the intricacies of the topic. It is, however, not a theoretical exam where a teacher or a professor is probing your deep knowledge about a given subject.

This being said, be aware that during the Q&A phase, the focus of the assessor's attention will be on your resilience, such as how you deal with difficult or unpredictable questions probing for details that may or may not be in the background documentation.

Imagine that you are listening to a colleague during a real meeting, somewhere inside the EU institutions. What would you think if that person started inventing stuff, guessing or outright lying, just to save face in front of his peers or bosses? Does this person realise that what he says – and does – may have an impact on the lives of EU citizens, and even beyond? This is not the behaviour one would expect of a real professional, a serious EU official, so an appropriate reaction must be found instead.

How do you handle this kind of question, or in other words, how do you best behave during the Q&A part of your oral presentation?

You could look the assessor in the eye and say "I remember this information was in the briefing, but I can't recall it right now. Let me check after the meeting and get back to you." In this way you essentially say, "I don't know", but the impression is very different, which has a direct impact on how the assessors will judge your resilience or even analytical skills. One word of caution, however, is that the assessors may have heard this line many times already, and it has therefore lost its original effect. You may want to brainstorm alternative formulations instead.

Do not be afraid to ask the assessor to clarify questions if you do not understand them. If you genuinely cannot respond to a difficult question, thank the assessor for raising the point, acknowledge its relevance, and concede this is not something you can offer an opinion on at the present time, but suggest that it is something you would be prepared to follow up later.

Remain calm under questioning and do not become defensive or nervous even if your views are challenged. The assessors are testing to see how you react under pressure so try to remain calm and relaxed in your responses, especially paying attention to keeping an "open" posture by resisting the urge to cross your legs, or fold your arms, or grab your notes with both hands, or look upwards when challenged.

The types of questions you will face from the assessors following your presentation are likely to be split into two types. Firstly, there will be more general ones seeking more information about your approach. The second type will be more specialised, relating to the specific issues contained in the brief.

Here are some typical questions you could expect. Give some thought as to how you would respond:

- Have you considered the impact of [a topic not covered in your presentation – e.g. broader economic picture, staffing issues, lack of resources, potential repercussions on other EU policies]?
- What alternative options did you consider? Why did you discard them?
- I am not convinced that [specific recommendation you made] is the right way to proceed. Have you considered [alternative option] instead?
- Why do we need to act at all? What is the problem with allowing things to continue as they are?
- Talk me through the [financial, people, resource] implications of your proposal in more detail.

Notes:

- I am not sure how popular this will be with other stakeholders [e.g. staff, the public, NGOs]. What arguments can you propose that would help me to persuade them that this is a good idea?
- What are the longer-term implications of your proposals?
- What concerns do you have over the long-term viability of your proposals?
- How might your proposal affect EU activities in other areas?
- What other information would you have liked to help reach your decision? Why?
- What was the most important factor in making your decision, as far as you are concerned?
- How would you communicate your proposals both internally and externally?
- What do you see as your role in this project going forward?
- What external knowledge or expertise would we need to bring in?
- What do you see as the biggest risk in your plan? How do you propose that we manage it?
- What contingencies do you think are needed?

You could consider trying to gamble a bit by intentionally "forgetting" to mention an important element during your presentation, thus hoping to draw a question from the assessors to which you will know the answer, and so impressing them with your swift and accurate response. This may seem like a risky endeavour, but experienced speakers frequently use this little trick.

Controlling Your Nerves

Being anxious about speaking in public is perfectly normal. Even the best and most experienced speakers get a bit nervous before they go on stage or speak in front of a large group. You should never expect yourself to be completely anxiety free. What you need to do is to turn that anxiety into energy for giving a great presentation, not holding you back from speaking.

Fear of public speaking – also known as glossophobia – comes from our fear of being judged or the fear of forgetting what we want to say. Doubts over our own ability combined with the knowledge that others are forced to pay attention to what we say creates a feeling of anxiety that is difficult to overcome. On top of that, our mind tends to focus on the mistakes we make, and our anxiety is then reinforced.

Many people nowadays spend large amounts of their time online, which not only requires no public speaking, but also allows for complete anonymity (no judgement). More and more people also use predominantly written communication in their work; emails, memos and the like. They have much more time to reflect on what they put on paper or a screen than if they were actually talking to someone. Written communication is mostly indirect or asynchronous (not happening in real time) – there is no physical presence of the audience. In short, in our modern way of life we tend to do less public speaking, so we are less used to it and consequently more afraid of doing it.

Obviously, practice is the most important thing you can do, but this is a long-term

A candidate's point of view

The oral presentation was definitely the most difficult and demanding part for me. The reason was the complexity of the subject and the various viewpoints described in the exam booklet given. The time allocated to preparation was as expected, but for me the topic was something I knew almost nothing about. Nevertheless, I did manage to hold a 9 minutes and 45 seconds presentation – the assessors alerted me twice, at the 8th minute and the 9-and-a-half minute marks that I had such and such time left. When it came to the questions, I tried to answer as well as I could, with some personal recommendations. One question was rather off-topic, but that was somewhat disguised by the assessor as being referred to in the exam booklet: I stumbled at first and then recalled the resilience competency and said that I will consult the relevant experts, etc...

approach. There are, however a few things you can do right before your presentation. No matter how simple they may seem, these tips could help to ease your anxiety and calm down your nerves.

Right before your oral presentation, visualise yourself giving the perfect presentation. Visualise the room, the audience, the whole physical environment and yourself, at the centre of attention and doing amazingly well. This positive thinking will give your self-confidence a boost and act like a self-fulfilling prophecy. Your initial anxiety will be transformed into the energy you need for a perfect presentation.

Remind yourself that it doesn't matter what people think. Don't go in there worrying about everything that can go wrong. Go in there reminding yourself that you've done what you can, and that no matter how well it goes you'll continue to get better. Having notes in your hands and a flipchart with cues and ideas about what to talk about will significantly reduce your anxiety.

Although you are told when you can begin the presentation, before you say anything, pause, take a couple of calm, deep breaths, and look at the assessors. When they are settled and ready, you can begin.

As soon as it's over, tell yourself you did a great job. Worry about any mistakes you may have made later.

Notes:

....

....

....

....

....

Some Tips for the Assessment

Opening styles

You can choose various opening styles for the start of your presentation as follows:

- You might start with a surprising fact: "Did you know that 2 out of 10 EU citizens do not believe in man-made climate change?"
- You might start with a personal element (though given the topic and professional context, this is less recommended unless you can really come up with a suitable example related to the topic of the briefing): "When I was a teenager, I always dreamed about becoming a lawyer. Now that I have become one, I am very excited to analyse the latest case law in this field."
- You might refer to an event: "When President Juncker announced the Commission proposals to improve the digital economy, he suggested that..."
- You might recall a story: "Two months ago one day, early morning three people gathered in a meeting room of the European Parliament to discuss something crucial for the EU's future. These three were..."
- You can be factual: "In 2005 when the Constitutional Treaty was rejected in two EU Member States, nobody thought it could be revived again."
- You might develop your opening based on a mixture of the above.

Adapt your style

Make sure the presentation is delivered in an appropriate style for the target audience: you must adapt your vocabulary, examples, expressions and facts accordingly. (It may have a detrimental effect on your evaluation if, for example, you are asked to present a communication strategy for the introduction of the euro in a Member State and you use expressions such as "convergence criteria" to a non-expert audience.) Keep things sharp, succinct and to the point. Do not over-elaborate, or babble for the sake of using up time or showing off knowledge for its own sake. Also, it is important to be articulate, and not to use slang (such as "the new regulation was viewed as a really cool one by the industry"). Throughout your presentation you must be professional.

Be specific

It is crucial to add concrete examples to support each of your points. When talking about e.g. the EU's performance audit efforts, make sure to provide specific projects you are familiar with or ones that you learned from the dossier; or when discussing the EU's plans to cut CO_2 emissions from cars, you can mention specific emission figures, thresholds, or a simple but powerful example of "if you have an Peugeot, its emissions will be regulated as follows, therefore when doing your shopping next Saturday in Strasbourg, think of the added value this policy has triggered". This will help your audience visualise what you are talking about and remember it much better. The key point is to bring a high-level scientific and/or abstract piece of information to a "digestible" level by using real-life examples with details that reinforce your point so the audience can truly visualise it. It may be very challenging to do this under such time pressure, but the quality of your communication and also the assessment of your analytical competency will be much higher as a result.

Concreteness

Provide specific examples from the background brief or from your outside knowledge. These give the audience something to think about and an interesting source for the later question-and-answer session. On the other hand, be careful with numbers. These, on the face of it, can seem good tools to bring concreteness into your presentation; however, numbers can be hard to remember. Instead, you can turn a figure of 20% into a more memorable "every fifth..." phrase. Or, instead of saying "50 million EU citizens are living below the poverty line", you can phrase it as "one in ten EU citizens". This makes dry figures easier to connect with and thus helps your communication scores. To take this one step even further, you can say "If I look out of this window and see ten people in the street, one of them will be living below the poverty line."

Easy style

You may wish to include some light humour, but always ensure that it is appropriate to the subject of the presentation and to the audience. Needless to say, it is completely inappropriate to make cynical comments or voice stereotypes about an EU Member State, race, religion or other sensitive matters.

Delivery

Aim for a conversational delivery, referring to brief notes or bullet points on the flipchart, rather than memorising and reciting, or reading from your notes. Try to establish eye contact with the assessors and aim to read their body language to gain reinforcement or feedback. Many candidates get buried in their notes, instead of looking up and just taking small "hints" and nuggets of information from their notes or the flipchart.

What you think

Do not be afraid to express your opinions. When you are expressing opinion rather than stating facts, always remember to make this clear by using expressions such as "I believe that", "in my opinion", or "to my mind". You can show how strong your beliefs are by slightly amending some of these expressions: "I firmly believe that", "I strongly believe that", "we are absolutely certain that", "we are pretty sure that".

Stay on track

Make sure that you only cover topics in your presentation that you know and understand at least fairly well based on the background briefing. Do not choose to introduce a subject you are less familiar with because you think it will be more impressive: you may well run into difficulties when questioned in more detail following the presentation. It is better to present confidently on topics about which you feel comfortable.

Pauses

Pause slightly between points to show the

Notes:

....

....

....

....

....

audience when you are about to move on to a different subject. Pauses are also an extremely useful tool to gain the audience's attention: if used wisely, a pause of a few seconds will allow everyone to catch up and focus their attention on you again. This certainly requires a lot of practice, but this is a worthy investment: improving presentation skills is not just useful for EPSO exams but later in your career too.

Corrections

Do not be put off if you make a mistake during the presentation (e.g. you realise you mixed up the date a Treaty was signed or you misread a piece of data). Apologise quickly and move on.

Interactivity

The assessors will not ask you questions during the presentation itself, only in the following question and answer session, so interaction will only be possible in the latter phase.

Use transitions

You can use transition statements as a signal to the audience that they should refocus. They may have got distracted for a couple of moments and then found it hard to get back on track with what you're saying. But if you make a transition statement such as: "So that's the problem we're facing, now I'll go onto my recommendation to address it", this gives them an opportunity to get back on board.

How to Prepare

As you will not know the topic of the background briefing in advance, it is difficult to prepare from a content perspective, except by following the same preparation as advised for the case study and the general tips for preparation.

You could improve your analysis and problem-solving competency by the following exercise:

- Imagine a topic, preferably EU related
- Take half an hour, and browse the internet using keywords that are related to the chosen topic
- Bookmark or copy-paste the relevant information on the topic into a draft document
- Then review the result, and try to make a coherent text of it
- Prepare a single page presentation slide as the one you would use for a presentation to a general public

When you do this a number of times you will "rewire" your brain to become more proficient for the preparation phase of your oral presentation (this, of course goes for the case study as well).

You can also consider your personal presentation style in advance by asking others (friends, colleagues, fellow candidates, or a coach) for feedback on the strengths and weaknesses of your communication style and how you tend to present information.

Practising giving presentations can be unappealing for some people, but it is definitely worth considering. Try to find opportunities to do so in advance of the Assessment Centre in order to reduce any tension or fear: even if you just present on a familiar topic to supportive friends or family members, it can still be extremely useful. You may also wish to have yourself recorded on video and then analyse your body language, voice strength and pace of speech, content vocabulary and other factors that assessors will be looking at. You ideally wish to get to the stage that:

- You are comfortable speaking from memory with only the need for brief prompts or bullet points on index cards
- You can ensure a presentation you give runs to a set time
- You feel comfortable projecting your voice and speaking at a measured pace
- Through feedback, you are aware of any distracting habits you may have, such as fiddling with your hair or repeating a particular phrase or expression (e.g. "yeah", "uhm" or "you know": these are much more common than most people imagine, it's just that speakers hardly ever notice these themselves). You should aim at least to get to the stage where you become consciously aware when they are happening and can take steps to stop them
- If you really want to become a proficient public speaker you might consider becoming a member of the worldwide Toastmasters Network. They empower individuals to become more effective communicators and leaders. Check it out on www.toastmasters.org

Key points to remember

- *Being nervous about giving an oral presentation is absolutely normal. The trick is to convert your stress into positive energy.*
- *Focus on different competencies, depending on the phase of the exercise you are in*
- *Keep it simple, concrete and try to use some storytelling*
- *Preparation, delivery and Q&A require different approaches and styles*

For a sample oral presentation exercise, see Annex 5.

Notes:

....

....

....

....

....

7. The Group Exercise

This exercise is currently suspended because of Covid and replaced by the situational competemcy based interview. See Chapter 10.

Introduction

Group exercises involve working with others as part of a team to resolve an issue you are presented with. These are the most effective simulations for measuring interpersonal skills and behaviours such as leadership, teamwork, negotiation, and group problem-solving skills.

There are various types of group exercise. In the EPSO group exercise there will normally be six candidates around the table, each presenting the position of a stakeholder. Each candidate receives the same "core" background information along with the position of the stakeholder he or she is supposed to be reporting back from. In the scenario the candidates are all of equal status, and it is expressly forbidden to designate a formal chair for the meeting. The objective is to reach an agreed position, as far as possible reconciling the interests of the different stakeholders.

The EPSO group exercise is an exercise in bureaucracy, NOT a political negotiation or a situation where the candidates have to defend a position and make sure that their position comes out on top in the resulting report of the meeting. You are supposed to have previously consulted your stakeholder and have to act merely as the "rapporteur", even if you personally don't agree with your stakeholder's point of view. This has important consequences in terms of how you should analyse the background information and how you are expected to behave during the actual group discussion.

The Exercise

The group exercise **tends to be the last exam of the day**, starting usually at 4pm. The assistant will invite you into the room and ask you to take your designated place (your candidate number within the group – see Figure 7.1). In front of you there will be a file with your background information (including the position of the stakeholder you are speaking for). You are not allowed to open this file until you are told to do so.

You will then get **15 minutes** to read the background documentation. Use this wisely and make rough notes on key messages before the discussion with the group begins. However, be aware that the time for this preparation is set deliberately short: you will not have enough time to read and digest everything in great detail. It would not reflect

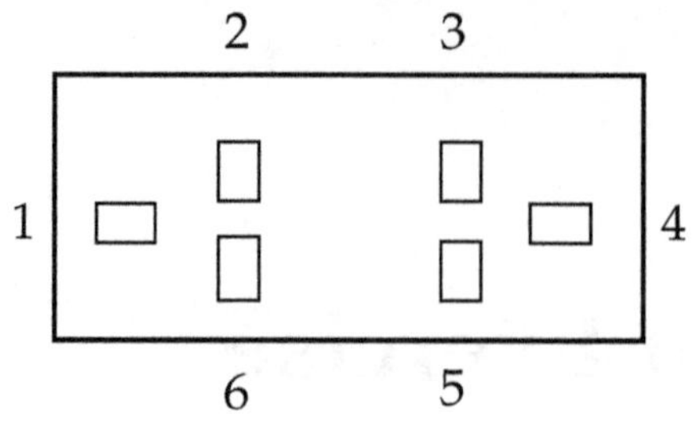

Figure 7.1

well on you if you spent the first five minutes of the subsequent discussion with your head down, catching up on reading the background information.
Given this, it is advisable to concentrate initially on **the first page (the assignment) and the last page (your stakeholder's position)**, as these contain the most important information. The other background information may contain interesting facts and figures but is not as important as the first and the last pages. During the initial preparation time you are not allowed to discuss the background documentation with the other candidates.

Once the preparation time is over, the members of the jury will enter the room and take their position in the corners of the room. Each member of the jury can observe the body language and facial expressions of three candidates, as he or she is facing three candidates. For example, in Figure 7.2 member D can observe candidates 2, 3, and 4. In this way, two members of the jury who can see their face observe every candidate. You will notice that these are not the persons who ran your competency based interview earlier that day. This is not a coincidence, because they want to avoid the "halo effect" mentioned in the first chapter (i.e. having a subjective bias, a good or bad impression of a person in mind while assessing that person's competencies through another exercise). During the exercise, the members of the jury act as a "fly on the wall". They will not intervene in any way. You can actually ignore their presence and don't try to make any eye contact either.

When the jury is seated, the assistant will give the signal that the discussion can start. You will be told that you have **50 minutes** for the discussion, and then the group is on its own.

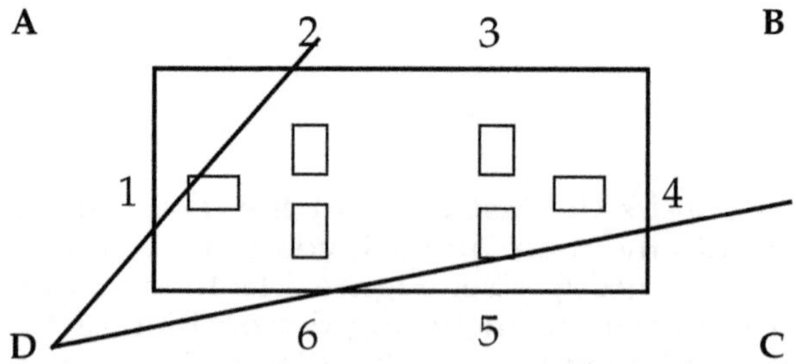

Figure 7.2

An assessor's point of view

It is sometimes very difficult to be "a fly on the wall" during the group discussion. As an assessor you know the details of the file they're discussing and it is tough to refrain from getting things going again when they are stuck. Luckily, we have seen many group exercises before – we actually practiced it ourselves during the training – so we realise that this is a very tough one. On top of that we are all tired. But we keep in mind that after the candidates have left the room we still have to discuss the results, so we'd better be attentive or otherwise the day will take us even longer...

The Phases of the Group Discussion

Ideally, the group discussion is conducted in three phases.

During **the first phase**, each candidates will normally explain the position of his or her stakeholder with respect to the items to be discussed as given in the assignment. The most efficient way of doing this is by a "tour de table".

An important note: as the group has no leader or designated chair, a member of the group must initiate a roundtable summary of this kind. This can be you or anyone else, but it's vital that if you are the one who proposes this exercise, you set clear instructions and time-limits. Simply saying "let's have everyone summarise their views" is going to lead to chaos, as some members of the group will take 2 or 3 minutes while others might spend only 30 seconds. It is therefore best to add "in two sentences" or "in 30 seconds" to set a limit. Even if people run over their time, there is a benchmark that they all know they should stick to, and you can even gently remind them (without being bossy as nobody has appointed you to have that role) that you had all agreed to keep it short.

One after the other, each participant can give a brief introduction about which stakeholder he or she has consulted, and then state what their stakeholder's position is. You should avoid giving your personal opinion at this point, or make guesses about the intentions of your stakeholder. There will be time for that during the next phase. At this stage, you are there simply to report your specific information to the other participants in the meeting.

Say there are three items to be discussed (A, B, and C) and there are six participants (1 to 6) around the table; then – at the end of phase 1 – the group as a whole should have a clear view of all the positions around the table. In other words, all the "Xs" in Figure 7.3 will be known.

Notes:

	1	2	3	4	5	6
A	X	X	X	X	X	X
B	X	X	X	X	X	X
C	X	X	X	X	X	X

Figure 7.3

Because everybody will have read the common assignment you will all agree on what exactly are the items to be discussed (A, B, and C) – and as everybody has hopefully also read the last page, with their personal stakeholder's position, it should be clear how to fill this matrix.

You may find that there are "Xs" missing, simply because some stakeholders did not express a position on one or other of the topics. There may also be information in the stakeholder positions that doesn't fit in this matrix (a topic "D" or "E"). In this case, the group will have to decide whether this point is to be taken into consideration or not.

The idea of **the second phase** is to have a "horizontal" discussion and to find a common solution. Most probably, some of the stakeholder positions will be wide apart, suggesting that it will be difficult – or even impossible – to find a compromise.

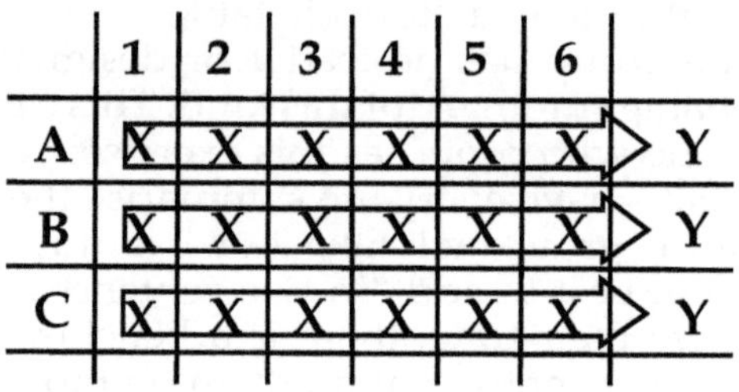

Figure 7.4

Remember that the group exercise is a simulation of a real meeting. Like in most real-life situations, the solution will not necessarily be the most obvious compromise. So, the outcome of the horizontal discussion may very well be that a decision by the hierarchy is required, or that more evidence is needed; maybe you have to propose a pilot project, a market study or consulting experts. All these are valid solutions, and can be the outcome of your discussion (Figure 7.4).

The discussion during phase two is the most challenging part of the group exercise. You should be aware of that and help try to converge rapidly on a solution, even if this does not entirely correspond to the expectations of your own stakeholder. Remember, this is not an exercise in negotiation but the simulation of a bureaucratic process.

The third, and last, phase is fairly easy. All you have to do is wrap up and make a summary of the solution(s). The group is not expected to deliver a written report. It is sufficient that, at the end, somebody presents the result to the group (not to the assessors) and gets the final agreement of the group on this (Figure 7.5).

The biggest danger during this phase is that the horizontal discussion of phase 2 is reopened. This could happen when you are ahead of time, and feel compelled to use the 50 minutes you have been given. Once the conclusions have been read, DO NOT re-open

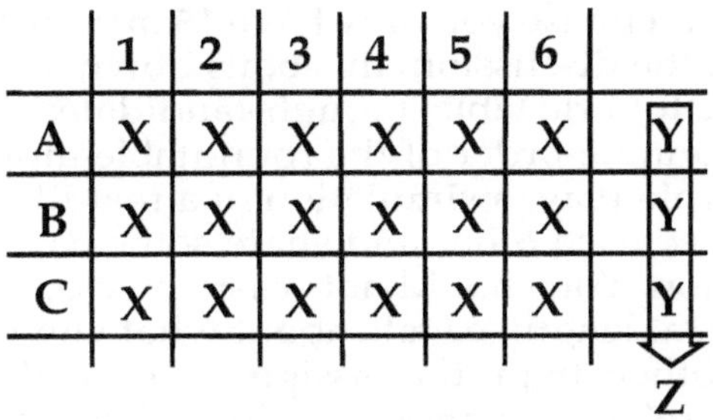

Figure 7.5

the discussion, or try to improve the formulation. By doing so, you would open up Pandora's box and ruin the whole exercise.

> ***A candidate's point of view***
>
> By the time I had to do the group exercise I was literally exhausted. The AC is a tiring experience and they keep one of the most difficult parts to the end. I was lucky to be part of a group with extremely good candidates and we worked well together, debating and agreeing, compromising and defending points. It is however almost impossible to see yourself from the outside and decide whether you are doing well or not and then adjusting yourself. But this is what one should do throughout the exercise. The best part is that the assessors become "invisible" to you once you start the exercise. There is so much focus on the talking points (we had 4!) that you barely notice that there are people looking at you and evaluating you. The worst part is that the time is extremely short for 6 people with different agendas to agree on 4 issues. It takes imagination, structure and good will.

Timing

You have 50 minutes for the discussion and have to go through these three phases to come up with the result. The timing is crucial. Now, let us have a look at these phases in reverse order.

If all went well, the third phase can be quite short. It must be possible to wrap up the conclusions in **10 minutes** or so. Avoid interrupting or correcting the person who is reading or suggesting the conclusions.

The second phase will probably the longest. It is not unusual to spend half of the available time (around **25 minutes**) on the horizontal discussion to reach acceptable solutions.

Notes:

....

....

....

....

....

This means that for the first phase you only have **15 minutes**. Assuming that you don't lose any time in setting up the discussion, this boils down to two and a half minutes for each participant during the tour de table, though candidates often tend to interrupt each other or intervene in the running order of the roundtable inputs.

The group exercise is a role-play, a simulation of a real-life meeting where the participants are supposed to know each other and share some common understanding of the background of the discussion. You should not waste precious time by introducing yourself – or your stakeholder – at length, or talk about what you may have read in the background documentation, other than the assignment or the position of your own stakeholder. The other "core" information should be brought into the discussion only during the second phase.

Roles and Duties

It will be clear by now that – in order to conduct a group discussion as described above – it is important that everybody around the table is aware of the general flow, and plays the game by the rules.

In the assignment it will be stated that you are NOT allowed to designate a formal chair for the meeting.

In practice, however, there are a number of roles to be taken on by members of the group. For example, a **moderator** takes on the role of an informal chair, and has to show awareness of the expected outcome (the mandate) and manage the sequence of events during the meeting by actively guiding the discussions and by making sure everyone gets a chance to contribute. Thus it is a high profile role in steering the group and achieving a successful outcome.

It is important to underline, however, that the moderator role is by no means one that is restricted to a single person: multiple participants, at different stages of the exercise, can take up the role of a moderator even if for short periods of time. The essential element is to summarise what has been said by the group members so far, and also to try to advance the discussions by closing as many open points as possible and then proposing the next step or the way forward. This should not be done in a dominant or bossy manner but by carefully establishing eye contact with the other participants to get their non-verbal feedback (nods, blinks, body leaning forward) so you know that your proposals are supported.

A second role is that of **timekeeper**. The timekeeper keeps an eye on the clock and warns the group when there is a risk of time overrun. There will be clocks on the walls of the room, so you should use them. Again, the timekeeper is not a stand-alone role and anyone, at any point, can remind the group of the time left and where you have got to in the discussion. Make sure not to overdo this role otherwise you risk antagonising the group and putting undue pressure on them.

In many professional meetings, there is a **secretarial** function for taking notes, but in the group exercise this role can be taken by any of the participants – and actually has much to recommend it, as it keeps you really focused on what is happening. There will be a flipchart in the room and you are free to use it. From experience we know that less than half of the groups do this, so it is in no way obligatory.

Apart from simple note-taking, somebody, the "**rapporteur**", has to draft the minutes. The rapporteur has to read back the conclusions at the end and get the approval of the group for them. Again, this is a self-appointed role that you need to be careful to get informal approval for from the rest of the group, rather than arbitrarily and unilaterally awarding it to yourself.

What the assignment explicitly forbids is for the group to designate a chair to take charge of all these duties. The idea is that all the participants have an equal "weight"; they are colleagues – equals – who have been tasked, as a group, to come up with solutions. This is a very important element of the exercise and those taking part have to be aware of this, because no one should try to tell the group what to do – you can only, assertively perhaps but respectfully, "suggest" they consider X or Y initiative and your proposed course of action.

On balance, we don't think it is a good idea to (explicitly) "volunteer" for one of these roles. Instead you should regard the logistics of your meeting as a collective responsibility.

An assessor's point of view

I have seen many group exercises where one person spontaneously took the lead at the start of the discussion by introducing the objectives of the meeting, proposing to start with a roundtable, and then giving the word to the first colleague to reveal his stakeholder's position. Unfortunately, in many instances, for the rest of the discussion this person disappeared into oblivion, thinking that by starting the discussion they had done their bit. There is nothing worse than being "invisible" during extended periods. A person who is "invisible" cannot be assessed as we cannot observe his behaviour. However, being too visible is not good either. Monopolising the floor by too lengthy interventions – as a participant, or in fulfilling one of the roles of the chairman – will be seen as bad behaviour in terms of working with others. A good balance has to be struck.

Composition of the Group

Isabel Briggs Myers and her mother, Katharine Briggs developed the popular theory of personality types based on the psychologist Carl Jung's work on psychology types. According to them, all human beings can be classified into one of sixteen personality types, regardless of ethnicity, sex, age, origin, education, or any other factor. These personality types are based on psychological preferences in how people perceive the world and make decisions.

As it is EPSO who invite participants to their Assessment Centre, using their own internal criteria and schedule to do so,

Notes:

....

....

....

....

....

you have no influence on the group composition and the people you end up with around the table. With six people in the group exercise there are 16^6 or 16,777,216 possible combinations of how your group will be composed in terms of personality types.

Though this is obviously an unimaginably large theoretical number of permutations, you will nevertheless in practice probably have got a fairly good idea about the basic characteristics of your fellow participants after having seen most (or all) of them during the day, and possibly even chatted with them during the breaks between the exercises. This will also help you decide how you should best react if there is a very talkative person in the group or someone who seems to be very reserved and shy. The group exercise is therefore a realistic approximation of your (future) working environment. You just have to accept this as a fact of life.

If you are interested in group dynamics, it is worth watching the classic movie "Twelve Angry Men" (or one of its remakes) as it gives a fascinating insight into how a discussion can be shaped by a single person in a group.

An assessor's point of view

I have seen many group exercises and none of them were similar. Not only were the discussions completely different but even the conclusions (if any) could go in various directions. It all depends on the people around the table, as is the case in real life situations. There is, however, one important distinction one can make. There are only two kinds of groups: "good" groups and "bad" groups. Good groups demonstrate that they have understood the purpose of the exercise; they work together, manage their time effectively and reach a conclusion at the end. Bad groups don't come up with a conclusion; they lose too much time in endless discussions, work against each other or simply don't grasp the concept of the exercise. On average, candidates who are members of a "good" group get higher scores than if they had been in a "bad" group. The bottom line is that it is in everybody's interest to behave like a good group.

Competencies

The exact competencies that will be assessed during your group exercise depend on the competition you are taking. It is strongly advised to check the the Notice of Competition to find out what will be important in your behaviour during the exercise.

Typically, the following competencies could be assessed: analysis and problem solving, learning and development, prioritising and organising, resilience, working with others, and – for the AD competitions – leadership.

Analysis and problem solving

"Identifies the critical facts in complex issues and develops creative and practical solutions."

For the group exercise, positive indicators are related to correctly interpreting the available information and dealing well with their complexity. You display your understanding of the issues at stake and link up the various elements of the scenario. This also means that you capture the overall context and demonstrate a clear insight into the complexities of the case by taking on board all the available information and fitting everything together. You analyse and interpret the available information correctly and comprehensively and are able to give a concise but systematic overview of the situation. You are not overwhelmed by the high volume of data or confused by conflicting information. You gather information from various sources (i.e. the other participants) and you manage to propose useful and practical solutions. This also means you can mention where a particular piece of information you are discussing with the group is from, or you can even cross-check it with another document in the background file to demonstrate your ability in critical analysis. You can also ask other members of the group how they see an issue, to show the assessors that you have an open mind and are willing to corroborate a piece of information with input from others.

Learning and development

"Develops and improves personal skills and knowledge of the organisation and its environment."

You actively gather information from the other participants and ask questions to improve your understanding of the problems at stake. You invite other participants to explain their position and encourage less active participants to have their say and contribute to the debate. You take information from the other participants and blend it together, drawing attention to the potential significance of new elements that come to light as the discussion unfolds. You make an effort to develop a clear understanding of the pros and cons of the arguments presented. Candidates often forget to ask the other candidates questions, as they are too busy interpreting the data and making sure they speak intelligently about the task. Make sure to avoid this trap. Ask a question every 5-6 minutes – it is also an excellent way to stay involved in the discussion even when you don't have anything to add: just ask a smart question or request clarification from someone.

Prioritising and organising

"Prioritises the most important tasks, works flexibly and organises own workload efficiently."

Your behaviour will be assessed as positive when you demonstrate a clear grasp of the remit of the group, identify the key issues and propose or establish an order of discussion. You zoom in on the essentials and don't waste time on trivialities. You rank points for discussion by order of priority. You can find common ground between diverging opinions and propose compromise solutions. You show awareness of the state of play. This is also demonstrated when you focus on answering the core questions of the exercise instead of being distracted by nuances or

Notes:

unimportant items. Stepping back and asking yourself and the group "what is our core task?" is a good way of keeping in focus instead of becoming bogged down in a discussion that may not lead anywhere.

Working with others

"Works co-operatively with others in teams and across organisational boundaries and respects differences between people."

Positive indicators for working with others are related to being friendly and approachable but assertive during the group discussion. You have an active and constructive attitude; you are friendly and enthusiastic in manner and body language. You adapt your own points of view to take into account input received from others. You encourage everybody to contribute, create a relaxed atmosphere conductive to effective communication and treat all participants as equals.

An easy and very practical way of demonstrating good skills in working with others is giving credit to group members. Without sounding too corny or artificial, you can always say "that was a very good suggestion from X and I think we can build on that" or "I really like your idea to phrase the message this way, this could be a good basis for further discussion".

If you are either "invisible" or too dominant you will be scored negatively on your working with others competency. Remaining on the sidelines or intervening only when compelled by other participants will be seen as poor behaviour. Also, showing more interest in defending your own personal views rather than building consensus will not be appreciated by the assessors.

Avoid engaging in lengthy bilateral or trilateral discussions while forgetting about the rest of the group. This requires a high level of awareness to avoid monopolising the floor and excluding others. A practical way of doing this is to make sure that even when you have a bilateral discussion (or even disagreement) with someone, you keep eye contact with everyone else in the group instead of just looking at the person in question. But do try to avoid going head-to-head with another candidate. The object of the exercise is to find a consensus agreement, not to score points or defeat someone else.

Resilience

"Remains effective under a heavy workload, handles organisational frustrations positively and adapts to a changing work environment."

Resilient candidates have strategies to cope with apparent lack of progress. They take remedial action when they see that their points are in danger of being ignored. They do not give up, but keep focused on the job until the end and display a consistently high level of performance from start to finish. They take on board negative feedback and turn it to their advantage. They help the group to manage time in order to reach the goal within the fixed deadline.

This competency is closely linked to leadership (see next) in the sense that even if there is a deadlock or positions seem quite wide apart, you manage to come up with a suggestion that puts the contentious issue aside and puts the focus on what you can agree on. Books like *Getting to Yes: Negotiating an Agreement Without Giving In* have helpful ideas about negotiating tactics, and at the EPSO group exercise you don't even have to negotiate in the classic sense of the word!

Leadership

"Manages, develops and motivates people to achieve results."

In the group exercise you are expected to contribute on how best to approach the task and also encourage others to contribute as best they can. You can motivate the others by your own commitment and enthusiasm, and how you explain things to other participants. A leader regularly takes stock of the state of play and knows who to ask for input or clarification on any given point. He or she regularly reminds the group of the main issues and brings the discussion back when the group gets side-tracked. This in practice means that you always keep your eyes on the ultimate goal of the exercise and drive the discussion forward. In other words, you are *result-oriented* and not *process-oriented.*

Making sure everyone is on board is crucial: nobody has a formal leadership role in the group exercise, and others may think that you hijacked the discussion if you impose yourself on them too much. Make sure, therefore, to ask questions and seek support from everyone before concluding on a certain point. Be aware of others' body language, and if you detect any opposition (folded arms, raised eyebrows, leaning forward because they want to say something), then let that person air their grievances before proposing an acceptable compromise. Books like *What Every Body Is Saying* by Joe Navarro can help you improve your ability to read others' body language, and careful observation of teams (during meetings or on videos or TV) also greatly improves this skill.

Weak leadership shows itself in a lack of commitment and enthusiasm or, conversely, when someone tries to impose their authority but only succeeds in alienating other group members because of trying to be overly dominant. Weak leaders have no clear strategic vision, send the group down false trails, or don't intervene to stop sideshows.

Some Tips for the Assessment

Understand what is being asked

Do not rush into a group exercise without first pausing to analyse and discuss the scenario. Planning and preparation are always the keys to success, so make sure that you properly review the situation described in the brief with the group before you rush into solving the problem. Candidates often spend too little time understanding the details of the requirements and therefore answer the wrong questions or give incomplete answers during the exercise – just because they didn't spend an extra 30 seconds on properly interpreting the instructions.

Start by analysing and qualifying the question, so that everyone is clear about exactly what is required from the exercise. For example, if the exercise requires you to outline ideas for a negotiation strategy with the Council of Ministers, make sure

Notes:

you do not misinterpret the task by adding the European Parliament as well; or, if the exercise requires you to describe the state of play on a certain piece of legislation on biofuels, make sure you keep your focus on the policy at hand instead of the underlying legislative procedures or going off at a tangent about wind energy. Then show clearly the thought processes and procedures you followed to arrive at your proposed solution.

The real problem

An excellent way of keeping focus is by asking yourself a simple yet powerful question: "what is the real problem we need to solve?" As an example, suppose you need to send a letter that has to arrive at its destination within a day. This means you would need to rush to the post office by bus to reach it before it closes. If you miss the bus, you could start thinking what other means of transport you could take, whether it is worth paying for a taxi, etc. However, the real issue is to get the mail to its addressee in time, so if you focus your attention on solving this instead of sticking to your original line of action (that is, how to get to the post office), you can come up with creative solutions such as finding a person who is going to the addressee anyway and asking him to take the letter. The same is true in a group exercise: make sure you are crystal clear about what the real problem is that you are requested to resolve instead of getting lost in a debate on a subtlety: keep your eye on the instructions as that will help you to keep your focus.

The beginning

Many group discussions begin with each person outlining their view of the presented material and their proposed solution. This is a good way to start but be sure that a) this does not take up too much of the allotted time, and b) each person has the chance to contribute equally. If you are the one proposing a roundtable discussion, make sure a cut-off time is specified so nobody will go over time (or if they do, can be politely asked to wrap up their remarks). Another common misconception is the overrated importance of being the first to speak. While it may show some leadership, your performance and continuous participation throughout the exercise is far more important than jumping in first.

Team skills

The best way to impress the assessors is to show yourself to be a good team player – flexible, full of ideas but willing to listen to and help expand the ideas of others. This demands constant self-reflection and a good sense of proportion. It also requires that you pay careful attention to what other members of the group say, take short notes on their input, and regularly summarise the various positions while adding your own take on the discussion. Moreover, keep in mind that you are being assessed in a group scenario. Make sure therefore that you demonstrate team playing skills (you ask questions, give credit, build on other participants' input) instead of simply voicing your own opinion as a stand-alone contribution.

Always remember that you are all in the same boat and that the exercise should not look like six individuals working in parallel but as a single team where everyone has their eyes on the same objective.

Be active

You need to contribute, otherwise the assessors will not be able to judge your performance; but you must never dominate. Be assertive, but not aggressive. If you are aware that you are usually a shy person who does not speak up, do your best to participate. If you know that you can sometimes be overbearing in groups, hold that tendency in check. Recognise other people's contributions both verbally and non-verbally (e.g. by saying "I think this is a very good point and we should take it on board", or conveying positive body language towards other team members by turning towards them, showing positive gestures, taking notes when they are speaking etc.).

Candidates often make the mistake of being extremely talkative at the beginning of the exercise; then they realise that they may have been "a bit over the top", so they then keep very silent for a period, before again trying to overcompensate. Figure 7.6 shows this sort of uneven distribution of the level of intensity, which is to be avoided:

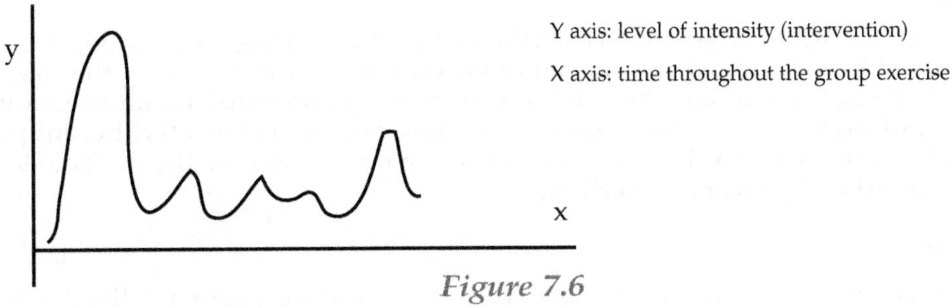

Figure 7.6

On the other hand, the right amount of activity would look like Figure 7.7:

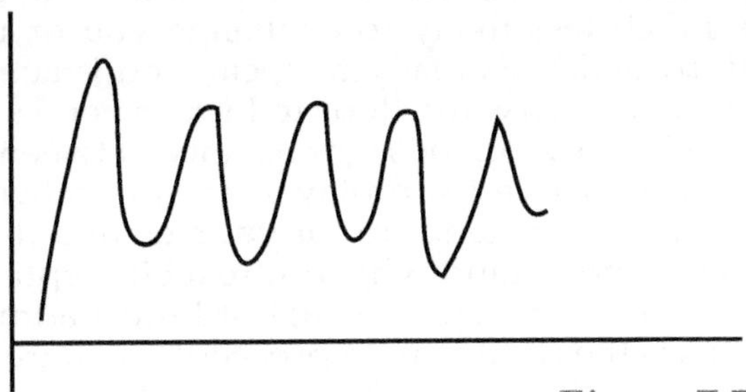

Figure 7.7

Be clear

Speak clearly and confidently. If you have a tendency to speak too fast, practice beforehand to consciously slow down and add pauses so the other group members can digest what you have said. You may wish to record your voice while talking freely about a certain subject and then evaluate your performance (don't read any text but instead try to express your thoughts as they arise; this is more similar to the situation you will be facing at the Assessment Centre).

Listen

Listen and do not interrupt. Be aware of what others in the group are contributing and acknowledge their views ("This idea

Notes:

about launching an information campaign to underline our communication efforts is very appealing"). You could try to draw out quieter members and seek their views ("You seem to have some reservations about this approach, is that correct?"), though choosing the right time to do so is vital as otherwise you may antagonise that person. Be sure to appear interested and attentive whatever topic is being discussed.

Note taking

It is very much recommended that you take notes at all times, even though the notes themselves must be kept short so you won't become disconnected from the discussion. The aim with the notes is to use them to your benefit by coordinating and reciting what others have said, so you can quickly summarise key points and recall different perspectives. If handled effectively, this can result in you being adopted as the de facto leader of the group without being overly assertive.

Be diplomatic

If one person is behaving in a dominant way, deal with this diplomatically. A good way of "disarming" a dominant or overly talkative member of the group is to politely suggest that another member may wish to contribute to the discussion and ask that third person (that is, not you or the "chatterbox" member) about his or her views. This way it is not you who "steals" the right to speak but you immediately pass it on to someone else, so the dominant member will be much less likely to challenge you or the third person. Make sure, however, that the third person is ready to speak and is actively following the discussion in the moment when you pass the floor to him or her.

Be prepared to compromise, but do this by striking the right balance between defending your own position while also being a proactive team-player open to others' ideas. Make your points and, if criticised, be prepared to stand up for yourself and diplomatically argue why your opinions are valid ("I understand why you're a bit sceptical about this idea, and in fact I used to have reservations myself as well; but I must admit all the evidence I've heard has persuaded me this is the right way to proceed"). Ensure that any criticism you give is constructive: if you challenge another person, follow this with proactive suggestions for finding common ground and don't just stop at saying "I strongly disagree".

Time management

Keep an eye on the time and stay focused on the overall objective ("We have covered points 1 and 2 so far and came to the following conclusions ... As we have 20 minutes left, I suggest we focus on the remaining items in the following way..."). From time to time, try to summarise the group's progress; this can also improve your stature as an effective member of the group by taking stock of where you are, though don't be a nuisance for the group by doing it too often.

Self-assess

About halfway through the group exercise, check the impact you are having on the discussion – is it visible, sufficient, too little? Make adjustments accordingly. Awareness is fundamental: though you are part of an exam scenario, try to look at the situation as an "outsider" so you can duly check your own and your fellow members' performance.

Eye contact

Assessors are trained not to hold eye contact with group members, or to respond to comments made during the course of the group discussion (even humorous ones!) even if

Group Exercise video recording

In its 2018 Management Plan EPSO announced the use of video recording for the group exercise. As far as we know this is the first time that a candidate's performance at the Assessment Centre will be recorded – EPSO has always been very scrupulous in preserving the privacy of the participants.

We believe that this is a very positive move for at least two reasons.

First, the presence of the assessors in the meeting room (sitting in the four corners of the room, observing the candidates and taking notes) could come over as quite intimidating as the participants were constantly reminded of the fact that they were being observed and this undoubtedly influenced – and disturbed – their behaviour during the exercise. With cameras, discreetly positioned across the room, the simulation of a meeting will be more realistic for sure.

Secondly, it was a very tough job for the assessors to observe six candidates simultaneously during 40 or 50 minutes and at the same time take meaningful notes for the scoring phase after the meeting. With video recording, the assessors can take their time to observe – and discuss – the individual behaviour of the candidates. This can even be done at a later time, after the exhausting day as an assessor in EPSO and in the quiet of a private office.

Our latest information is that already one meeting room is fully equipped with the video recording gear and that EPSO will soon start using this new facility, so you can maybe already expect this new method to be used for your Assessment Centre.

partially addressed to them. Do not be disheartened if your contributions do not seem to be having an effect on the assessors: they are merely trying to ensure that they do not unduly influence your behaviour and that they remain as objective outside observers.

Play the game

Whatever the scenario is in the group exercise, immersing in it will be a positive factor. If you are to represent a European Parliament working group, making references to the Parliament staff as "our colleagues" will demonstrate that you fully understood the scenario (and that you read the instructions carefully, so you paid attention to the details), which can yield some extra goodwill from the assessors.

Missing candidates

On occasion, a candidate may drop out from the Assessment Centre. In this case, all participants in a group exercise may be given their brief and asked to consider it as part of their overall decision. Do just as you would in real-life if someone could not be present: ensure that their views are

Notes:

....

....

....

....

....

represented fairly in their absence. EPSO always tries to keep the number of participants to a minimum of 4 and a maximum of 7, the most common group size being 6.

Do's and Don'ts for the Group Exercise

DO...

- Be as natural as possible, don't act artificially
- Keep eye contact with every team member while speaking (which might require you to constantly turn around but it's worth the effort)
- Take time to organise your thoughts. Think of what you are going to say, or write a few keywords down before intervening
- Initiate the discussion if you understood the topic clearly, or just ask questions
- Seek clarification if you have any doubts regarding the subject
- Listen to others to learn about their position or ideas
- Be assertive not dominating: finding the right balance is hard but pays off
- Allow others to speak by passing the ball to them, saying "...and what do you think?" in a friendly and encouraging way, addressed to a specific person instead of the whole group
- Keep positive body language by leaning forward, hands open and on the table. Show interest in the discussion and don't pull your chair back or cross your legs or arms
- Support your point with some facts and figures, referencing the background files
- Make short contributions of 25-30 seconds rather than staying silent for 10-15 minutes
- Speak politely and clearly
- Motivate the other members of the team to speak by encouraging them
- Use simple and understandable words while speaking
- Respect contributions from other members by not interrupting them
- Disagree politely and agree with what is right
- Make sure to keep the discussion on track by giving the floor to another person when you are finished instead of simply finishing a sentence and keeping silent
- Summarise the discussion on a regular basis

DON'T...

- Try and be someone you are not
- Be "invisible" by not speaking regularly

- Look at the assessors
- Initiate the discussion without being on top of the brief
- Try to dominate the discussion
- Take unilateral decisions to allocate jobs (such as moderator or timekeeper)
- Interrupt anyone while they are speaking
- Talk to another person while someone else has the floor
- Act in a manner that might be considered as verbal aggression or bullying
- Ridicule what someone else has to say or be sarcastic
- Speak too long
- Take comments and arguments personally
- Intervene and snatch someone else's chance to speak
- Speak just to increase your speaking time
- Say irrelevant things and distract the discussion
- Display low self-confidence with shaky voice and trembling hands
- Adopt negative body gestures like leaning back in your chair, knocking the table with a pen etc…
- Engage in sub-group conversation

How to Prepare

It can be difficult to prepare for group exercises, especially as you have no prior idea about the composition of the group (the other candidates) and the mix of personality types can be very different. However, you may get a basic idea of what the group will be like if you mingle with the other candidates throughout the assessment day. So, if you get a chance to socialise with others and identify who could be in your group, you can get a "feel" of their personality types and communication styles, which can prove useful in the exercise. You may also need to show different aspects of your own personality in the exercise – for example, if there is one constant talker who threatens to take over the whole discussion as compared with a group where everyone is more or less equally expressing conflicting views and priorities.

Notes:

……………………………………………

……………………………………………

……………………………………………

……………………………………………

……………………………………………

A candidate's point of view

In between the various individual exercises we had a lot of time to socialise with the other candidates. One could see them as competitors; after all they too are competing for a limited number of places on the reserve list. I looked at this in a different way. In fact, I considered the other candidates as (potential) future colleagues, who I would have to work with in the group exercise later that day. So I took the opportunity to get to know them, making sure that we were not total strangers meeting for the first time around the table for the group exercise. Working with others is an important competency and the group exercise is the only exercise in which you can display this competency in real-time, so you can better have an idea of what they are like.

A good way to prepare yourself for the group exercise is to become more self-aware as to how you actually act during the meetings you undoubtedly have in your current working environment. Actively step out of your comfort zone and take the floor as often as you can. Don't be afraid that the others will judge you; on the contrary, they will appreciate you for that.

You can also follow a classroom training with eutraining.eu. In this you will have the opportunity to practice the EPSO group exercise with a number of fellow students, under the supervision and guidance of an experienced coach.

It can be useful to ask for feedback as part of your preparation, from those who know you well and what role you tend to play in a group situation. "Group situation" can refer to either your work or social life. It is worth considering issues such as the following: Are you the one who always suggests where to go next when out with friends? Or do you tend to follow the group decision? Do you tend to clash with others in a group if you have a strong opinion, or do you tend to avoid conflict at all costs? Do you like having a close ally with whom you can share feelings about the group as a whole? Or do you prefer being everyone's friend? Do you always try to make sure everyone in the group is included in a conversation, or does it make no difference for you if some are quiet or inactive?

All of these traits can have both positive and negative implications. How, then, might your typical behaviours impact upon your performance at the Assessment Centre? Generally, the key is being flexible in your relations with other people.

For example, you may need to become more directive and assertive when faced with a group that is failing to reach decisions quickly enough ("I suggest we focus on the task at hand as we are running short of time" or "I guess we should split the tasks among us as follows..."). Equally, you may also need to be more facilitative and questioning ("what do you think about developing a public consultation on the research policy?" or "why not produce a checklist of issues that must be considered when launching a tender procedure?") in a group that is making quicker, less reasoned decisions. Make a conscious effort to behave in a manner opposite to your "natural" style when in group settings and gain feedback on how effective you were from someone else.

If you have the time, we can also recommend you read the book *Six Thinking Hats* by Edward de Bono. The author shows how meetings can be transformed to produce quick, decisive results every time. This is a must-read for anybody who frequently participates in meetings.

Key points to remember

- *The group exercise is an exercise in bureaucracy, not a negotiation round. Group collaboration is key, and understanding that there are no winners or losers*
- *During the preparation time, focus first on the first page (the assignment) and the last page (your stakeholder's position) of the file, as these contain the most important information*
- *Listen carefully to what the others have to say and don't impose your stakeholder's point of view*
- *Be aware at all time of the progress of the meeting, and keep an eye on the time*
- *Always be constructive and give credit to others, ask genuine questions and summarise the discussion from time to time without being too dominant*

For a sample group exercise, see Annex 6.

Notes:

8. The Interview in the Field

Introduction

The interview in the field is only used for specialist competitions. However, while at one time competitions for specialists represented only a minority of the selections for permanent staff, this has steadily changed over the last few years. In the period from 2010 (when the current testing system was introduced) to 2015, generalist Administrator and Assistant positions were at the core of EPSO's process. Today, in contrast, specialist competitions dominate. Indeed in 2019 there was only one generalist competition among the 37 published – all the rest were considered to be "specialist" ones, using a talent screener and having an interview in the field as part of their process. While not changing the overall EPSO selection process, this has significantly modified it.

Why this shift has happened? The underlying reason is that EPSO is emphasising the selection of professionals who are able to do the job from day one. This is a request coming from the recruiting services, reflecting the view that the generalist competitions were not producing fully satisfactory results from an operational point of view.

The result is that while in the past specialist competitions were organised only for very specific jobs, such as nuclear engineers or security specialists, today they are organised broadly for many areas both at Assistant and Administrator levels. In many cases, the Notice of Competition even states which particular Directorate General intends to recruit from the reserve list. The Notice of Competition will normally have a detailed list of responsibilities and tasks that the successful candidate will need to carry out on a daily basis. This list is the "duties" attached as Annex 1 to the core text of the Notice of Competition. Usually these duties are tasks that the candidate needs to have either performed or to be familiar with to some extent from previous jobs.

These specialist competitions now dominating EPSO's selection palette are usually smaller in scale than generalist competitions, especially the AD5 graduate Administrators competition. The reserve lists are typically smaller but so too are the numbers of candidates. There can be considerable variation in the specialist tests used and how they are evaluated.

The Selection Process

In comparison to the generalist selection process, there are some significant differences in the process for specialists.

1. **The first phase of the selection is based on the talent screener**. In order to allow the Selection Board to carry out an objective assessment of the comparative merits of all candidates in a structured way, all candidates in the same grade must answer the same set of questions in the talent screener section of the application form. At this stage, the panel first screens the detailed CVs of the applicants, evaluates the technical competence of the candidates and allows only the best to pass on to the next phase. We will give a more detailed overview of this process later in this chapter. What is important to emphasise is that while in generalist competitions, the application form has little importance at the beginning of the process as applicants will automatically be invited to the next phase, in the case of the specialist competitions the talent screener has the utmost significance, acting as a pre-selection tool.

2. The second major difference to the generalist competitions is that **often the verbal, numerical and abstract reasoning tests are done on the Assessment Centre day** and not used as a pre-selection tool. This happens when number of qualified candidates is BELOW a threshold determined by EPSO. In this case while the tests are eliminatory, the marks obtained will NOT be added to those awarded for the other Assessment Centre tests in the calculation of the total score. In other words, the verbal, numerical and abstract reasoning are only used to assess if you meet the *minimum requirements* of the MCQ tests. In the generalist competitions, in contrast, candidates need to perform to their very best because this is one of the major tools to select only the best performers. While specialists who get to take the verbal, numerical and abstract reasoning tests at the Assessment Centre still have to get the pass marks, obviously reaching a minimum level is easier than having to be one of the best among all who get the pass marks.

   If, however, the number of eligible candidates is ABOVE the threshold set by EPSO, then the computer-based MCQ tests will be organised as a preliminary stage to reduce numbers. In this case the files of the applicants will be checked for eligibility in descending order of the marks obtained in those tests. For this reason candidates need to get the highest scores they can.

3. Finally, **the third major difference is the use of the field-related interview**. This interview in the field of the competition has far higher importance than the assessment of generic competencies via the general competency-based interview, the group exercise and the case study because of the points allocated to it. The field interview counts for 100 points while in total the generic competency exercises count for 80 points in the case of Administrator positions and 70 points for the Assistant positions. In order to make sure that those recruited can be "operational from day one", therefore, **for specialists competency in the field has a greater weight in the overall scoring** than their general competencies.

The Talent Screener

Even though the talent screener is not part of the Assessment Centre as such, it is important to say something more about it at this point to understand the rest of the chapter. Furthermore, the talent screener provides the basis for your preparation for the Assessment Centre and is also excellent guidance for the likely content of the field-related interview.

Some typical talent screener questions, taken from a recent competition

Question 1a:

Do you have any professional experience in a monitoring centre of an international organisation, private body, or NGO?

Question 1b:

If so, please give the name of your employer and indicate what you were responsible for, the nature of your duties, and the total length of that experience in months.

Question 2a:

Do you have any professional experience of processing sources in real time (audio-visual, press agencies, social networks) requiring rapid reaction?

Question 2b:

If so, please give the name of your employer and the total length of that experience in months. Please give details of the sources processed, indicating the type (audio-visual, press agency, social network) and name.

Question 3a:

Do you have any professional experience of taking swift decisions in high-risk contexts?

Question 3b:

If so, please give the name of your employer and the length of that experience. Please give details of the type of experience in a high-risk context requiring swift decision-making.

The questions in the talent screener section of the online application form are based on the selection criteria given in the Notice of Competition. All candidates in a competition answer the same set of questions. In this way, the Selection Board is presented with each candidate's answers in the same structured framework, helping the Board to carry out a careful objective assessment of the comparative merits of all candidates.

A few practical considerations to keep in mind:

- **Alternative CV**. The talent screener is like an alternative CV. Normal CVs are pretty much non-standardised as you are free to give the information in whatever detail or style you prefer (even if you use a standard format such as Europass). In a regular CV you can make a self-assessment (e.g. "I am an experienced project manager") without any formal proof. You can draw a veil over your weaker areas and put a favourable gloss on reality. In a talent screener, on the other hand, you are forced to stick to the facts, to measurable realities and figures. That is why a talent screener is considered to be more objective than a regular CV – you need to answer specific questions and systematically cover various points as opposed to describing your professional background in an unstructured way.

- **Honesty is essential**. The information you provide will be used to rate your application against other candidates and identify the best to be invited to the Assessment Centre stage of the competition. It is essential that you are completely honest in your answers as they will be validated and any attempt to deceive the Selection Board will result in disqualification from the competition. All your answers will be verified by the Selection Board and validated against your application form. The Selection Board will then score your answers.
- **Your options**. You must reply "Yes" or "No" to each question by clicking on the appropriate button. If you reply "Yes" to a question you must also reply to the question underneath by entering your answer in the text box. If you reply "No" to a question you will not be able to enter anything in the text box or to save any text that you may have already written there. You should explain and justify your "Yes" answer by listing all the verifiable elements of your educational and professional background, including details such as names of universities, employers, dates, locations, titles or certificates obtained, etc.

Answering the Talent Screener

Even though this is clearly stated at the beginning of the talent screener section of the application form, it is worth emphasising that the **scoring of your answers will only take account of the text you write in the boxes provided for this purpose.** Any reference to other sections of the application form, or external documents, will not be considered.

In addition, you are expected to provide **complete and standalone answers**, even if this means that you have to repeat information that has already been provided for other questions in the talent screener. The reason for this is that your answers will not necessarily be scored by the same people and hence they may not have access to the entire content of your talent screener.

Your answers should be concise (usually limited to 4000 characters) but at the same time comprehensive. So don't limit yourself to the most important parts of your career but also mention the less important – or shorter – episodes that may contribute to the total length of your relevant experience for a given question. And since the main element influencing your score consists of the length of your experience it is also a good idea to totalize the length of your experience at the beginning or the end of your answer.

Please note that the questions in the talent screener have a different "weight" – some are more important that others. The weights will only be revealed when you get the results of the talent screener phase but you can get an idea of which questions are more important by reading carefully the Selection Criteria section of the Notice of Competition. You should obviously pay particular attention to your answers for the most important questions.

Scoring your answers

In the second step, the Selection Board examines the content of the candidates' answers to the questions and awards 0 to 4 points for each answer. If they give you zero points even if you answered "Yes", this means that your answer is not considered to be good enough to justify a "Yes". You may have given insufficient evidence, information that was not asked for, or fall below a certain threshold as set previously by the Board. The scoring is actually done by using a "scoring grid", a table pointing out the correspondence between pre-defined criteria and a score to be given. Say – for example – that a question asks for the number of years of (relevant) experience in a given area. The corresponding line in the grid might look like this:

Question	0-12 months	12-24 months	24-36 months	37-48 months	49+ months
2	0	1	2	3	4

Obviously, the content of this scoring grid is secret, and it will never be revealed to the candidates, not even when the talent screener phase is over, or when a candidate does not agree with a score given. This scoring grid is exactly the same for all candidates, regardless of their own opinions about their personal experience or background.

The points are then multiplied by the weighting for each question and summed up to obtain a total score for the talent screener.

- **Human scoring**. It is important to realise that the scoring of your talent screener is done by humans – the members of your Selection Board. The members of the Selection Board have to go through each and every piece of text you write in the second part of your answers to the questions. As you can imagine, this is a labour-intensive activity (that is why the pre-sifting is used to eliminate the obvious "lesser" candidates). When drafting your answers you should bear this in mind. Be concise but comprehensive, and answer *only* and *exactly* what is being asked (you in any case cannot exceed 4000 characters per answer). Avoid abbreviations, and if you use acronyms, always explain them as they may be unfamiliar to the Selection Board members. Give a clear structure to your answers, break down the answers into paragraphs, use bullet lists, and emphasise keywords. In short, make their lives easy. It is also worth considering all the tips in this book given for the communicating competency and the case study exam, as applying those techniques can significantly enhance the impact of your talent sifter and, ultimately, the scores you get.
- **Standalone answers**. Be aware that this selection is made solely on the basis of your responses to questions in the talent screener tab of the online application form, so there is no point in referring to your CV or any other document. The information herein will NOT be taken into account for your talent screener scoring.
- **Talent screener as pre-selection**. The candidates with the highest points go through to the assessment phase. **From this point onwards your score for the talent screener will not be taken into account anymore**. The final score you obtain for your competencies in the field will be determined in the Assessment Centre. It will be based on the results you obtain for the case study, the professional tests and/or the field interview.

Notes:

Who scores your talent screener?

As for every competition that EPSO organises, there is a Selection Board composed of EU officials of the same or higher grade than those being selected (e.g. if you are applying for an AD7 exam, the Selection Board members need to have at least AD7 grade). Moreover, given the highly specific nature of specialist competitions, the members of the Selection Board, who also act later as assessors, will be coming from the same field as the competition (e.g. if you are applying to be a macroeconomist, the members will have this background as well, likely coming from e.g. DG ECFIN).

This also means that they are very familiar with the diplomas, professional experience and overall context of that field, so if you apply for an economist position, you will not need to explain what your job was when dealing with "quantitative easing". At the same time, if you did something less ordinary, e.g. volunteer work in a 3rd country for an NGO, or obtained a diploma in a non-European MBA program, this will certainly not be obvious to them so it is worth adding further details.

How to Use the Talent Screener in preparation for your Field Interview

We have talked about the evaluation of the talent screener. However, after passing the pre-selection stage, the talent screener once scored is an excellent source for your preparation for the field-related interview.

First, the Selection Board will assign each selection criterion a weighting that reflects its relative importance from 1 to 4. As a basic rule, whatever has higher weight in their assessment is the sort of experience that they are particularly looking for, experience that is lacking in the recruiting services. For example, if a question is given the weight of 1, it is probably less important than a question given the weight of 3. This can help in your preparation in identifying potential questions that might be asked during the interview.

Second, you will see where you scored lower or higher in the talent screener, as each of your answers will be awarded from 0 to 4 points. It is logical that you will be stronger in some areas than others. To use the example of competition lawyers, an expert in this particular field may not have the same amount of experience in mergers, in state aid or in anti-trust. Therefore, it is normal to score higher in some areas and lower in others.

Following from these two points, it makes sense that whatever carries a high weight and where you scored high could potentially be the most relevant areas for your interview.

Purely factual information, such as "Do you possess a recognised audit certification or professional qualification?" or questions related to your education such as "Have you obtained a university-level diploma, in addition to the one required to access the competition, in one or more of the scientific domains?" will ONLY be assessed in your talent screener. You need not expect questions on such matters during the interview. These are easily quantifiable questions, for which you will have already received the applicable points in the talent screener's scoring phase, therefore there will be no further assessment of them.

The fact that you have passed the talent screener phase means that on paper you do in fact have the right experience and expertise to do the job. Your task is to prove at the interview that you *really do know* in detail what you *seem to know* on paper. Therefore, as a general rule it is better to devote your energy to focusing on those areas where you got higher scores. You might face some conceptual, theoretical questions on the topics where you have less experience. However the interviewers usually "dig deep" into your experience in areas where you seem to know a lot, where you claim an expert-level knowledge. This does not mean that you won't face some questions in areas where you scored less, but predominantly the questions will be related to things that you seem to be an expert in.

Your preparation for this interview should therefore focus on making sure you are able to describe what you have really done in your past, not on spending weeks learning about things that you have never dealt with. You might be asked to give a general overview of particular processes in areas with which you are less familiar. But most questions will target what you are an expert in. To go back to our example of the competition law field, do not devote immense energies trying to learn how to investigate state aid cases from books if you have never done it in practice. But do make sure you are properly prepared to describe in detail a particular merger case that you handled in your competition law practice.

Finally, whatever you mentioned in your talent screener may potentially be a source of questions in your interview. The interviewers in your panel will likely read your talent screener before you enter the room, or they may even have it in their hands while conducting the interview. Therefore, anything you mentioned as an example in the talent screener might be used as a basis for further questions. What is important to bear in mind is that assessors often do not take into account if it is a recent experience or something from long-ago. They may not take into account that you might have forgotten some details of something that you dealt with several years ago. Therefore, it is clearly your task before the interview to refresh your memory about anything that is mentioned in the talent screener, making sure to cover every possible detail of each particular example.

Practicalities of the Field-related Interview

The interview usually lasts somewhere between 40 minutes and an hour depending on the competition, but the length of the interview is the same for every participant in the same competition. In general, the panel is at liberty to decide the length of the interview and the questions, but whatever applies to you will apply to all the other candidates in the same competition.

The pace of the interview is rapid, somewhat similar to the competency-based interview. There are many questions and follow-up questions, so be prepared for that. You will not have the time to elaborate in depth on some of your ideas. You will need to be ready to follow the interviewers in your responses, recognising that they are the ones in the driver's seat, steering the interview. You will need to get to the point rapidly in your responses.

Notes:

The assessors are not supposed to give you any feedback, therefore there is rarely a nod or a smile during the interview. It is important to mentally prepare for this and bear in mind that if you feel that the evaluators are being "cold" with you, most likely it has nothing to do with your performance. You might feel they are challenging or "not nice" but it is only because they are trained not to reveal anything positive or negative and to act as neutrally as possible. This is likely to be a bit different from other interviews you have experienced.

Who are the assessors?

Similarly to the competency-based interview, **you will be assessed by a panel of two**. At least one of the assessors conducting this interview will be a specialist in your field. So, if you apply for an IT specialist position one of the interviewers will be an IT specialist. While the second assessor might not be a specialist, he or she will be knowledgeable about the Assessment Centre procedures and will be able to judge the credibility of the answers you give. The Assessors, as members of the Selection Board, will be EU officials of the same or higher grade than those being selected.

You might find that the assessors have a background in a related area to your sub-field of specialist knowledge rather than being themselves experts in that area. You need to be aware of this, and if you sense that some things are not completely clear to your assessors, be prepared to add an additional layer of explanation of the technical details. The interview is always a two-way process and it is very important that you are clear and understandable to your panel.

If your background is in a very specialised field or if you have been working in a particular field with or inside the EU institutions, it's possible that you might end up having assessors on your panel whom you already know through your professional network. Selection Boards are asked to declare any such situations. However, EPSO has a narrow understanding of conflict of interest, which only refers to family relationship or a hierarchical link between a candidate and a Selection Board member. What this means is that you might end up being interviewed by somebody whom you know from professional circles.

The names of the Selection Board members are published on the EPSO website (www.eu-careers.eu) before the start of the Assessment Centre phase; there is no e-mail sent to your account about this therefore it is up to you to have a look. You will find the list on the main page of the particular competition that you are taking, on the right-hand side under the "Related News" section. It is always a good idea to examine the list. You will not know who will be the assessors on your day but it is still advisable to check if you know anybody. To ensure the Selection Board's independence, it is strictly forbidden for candidates or anyone outside the Board to attempt to contact any of its members. If you end up being interviewed by somebody you know, act naturally and always explain everything from A to Z and do not consider that the person might know the "story" you are sharing as you are assessed by both panel members.

Methodology of the Field Interview

In order to demystify this interview, which has such great importance, we will now look in detail at some key points that could provide real help for you in preparing. Because, believe it or not, whether you are in a competition for "taxation", "researcher", "international cooperation", "managing aid to non-EU countries" or virtually any other specialist role, there are some common modalities and practical ideas that anybody can use in order to prepare for such an interview.

The interview in the field is primarily intended to assess your applied knowledge in the field. This means that while the assessors may ask some theoretical or conceptual questions the main emphasis will be on questions that are practical and frequently related directly to your own personal experience. They often pick examples themselves and ask for details of those cases, while sometimes they allow you to choose the examples yourself.

The greatest source for preparation besides the talent screener is the Notice of Competition. It is important to emphasize this because the evaluation of the candidates is solely on the basis of the criteria that are mentioned in the Notice of Competition.

In the case of specialist competitions, there is normally a description of the responsibilities of the job at the beginning of the Notice of Competition. Annex 1 contains the detailed list of duties expected from the candidate once selected and recruited. As explained earlier, the expectation in the case of specialist competitions is that people selected should be able to perform these duties from day one, without major investment in training. And the only way to guarantee that is to evaluate and assess at the interview if they have had these responsibilities in the past. Therefore, the focus of the field interview will be to assess what tasks you have carried out in the past on the assumption you will be able to do them in the future as well.

Consequently, **the list of duties in Annex 1 is clearly the key guidance** for you in preparing for the interview in the field. Whatever roles and responsibilities are mentioned could be a source of a potential question during the interview. And very often whatever is clearly outside the scope of the duties should not be expected as an interview question.

In terms of methodology, the field interview is a bit of a special case, as compared to the other exercises. The field interview does not involve using positive and negative indicators to observe your behaviour, like the other exercises do. Instead, the assessors want to get a clear and precise idea of what you are worth as a professional in your field.

In the field interview, the subjective elements of the assessment are reduced as far as possible. Nevertheless, you still have to consider it as like an interview where you are "pitching yourself" to a future employer, so in that sense it is a sort of job interview. The best proof of this can be found later on, once you have received your competency passport; you may find very different scores between your talent screener and the results of your Assessment Centre (i.e. case study and field interview). Say, for example, that you had a score of 80/100 for your talent screener and barely a pass mark for the AC. This would then mean that you had not been able to convince the assessors (and markers) of your capacity to effectively apply your knowledge in the field; you had not "sold" the intrinsically proficient professional you are.

Notes:

....

....

....

....

....

What kind of questions should you expect?

The objective of the field interview is to validate the image you have given of yourself as a professional in the field. This means that you will be asked mainly practical questions about areas where your expertise seems to lie. However you might also be asked about the legislative framework for a procedure that you need to follow step by step for a particular activity. You might be asked about stakeholders, about issues you encountered, about decisions you made. And as said before, usually by illustrating with concrete examples.

Let's explain through an actual concrete example what to expect. One of the duties mentioned in the Notice of Competition for "Administrators in international cooperation and managing aid to non-EU countries" is given as "Professional experience of managing crisis situations and security related issues in the field of the competition".

Possible questions you might expect are:

- Could you please tell us about an example of when you needed to manage a crisis situation?
- What was your exact role? What was your contribution to the whole operation?
- Could you please describe what you did step by step?
- Were you in touch with any external stakeholders?
- What was the legal basis to your work?
- Did you encounter any particular difficulties? How did you deal with those? Do you think you made the right decisions? Please explain why.

Most of these are follow-up questions that are probing in depth the example that you provided. The basic questions will be exactly the same for every candidate as it is a structured interview and the list of questions to be asked, as well as the way your answers are scored, is predefined. However, the follow-up questions might well vary depending on what you say.

While each candidate gets the same basic questions, sometimes, because of the highly-specific nature of specialist profiles, they get asked questions related to *process* rather than content. For example, one candidate might be asked about state aid while another might be asked about mergers. But while the topics might differ, questions will in both-cases relate to the process (for instance – the process of investigation). In some competitions, however, the panels very strictly use the exact same questions for all candidates.

An example may clarify this. Say that one of the questions of the talent screener probed for your experience as a project leader. One candidate replied that he had over five years of experience as a project manager, working for a large multinational company. He did not say, however, that he was working for a local subsidiary of that organisation on a small, one-person project. In fact, he didn't even realise that he was not a "real" project manager, with authority over other people, but merely responsible for a less important aspect of a bigger process. Another candidate, who had been in charge for over five years of a 100-person project team, defining, monitoring and controlling the whole project, gave a similar answer to the first person in our example. Neither of them lied when replying "Yes" to the question, but while the first person – maybe even without knowing – provided an overly inflated image of his role, the second person – in all modesty – gave an understated impression of his. As a result, both got the same score for their answer to that question.

The whole idea of the interview in the field is therefore to "debunk the junk" – to get a realistic view of the candidate's experience and skills by asking more detailed questions, clarifying areas that are unclear. Obviously, during the field interview the second candidate in our example will (or at least should) get a higher score than the first one on this aspect.

It will be clear by now from what we have been saying that the interviewers will have seen your file (application form, CV, talent screener) before the interview. This is yet another difference with the other structured interview, the general competency based interview, where the interviewers know nothing about you when starting the interview. For this reason the interview may or may not start with an introductory presentation by yourself. If the assessors do ask for this, they will be looking for a brief two-minute introduction just to remind them of the details of your past experience. However, they might decide to completely skip this and, after a short introduction of the panel, go immediately into asking questions.

The scoring of the field interview is also done based on a scoring grid, much like for the talent screener. They often score each question on a scale from 1 to 5 or from 1 to 10. This grid may be different, but as it is meant to be a tool for the assessors only, this does not really matter for you. Obviously, this grid will not be revealed to the candidates.

Some Tips for the Assessment

Here are a few tips to help make sure you are not scored lower than what you should deserve based on your achievements and overall profile. Always make sure, nevertheless, to provide truthful and relevant information, and never invent anything that is not "rooted in reality".

- **Remember it is a subjective exercise**. The interview in the field is purely scored by humans and not by computer algorithms. While in certain private sector jobs computer programs would "screen" your application or CV in search of industry-related keywords, EPSO does not resort to such automatic or automated methods.
- **Terminology matters**. At the same time, using relevant terminology or references to your job-related (or competition-related) activities can have an important impact on your scores. Moreover, the way you communicate your specific knowledge during the interview will also influence the assessors' understanding of your professional background. Therefore using a clear structure, clear references and short, to-the-point answers will add a lot of value to your performance.
- **Less is more**. To paraphrase Einstein, "everything should be as short as possible, but not shorter". This means that while you need to provide extensive information about your achievements, job-related expe-

Notes:

....

....

....

....

....

rience and qualifications, no assessor will want to hear a lengthy reply to the various questions in the field interview (or in the talent screener, as a matter of fact). Remember that the duration of the interview is strictly limited in order to give every candidate the same fair chance.

- **EU institutions and EPSO like formality**. Many candidates, especially those coming from outside the "EU bubble" tend to overlook the fact that EU institutions, and EPSO especially, are keen on using the right formal terminology and expressions. You are also expected to be precise. Thus if you are asked to provide evidence of your experience in "developing social, economic or political studies in the area of….", then they are only interested in such studies, not conferences you organised or internal memos that you had been tasked with drafting. On the other hand, your contribution to a peer-reviewed journal or an analytical website would certainly qualify, and so may your MA thesis.
- **Keep the instructions in mind**. Similarly, if you are asked to provide evidence of your experience in "contributing to the decision-making process of the European Commission", focus on the word "contributing" and carefully consider its interpretation – the activities you mention may include not only specific files you were in charge of but a broader set of activities such as coordinating a stakeholder conference or liaising with Member States' permanent representations in Brussels. Or, if your main activity was in the field of communication, make sure to mention how you contributed to the formulation phase of a policy or legislation, not only to its communication once it was adopted.
- **Team management vs. list of projects**. Another example is a question on "your experience in managing a team". Here you should avoid simply listing the projects or legislative files or clients you dealt with, and instead focus on the personal and human side. Explain how many people were involved in the team you worked with, how many units or European Parliament or Commission Directorates General (DGs) you coordinated with, and the level of responsibility you had. In a case like this, it is also worth mentioning any skills and competencies you gained as a result of such experience.
- **Dig deep and remember it all**. When thinking in advance about possible questions on, for instance, your team-management skills or drafting reports, search your memory and go through your CV thoroughly – you may find some hidden treasures that you can include in your answer. This may be your Master's thesis that you wrote on a related topic, a conference where you were a speaker, a short training course you followed and received a certificate for, or any other achievement or contribution that you can leverage for the purpose of the field interview. Remember, you need to present all relevant information in a highly structured manner to make sure that the Selection Board can tick the right boxes, understand your profile better and give you a higher score based on hard evidence, i.e. facts, figures, places and dates.
- **Don't boast**. No Selection Board member wants to see an overconfident candidate who is too full of himself. There is no need to say "I am a best-of-breed, 100% focused person who is happiest at the sharp end and personally passionate about European integration." This sounds bombastic and ultimately trite and will not result in higher scores. Be specific about your achievements and positive but not over-the-top about your potential contribution: "I have 3 years' work experience gained at the European Commission's Joint Research Centre in Sevilla – my work there has reinforced my commitment to the EU's

role in advancing science and technology, and I am eager to effectively contribute to further research building on my PhD and the Sevilla experience."

- **Link your achievements to the competition's objectives.** Even when a question relates to "your" commitment, motivation, achievements or experience, always make sure that you link your personal background and work experience to the needs of the EU or institution that will ultimately hire you. You may think that the question is about you – but in fact, it's about how your background fits the profile they are seeking to select candidates for. In short, say what you have done, but make sure to add in what way that is relevant and beneficial to the EU institutions.
- **A small detail for you can be an important piece of information for them.** Candidates occasionally "undersell" themselves. They may list various activities they have done (e.g. "I was in charge of writing memos, articles and press releases") when they could spell each item out in much more detail, thus boosting their profile and revealing more about these achievements. In the above example, if the candidate wrote memos, that could be showcased as a standalone achievement, adding more information about the kind and type of memos he or she was drafting. Press releases can also be important elements in demonstrating your ability to communicate EU policy and draft under time pressure, so why not list that as another standalone achievement? If you list these as part of a long collection of items, they lose their uniqueness and attract less attention from the Selection Board members. This is not "just" a presentation/communication issue – it can have a serious impact on your overall scores.
- **Concrete vs. abstract? Concrete wins every time.** When you talk about your professional background, make sure that you don't fall into the trap of making it too abstract. For example, if you say that you have worked on impact assessments, make sure to give dates for when you did this as well as other facts and figures that underline the importance of the responsibility you had (e.g. "coordinating work with 6 Directorates-General", or "supervising a budget of 8.3 million EUR", or "having an impact on 73 major businesses in Europe"). This concrete detail makes what you say far more relevant.

  If you were involved in a scientific study, you can make it more concrete by adding information such as "I liaised with 4 EU and 2 non-EU research centres", or "the project was financed by the Leonardo da Vinci program". Simply saying "I was a member of an international research team" may have the same meaning from your perspective, but it has a very different impact from the Selection Board's point of view.
- **Remember that the interviewers are bound by confidentiality.** Therefore, the interview is a "safe space" to use examples that may be confi-

Notes:

dential to some extent. At the same time, this is something that should be subject to your own judgement. For instance if you are working on an ongoing merger case as a competition lawyer, you might not be able to mention some things. The same applies for security experts as they might not be able to disclose some aspect of some operations. There are many other possible examples. It is also important to consider that the interviewers might know some people in your close professional circle, so it is better to avoid using personal names while still aiming to be as concrete as possible.

- **Your role should be clear**. Make sure that your role is crystal clear for each example you give. Don't just say "I participated in the working group on counterfeit medicines" but say "I was the team leader of the working group on..." or "I was the chief coordinator of the working group on...". This gives a clear indication to the assessors of what role you had in that project and you don't lose points because of being too vague or modest. Also avoid using "we" and instead use "I" whenever possible. It is not that you should try to take the credit for things that you have done as part of a team, but it always needs to be very clear what your personal role and exact contribution was.
- **Don't forget the relevance (and vanity) factor**. As with every organisation, EU institutions are keen on seeing job experience that is related to their own activities, in this case, supporting European affairs even if it is from a technical perspective. This is not to say that someone who has no EU experience would be disadvantaged when applying for a specialist EU competition, but bear in mind that if your experience was not gained inside or in relation to EU institutions, you need to make sure you explain why it is relevant for the profile they are seeking candidates for. If EPSO is searching for food safety experts, and you have worked on EU-related files and cases, make sure you put them high up on your list when mentioning your field-related expertise. This will be regarded positively and can have another positive impact on your application.

How to Prepare

Earlier we contrasted this type of interview with more typical job interviews and also with the generalist selection. The EPSO interview in the field is totally structured, therefore you can certainly prepare well for it.

It is worth recording yourself and then analysing your answers in light of the above tips. Were you concrete enough? Did you highlight your own role? Did you use the right terminology? Did you talk too much or share too few details? Such an exercise can significantly help your awareness of how to present your experience to the assessors.

You could also benefit from reviewing any weaknesses in your CV as shown up by the talent screener, and to some degree "pre-script" effective answers to the questions that might probe those weaknesses. You could practise by trialling with a friend acting as an interviewer and working from the data used for the talent screener and the duties list of the Notice of Competition. You could work with somebody preparing for the same competition, or prepare with the help of a colleague by doing mock exercises, or use a professional coach. It is crucial to practise aloud your responses before the actual date.

At the very least it would be essential for you to be 100% on top of every fact and figure, especially things like exact dates of employment, exact line management responsibilities and the like, that you mentioned in the talent screener. Interviewers get nervous about any inconsistencies that emerge in discussing a CV as they worry about what else might be hidden – so it would be most useful the day before the Assessment Centre to systematically review your CV in your head so you can give exact chapter and verse on everything.

Some Frequently Asked Questions

Here are some questions commonly asked by candidates preparing for the Assessment Centre field interview. Of course, depending on which competition you are preparing for, you might have different elements during the interview. The panel has quite some liberty to define the questions it uses to assess the candidates' knowledge and expertise in the field. Nonetheless there are many common elements.

Question 1: If I got 0 points for a question in the talent screener, will they ask me further questions on that?

As mentioned earlier, usually the interview is intended to assess if you are really an expert in the areas where you seem to be one on paper (on the basis of the talent screener). However, there could potentially be other subject areas which the Selection Board considers very important. Such areas will be indicated by being given heavy weighting in the talent screener scoring. So where you scored low but the Board gave a topic a high weight, it is advisable to revise that particular topic. In addition you should check if there are references to it in the Notice of Competition. It is obviously far better to respond "Yes, I know a bit about this subject even though I have never really dealt with it myself…" and then give some overview of what you know about it, rather than simply shrugging your shoulders and saying that No, you don't know anything about it. Also take the opportunity to bring in interlinking experiences related to the topic.

In rare cases panels may decide not to review the talent screener at all before the interview in order to start the interview without any influence or preferences. In that case they will follow very much the list of the duties from the Notice of Competition and will ask you about each of those responsibilities. You should accept that it is absolutely normal that for some areas you might not have any experience. Other candidates will have the same problem. What you should make sure to do is to respond as well as you possibly can about what you DO know about in practice, and be able to at least cover theoretically the basics about areas in which you are not an expert.

Question 2. What if I know one of the interviewers?

This is actually quite a common situation as many candidates have been working in the field of the competition for

Notes:

several years and have a professional network. If you end up being interviewed by somebody you know in a professional context, just act naturally and never exclude the other panel member from the conversation. Keep eye contact with both and be ready to explain situations that the person you know might be familiar with already. Be prepared to present yourself as if they did not know you at all, and never make reference to having worked together or come into contact. You can certainly mention a situation where you had such contact, but if you do so, don't refer to the interviewer as having been involved or already knowing about it.

Question 3. If they ask for an example, may I also use the STAR method for response?

The STAR method is a way (discussed already in Chapter 5) of responding to example-based questions. However, while in the general competency-based interview, your response should mainly focus on HOW you dealt with a particular situation, in the field-related interview, your answer should predominantly respond to the WHAT you did question. It needs to cover the technical details of the example. Therefore, while the structure of your response may follow the STAR model used for the general competency based interview, the content of the answer needs to be different.

Question 4. What are the best examples to choose from my past?

It is best of all if you can choose outstanding examples of where you were involved in a very interesting case that is well-known, or where you managed a project from the beginning until the end, or where you were responsible for a larger budget, or where you dealt with something that the assessors might know about.

It is essential to choose examples that tell a positive story about your experience. Remember that the panel is bound by confidentiality, so you may to some extent mention things that might not be public information. At the same time, always keep in mind not to cast any negative light on your current or previous manager, or your current or former organization. If your field is particularly confidential, for instance you work in the area of "Armed Security", you might choose not to share some details. But in general, it is great to choose some outstanding examples that speak well of your expertise, that will be interesting to the interviewers. For example, if you worked for a while in Mozambique on a project, this is quite exotic so the panel will remember you better than if you mentioned a plain example from Brussels. Be concrete and to the point as much as possible.

Question 5. This is an interview in my field. Do I still need to prepare for it?

Definitely, yes. There are several reasons why you need to prepare. First of all, because while you might easily remember details of a project that you worked on two years ago, you might not be able to recall details of something that happened 12 years ago. You therefore will need to refresh your memory. Go through the Notice of Competition, thinking about what specific examples you could mention to demonstrate those technical skills and competencies. Revise workflows, processes, procedures, stakeholders, issues you encountered, solutions you had, innovative ideas, etc. The panel may ask some more theoretical questions as well. And as a second step after the revision, it is also important to practice aloud.

Question 6. If I'm specialised in one particular area and I know that the jury members are mainly specialists in another, what shall I do?

This most likely will not at all affect the content of the interview. You may be asked about anything that is mentioned in the Notice of Competition, but the background of the panel will not influence the questions they ask. Of course, if a person is an expert in a particular field they will be better positioned to assess your knowledge and expertise related to that particular area.

Question 7. What should I revise before this interview?

It is important to revise everything you have done previously in your career. For the revision, it is a good idea to use the talent screener and the duties in Annex 1 of the Notice of Competition as a basis. It is also wise to get up to date on current hot topics related to the area.

Question 8. How can I practice for this interview?

A very important step is to practise your answers out loud. You may do this by yourself, with a helpful colleague, with another candidate or with a professional coach. This will sharpen your answers, you will learn to respond much more to the point, with more confidence and more directly – all of which is crucial in a rapidly paced interview like this one.

Key points to remember

- *The field interview is only applicable for specialist competitions*
- *The interviewers will be experts in the field of the competition*
- *The idea is to get a clear picture of the candidate as a professional in the field of the competition*
- *The interview in the field is also a "structured interview" because the same questions are asked of all the candidates*
- *The tips relating to clear communication are just as relevant here as for other exercises*

Notes:

....

....

....

....

....

9. The Motivational Interview

The motivational interview is a new feature of the Assessment Centre. It is currently used as a formal component of the assessment only for the annual AD5 graduate Administrator competition.

However it is worth reading this chapter even if you are taking a different competition. The reason is that evaluation, even if only on an informal level, of your motivation to work for the EU is likely to seep into more and more aspects of the assessment for all candidates.

Introduction

Before 2010 the open competitions (as originally organised by the institutions themselves and later by EPSO) had a sort of motivation test using general EU knowledge as a measure. Usually, this test was in the form of an interview where a panel questioned the candidate in a rather unstructured and random way about the facts and figures of the EU. They asked questions about the inner workings of the EU and its institutions, hoping to get an idea of how well the candidate had studied this vast body of knowledge, and taking this as an indication of how thoroughly the candidate had prepared for the competition – in other words, how *motivated* they were.

The problem with this method was that it was often a lucky shot for the candidate to know the right answers (since the jury could not use the same questions for all the candidates; people talk to each other). Moreover, with successive treaty changes and enlargements, the body of knowledge to master became so large that the questions could only probe in a haphazard way the real knowledge – and understanding – of the candidate.

When the Assessment Centre was introduced in 2010 the idea was to embed some "applied EU knowledge" in the general competencies performance tests. The topics of, for example, the case study, the oral presentation, or the group exercise, would be EU-related, and for specialists even related to the field of the competition. As a result, candidates with a good knowledge of the EU (in the field of the competition) would have an advantage and perform better, even if the tests were formally only assessing some of the "general" competencies.

However, the notion of motivation disappeared entirely from the competition, leaving the doors wide open for candidates who might be bright and good professionals but were without any real motivation to work specifically for the EU. Then, in 2014, a mandatory "self-assessment" of motivation and EU knowledge was introduced in the application procedure, aiming to filter out those candidates who didn't want to make the effort of going through the self-assessment, and those who realised that working for the EU was not their thing after all. Nevertheless, the number of candidates remained very high and the tools to filter out the high potentials (CBTs and/or talent screener) did not look at motivation (or EU knowledge) at all. This problem was reinforced by the economic situation and young adult unemployment in certain Member States, feeding the suspicion that many candidates were only interested in getting a job in the institutions for the salary and benefits. There was also the rise of anti-EU sentiment across the continent, increasing the risk of hiring Trojan Horses aiming to destroy the EU from within.

Then, in its 2016 Management Plan, EPSO started talking about the adoption of a **strength-based approach** in combination with the STAR method (Specific Objective #3). (For STAR, see Chapter 5.) A strength based interview focuses on what you *enjoy* doing, rather than what you *can* do (as in a competency based interview). Strength based interviewing has its foundations in positive psychology. The theory is that by identifying your strengths and matching them to the role you'll be happier in your work, perform better, learn quicker and stay with the organisation for longer. Unlike their competency counterparts, strengths interviews are more personal and allow recruiters to gain a genuine insight into the personalities of candidates and to see if they are likely to be a good "fit" for the organisation.

The first signal of change popped up in January 2018 when the candidates for the 2017 AD5 generalists (graduate) competition were asked for their motivation when presenting themselves at the beginning of their (general) competency based interview. Instead of the usual two minutes of self-presentation they got four minutes, not only to tell the interviewers about their educational and professional background but also about their reasons for participating in the competition – in other words, their motivation. From the feedback we received from candidates for other competitions in 2018 we learned that this has now become standard practice.

The first "official" sign of EPSO's new approach came with the Notice of Competition for the **2018 AD5 graduate competition:**

> "Eight general competencies and your motivation to join the EU institutions will be tested at the assessment centre through five tests (case study, oral presentation, competency-based interview, group exercise and a motivational interview)."

It looks like this extra test for generalists is in a way mirroring the "interview in the field" given to specialists, because for generalists their "knowledge in the field" is in effect their (general) knowledge of the EU.

The motivational interview was used again in the 2019 AD5 graduate competition.

What is Motivation?

Motivation is the force that initiates, guides, and maintains goal-oriented behaviours. It is what causes us to take action, whether to grab a snack to reduce hunger, enrol in college to earn a degree – or to participate in an EPSO competition to become an EU official.

A lot has been written about motivation and how it operates in our personal and working lives. However, I would like to mention particularly some of the ideas in Daniel Pink's 2010 bestseller *Drive: The Surprising Truth About What Motivates Us.*

When Pink discusses motivation he breaks it down into two specific types: extrinsic and intrinsic. *Extrinsic* motivation is driven by external forces such as money or praise. *Intrinsic* motivation is something that comes from within and can be as simple as the satisfaction felt from accomplishing a challenging task. He identifies the three elements of "true motivation" in the 21st century workplace as being "autonomy", "mastery" and "purpose". The degree to which these three elements are found in any workplace – including the EU institutions – of course varies greatly, but in respect of the Assessment Centre motivation interview the relevant element is clearly "purpose". Pink argues that, for instance, it is actually more important for one's motivation to see "the bigger picture" and understand the objectives of the organisation than to be highly paid (as long as your pay check compares with that of your peers).

Public Service Motivation

So what then are or should be the specific motivators for public servants, people working for national or international government or not-for-profit organisations?

Public service motivation refers to the motivation to contribute to society and to the general interest. Research suggests that the choice to work in the public or non-profit sectors reflects a set of values, a desire to do work that is socially meaningful and that allows the individual to serve a broader public interest. It is closely related to the "purpose" element in Pink's theory on motivation.

Based on his research ("Measuring Public Service Motivation: An Assessment of Construct Reliability and Validity", *Journal of Public Administration Research and Theory* 6, no. 1 (1996): 5-23.), James Perry detected four dimensions of public service motivation:

- Attraction to policy making
- Commitment to the public interest and civic duty
- Compassion
- Self-sacrifice

These are general public values that have been documented as a basis for public service motivation throughout the Western world, as these cultures share, to some extent, a common Greco-Judean background and have developed similar political cultures and public institutions. However, Wouter Vandenabeele ("Development of a Public Service Motivation Measurement Scale: Corroborating and Extending Perry's Measurement Instrument" *International Public Management Journal* 11, no. 1 (2008a): 143-67.), refers to another public service motivation dimension, democratic governance, which refers to administrative values in democratic governance systems.

Public service motivation has been shown to relate to job and organisational performance, sectorial and employer pref-

Notes:

erence, decreased turnover and increased job satisfaction, incentive preferences and whistle blowing.

Public service motivation is, of course, not the sole motivation of employees working in the public sector. It is only one of the multiple motives that explain organisational behaviour in public service or governmental organisations. The other components of public sector motivation include, among others, job security, retirement pay or pension rights, salary, promotion opportunities and work-family balance (Lewis, Gregory, and Sue Frank, "Who Wants to Work for Government?" *Public Administration Review* 62, no. 4 (2002): 395-404).

Furthermore, an individual's motivations may shift over time or in relation to different behaviours. The motivation to accept a job can be quite different than the motivation that is shown on a day-to-day basis. However, one can assume that the initial motivation to join affects the motivation for other types of behaviour and that the underlying variable is a stable "public service identity". This is also related to the discussion of whether public service motivation is something one brings to the organisation or whether this type of motivation develops over the course of employment in the organisation.

Motivation in the EU Administration

What, then, more specifically can be said about the motivation of those who work for the EU administration?

On this topic Wouter Vandenabeele (Public Management Institute, Catholic University of Leuven) and visiting scholar Carolyn Ban (Graduate School of Public and International Affairs, University of Pittsburgh) presented an informative paper at the European Union Studies Association meeting in April 2009 (available at http://aei.pitt.edu/33022/1/Ban._Carolyn.pdf.). The paper was based on a survey of all employees of the European Commission, done as part of their annual satisfaction survey, which had a response rate of 28 per cent.

Some 39.5% of those who responded cited "build Europe" as one of their motivations for entry to the EU civil service. This was less than salary/benefits (50%) or even "work in in an international organisation" (59.7%), suggesting that the majority of EU officials can hardly be classified (as they are often are by Eurosceptics) as zealots for the European cause. However it is also clear that for significant numbers of EU officials the challenge of working in an international organisation and contributing to building Europe are and remain important factors. Inevitably, in the real world, motivations are mixed. While building Europe may be a consideration, an *intrinsic* motivation (using Daniel Pink's terminology, as above), without doubt fewer EU civil servants would have found this sufficient reason to uproot their lives and come to Brussels without also having the prospect of a good salary and working conditions.

It is often said that older officials were more incentivised by "altruistic" motives like building Europe than are the younger generations. The Vandenabeele/Ban study gives some support to that idea. Of those in the age cohort 30-39, for example, only 38% gave "build Europe" as a motivation for entry, compared with 51% of those over 60. However such data, as the authors point out, have to be used with caution: memory of actual motivations can be fallible and surveys of national government civil servants show similar results. We are often more idealistic in retrospect than we were at the time. Of course, it must also be said that those who are over 60 are particularly likely, having in many cases spent their entire career working for the EU, to have a strong attachment to the EU's values and indeed to have pursued successful careers within its institutions. For them it has been a lifetime's work and they will tend to attribute to it a meaning and significance beyond simply making a good salary. It would be a fair guess that those who sit on EPSO panels would also tend on average to be towards the more idealistic end of the spectrum, and this is worth keeping in mind in thinking about your interview preparation.

Finally on the findings of the Vandenabeele/Ban paper, it is worth noting that its authors found variation by function group. Whereas 46% of Administrators gave "build Europe" as an entry motivation, this was true of only 35% of Assistants. This can hardly be surprising given that the opportunities for Administrators to participate in policy-making are so much greater.

The importance of national factors should also not be underestimated. Take the case of EU officials coming from Britain. The first waves of British officials who went to Brussels after accession in 1973 included many who were enthusiastically pro-European. They were a self-selected group who saw Europe as the future for their country. With the strong endorsement of British membership of the Community given in the 1975 UK referendum, these pioneering officials could also feel that British opinion was on their side. But in later decades, with the slow but steady rise of Euroscepticism, that conviction faded. Inevitably the idea of working for the EU when it was consistently disparaged by many at home began to lose its appeal. It became ever harder to find qualified candidates from Britain to take EU jobs and Britain became underrepresented in the institutions.

This is not a phenomenon unique to Britain. The Eastern enlargement of the EU in 2005/2007 has resulted in proportionately much larger numbers of candidates in EPSO competitions coming from those countries than from the older Member States. Of course economic factors have been a significant factor in that. However, Poland, a country where Euroscepticism has strong roots, has consistently produced fewer EPSO candidates, relative to its population, than many of the older Member States. This is despite a substantial diaspora of Poles to work in Western European countries. Only 3.76% of the candidates for the 2017 generalist Administrators competition, and 3.89% for the 2018 competition, gave Polish as one of their languages despite Poland having 7.4% of the EU population. It can be assumed that some potential candidates are discouraged by domestic attitudes to the idea of working for the EU.

The Motivational Interview

According to EPSO:

"The motivation to join the EU Institutions is multifaceted, involving several elements: the origin of the interest to work for the EU, the awareness about and commitment to EU values, the understanding of present and future challenges of the EU, the expectations regarding an EU career, knowledge of the EU and its origins, of the EU institutions and of the main EU policies.

On this basis, a motivational interview has been developed and con-

Notes:

sists of a 20 minute structured interview by two members of the Selection Board. The EU motivational interview will test each of the above elements.

Test Pass mark for the motivational interview: 5/10. The marks obtained in the motivational interview will be added to the marks obtained in the other assessment centre tests to give candidates their final overall mark.

A comprehensive explanation of the content and the method will be made public (EPSO website)."

A careful analysis of these few lines of text allows us to give some hands-on advice on what to expect from this interview.

First of all we have to note that this interview is less important than the other tests: you can earn a maximum of 10 points out of 90 (11% or so) while the other five tests combined can bring you 80 points out of 90 (16% per test). Because the pass mark is 5/10 (meaning that the difference between the worst and the best performer with a pass mark is a maximum 5 points) one can even say that the relative importance of your total score is only about 6% (5 out of 90).

However, this test is still very important because of the pass mark; **if you don't get at least 5/10 you are out of the competition**. The good news is that you can prepare very well for this kind of test, whereas it is much more difficult to obtain excellent scores on the general competencies tests (because you cannot change your "natural" behaviour overnight).

It is a **structured interview**. Structured interviews follow a fixed script, meaning that all the candidates will get to answer the same questions on a fixed set of anchors. A positive corollary of this is that the questions will have to be very "high level" because too detailed questions would rapidly spread amongst the candidates via social media. Despite the fact that the main questions will be rather "high level" you can nevertheless expect a few very detailed follow-up questions; this will allow the interviewers to distinguish between "good", "very good" and "excellent" answers.

The interview will last for only 20 minutes which means that there will only be a very limited number of questions.

The topic of the questions will be organised around the following anchors:

- The origin of your interest in working for the EU
- Awareness of and commitment to EU values
- Understanding of present and future challenges of the EU
- Expectations regarding an EU career
- Knowledge of the EU and its origins, the EU institutions and the main EU policies

Let us now discuss these anchors in more detail, allowing you to prepare in a more focused way.

The origin of your interest in working for the EU

Here you would explain where your interest in working for the EU came from in the first place. Maybe (one of) your parents have been EU officials and you studied in a European or other international school. Maybe you studied international or EU politics – or economics – or graduated at the College of Europe. You may have participated in an Erasmus program or otherwise studied abroad. You may have been living and working abroad, being embedded in another culture or language. You may have done an internship (Blue Book or the like). You may have worked as a contract or temporary agent, or as an external service provider for one of the EU institutions or agencies. Your work may have brought you into contact with the EU institutions or agencies, perhaps in another national or international organisation or NGO.

You will probably have to present yourself; grab the opportunity to highlight these aspects of your personal history and explain why they raised and reinforced your interest in working for the EU.

Awareness of and commitment to EU values

The European Union's fundamental values are respect for human dignity and human rights, freedom, democracy, equality and the rule of law. These values unite all the Member States – no country that does not recognise these values can belong to the Union.

Here you would explain how you became aware of the values of the EU. You may have been raised in a country that was not at that time a Member State, and have personally experienced the (economic, social, cultural, political) advantages brought by EU membership. You may have lived and worked outside the EU and have had the opportunity to observe the differences. You may have studied EU or international politics, or economics. If none of the above applies to you the least you can do is to read about these values as much as you can. A good starting point is https://europarlamentti.info/en/values-and-objectives/values/

Try to explain why these values matter to you personally, and demonstrate that you are committed to them.

Understanding of present and future challenges of the EU

Our advice to prepare for this kind of question is simple: read as much as you can on what is happening in the EU and try to make sense of it. A good place to start is the Commission's White Paper on the future of Europe.

If you Google the terms "present and future challenges of the EU" you will get a host of older and fresh information on this topic as well. We further suggest following the specialised press like Politico or EUObserver; this will keep you up to date.

Notes:

Expectations regarding an EU career

Here we would advise you to read the previous pages again and try to figure out for yourself what your personal motivation to work for the EU looks like. It is very important that you are really honest with yourself, because you might otherwise land a job that is not a good match with what makes you tick, resulting in an unhappy career. As we saw earlier, the motivations of current officials are very varied and not necessarily only altruistic, so there is no "politically correct" answer to this question. Remember that the assessors are "real" EU officials too, so they will easily detect if you are trying to fool them with overly idealistic blah blah.

> It is a good idea to subscribe to the Facebook forum on the EPSO competitions because candidates share a lot of useful information that is not available on the "official" EPSO website. And eutraining.eu is another useful source of information.

Knowledge of the EU and its origins, the EU institutions and the main EU policies

Here again, preparing for this question is a matter of reading and learning as much as you can on the history and the organisation of the EU. There are some very good entries on the origin and the organisation of the EU as we know it today on Wikipedia:

- https://en.wikipedia.org/wiki/Timeline_of_European_Union_history
- https://en.wikipedia.org/wiki/European_Union

Of course, much more detailed information will be found on the websites of the various institutions, and there are many excellent books available.

How to Prepare for this Interview

After this lengthy description of the underlying principles it is now time for some hands-on ideas to prepare well for this interview. In Annex 7 we have given some of the possible topics that might come up. Because the exact questions are not known in advance it is impossible to "learn" the answers by heart. But you can still do some practical things to prepare yourself for the possible questions you will face.

Review your application form

You may remember that in the early stages of the competition you had to fill out an online application form. You had to tell EPSO about your motivation for the job and what value you could – in your opinion – bring to the EU institutions.

Before the introduction of the motivation interview this part of the application form was more of a formality for the selection process. The first time anybody even looked at your answers was when you were already on the Reserve List, by the recruiters looking for candidates to invite for a job interview. With the introduction of the motivation interview it is highly likely that things have changed. Our bet is that the interviewers will now have a close look at these sections of your application form before they even start with the interview. So the advice would be to review your application form to make sure that you don't tell them totally different things during the interview.

It is quite possibly too late now to think about what to say at the application stage because you may well be past that stage. You may not have given too much thought to this issue when you filled out the form, but the least you can do when you reach the Assessment Centre is to try to be consistent with what you said in applying for the competition.

Think about what really makes you tick

You could draw up a list of "entry motivations" and try to establish the order that applies in your case. For example, in the Vandenabeele/Ban study discussed above the range of entry motivations measured comprised "Build Europe", "Shape European Policy", "Specific Policy Area", "Work in an International Organisation", "Work is Challenging and Interesting", "Career Enhancement", "Natural Progression", "Salary/Benefits" and "Personal/Family". You could give a score or use percentages (adding up to 100%). This exercise will force you to think in a more systematic way about your own motivation. Obviously, you would have to remember the top scores on your list.

Usually there will be only 2 or 3 items in this shortlist (this is based on the Pareto principle which says that often 80% of the effects are caused by 20% of the causes). Then think of a good narrative to explain why these are your main motivators. If applicable you can tell them about specific events, or periods in your life, when these things became a motivator.

Study, study, study

Most of the questions in the motivation interview will be about your knowledge and understanding of the EU. The only way to acquire this knowledge is to study. Read books, websites, newspapers and articles on the EU or EU-related topics. Whatever you can get hold of. Study as if you were back at university preparing for an exam. This is the only way to brush up your knowledge of the EU and be prepared for this important challenge.

We suggest you make your own case study type of exercise and create a written summary which you can review a couple of days before the interview. Another exercise could be to prepare an oral presentation on these topics to a group of friends (or family).

Notes:

Some Further Reflections on EPSO's Motivation Interview

Behind the scenes we have heard some fierce criticism of the concept of the motivation interview. Some of the trade unions consider this to be a breach in the wall of objectivity and impartiality around the EPSO competitions. After all, it is very difficult to define exactly what motivation is about (even scientists don't agree) so it must be impossible to measure it in an objective way. Some even see this as an attempt to go back to the early days of the EU, when staff were commonly hired on political, national or nepotistic grounds, not on merit or competence.

It is always a good idea to inform yourself about any potential future employer and the specifics of the post you are applying for. Exactly the same applies when you take an an EPSO competition.

Knowing about the mission of the employer and your role within the new working environment is not only a sign of motivation which can help you land the job but it has another pleasant side-effect: it will also increase your motivation once you have the job. The reason for this can be found in Daniel Pink's theory on motivation, more specifically in the "purpose" element. Seeing "the bigger picture" and understanding the objectives of the organisation will increase your intrinsic motivation and you will therefore be a happier and more effective employee. This is what every employer is ultimately looking for.

We believe that some nuance has its place here.

It is true, for a start, to say that in recent years the issue of a candidate's motivation has been neglected during the selection process. Only at a very late stage (the job interview) has some attention been paid to this very important aspect of prospective hires. And job interviews are typically conducted by managers using their gut feeling, rather than more systematic techniques, to decide whether or not they want to hire a candidate.

The motivation interview, in contrast, will be conducted by professionals who are trained and experienced in the field of human resources; it is highly likely that only "permanent members" of the jury will be allowed to conduct this kind of interview. Moreover, while the effect on the candidate's total score will only be marginal (5-6% at the most), the threshold will allow the interviewers to single out those candidates who are clearly applying for the wrong reasons, or couldn't make the effort to learn about their potential new working environment. This is a very valid argument in favour of this interview.

Key Points to Remember

- *Motivation is a complex and multidimensional concept and it is difficult to measure in an objective way*
- *An important part of motivation is measured with questions about the (general) knowledge of the EU, its history, guiding principles, organisation, challenges and future*
- *While the impact of the motivation interview on your total score will only be marginal, it is essential to obtain a pass mark*
- *It IS possible to prepare well for this interview; it's not a lottery!*

10. The Situational Competency Based Interview

Introduction

Due to the Covid-19 outbreak, and to conclude the open competitions within a reasonable period, EPSO decided to organise online testing – remotely – for the Assessment Centre tests. Remote online testing allows candidates to sit the tests at home or in the office without needing to travel to an EPSO testing centre. The testing takes place via online videoconferencing.

To ensure equal treatment, all candidates must take the same tests. However, the group exercise cannot be conducted remotely in a satisfactory way. As discussed in Chapter 7, the group exercise very much depends on the inter-personal dynamics that are created by having a group of people sitting around a table engaged on a common task. This would be near-impossible to replicate satisfactorily online. Furthermore, if the internet connection to any participant was lost or became unstable, the group dynamic would be lost and the exercise difficult to complete in a meaningful way.

For this reason, rather than simply shift the group exercise online, as with other tests, EPSO have introduced another test to substitute for it, the situational competency based interview, the SCBI.

The SCBI is intended as a way of assessing general competencies normally measured by the group exercise, i.e. analysis and problem solving, learning and development, prioritising and organising, resilience, working with others, and leadership. It looks at how candidates would react in a specific situation.

Schedule and arrangements

The situational competency based interview consists of a one-on-one online meeting with a trained interviewer.

Approximately two to three weeks before the SCBI testing period, candidates will receive a written assignment and background information to help them prepare. In the assignment, candidates are asked to replace a colleague and assume responsibility for various tasks and situations to be discussed during the interview. Additional situations, not based on the assignment, will also be included. Candidates are allowed to consult the written assignment and background information during the interview.

For the SCBI, candidates will be interviewed by an EU staff member. Two Selection Board members observe and assess the performance of each candidate and score the competencies covered by the test. The interviewer is not involved in the assessment of the candidate. The interview is not recorded for data protection reasons. The interview itself lasts between 30 and 40 minutes.

The very first SCBI was used for the EPSO/AD/374/19 competition, in December 2020. In this competition, the interview lasted 40 minutes. Additional time was added when there were interruptions in the connection.

Comparing the SCBI with the other Assessment Centre tests

Even though this is a new test, substituting for the group exercise, the SCBI fits nicely in the portfolio of the EPSO Assessment Centre test suite. For this reason, it makes sense to compare the SCBI with some of the other tests, in order to get a better understanding of this test and thus help in achieving a better performance when taking it.

Compared with the case study and oral presentation

At first sight, the assignment for the SCBI looks and feels a lot like the assignments for the case study and the oral presentation. After the cover page, the very first document in the bundle is the assignment itself. It describes the general situation, your position, and the tasks you have to perform. In a way, the assignment contains the "metadata" of the exercise. A list of abbreviations used follows.

In the rest of the bundle there is a collection of press articles, webpages, emails, notes, and other documents giving more details on the situation and the problem to solve.

Despite the fact that the assignment (the first page) looks similar to that of a case study or oral presentation, there is a striking difference. The "Important Notice" (printed in red, top of the page) says that "Candidates are advised to *rely mainly* [our italics] on the information presented in the exercise, although candidates may use information from other sources when answering questions."

In contrast, in the case study and the oral presentation (and the group exercise for that matter), candidates are supposed to *rely solely* on the information provided. In fact, **the "Important Notice" is suggesting you do some extra research** so as to clarify your understanding of the file. You can also rely on your own knowledge of the topic, which is not the case for the other exercises.

The fact that you can do additional research, and ask questions during the interview, is also clearly indicated in the front matter on the flip side of the cover page.

We believe that "doing extra research" can be interpreted in the widest possible sense. You can use Google, the Commission's websites, talk with people who know more about the topic, read books, etc. In showing that you did extra research you will definitely display some positive indicators for learning and development. Keep in mind, however, that this is still an "open" competition, meaning that people who have never worked for the EU institutions must get a fair chance too. It is therefore NOT advised to use information that only insiders have access to (the Commission's intranet, for example).

Another important difference has to do with the preparation time allowed. For the case study and oral presentation (and indeed the group exercise) you only get a very limited amount of time to go through the background documents and make sense of them. For the SCBI you get at least 2-3 weeks (even more if you come at the end of the SCBI period). This means that the expected level of understanding and familiarity with the background documents will be much higher. Showing your deep and intricate understanding of the scenario is an opportunity to display positive indicators for the analysis and problem solving and learning and development competencies.

On the other hand, in the case study and the oral presentation, and also the group exercise, your prioritising and organising competency is mainly tested "on-the-fly", that is while you are doing the exercise. In the SCBI you will have to demonstrate that competency by the way you go about organising and prioritising the actions and activities that you are planning to do in the context of the scenario. Which is a different thing.

Finally, one might find another parallel with the case study in the sense that the interviewer will be a regular EU official, and not a member of the Selection Board. Remember that the markers for the case study are equally regular EU officials.

Compared with the group exercise

We have already seen in the previous section that the SCBI differs from the group exercise in that (1) you are not expected to rely solely on the documentation provided, (2) you have much more time to prepare, and (3) the way your prioritising and organising competence is demonstrated is different.

There is another difference.

If you take a closer look at the background documents for the SCBI, you will see that there are six "stakeholder positions" at the end of the bundle.

As we saw in Chapter 7, for the group exercise each participant gets one stakeholder position to present during the meeting. In the group exercise you are NOT "representing" or "defending" this position; you only have to make sure that this position is known by the other participants and taken into account during the discussion. The same is true for the SCBI: you have to take all the stakeholders' positions into account in your analysis and problem-solving activities. The difference with the GE, where you are on your own, is that *you have all six of them available* without having to rely on the other participants to know them.

Compared with the general competency based interview

Much like the general competency based interview (GCBI), the SCBI is a behavioural interview. During a behavioural interview, the interviewers are not asking if you have a skill; they're going to ask you to show them how you have implemented that skill in or out of the workplace. Behavioural interviews focus on the past, allowing the interviewers to predict the future.

In the general competency based interview you can take that literally as most of the questions will be formulated like:

> *"Tell us about a situation where XYZ happened – what did you do and what were the results of your actions?"*

Notes:

....

....

....

....

....

So, in the general competency based interview they are asking about how you implemented a given skill (competency) in your past. The GCBI is strictly organised – structured – around a set of well-defined situations (anchors) and that is why it's commonly referred to as "the structured interview."

While in the GCBI the questions are directly related to the anchors (check out Annex 4 of this book), this not the case for the SCBI. The questions asked during the SCBI will be about the situations as described in the assignment, and these may cover multiple anchors simultaneously. Examples of SCBI questions based on the assignment could be:

"Based on the assignment, if you were to take a leading role, how would you manage the conflict between X and Y?"

Or

"How would you decide what is relevant and what is less relevant in the information provided by Z?"

You can also expect some questions that will not be based on the assignment, like:

"How would you deal with a colleague that…?"

Or

"How would you react if your project receives comments that…?"

The SCBI is "semi-scripted", meaning that not all the candidates will get the same questions (or anchors in the GCBI). Instead, the interviewer will have the choice of a list of questions from which he or she can freely choose during the interview. This also means that it will be a bit more difficult to prepare for this interview, as there is more uncertainty involved. This will, however, allow them to test your resilience in a better way than by just asking you questions about it (for which you can prepare very well).

Compared with a situational judgement test and e-tray exercise

In a way, the SCBI can also be compared with the situational judgement test found in some Administrator competitions and with the e-tray exercise. The difference with these exercises is, however, that they are multiple-choice questionnaires, in a computer-based environment and that the scenarios of the SCBI are more detailed and complicated.

The SCBI as a Role-Play Exercise

The SCBI is also a **role-play exercise**. You are explicitly asked to "replace a colleague and assume responsibility for various tasks and situations to be discussed during the interview", so, during the interview you are "playing the role" of that person.

In the feedback we have received, some of the candidates were even asked to play the role of being the chairperson of a meeting and to introduce the meeting by explaining the assignment. On another occasion, the interviewer played the role of being one of the persons mentioned in the background documents, calling you on the phone to ask you what you have done to solve their problems.

The assignment documents

As part of the assignment you are provided with a number of documents in various formats: pages with text and figures, emails, press articles, notes for the file, webpages, etc. Most of the documents will have a clear date of validity and for those that don't you can assume that they were available to you before the "Today" date as indicated at the bottom of the assignment document, which is the first document after the front matter.

Figure 10.1: Classification of SCBI documents

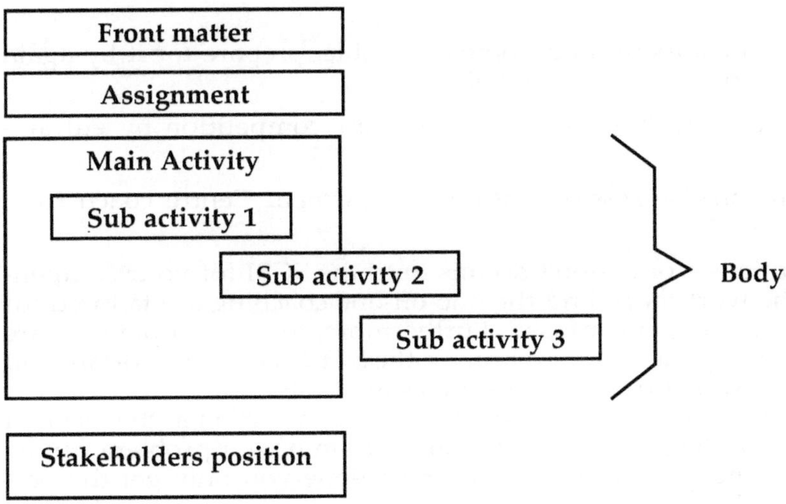

Equally, for most of the documents it will be clear who the originator is. If it is not clear, you can assume that the document/page contains "metadata" about the exercise. Generally speaking, one could classify the documents/pages as presented above in Figure 10.1

The so-called "main activity" is what is explicitly at the bottom of the assignment (printed in bold and with 2-3 bullet points) that you are asked to carry out. The "sub-activities" are – intentional – distractions from your main tasks. These may be entirely or partially related to the main task, or even be totally unrelated.

The "stakeholder positions" will be grouped separately at the end of the assignment and are related to the main task. The positions will be contradictory, meaning that you have to analyse them and come to a reasoned conclusion.

Notes:

Preparing for the SCBI: Strategy

Provided you have the time to prepare for the SCBI well in advance, we would advise to apply the following strategy:

1. Check on the EPSO website to see if there is a current SCBI test and access the file. Try to identify and classify the various documents following the model as given in figure 10.1.
2. Use the SCBI assignment you have downloaded as a basis for a simulated preparation by following the step-by-step approach as given below. This will familiarise you with what is involved.
3. Once the SCBI of your own competition becomes available, prepare for it by again following the step-by-step approach as given below.
4. (Optionally) take part in a workshop organised for your competition by eutraining.eu
5. (Optionally) reserve a one-on-one session with an Assessment Centre coach from eutraining.eu

If you are able to go for options 4 or 5, don't do this until the SCBI for your competition is actually published. The workshops and the one-on-one coaching are tailored for a specific competition and you may get confused. Furthermore, for the people who are in the running for that competition, their preparation for the SCBI is more important and more urgent than it is for you. And eutraining's resources are finite.

Taking part in a workshop has the advantage over a one-on-one session in the fact that you will learn from the other participants as well. You will see how a problem can be viewed from different angles and perspectives. In a one-on-one you only get the perspective of one person, the coach.

Preparing for the SCBI: A Step-by-Step Approach

1. Read the assignment. Try to imagine the general context is which you are put and **understand exactly what your tasks are** (the text printed in bold at the bottom of the page).
2. Go carefully through the entire package of documents. Try to **identify which documents are part of the "main" activity**, and which are sub-activity related. In doing so, you will have an oversight of the entire package.
3. Go through all the documents in the "body" of the assignments, in detail. Note down, or mark on the documents, the following information:
   a. Main activity or sub-activity (number the sub-activities)
   b. Origin of the document
   c. Recipient(s)
   d. Validity date

   e. Keywords summarising the content of the document

4. **Create a table (Excel) that looks like this:**

Document	Date	Origin	Recipient(s)	Keywords	Importance	Urgency	Priority

5. Complete the table with the information you collected in point 3. You can leave the fields "Importance," "Urgency," and "Priority" blank for now.
6. Go through all the documents in the "Stakeholders Positions" and try to identify the different issues they have positions, pros and cons, and proposals on.
7. **Group the issues into four categories:**
   a. Issues related to the scope of the "main" activity
   b. Issues related to the resources needed to complete the "main" activity
   c. Issues related to the timeline and/or the deadlines of the "main" activity
   d. Issues related to the sub-activities
8. Do whatever additional research you deem necessary to better understand the issues that need to be addressed.
9. **Create another table (Excel) that looks like this:**

Stakeholder	Scope	Resources	Timeline

10. Complete the table with the various positions in each category for every stakeholder.
11. Complete the first table with the "Importance" and "Urgency" for every document. As a rule, things that are directly related to the main activity may be important, while those that are referring to the sub-activities will most likely be less important. On the other hand, based on the validity date of a document, and the originator, you could also make an estimate of the urgency.
12. Using the **Eisenhower matrix** (see textbox) you can now determine the priority of each document.
13. Reorder the table so that the **docu-**

Notes:

....

....

....

....

....

ments with the highest priority (both "Urgent" and "Important") come on top of the list. This will help you in prioritising the actions you will have to describe when answering the questions during the interview.

14. You now have a good overview of the background information, summarised in two simple tables, probably less than two pages long. It is now time to start thinking about **the questions you may expect** during the interview.
15. **Start with reviewing the tasks** as given in the assignment (the bullet points, printed in bold at the bottom of the page) and think about possible questions related to these tasks. Think of listing and prioritising issues, proposals or recommendations to solve the issues, roadmaps, required resources, governance, budgets, etc.
16. Now look at the side issues as discovered in the sub-activities. Think of possible questions that may arise from the scenario, and how they will relate to EPSO's behavioural competencies (re-read Chapter 2 of this book).
17. Try to figure out your answers to all the questions you have listed in 15 and 16. Usually, there is not one single best answer. And don't think that you absolutely have to come up with the answer that the interviewer had in mind. **What is expected of you is that you can explain how you came up with this answer, the rationale.** On the flipside of the cover page, EPSO says that: "The problems have not been fully elaborated, information is partial, additional research is allowed, and candidates will be allowed to ask questions during the interview." This means that, if you make a hypothesis when thinking of an answer, or if you base your answer on additional research, you had better say this at the start of your answer. In this way you will display a positive indicator for analysis and problem solving.
18. Have another look at each page of the assignment and how each of them connects with your recommendations and priorities.

If you want to prepare for the questions that are not based on the assignment, then take a look at Annex 1 of this book. You will find hundreds of indicators for all the competencies they can use to assess your behaviour.

The Eisenhower matrix

Although it was Stephen Covey who made this method popular in his book *First Things First*, the concept is originally credited to US President Dwight D. Eisenhower. Whenever confronted with something that needed to be done, he would ask himself two questions: First, is the task important? Second, is it urgent? Based on this, the task would end up in one of four categories: important and urgent, important but not urgent, not important but urgent, and neither important nor urgent.

Obviously the first priority has to go to the tasks that are both important and urgent (quadrant No. 1 in the matrix in the figure opposite). However, what is not so obvious is that tasks labelled important but not urgent get the next priority (No. 2). This is what Eisenhower's point was all about: "What is important is seldom urgent and what is urgent is seldom important". Tasks that are in quadrant No. 3 are typical candidates for delegation, and the ones in No. 4 can even be dropped because they are neither urgent nor important, so why bother?

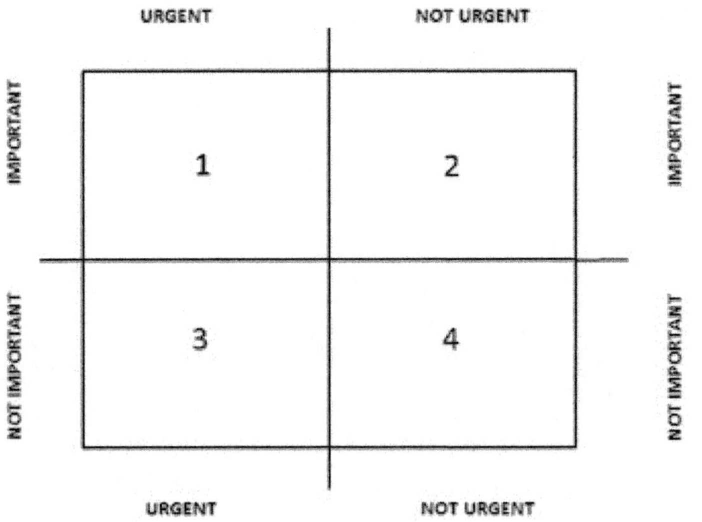

Key Points to Remember

- *The SCBI is not a mystery. It is a methodologically correct exercise that fits very well in the EPSO Assessment Centre test suite.*
- *It is possible to prepare very well for the interview, but this may take a lot of time. The good news is that you will get the time.*
- *You can ask for the support of an Assessment Centre coach, or participate in a dedicated workshop, to help fine-tune your answers for the interview.*

Notes:

....

....

....

....

....

11. Recruitment

You have passed the EPSO selection tests, and you are on the reserve list – congratulations! The next challenge is actually finding a job in the EU institutions. Unfortunately, many candidates think that passing an EPSO competition somehow guarantees a job, which is not the case. As EPSO's name suggests, they only do the "selection" process for suitable, "recruitable" candidates; they do not deal with the actual recruitment at all. It is up to the various EU institutions, and especially their human resources departments, to look into suitable candidates, interview them and eventually hire them.

More about "working for the EU"

This chapter is intended only as an introductory overview of some of the main issues involved in actually getting a job. It is a complex subject and there are many alternative pathways, some of them far from obvious. For a complete account – including alternative "ways in" if you don't succeed in your EPSO competition – you should read *Working for the EU: How to Get In* by Johannes de Berlaymont. Johannes (the nom de plume of a former senior insider) offers a wealth of advice and guidance, including many vital points not available in "official" EU sources. Make sure to read it!

Reserve List and Hiring

It may seem deeply frustrating and disappointing to discover that, having battled to get onto the reserve list, you are still not certain of actually getting a job. There are two points to consider here. One is that sometimes candidates themselves change their minds after being placed on the reserve list (because they take up a new career, their life circumstances change, they move to another country, etc.) and even if they are offered a job, they would no longer wish to take it. This obviously is a cost to the European taxpayer as, on average, EPSO spends several thousand euros per successful candidate and if they then do not end up being recruited by an EU institution, this is money wasted.

The other consideration is that some candidates, despite having all the necessary competencies, may not be fully suited for any specific job that is available in the year(s) after the publication of the reserve list. This can be due to personality, knowledge, "cultural fit" or other factors, or even poor interviewing skills. This might sound strange since everyone on the reserve list has demonstrated through the selection process that they possess the necessary skills and competencies, yet when it comes to a specific position, this may not always be sufficient.

That is why it is vital to understand that the process does not end at the moment you are placed on the reserve list. Instead another, very different, type of "competiton" starts, which is much like a "real" job hunt in the private sector. More details and tips follow in this chapter on how to make it a success.

Work Experience

While for AD5 competitions no work experience is required to apply (and for most AD5 competitions, even those in their last year of study are eligible, provided they do get their university degree by the cut-off date), this lack of such experience can be a hindrance when it comes to actual employment prospects.

A candidate's point of view

I have relevant work experience and I sent off dozens of job applications after I had been placed on the reserve list. I was invited to a couple of interviews, but unfortunately none landed me a job. It was quite frustrating as I didn't know what I was doing wrong: I'd passed the competition, was on the reserve list, and yet I couldn't succeed in securing a job. After some feedback, I realised that I took it for granted that I'd get a job once I was on the reserve list, and probably didn't present myself, both in my cover letters and at the interview, in the best possible way as if it was a "real" job interview, thinking it was more of a formality than an actual test. After realising this, I changed my approach, my CV and cover letter to better reflect how I could be useful for the given post, and managed to find a job fairly fast.

To counter-balance this, candidates need to convince potential interviewers such as Heads of Unit that, despite their lack of work experience, they possess the necessary skills and the right attitude to be hired for a job. Summer internships gained before you obtain your degree are formally not considered as work experience, but they can nevertheless become an important "selling point" in demonstrating your work ethic and domain-related experience even if you are a fresh graduate. Also, extra-curricular activities can be very useful as evidence of your ability to cope with employment even if it is your first real job.

In the following sections of this chapter, we will go through each step related to the recruitment phase, with tips and advice on how to make the most of it and find your dream job.

The Competency Passport

Whether you succeeded in the Assessment Centre or not, you will get detailed feedback on your performance there in the form of the competency passport. This document, with specific and personalised comments on how you did in each of the 7 or 8 competencies, is given to you with two goals. On the one hand, if you passed, it can serve as a baseline for your future professional development and also be used to help make a hiring decision when you interview for a specific post.

On the other hand, for those who failed the Assessment Centre, the competency passport lets you know exactly which competencies and skills you should improve in order to be successful next time. Even if you decide not to sit an EPSO competition again, the competency passport can be very helpful for your own development, independent of EPSO, as it provides honest and impartial feedback about your performance. Bear in mind that this feedback is about how you did in the Assessment Centre – it is not necessarily a final verdict on either what you are now or what you are capable of in the future. Whether it reflects very well or poorly on you, keep in mind that the assessors could only base their evaluation on how they perceived you through the various exercises you did on one particular day.

The competency passport, as you can see from the examples in Annex 8 of this book, includes a detailed account of how your final score was calculated, so it serves as a report card and a transparent feedback form. It also provides a "spider's web" chart of your competencies, as discussed in Chapter 2, and tells you how you compare to objective benchmarks, such as the pass mark.

Some candidates who fail are tempted to challenge the assessment and scores they have been given. You should be aware that this is futile unless a blatant violation of the rules happened (e.g. your linguistic skills in a language that was not required for the given competition were tested in the competency-based interview), but that is grounds for an official complaint rather than a request to review the evaluation. As many as four assessors have seen you in the Assessment Centre, and most likely two other markers have checked your case study essay, and between them they have come to the conclusion that you see in the competency passport. It may feel unfair, but challenging the verdict and being granted a re-evaluation is nearly impossible.

Once you are on the Reserve List

When you are informed that you have passed the competition, EPSO will let you know that your name will appear on the reserve list, which will be published in the EU's Official Journal. This not only formalises your achievement – it can also serve as a strong motivating factor that

Notes:

....

....

....

....

....

your success is publicly available for everyone to see: it shows you have what it takes to be an EU official.

The next step in the process is that your name, together with those of all other successful candidates, will be made available to EU institutions in an electronic database, along with your CV as it was uploaded in your EPSO profile. You have the opportunity to update your CV if your contact details or other elements have changed, and you will probably want to double check that it indeed reflects in the best possible way on you in order to maximise your chances of success.

The **period of validity** of the reserve list is an important factor to consider: the default rule is that the lists are valid for one year, given the fact that for generalist Administrator, Linguist and Assistant exams EPSO organises selection competitions once a year. On the other hand, for specialist competitions the lists are usually valid for three years as these are organised on an ad hoc basis. The validity is an important piece of information that is worth checking as EPSO will only prolong the validity of a list in exceptional cases. (This is usually when there are still many candidates on a list and they have not yet been hired because of lack of open positions in the EU institutions, and not because candidates are no longer interested or available.)

Another important issue to consider is that the EU institutions are asked, on a continuous basis, about their expected staffing needs in the next 1-3 years. This is the information on which EPSO bases its planning for how many places there should be on any given reserve list. Given that a certain percentage of candidates will *not* be hired from any given list, there is a careful balancing act that needs to be done between having a sufficient number of candidates on a list while not making successful candidates frustrated by raising false expectations if there aren't enough vacant posts available in a given year. Moreover, there are huge variations in the number of laureates who actually end up on a reserve list – for some specialist competitions, or for Linguist exams that aim at lesser-spoken languages like Maltese or Danish, there could actually be fewer laureates on the list than the number initially foreseen in the Notice of Competition. This is of course a lucky situation from the candidates' perspective as it creates an excess of demand over supply in the "market" so that, at least in principle, all laureates on the list can be hired.

Once you are on the reserve list (and in some cases, already at the time of application for an EU competition), you will be asked about your preferred EU institution to work for, or the policy area in which you'd like to work. This is by no means a guarantee that you will actually get a job in that institution or in that policy area, but it is still a factor to consider when institutions look at your CV and try to establish a match between their needs and your profile.

The Recruiter Portal

The institutions can find out which laureates are available for recruitment via the so-called Recruiter Portal. (This has replaced the old "flagging" system.) The Recruiter Portal shows whether a candidate is "Available", "Not Available" or "Recruited".

The Recruiter Portal allows recruiters to search for candidates using multiple criteria and across different lists of laureates. It has been one of the factors in ensuring a closer match between the number of laureates selected and the numbers actually recruited – previously there were often too many laureates for the jobs available in the institutions, causing frustration to candidates and waste of money for the EU. Laureates, through their own portal, are also able to see what vacancies (though not all) may be available.

What do I do to Find a Position?

In theory, initiation of recruitment should always come from the EU institutions and not the candidates – though the actual practice can be different.

When the institutions contact you

The institutions have access to the list of available candidates for any given vacancy. However, the first objective precondition is that the level at which an institution wants to fill a post needs to correspond to the level of the competition you succeeded in. In practical terms this means that if a vacancy is available at AD7-AD12 level, only those candidates can be considered that have succeeded at a competition of AD7 or above. In such cases, even if your profile matches the vacancy 100% but you succeeded in an AD5 competition, institutions cannot make an exception.

Another important issue to bear in mind is that the **order of priority**, when it comes to recruiting, is a formal rule of the EU Staff Regulations. Internal candidates – i.e. officials working for the institutions already and wishing to transfer to the new post – have preference, and those working in the vacant post's institution have an even higher priority. This may sound discouraging, but from the institution's perspective it makes sense to check if they can fill a post via internal recruitment before hiring new staff.

Finally, when EPSO organises an **internal competition**, which usually happens once every 2-3 years, its laureates are eligible for posts as well. Since they are, by definition, officials and temporary agents who already work for the institutions (otherwise they would not be eligible to participate in the internal competition), they have a higher priority to be hired than external laureates.

Over recent years a cumulative staff cut of 5% has been required from all EU institutions, which made them even more likely to seek suitable candidates internally first. On a more positive note, the EU institutions have still been hiring about 1000 new staff each year despite the cuts because of staff turnover and retirement. When the institutions send EPSO their planned staffing needs to establish the number of places on a reserve list, they have become more realistic or conservative in their estimates. This is partly bad news as it intensifies the competition (fewer places on the reserve list), but also good news as those who do make it to the reserve list have a much better chance of getting hired eventually.

Bear in mind that for any given vacancy there are likely to be dozens of candidates who apply. Some will clearly have no chance of being hired as their profile may be vastly different (e.g. a biologist applying to deal with competition law), while others may not correspond to all the selection criteria for the given post (e.g. security clearance is needed, or experience in data protection that they may lack). On the other hand, this is the point at which you

Notes:

need to convince the employer – in most cases a Head of Unit and a few others involved in the recruitment process – that you are the most suitable candidate for the post.

Recently, EPSO has initiated a new process whereby the institutions make some, though not necessarily all, of their vacancies available for laureates of open competitions. This way you can see in your EPSO profile the list of open positions where institutions accept "external" candidates who are on a reserve list. This is the easiest way to learn about open positions, though of course this information is available to all other candidates on the list so there could be fierce competition. Moreover, sometimes a given unit or institution's HR unit will contact you directly if they have a suitable vacancy and they have pre-screened your profile and concluded that you could potentially be a good fit for the position.

When you contact the institutions

Apart from waiting for the institutions to either make these posts available or contact you directly, there is also an **internal list of vacancies** published on the intranet of EU institutions.

In any case, it is definitely a good idea to be proactive and contact Heads of Unit in areas you are targeting for employment. Note, however, that the "machine gun" approach of firing off CVs to anyone and everyone you can find in the EU Who-is-who will certainly not work. You need to be focused in your approach.

Whenever you send off an application, make sure to include a covering letter. This does not necessarily have to be a separate document but could be simply a well-crafted email to which you attach your CV. (For the EU institutions, using the Europass format is often required. Even where this is not explicitly asked for, make sure you use a structured and well-presented format.) In your covering letter, you can also include (for example) a hyperlink to your LinkedIn profile if you have one, for additional information and to showcase any endorsement or recommendation that it may include.

It is vital that you mention, either in the subject line or at the very beginning of the email, that you are a laureate of XYZ competition and that you are on a reserve list. You may also wish to provide a hyperlink to the Official Journal in which your name appears, in order to substantiate your claim – even though, as soon as your application is seriously considered, the first thing the Head of Unit or HR staff will do is double check your name in the electronic database of eligible candidates.

In your covering letter, make sure to highlight all the elements that make you suitable for the job concerned; if you have the detailed job description, you can explicitly connect your academic and professional achievements to the requirements for that job so as to reinforce the idea that you are indeed a suitable candidate.

One of the most common mistakes candidates make is that they talk too much about their skills and achievements without actually linking them to the specific job they are applying for. Instead of saying, for example, that "My expertise in project management can prove helpful in your unit as I understand the EU financial regulations and how to run multiple accounts at the same time", they might say "I have extensive experience in project management and running multiple accounts at the same time". The latter does not connect the skill set with the need, and therefore it requires the reader (the potential employer) to establish such a link for themselves, something which easily doesn't happen given the limited time spent on looking at any given application. If you do this mental shortcut for them, your chances of raising their interest level and inviting you for an interview increase significantly.

Moreover, the rules and best practices listed for the case study apply here as well: a good visual presentation of both your covering letter and your CV are essential for success. Bullet points, moderately but strategically used; highlights or links in the covering email; short and well-defined paragraphs; an overall 100-150-word length – all can add a lot to your application.

The best approach is to try to think with the recruiter's head. Imagine for a second that it is *you* on the receiving end. You announce an internal vacancy and receive several dozen applications both from inside and outside the institutions. You probably don't know 90% of the applicants and therefore don't know whether or not they are really the reliable, trustworthy professionals they claim to be. They need to validate these claims, at the minimum by sending you a professionally written message that immediately demonstrates the excellent drafting skills they claim to have.

As you read through these messages and CVs, a number of questions come to mind that you expect to be answered; otherwise you are likely going to reject or ignore those applications. Some of these are listed below:

- Is the candidate formally eligible for this post?
- Is he or she on a reserve list that matches the job profile, seniority and grade?
- Do they speak the required languages?
- Is their job experience relevant to the specific tasks they would need to do in this role?
- Which specific elements of their profile would fully correspond to the tasks?
- Do they have the right skills that were spelled out in the vacancy notice, or those that were not written there but are implied by the job description?
- Do they have good team working, communication and diplomatic skills? (This can be seen in the competency passport but it's still good to reiterate here.)
- Do they have any EU experience, and if not, which parts of their experience would be similar to what I am seeking?
- Will it take a long time for them to get started in the job, and once they get started, will they need to learn a lot before they become autonomous and operational?
- Are they available for an interview in person, or they would need to travel from far away (which may add complexity, time and administrative burden to the hiring, and unless they are a stellar candidate, others may be more accessible)?
- Do they have the right attitude and "cultural fit" for our unit?
- Are they extroverts, or more analytical, or both, depending on what I am seeking?
- If they already work for one of the institutions, is their current job relevant to the new post? Do they have anyone as a reference I could speak to?
- What is their nationality and gender? In theory these are not factors but in practice they often are.

Notes:

....

....

....

....

....

If you manage to answer or take away these "anxieties" in the covering letter and the CV, you will have a much better chance of being invited to an interview. As mentioned above, many candidates only give a "static" description of their strengths and experiences, without directly linking these to the specific requirements of the job. The most important principle here is to answer the question: "how can you be an asset to my team?"

A good approach can be to carefully analyse your covering email and weed out sentences that start with "I", turning them into sentences that follow the formula of "My [experience/personal trait/knowledge] can contribute to your unit's work by [mention how]." In every paragraph this link must be apparent, otherwise the covering letter will fail to stand out or to establish you as a highly relevant candidate in the eyes of the person doing the recruiting.

Finally, in thinking about which EU institution or body to apply to, consider Table 10.1, outlining the number of staff, place of work and kind of profiles that are typically sought in those institutions (excluding the EU agencies, which are scattered around the Member States and recruit a mix of generalist and highly specialised staff). Obviously, there are many exceptions and even if you have an atypical background, e.g. in natural

Name of EU institution	*Staff (only officials and temporary agents, approximate numbers)*	*Place of work*	*Type of profile sought*
European Parliament	5500	Brussels, Luxembourg, Strasbourg	Lawyers, IT, Economists, Political scientists, Assistants, Translators, Interpreters
Council of the EU	3100	Brussels	Lawyers, Lawyer-linguists, Assistants, Event managers, Translators, IT
European Commission	32000	Brussels, Luxembourg	Lawyers, IT, Economists, Scientists, Translators, Finance experts, Assistants
European External Action Service	n/a, about 60% of staff are EU officials, others are seconded by member states	Brussels; 144 delegations around the world	Diplomats, political scientists
Court of Justice of the EU	2000	Luxembourg	Lawyers, Lawyer-linguists, Interpreters, Assistants, IT
European Court of Auditors	1000	Luxembourg	Auditors, Translators, Assistants, Administrative staff
European Ombudsman	70	Brussels, Strasbourg	Lawyers
European Data Protection Supervisor	50	Brussels	Lawyers, Data protection experts
European Economic and Social Committee	800	Brussels	Lawyers, Economists, Translators, Scientists, IT, Assistants
Committee of Regions	500	Brussels	Lawyers, Economists,Translators, Scientists, IT, Assistants

Table 10.1 Where to find a job and for which profiles (excluding agencies)

sciences, that can easily prove to be an asset as it makes you stand out and you can offer to provide a different mindset or a better understanding of technical matters than other candidates.

The Job Interview

When *that* phone call or email comes and you are invited to an interview, this means you have been shortlisted along with 4-5, sometimes 6-8 other candidates.

The way the interviews are organised can differ from one institution to another, or even from one DG to another. It is nevertheless required that there is a panel of at least two persons (in most cases there are actually three) who interview you, one of them almost certainly being the Head of Unit. For some high-profile posts, there could even be two or three rounds of interviews: once you pass the first one with the panel, the Director or even the Director General of the DG may want to vet you too before you are offered the post.

The interview itself, however, is not structured or streamlined across the institutions. It can be partly competency-based (just like it was in the Assessment Centre, with the difference that here it will not be directly linked to specific competencies) or "classic", where they ask you questions in no particular order about your academic, professional and other achievements, your interest in the job, and may even probe your professional knowledge (e.g. where sectoral policy or technical knowledge would be necessary).

It is in any case a very good idea to check the relevant DG's organisational chart and see where the unit fits in and who they report to, and also to look into the activities of the DG as a whole. Generally speaking, annual reports make for boring reading – but in this situation they can be a goldmine of information so you know all the right names and terminology for the work and programmes the DG or institution has been involved with in the preceding year.

Many of the tips in the previous chapters about the oral presentation and group exercise are relevant to how you should act, listen and interact with the interviewers. And keep in mind the points mentioned earlier about the covering letter: in the face-to-face interview, underlining the link between your profile and the requirements of the job is vital to success.

Make sure to prepare one or two questions that you can ask either during or after the interview as they will likely invite you to do so anyway. Generic questions such as "when will you know the results?" are practical but they don't contribute to a better impression about you. Rather, think of something that is related to the job, but be careful not to ask something that you would be expected to know from your preparation for the interview or from their very own website.

Notes:

....

....

....

....

....

Is it the Right Job for Me?

In terms of your long-term career prospects and your job satisfaction, try to identify the sort of job that best fits your personality.

Are you more of an organiser type or an analytical type? This is an over-simplification, of course, and quite a basic way of approaching your personality type. However, some people are more inclined to be an organiser type, where they are more "agile" and like fast moving workplace situations, and others are more the analytical or "PhD-type", who would rather go deep into a given file.

If you consider jobs that require a lot of analysis, maybe in legal affairs or as a translator or lawyer-linguist, analytical types get more satisfaction and tend to stay longer in these jobs than organisers. At the same time, even these jobs have lot of organisational issues to handle, such as managing stakeholder contacts, research projects or on-site visits. Therefore just because a unit or DG deals with a given topic, don't prematurely decide whether or not it is the right fit for you.

The other thing to consider is whether you prefer a "flat" or a "hierarchical" organisation. If you feel more comfortable in a relatively flat organisation, then smaller EU bodies may be a better fit for you as there is less hierarchy in these than in, say, the European Commission.

Another point to consider is whether, if a job opportunity comes up, you simply look at its immediate attractiveness (e.g. how much it pays) or whether you want to think longer-term about its fit with the CV you are trying to build. Would the job contribute to a consistent, coherent profile of the sort you want? Or would it be instead just a short-term opportunity and maybe not such a good fit when it comes to your overall profile and the impression it would give to a potential future employer? Your own circumstances will dictate what you do in such a situation, but it is a good idea to try to step back and take an overview of this sort so you can act in a measured way.

You may also recall our reference to Daniel Pink, in the competency based interview chapter, about the three key factors in job satisfaction: autonomy, mastery and purpose. These are important considerations as even within the EU institutions these factors can vary to a great extent, depending on which job you do.

Location can also be a key consideration. The working environment of cosmopolitan Brussels, at the heart of EU politics and policy making, is, for example, very different from Luxembourg, where most of the jobs are in "back office" roles. Your personal tastes, aspirations, career goals and perhaps family commitments will all be relevant issues.

Finally, an important comment on strategy: sometimes it is worth accepting a job offer that may not be 100% your dream job, but is nonetheless a good entry point to the institutions. As you are most probably planning for the long-term, and given the fact that you can switch jobs while keeping your administrative grade (and hence your salary) even when going to another EU institution and DG, you can transit into a new position after 2-3 years. It is indeed a bit of a gamble to refuse an offer when you get one, hoping that a better option comes along, so it is best only to do so only if you are absolutely certain that the job in question is not for you. Generally speaking, it is far better to "get in" first because it is far easier to build a career once you are already "inside".

A recruiter's point of view

Sure, I will consider your qualifications, but what I am really looking for goes far beyond that.

I want to work with people I like and who like me. A candidate who makes a great first impression and sparks a real connection instantly becomes a big fish in a very small short-list pond. You may have solid qualifications, but if I don't think I'll enjoy working with you, I'm probably not going to hire you.

I want you to stand out. A sad truth of interviewing is that later I often don't recall, unless I refer to my notes, a significant amount about some of the candidates. The more people I interview for a job, the more likely I am to remember a candidate by impressions rather than by a long list of facts. I will remember you by "hooks" – whether flattering or unflattering – so use that to your advantage. Your hook could be your clothing, or an outside interest, or an unusual fact about your life or career. Instead of letting me choose, give me one or two notable ways to remember you.

I need to know whether I should hire you, but just as importantly I need you to make sure my job is a good fit for you. So I want you to ask questions. You are the only person who knows what makes you tick. I don't. There's no other way to really know whether you want the job unless you ask questions.

I know you want a positive work-life balance, but let us first find out if you're the right person for the job, and whether the tasks, responsibilities, duties, etc. are right for you. Then we can talk about the rest.

I also appreciate a brief follow-up note. A follow-up note is nice. But "nice" may not separate you from the pack. What I really like is when you follow up based on something we discussed. The more closely you listened during the interview, the easier it is to think of ways to follow up in a natural and unforced way.

Remember, we're starting a relationship – and every relationship is based on genuine interactions.

Working for the EU

There is nothing wrong with being curious about certain – more delicate – aspects of working for a future employer, yet many people are afraid to ask. When informing yourself about working for the EU you don't need to worry about this, because everything is out there, in the open. The EU as an employer makes no secret of the salaries, the working conditions or other things that affect their employees in their well-being at work. In fact, all the information you need to know is written down in the Staff Regulations. However, this is a typical EU legal docu-

Notes:

....

....

....

....

....

ment, which means that it is very complete but can be difficult for the uninitiated reader to understand. This is why you will find straightforward answers to some common questions below.

Remuneration

Before considering the question of your future remuneration, keep in mind that the EU's career system consists of a single pay scale with 16 grades. Within this pay scale, Assistants (AST) can occupy grades 1 – 11, Secretaries/Clerks (AST/SC) can occupy grades 1-6 and Administrators (AD) can occupy grades 5 – 16.

Each grade has five "seniority steps": you automatically advance through these steps according to your seniority as an EU employee. You move up one step every two years until you are promoted to the next grade or until you reach the last step in the grade. The very top grade (AD 16) has just three seniority steps.

EPSO open competitions are generally organised at specific grades between 5 and 8 for ADs, or 1 and 3 for ASTs. On rare occasions, EPSO organises a competition for senior grades (AD9 – AD12). As a newly recruited official you will be appointed to the grade set out in the Notice of Competition for the competition you took part in.

When you are first recruited you will normally be put on the first step of the grade to which you have been appointed. However, your professional experience is taken into account if it goes beyond the minimum period required in the Notice of Competition, and this may result in classification in the second step of the grade.

Basic monthly salaries range from around €2,300 per month for a newly recruited AST1 official to €18,300 per month for a newly appointed top level AD16 official. The complete salary table is available in the Staff Regulations (Article 66).

The basic monthly salary is just the starting point. To know how much you will get, you then have to add the allowances you may be entitled to, minus social security contributions (pension, health and accident insurance) and other taxes (income tax and a special EU levy). If you have left your home country to come and work for the EU, you are entitled to an expatriation allowance equivalent to 16% of your basic salary. Some family-related allowances are available to EU officials according to their family situation. These include a household allowance, a dependent child allowance, an educational allowance and a pre-school allowance. These allowances can help to cover the costs of looking after a family while working for an international organisation.

You will be exempt from national taxes on salaries, wages and emoluments paid by the EU as laid down in the Protocol on the privileges and immunities of the European Communities.

To give you a more concrete idea of what you would earn as an EU official there is a handy calculator available at https://eutraining.eu/salary-calculator. This tool only gives you an approximation of the real salary because there are many other things that are not factored in, but you'll get the idea.

Flexible working environment

Telework and flexitime were introduced in 2007 as part of the institutions' modernisation. These flexible working arrangements give employees more freedom in the organisation of working time by making use of information technology. They focus on results-based management and objective-driven performance, which do not necessarily require staff to be physically present in the office. While in most cases only a limited number of staff are usually granted telework, it largely depends on the actual job whether or not this is allowed or feasible (e.g. if your job requires regular contacts with the European Parliament or other institutions, most in-person meetings cannot be substituted by conference calls instead of joining a Parliamentary committee meeting).

Leave and absences

EU officials are entitled to annual leave of 24 working days. On top of this entitlement, you may also be granted leave for time spent travelling between your home country and the place where you work. In addition to annual leave, there are rules for special leave for marriage, moving house, death of relatives or serious illnesses, births, etc. In exceptional circumstances, you may also apply for unpaid leave on personal grounds.

Personal life

A range of measures is in place to help ensure that working for the EU is conductive to a healthy professional, personal and family life. These measures focus on parental and compassionate leave, a solid infrastructure of childcare and schooling and modern working arrangements. In particular, mothers are entitled to 20 weeks maternity leave and fathers 10 days paternity leave on the normal salary, while 6 months parental leave per child is available on a basic monthly allowance.

There are many leisure, sports and cultural clubs open to EU staff and their families, including athletics, dance, theatre, art and language exchange.

Sickness insurance

As an EU official, you and your family are entitled to benefit from the Joint Sickness Insurance Scheme (JSIS) of the European Communities, which covers medical expenses at a reimbursement rate of 80% for most kinds of treatment (subject to maximum limits). You are also covered by accident insurance and insurance against occupational diseases. The Joint Sickness Insurance Scheme is funded through a contribution of about 2% of the basic monthly salary from each official. You are also required to undergo a preventive medical check-up every year.

Career path

If you start at the Commission, for example, you will do so as a "probationary" official. At the end of a 9-month initial period, a report on your performance will be drawn up. If you successfully complete the probationary period, you will be established as a "permanent" official. Like all other officials, your performance will continue to be assessed regularly in the annual staff appraisal exercise, which has a direct influence on the progress of your career, including promotion to the next grade in the salary scale.

Officials who join the EU in the

Notes:

Assistant category can pass to the Administrator category by following the "certification" procedure. This allows selected staff that have demonstrated the right potential to follow a set of mandatory training modules and sit final exams. If they succeed, they are able to apply for AD posts. However, this is not a straightforward process and candidates aiming at AD-level jobs are well advised to prioritise AD-level competitions.

Where will I work?

The answer to this question depends entirely on which bit of the EU you work for, as the EU institutions, bodies and agencies are quite widely dispersed. However, over the years Brussels has become the primary centre, leading to it being colloquially referred to as "the capital of the EU". By far the greatest proportion of Commission jobs are in Brussels. So, too, are a lot of the European Parliament jobs, though many "back-office" and translator jobs are in Luxembourg. In round figures, the distribution of EU officials looks like this:

Brussels	72%
Luxembourg	13%
Member States	10%
Outside EU	5%

As mentioned above, if you leave your home country to come and work for the EU, you are entitled to an expatriation allowance equivalent to 16% of your basic salary.

Retirement

It may appear a bit premature to talk about retirement at the stage when you have not even been recruited, but especially for those who have already built a career and are not "first-jobbers" in any sense, this may be an important issue to consider before making the decision to work for the EU.

It is impossible to predict the future, especially when this is 20, 30 years from now. Our society is changing rapidly and the EU institutions are no exception to that. Two reforms (2004 and 2013) of the Staff Regulations prove this point. Hence, it is only possible to describe the situation as of today, without making any assumptions for the future.

EU officials in service before 1 January 2014 retire at 65 and EU officials recruited after 1 January 2014 retire at 66. However, it is possible to take early retirement with a reduced pension from the age of 58, or to work up until the age of 67 or, exceptionally, until the age of 70.

Pensions are paid as a percentage of the final basic salary. Officials accumulate 1.8% pension rights every year and are entitled to a maximum pension of 70% of their final basic salary. Whilst working at the EU, your contribution to the pension scheme will correspond to 10.3% of your basic salary.

As mentioned before, the average age of entry for AD5 (entry-level) staff in the Commission is 34 years old, and of course this means that some are starting at significantly older ages than this. Your age at entry, therefore, will determine how "complete" a career you have in terms of pension rights. Most importantly, of course, your final grade and step at the moment of your retirement will determine your final basic salary and therefore pension entitlements.

Staff can apply to transfer pension rights they already have from a previous job or as a self-employed person. Similarly, you can also transfer the pension rights you gain while working at the EU into another pension fund.

It is important to note that the transfer of pension rights is not mandatory; within 2 years from your appointment you can decide to do this or not. Very often, especially when you have been working in the private sector before, or if you have been self-employed, this transfer is not interesting, because the accumulated amount is converted into an "equivalent" number of years of contribution and this figure can be very disappointing. Under these circumstances it can be beneficial to aim for a "mixed" pension; one part being paid on the basis of your previous career and the other part by the EU.

Key points to remember

- *Being on a reserve list is a necessary but not sufficient condition to be recruited by the EU institutions*
- *You have to be proactive in your search for a job at the EU, much like you would be in looking for any other job*
- *You have to keep your CV and EPSO file up-to-date*
- *Inform yourself thoroughly about the future employer, and the position that is offered before going to the interview*
- *A job interview is a "sales" operation; use all your objective and subjective arguments to convince the employer that you are the best candidate for the position*

Notes:

....

....

....

....

....

12. What if You're Not on the Reserve List?

"You may have to fight a battle more than once to win it", *Margaret Thatcher*

Introduction

This very short chapter has been in many ways the most difficult one for us, the authors, to write. After all the information and advice we have been giving you throughout this book, with the express intention to help you through the Assessment Centre and put you on a reserve list, we are very sorry if you didn't make it. We thought, however, that it was our duty to write a "complete" book on the EPSO Assessment Centre, and to give you a bit of advice – and moral support – in the unlucky situation where you do not make it to the reserve list.

Resilience

Previously, we have defined resilience as an individual's ability to adapt to stress and adversity. Individuals demonstrate resilience when they face difficult experiences and rise above them – or "bounce back".

It goes without saying that not making it to the reserve list is a difficult experience. You have put a lot of time and effort into this, and it is absolutely normal that you will be disappointed at this stage. It is a mistake to think that people who are resilient experience no negative emotions or thoughts and display optimism in all situations. That is rarely the case. The truth remains, however, that resilience is demonstrated by individuals who can overcome disappointments, finding ways of navigating their way around negative experiences and using effective methods of coping with them. Sometimes candidates indeed very effectively demonstrate their resilience competency by coming back to the Assessment Centre, in another competition, and this time succeeding.

Think How to Make the Most of it

You should keep the thought that you are one of the few to have made it to the Assessment Centre. Most of the participants in your competition didn't make it that far. They were either not admitted on formal grounds, or they were eliminated from the competition during the pre-selection phase. It is an achievement in itself to have got as far as you did.

There is absolutely no reason for self-doubt, or a dip in your self-esteem. You have proven that – at least intrinsically – you have what it takes to become an EU official. Consider that from a small town of say 10,000 people, somewhere in Europe, on average only one will become an EU official (there are roughly 50,000 people working for the institutions compared to a total population of 500 million). The fact that you were invited to the Assessment Centre means that your dream of becoming that one person has been seriously considered.

The EPSO competitions are exactly what the name says: *competitions*. Only the very best win. You could compare them with the Olympic games: only the very best (at that given moment in time) make it to the podium. This doesn't mean that the others are bad athletes. On the contrary, they were the best in their country, but they didn't make it to the podium. What is more, the athlete who didn't get among the medals still has a chance of coming back to the Olympics and succeeding on another occasion.

You Have Learnt a Lot

There is at the very least one positive outcome to your endeavour of participating in an EPSO competition: you will have learnt a lot.

First of all, you have learnt a lot about yourself. You are now aware of the fact that you are actually capable of doing this. You are smart enough, skilled enough and motivated enough to try it again another time, with the right preparation and building on your experience.

In your competency passport EPSO will have given you an overview of your strong points, your relative weaknesses and the ways to further develop yourself. Much like an Olympic athlete you know where to improve so that you can compete better during the next games. Take what the competency pasport says seriously, and don't just ignore the things it says that you prefer not to hear. It is the work of a team of experienced assessors who have done their best to evaluate you as systematically and as objectively as possible. Most people have never had the opportunity of such a thorough inde-

Notes:

pendent review of their work-related strengths and weaknesses, so take the chance to learn and benefit from it.

You have experienced first hand how the EU selects staff. From the exercises you have had a glimpse of what working for the EU looks like, feels like. This is very important, because you now know exactly what is expected.

A candidate's point of view

Maybe my professional profile is not suitable for the EU and EPSO made an error when inviting me for the Assessment Centre. Or maybe I had a bad day when I was being assessed. Or maybe I am simply unlucky. But maybe, the best answer is another one: I was a bit naïve. If I asked around I would have found out what is expected at the Assessment Centre and I would have prepared accordingly. I may actually go for a temporary/contractual/AST competition, just to get into an Institution. Once you are an EU official of any type and grade it is probably much easier to secure your dream job, through internal mobility, promotion or even another competition. The more routes I try, the more chance I have to become an EU official.

Consider Your Options

After your (first) EPSO experience you may have come to the conclusion that a position in the EU is not after all what you were really dreaming of. You may have had the wrong idea about what it is like. This happens, and there's nothing to be ashamed of.

On the other hand, if you are still convinced that an EU career is really something for you, you could consider taking another competition than the one you did this time. Walt Disney put it this way: "The difference between winning and losing is most often not quitting."

Think about what sort of competition you should apply for. If you apply for a generalist competition (like AD5 Public Administration), while the number of jobs on offer may be relatively large, the number of candidates will likely be enormous. Even though the numbers will be whittled down for the Assessment Centre to a ratio of maybe 2.5 candidates per available post, EPSO is selecting from a very large pool. So consider if there are any more specialised competitions you might apply for, where the pool isn't so large, and the competition might be less fierce at the Assessment Centre.

A point to highlight is that whatever score you got in the Assessment Centre (as in the pre-selection) is only relevant to the competition in question and has no impact on any other competition you may take part in. **Your results are not carried forward from one competition to another, either officially or unoffically**. Therefore there is no penalty whatsoever in not succeding the first time. If you come back to the Assessment Centre a second or third time you always start with a clean slate – all the while having much more experience and insight about the exam itself, giving you every chance of improving your scores.

Finally, do bear in mind that there are other "ways in" to the EU administration that do not involve the formal Assessment Centre route. Indeed these positions are becoming ever more frequent as the EU administration tries to balance the constant upward political pressure to "do more" with the constant downward pressure on budget and headcount. There is a great deal on the topic of "other ways in" in the book *Working for the EU: How to Get* In by Johannes de Berlaymont.

Most important of these roles are the so-called **Contract Agent for Specific Tasks (CAST)** positions. The CAST (Permanent) selection process is different from the "regular" EPSO open competitions because although EPSO is involved in the selection process there is no Assessment Centre, and only a limited number of pre-selected candidates will be tested via the computer based tests (CBTs). Submitting an application does not mean that you will automatically be invited to sit the CBTs. Only candidates shortlisted by the recruiters will be invited to sit the selection tests when a vacancy arises. If you pass the selection tests, you will be invited to recruitment tests organised by the recruiting services. Such tests will comprise an interview and optionally other forms of evaluation. It is up to the recruiters to determine exactly which interviews and evaluation tests you will have to undergo, and some of these tests may be very similar to the ones described in this book.

Likewise **temporary agent** positions are available. The EU institutions and agencies have a limited number of posts in their "establishment plan". This is fixed on a yearly basis by the Budget Authority and it is part of the annual budget (so there is a corresponding amount of money available to pay the salaries and other staff-related expenditures). There are many reasons why the establishment plan cannot be filled up completely. Often, the reason is that the institution simply doesn't find a permanent official (in-house, from another institution or on the reserve lists), then they will try to fill the post with a temporary agent. These vacancies are usually published on the EPSO website, but the selection procedure is carried out entirely by the institution or agency. The word "temporary" can be a bit misleading as these posts can be for up to six years and in practice it is not uncommon for them to be used as "stepping stones" to permanent jobs.

Working in these sorts of roles will give you the opportunity to find out whether the EU administration is a good match for you, or not. Having worked for the institutions for a couple of years will also, inevitably, give you an advantage over other candidates in any further competitions you enter, because you will have a better idea of how the EU works, and what it expects from its employees. The fact that you got to the Assessment Centre shows that the CBT tests are not your problem – and a period of working other than as a permanent official may well be the way to polish up the interpersonal and other soft skills where you maybe fell short at the Assessment Centre. And, for sure, you will be able to be more confident if and when you do get that permanent job.

You can consult the currently vacant positions at https://epso.europa.eu/apply/job-offers_en. If you are interested in an even wider range of EU Affairs jobs you can also go to https://www.linkedin.com/groups/3934764.

Notes:

Key Points to Remember

- *It is not a sign of failure if you are not on the Reserve list. The fact that you made it to the Assessment Centre shows you have what it takes to become an EU official but some other candidates just happened to be judged stronger than you in that particular competition*
- *You will have learnt a lot about the EU, the competitions, and especially about yourself, and this will be useful for the rest of your career, inside or outside the EU administration*
- *You can always try again and there are plenty of other opportunities to build an interesting career with the EU*

Annex 1 Competencies, anchors and indicators

Note: This Annex should be read in conjunction with Chapter 2, which explains the EPSO competency framework.

You can also carry out a free self-assessment of your competencies using the online tool created for *The Ultimate EU Career Development Book*, at https://www.johnharper-publishing.co.uk/the-ultimate-eu-career-development-toolkit/

Analysis and Problem Solving

Anchors

1. Analyses and prioritises situations to identify and solve problems.
2. Solutions increase efficiency and improve quality.
3. Involves others in solving problems and making decisions.
4. Factors organisational goals into decisions.
5. Makes clear, transparent and timely decisions.
6. Dealing with complexity.
7. Identifying the relevant aspects from a mass of information.
8. Proposing useful and practical solutions.
9. Gathering information from various sources and critically evaluating it.
10. Using judgement and analysis to find solutions to problems.

Indicators

	UNSATISFACTORY	IMPROVEMENT NEEDED	MEETS EXPECTATIONS	EXCEEDS EXPECTATIONS	EXCEPTIONAL
anchor	1 - Extremely Weak 2 - Very Weak	3 - Weak 4 - Fair	5 - Satisfactory 6 - Good	7 - Strong 8 - Very Strong	9 - Excellent 10 - Outstanding
1.	Has difficulty distinguishing between critical and non-critical issues. Loses focus when resolving larger issues. Misunderstands or misinterprets key elements of information.	Needs help with analysing and prioritising problems. Tends to focus on simple operational issues.	Solves urgent, high impact problems first.	Analyses and prioritises critical problems. Stays focused on critical problems until they are successfully resolved.	Analyses and prioritises critical problems accurately and quickly. Maintains a sense of urgency in solving even complex problems.

Analysis and Problem Solving Indicators – continued

	UNSATISFACTORY	IMPROVEMENT NEEDED	MEETS EXPECTATIONS	EXCEEDS EXPECTATIONS	EXCEPTIONAL
anchor	1 - Extremely Weak 2 - Very Weak	3 - Weak 4 - Fair	5 - Satisfactory 6 - Good	7 - Strong 8 - Very Strong	9 - Excellent 10 - Outstanding
2.	Rarely proposes innovative solutions. Produces 'quick fixes' that do not yield lasting or quality results.	Proposes solutions that are usually short-term. Is rarely transformative in terms of greater efficiency and/or improved quality.	Finds solutions that effectively address issues and are easily sustainable.	Finds solutions that change the workplace both in terms of increasing efficiency and enhancing the quality of products and services. Makes processes more efficient.	Finds solutions that consistently transform the workplace. Delivers products and services that improve quality significantly.
3.	Rarely collaborates with peers and stakeholders. Doesn't look for more efficient ways to do things.	Collaborates with others only when asked to. Prefers to solve problems independently.	Collaborates effectively with others to solve problems and make decisions.	Is highly collaborative in terms of seeking input to solve problems and make decisions.	Consistently and effectively seeks input from all peers and stakeholders. Is agile and decisive.
4.	Makes decisions that have minimal or no impact in terms of improving the quality of products and services, or in aligning with department goals.	Makes decisions that focus on immediate, short-term issues, losing sight of larger departmental goals and initiatives.	Keeps organisational and departmental goals in mind when solving problems and making decisions.	Makes decisions and takes actions that align with organisational and departmental goals and initiatives.	Always has 'big picture' in mind and helps others see it. Consistently aligns decisions and actions with organisational and departmental goals and initiatives.
5.	Has difficulty articulating rationale for decisions. Often defers decision-making to others.	Makes decisions that are sometimes not clear. Tends to put off decisions on more complex issues.	Makes sound decisions based on facts and experience.	Makes decisions that consistently support and facilitate desired outcomes.	Consistently makes clear, transparent, and timely decisions. Makes decisions that consistently align with organisational and departmental goals.
6.	Does not gather a sufficiently clear picture of the problems in their full complexity. Omits important facts and details from analysis.	Captures the global picture but misses a number of important details.	Understands and summarises the main issues involved.	Understands the problem and links up the elements. Takes on board all the available information and fits everything together.	Analyses and interprets the available data correctly and completely. Gives a concise and systematic overview of the situation.

Analysis and Problem Solving Indicators – continued

	UNSATISFACTORY	IMPROVEMENT NEEDED	MEETS EXPECTATIONS	EXCEEDS EXPECTATIONS	EXCEPTIONAL
anchor	1 - Extremely Weak 2 - Very Weak	3 - Weak 4 - Fair	5 - Satisfactory 6 - Good	7 - Strong 8 - Very Strong	9 - Excellent 10 - Outstanding
7.	Is overwhelmed by high volumes of information and gets lost. Focuses more on the superfluous than the essential.	Misses logical links between items of information. Is distracted by side issues.	Tackles main problems and is not distracted by secondary issues. Distinguishes between relevant and less relevant information.	Simplifies the complex without neglecting key issues or details that matter.	Differentiates clearly between the relative importance of the different issues.
8.	Proposes solutions that do not tackle main issues to be addressed. Proposes solutions that contain elements used as justification for rejecting alternative options.	Proposes solutions that are impractical because of their implications. Proposes solutions that do not take all the factors into account.	Proposes reasonable but not particularly visionary solutions. Proposes workable solutions.	Proposes solutions that deal effectively with all aspects of the problem. Proposes solutions that exceed the expectations of the stakeholders.	Consistently proposes solutions that reflect a balanced analysis and sound judgement.
9.	Does not identify inconsistencies or contradictions in available information. Bases analysis on information from only a few of the available sources.	Is more descriptive than analytical in approach.	Takes into account different sources of information available. Compares and contrasts information drawn from different sources.	Analyses problems by comparing and contrasting drawn from all available sources.	Refers to the available sources and assesses the relative significance of each one. Identifies and resolves inconsistencies or contradictions in available information.
10.	Relies more on intuition than on analysis. Ignores options that should be explored.	Makes proposals without thinking through their implications. Does not make a convincing case for their recommendations.	Explores different options in search for solutions. Considers the implications for their proposals.	Tests different options to determine which provides the optimum solution. Weights up options and anticipates possible objections to preferred choices.	Considers all the options before deciding on the best way forward. Reacts to developments as the implementation unfolds.

Prioritising and Organising

Anchors

1. Understands goals and implements plans to achieve them.
2. Mobilises the appropriate resources to achieve goals.
3. Develops and implements metrics to measure results.
4. Anticipates and solves problems.
5. Sets realistic deadlines and milestones.
6. Manages workload efficiently and effectively.
7. Prioritises tasks appropriately.
8. Links up the various elements of the work.
9. Is flexible in taking into account new aspects coming in.
10. Collaborates effectively with others.

Indicators

	UNSATISFACTORY	IMPROVEMENT NEEDED	MEETS EXPECTATIONS	EXCEEDS EXPECTATIONS	EXCEPTIONAL
anchor	1 - Extremely Weak 2 - Very Weak	3 - Weak 4 - Fair	5 - Satisfactory 6 - Good	7 - Strong 8 - Very Strong	9 - Excellent 10 - Outstanding
1.	Does not follow an orderly method of setting objectives, scoping out difficulties, detailing work, or planning for task completion. Fails to prepare in advance.	Does not have a clear picture of unit or Institution goals; lacks perspective to pull elements into a strategic view; plans often lack substance and specificity.	Creates effective plans with defined purpose and outcomes. Breaks complex tasks into process steps, prioritises activities, itemises resources and estimates costs.	Plans with unit and Institution goals in mind. Plans clearly identify roles, responsibilities and timeframes.	Creates innovative, ambitious plans, which align with unit and Institution goals and serve as reliable roadmaps to desired outcomes.
2.	Is not able to integrate multiple activities and resources into a cohesive, actionable plan.	Has difficulty marshalling and informing resources to work together to achieve desired outcomes.	Organises, informs and supports resources to achieve goals.	Informs and mobilises resources – staff, stakeholders, technical experts – to achieve shared vision, mission, and goals.	Effectively influences, informs, and mobilises resources – staff, stakeholders, technical experts – to achieve shared vision, mission, and goals.
3.	Is unwilling/unable to create or track metrics. Allows work to continue without monitoring.	Has difficulty defining and implementing appropriate metrics to measure success. Becomes ineffective when plans need to change.	Monitors progress and determines how processes may be changed to improve quality and/or efficiency. Adapts to changes in plans effectively.	Implements metrics that effectively and efficiently measure results. Recommends improvements based on results.	Develops and implements reliable, effective metrics to measure outcomes; identifies and recommends changes to improve efficiency and effectiveness.

Prioritising and Organising Indicators – continued

	UNSATISFACTORY	IMPROVEMENT NEEDED	MEETS EXPECTATIONS	EXCEEDS EXPECTATIONS	EXCEPTIONAL
anchor	1 - Extremely Weak 2 - Very Weak	3 - Weak 4 - Fair	5 - Satisfactory 6 - Good	7 - Strong 8 - Very Strong	9 - Excellent 10 - Outstanding
4.	Ignores small problems until they become significant, jeopardising deadlines and effective utilisation of resources.	Identifies problems but does not effectively address them.	Addresses problems in process or resourcing quickly and effectively.	Anticipates and adjusts for problems and roadblocks. Resolves problems in early stages.	Proactively anticipates, analyses and solves problems and motivates others to do the same.
5.	Sets unrealistic deadlines and milestones.	Sometimes sets unrealistic deadlines and milestones.	Sets realistic deadlines and milestones.	Factors in 'what if' and plans for contingencies.	Consistently sets realistic deadlines and milestones, and always has a 'Plan B'.
6.	Works inefficiently or becomes overwhelmed with workload. Procrastinates.	Neglects work-life balance. Uses overtime as only strategy to cope with heavy workload or tight deadlines. Is overly perfectionist, indecisive, or impatient with others.	Manages to get all their work done in time and to a good quality standard.	Combines good work-life balance with efficient and effective behaviour at work.	Manages own workload as well as the workload of others effectively and efficiently.
7.	Does not identify main points and gets distracted by side issues.	Leaves the task of establishing priorities to others. Does not play an active role in identifying the issues and prioritising accordingly.	Identifies some of the key issues but overlooks others. Identifies issues that are priorities for him/her but not necessarily for their co-workers.	Has a clear picture of the remit of the unit, identifies key issues and proposes priorities.	Prioritises tasks appropriately, both for himself/herself and for the unit. Differentiates clearly between matters of primary and secondary importance.
8.	Does not grasp the general picture.	Makes few if any links between separate items of information.	Has a clear understanding of his/her mandate but is less successful in grasping the overall picture and priorities.	Sees how different elements fit together.	Focuses on both the general elements and the details of the situation. Has a clear understanding of the bigger picture. Fits things together and draws conclusions.

Prioritising and Organising Indicators – continued

	UNSATISFACTORY	IMPROVEMENT NEEDED	MEETS EXPECTATIONS	EXCEEDS EXPECTATIONS	EXCEPTIONAL
anchor	1 - Extremely Weak 2 - Very Weak	3 - Weak 4 - Fair	5 - Satisfactory 6 - Good	7 - Strong 8 - Very Strong	9 - Excellent 10 - Outstanding
9.	Sticks to own views despite consensus.	Puts most of their energy into defending own views. Is not inclined to organise and prioritise on the basis of points that emerge	Understands and defends their own position and links up with new elements. Shows good use of judgement in appraisal of new elements	Sees how new input affects the state of play and reassesses the situation if necessary.	Builds new elements into the work plan to ensure a well-balanced end result.
10.	Does not collaborate with co-workers and partners. Says 'Yes' to everything. Does everything by themself.	Keeps communication to a minimum and is reticent to share thoughts and ideas.	Maintains an open and honest dialogue with co-workers and partners. Delegates when appropriate.	Encourages others to share ideas and integrates others' thoughts and opinions in own plans and priorities.	Consistently and effectively seeks and incorporates others' ideas to ensure optimal results.

Delivering Quality and Results

Anchors

1. Taking responsibility.
2. Taking initiative.
3. Overcoming obstacles.
4. Delivering quality work on time.
5. Working to a high standard of quality.
6. Manages workload efficiently and effectively.
7. Understands the value of innovation and of quality improvement.
8. Links up the various elements of the work.
9. Demonstrates efficiency and effectiveness in own work.
10. Manages and sustains change initiatives.

Indicators

	UNSATISFACTORY	IMPROVEMENT NEEDED	MEETS EXPECTATIONS	EXCEEDS EXPECTATIONS	EXCEPTIONAL
anchor	1 - Extremely Weak 2 - Very Weak	3 - Weak 4 - Fair	5 - Satisfactory 6 - Good	7 - Strong 8 - Very Strong	9 - Excellent 10 - Outstanding
1.	Finds excuses for not dealing promptly with problems and requests. Refers problems to third parties instead of tackling themself. Blames external factors for failure to deliver quality work.	Does not always take responsibility for dealing promptly with problems that arise at work. Is slow to react to developments that affect achievability of results.	Takes his/her work seriously and applies themself to tasks. Is quality-conscious and does what is necessary to achieve high standards. Reacts to urgent requests.	Tackles assignments and accepts full responsibility for the outcomes. Reacts to developments that affect achievability of objectives.	Has a highly developed sense of responsibility and accountability. Anticipates problems and has solutions already worked out in advance.
2.	Does not do more than the minimum required to complete tasks. Sticks strictly to own job description.	Is reluctant to go beyond the call of duty. Never or rarely questions procedures or ways of working in place.	Understands procedures and workflow within their department. Follows established guidelines where appropriate. Works beyond the confines of job description if necessary.	Keeps up with events and takes initiatives that have a positive impact on quality of work. Acts without waiting to be told: takes initiative.	Goes the extra mile to ensure best possible results. Takes initiatives to make procedures and workflows more efficient or effective.
3.	Is deflected or stopped by obstacles and does not find ways around them. Goes round in circles instead of narrowing-in on solutions.	Does not deal adequately with complex tasks. Takes the first solution that comes along without standing back to weigh other options.	Achieves satisfactory results when faced with obstacles or complex tasks. Deals appropriately with unexpected developments.	Systematically ensures that desired results are delivered, notwithstanding difficulties. Thinks 'out-of-the-box'.	Demonstrates resourcefulness in finding ways around difficulties. Anticipates problems and has solutions ready.
4.	Underestimates work, gets their planning wrong and runs into time trouble. Spends too long on tasks that add little or no value to the end result.	Does not always take the right decision at the right time. Is perfectionist and loses sight of time constraints.	Deals with matters in appropriate and timely manner. Strikes acceptable balance between quality and deadlines.	Takes remedial actions when quality is in danger or compromised by deadlines. Sees where corners can be cut to meet tight deadlines.	Finds ways of delivering the best possible results under difficult circumstances and tight deadlines.

Delivering quality and results Indicators – continued

	UNSATISFACTORY	IMPROVEMENT NEEDED	MEETS EXPECTATIONS	EXCEEDS EXPECTATIONS	EXCEPTIONAL
anchor	1 - Extremely Weak 2 - Very Weak	3 - Weak 4 - Fair	5 - Satisfactory 6 - Good	7 - Strong 8 - Very Strong	9 - Excellent 10 - Outstanding
5.	Settles for quick and easy solutions.	Does not always meet expectations.	Performs to expected standards and in accordance with procedures in place.	Sets themself demanding standards and does not settle for second best.	Seeks to continuously exceed expectations. Puts a large amount of personal effort and creative thought into work. Thrives in challenging situations.
6.	Works inefficiently or becomes overwhelmed with workload. Procrastinates.	Neglects work-life balance. Uses overtime as their only strategy to cope with heavy workload or tight deadlines. Is overly perfectionist, indecisive, or impatient with others.	Manages to get all their work done in time and to a good quality standard.	Combines good work-life balance with efficient and effective behaviour at work.	Manages own workload as well as the workload of others effectively and efficiently.
7.	Resists change: prefers to continue to do things as they always have been done.	Has a limited perspective and understanding of the importance of quality improvement.	Understands the value of quality improvement. Identifies weaknesses that impede processes and recommends changes.	Understands and communicates the importance of quality improvement.	Clearly defines the value and imperative for continuous improvement. Consistently offers original, inventive ideas for improving products and services.
8.	Does not grasp the general picture.	Makes few if any links between separate items of information.	Has a clear understanding of their own mandate but is less successful in grasping the overall picture and priorities.	Sees how different elements fit together.	Focuses on both the general elements and the details of the situation. Has a clear understanding of the bigger picture. Fits things together and draws conclusions.

Delivering quality and results Indicators – continued

	UNSATISFACTORY	IMPROVEMENT NEEDED	MEETS EXPECTATIONS	EXCEEDS EXPECTATIONS	EXCEPTIONAL
anchor	1 - Extremely Weak 2 - Very Weak	3 - Weak 4 - Fair	5 - Satisfactory 6 - Good	7 - Strong 8 - Very Strong	9 - Excellent 10 - Outstanding
9.	Is extremely disorganised and unable to separate 'need to do' from less important tasks. Cannot handle more than one project at a time.	Has difficulty handling more than one task or project at a time. Disorganisation often results in poor quality work.	Successfully manages several projects to achieve desired results.	Manages several projects effectively and efficiently. Results enhance productivity and quality of the department.	Models efficiency by getting more done in less time while maintaining quality of results. Effectively manages multiple projects to achieve desired outcomes.
10.	Moves to next project before ensuring successful, sustainable implementation of previous projects.	Rarely monitors change initiatives after implementation	Sustains change through clear documentation and regular monitoring.	Ensures that operational changes are successfully implemented and sustained over time.	Employs clear post-implementation strategies to ensure sustainability. Encourages continuous improvement.

Working with Others

Anchors

1. Treats others with respect.
2. Cooperates and collaborates with colleagues.
3. Includes relevant others in decision-making.
4. Working with other cultures.
5. Utilising other backgrounds, skills and motivations.
6. Shows empathy and sympathy.
7. Assertiveness.
8. Balances individual and team goals.
9. Resolves conflicts among team members.
10. Builds productive working relationships.

Indicators

	UNSATISFACTORY	IMPROVEMENT NEEDED	MEETS EXPECTATIONS	EXCEEDS EXPECTATIONS	EXCEPTIONAL
anchor	1 - Extremely Weak 2 - Very Weak	3 - Weak 4 - Fair	5 - Satisfactory 6 - Good	7 - Strong 8 - Very Strong	9 - Excellent 10 - Outstanding
1.	Exhibits behaviour that negatively impacts the morale and accomplishments of the team.	Sometimes displays behaviour inconsistent with workplace courtesy and respect.	Treats others with respect. Encourages and appreciates individual contributions.	Is respectful and welcoming. Reaches out and engages with other people.	Promotes, supports, and influences a culture of respect and courtesy among team members. Inspires collaboration by bridging gaps among diverse individuals and units.
2.	Is not a team player. Does not seek consensus and co-operation with others. Often disrupts team process, jeopardising progress toward common goals. Ignores or belittles the contribution of others.	Has difficulty collaborating with others. Often prefers to work independently. Sees little value in letting everybody have their say.	Works effectively and cooperatively with others. Shares information and knowledge with others. Encourages others to express their views. Takes account of dissenting opinions.	Is highly collaborative. Praises the contributions of others. Seeks new alliances to expand sphere of influence and enhance quality of work.	Models cooperation and teamwork. Actively involves colleagues in decision-making processes. Creates opportunities for self and others to improve working relationships and work outcomes.
3.	Makes decisions in isolation without consulting others. Leaves to others the task of liaising with other departments and external stakeholders.	Adopts a silo mentality, does not co-operate with other organisational boundaries. Takes little interest in what other parts of the organisation do. Lacks understanding of priorities and key issues for other stakeholders.	Liaises with people outside immediate working environment. Sees when assistance is needed from other departments. Has contacts elsewhere in the organisation to call for support if necessary.	Works co-operatively across organisational boundaries. Is constantly in touch with colleagues from other departments.	Includes relevant others in decision-making. Engages with people outside own team to achieve common objectives.

Working with others Indicators – continued

	UNSATISFACTORY	IMPROVEMENT NEEDED	MEETS EXPECTATIONS	EXCEEDS EXPECTATIONS	EXCEPTIONAL
anchor	1 - Extremely Weak 2 - Very Weak	3 - Weak 4 - Fair	5 - Satisfactory 6 - Good	7 - Strong 8 - Very Strong	9 - Excellent 10 - Outstanding
4.	Shows lack of cultural sensitivity. Sees cultural differences in terms of national stereotypes. Is prejudiced and biased against people from other cultures, judges them based on personal standards.	Is aware of cultural differences but makes little or no effort to adapt to them. Shows little curiosity for understanding the reasons why people behave as they do.	Is aware of cultural differences and makes an effort to adapt to them. Makes an effort to understand other people in the context of cultural differences.	Mixes with people of other nationalities. Understands the importance of non-verbal communication patterns.	Bridges gaps between cultural differences. Is receptive to other cultural approaches. Enjoys working with people from different cultural backgrounds.
5.	Fails to consider individual differences in background, skills, or motivations. Sees things in terms of black or white.	Is dismissive of ideas that are not his/her own. Holds strong views and is reluctant to see things from other angles.	Holds strong views but is willing to consider other opinions. Listens to reason. Sees the shades of grey between black and white.	Encourages people to voice their opinions and express their views.	Effectively utilises the diverse range of backgrounds, skills and motivations of others. Actively seeks input from others.
6.	Shows no concern for the emotional state of others. Does not take steps to deal with underlying tensions at work.	Misreads other people's feelings or states of mind. Steps on other people's toes. Is dismissive of ideas that are not his/her own.	Is sensitive to the feelings of other people. Assists colleagues when asked to do so.	Is diplomatic when drawing attention to errors in other people's work or understanding of a situation.	Shows a genuine concern for the emotional state of others. Speaks up for colleagues in distress.
7.	Has low self-esteem. Allows themself to be dictated to by other people. Is 'invisible' in group discussions. Plays games, is sarcastic, or remains silent.	Bottles up feelings that eventually explode, leaving no room for communication. Is not sufficiently assertive when defending his/her views.	Is clear about what he/she feels and needs and how it can be achieved. Is able to communicate calmly without attacking other people.	Is happy to defend own position, even if it provokes conflict. Is able to say 'no', rather than agreeing to do something just to please someone else.	Understands how to negotiate if two people want different outcomes. Is able to talk openly about self and able to listen to others.

Working with others Indicators – continued

	UNSATISFACTORY	IMPROVEMENT NEEDED	MEETS EXPECTATIONS	EXCEEDS EXPECTATIONS	EXCEPTIONAL
anchor	1 - Extremely Weak 2 - Very Weak	3 - Weak 4 - Fair	5 - Satisfactory 6 - Good	7 - Strong 8 - Very Strong	9 - Excellent 10 - Outstanding
8.	Is unwilling to work outside comfort zone to support team goals.	Resists new challenges. Seems uninterested in building skills and knowledge.	Demonstrates flexibility and willingness to step out of comfort zone to support team and goals.	Is always willing to try something new. Balances individual and team goals.	Consistently goes beyond direct responsibilities to achieve team and department goals. Welcomes new challenges.
9.	Often avoids conflict. Is not prepared or willing to resolve conflict.	Is unable to resolve or constructively manage conflicts.	Works effectively with others to resolve conflict.	Manages conflict competently and efficiently. When possible, looks for and proposes middle ground solutions.	Skillfully and proactively addresses conflict. Seeks and achieves 'win-win' resolutions.
10.	Shows lack of interest in and respect for peers and partners.	Has difficulty building strong, mutually beneficial working relationships.	Builds and maintains effective working relationships with peers and partners.	Successfully builds productive, mutually beneficial relationships to solve problems and achieve common goals.	Leads colleagues to inspired cooperation and teamwork in support of department and organisational goals.

Communicating

Anchors

1. Demonstrates effective written communication skills.
2. Adapts written communication to the level of the audience.
3. Writes clearly, in a visually appealing manner.
4. Explains ideas clearly, simplifies the complex.
5. Methodical, structured and precise in speech.
6. Adapts verbal communication to the level of the audience.
7. Communicates clearly and knowledgeably.
8. Shares information with others.
9. Seeks input from others.
10. Protects private and confidential information.

Indicators

	UNSATISFACTORY	IMPROVEMENT NEEDED	MEETS EXPECTATIONS	EXCEEDS EXPECTATIONS	EXCEPTIONAL
anchor	1 - Extremely Weak 2 - Very Weak	3 - Weak 4 - Fair	5 - Satisfactory 6 - Good	7 - Strong 8 - Very Strong	9 - Excellent 10 - Outstanding
1.	Creates documents that are poorly written, unstructured, grammatically incorrect, or contain too many spelling errors. Uses incomplete sentences or bad punctuation.	Creates documents that are disorganised or contain many grammar or spelling errors. Uses sentences, that are too long, too verbose, or overly complex.	Keeps sentences and paragraphs short and concise. Leaves out words that do not contribute to the main focus of the communication. Writes documents that are syntactically and semantically correct.	Creates documents that are consistently clear and persuasive.	Writes documents that are always complete, concise, clear, concrete, correct, considerate and courteous.
2.	Creates documents that are either overly simplistic or too complex and therefore not adapted to the audience.	Creates documents that are somewhat disorganised and/or not appropriate for the audience. Uses slang, jargon, acronyms, or unexplained concepts or ideas.	Focuses on the needs of the audience. Uses simple language, without overusing clichés, jargon, and expressions or trying to impress with difficult words.	Creates documents that are concise and comprehensive and convey all the ideas that need to be addressed.	Writes documents that consistently address all the needs of specific individuals and groups within the audience.
3.	Creates visually unappealing documents; large blocks of continuous text without punctuation or white space.	Makes inappropriate use of colour coding, text formatting, capitalisation, etc. Uses no illustrations or visual elements.	Creates visually appealing documents with appropriate use of white space, indentations and graphical elements.	Makes appropriate use of colour coding, text formatting and capitalisation, enhancing the underlying structure and ideas.	Writes visually engaging documents, illustrated with tables and graphs enhancing the messages to be conveyed.
4.	Does not finish sentences or stops mid-sentence and expects the audience to second-guess and draw conclusions. Gets blocked and has difficulty in finding the right words to express themself. Speaks too fast and is difficult to follow. Has bad articulation or truncates their words.	Does not always clearly structure ideas; has difficulty in articulating his/her thoughts. Is hesitant and transmits uncertainty with body language or tone of voice. Does not engage spontaneously with audience.	Speaks clearly, connects with his/her audience and gets messages across with relative ease. Engages spontaneously with his/her audience.	Explains issues and ideas clearly and succinctly. Strikes a good balance between detail and the need for clarity.	Explains even complex issues and ideas clearly and succinctly, simplifies the complex. Convinces sceptics and opponents of his/her points of view.

Communicating Indicators – continued

	UNSATISFACTORY	IMPROVEMENT NEEDED	MEETS EXPECTATIONS	EXCEEDS EXPECTATIONS	EXCEPTIONAL
anchor	1 - Extremely Weak 2 - Very Weak	3 - Weak 4 - Fair	5 - Satisfactory 6 - Good	7 - Strong 8 - Very Strong	9 - Excellent 10 - Outstanding
5.	Speaks in an unstructured fashion, jumps from one point to another, does not get to the point, or does not achieve flowing delivery of ideas. Makes contributions that are often unclear or inaccurate. Gives minimalist or no answers to questions.	Gets lost in complexity and does not succeed in making points clearly. Dwells too much on detail and does not get to the point. Is rather vague or evasive when answering questions.	Speaks clearly, persuasively, and concisely. Focuses on the needs of specific individuals and groups. Keeps to a logical order when explaining things. Copes well with questions and provides relevant information.	Uses verbal communication that is consistently clear, persuasive, and adapted to the audience. Goes straight to the point when answering questions. Illustrates answers to questions with appropriate and relevant examples.	Is methodical, precise and structured in speech, is articulate and makes good use of language and gesture. Anticipates information needs and gives full and complete answers to questions.
6.	Has difficulty tailoring communication to the needs of others; communicates 'too much,' 'too little,' or 'too late.'	Does not always keep the audience in mind.	Tailors information to audience and individual needs.	Effectively adjusts the level of detail and tone to the audience.	Effectively adapts verbal communication to audience; effectively distinguishes between 'need to know' and 'nice to know.'
7.	Appears distracted or uninterested; frequently interrupts others. Does not listen to what others say.	Interrupts others to express own point of view. Has difficulty getting to the point. Uses facts that are not always accurate or relevant.	Appears knowledgeable and concise. Actively listens to and synthesises perspectives of others.	Appears credible and reliable. Actively listens to and integrates diverse contributions.	Speaks with conviction and authority. Listens to, synthesises, and integrates others' ideas.
8.	Does not share information in a timely manner, creating problems for colleagues and stakeholders.	Has difficulty distinguishing between critical and non-critical information.	Gives others the information they need in a timely manner.	Shares accurate, timely information with the right people in the right format.	Displays openness and transparency in sharing information with partners and stakeholders.

Communicating -Indicators – continued

	UNSATISFACTORY	IMPROVEMENT NEEDED	MEETS EXPECTATIONS	EXCEEDS EXPECTATIONS	EXCEPTIONAL
anchor	1 - Extremely Weak 2 - Very Weak	3 - Weak 4 - Fair	5 - Satisfactory 6 - Good	7 - Strong 8 - Very Strong	9 - Excellent 10 - Outstanding
9.	Avoids contact with co-workers and partners. Is monosyllabic in conversation.	Keeps communication to a minimum. Is reluctant to share thoughts and ideas.	Maintains an open and honest dialogue with co-workers and partners.	Encourages others to share ideas and integrates others' thoughts and opinions.	Consistently and effectively seeks and incorporates others' ideas to ensure optimal results.
10.	Discloses and uses private and confidential information inappropriately, putting the organisation or other individuals at risk.	Does not consistently follow the organisation's confidentiality or privacy practices. Sometimes shares private or confidential information with unauthorised or inappropriate individuals.	Consistently follows confidentiality and privacy policies and practices. Only discloses confidential information to authorised individuals.	Understands and implements confidentiality and privacy policies.	Clearly understands and follows confidentiality and privacy policies and practices. Actively develops practices to protect confidential and private information.

Resilience

Anchors

1. Social support.
2. Healthy mind in healthy body.
3. Positive thinking.
4. Communicating and problem solving.
5. Coping with heavy workload and tight deadlines.
6. Adjusting to peaks and troughs in workload.
7. Handling failures and setbacks.
8. Working with management.
9. Facing changes.
10. Self-control.

Indicators

	UNSATISFACTORY	IMPROVEMENT NEEDED	MEETS EXPECTATIONS	EXCEEDS EXPECTATIONS	EXCEPTIONAL
anchor	1 - Extremely Weak 2 - Very Weak	3 - Weak 4 - Fair	5 - Satisfactory 6 - Good	7 - Strong 8 - Very Strong	9 - Excellent 10 - Outstanding
1.	Is socially isolated. Has few or no social contacts with colleagues, friends or family.	Has an operational network, but no personal or strategic network to rely upon. Neglects work-life balance.	Has both an operational and a personal network to rely upon.	Has good operational, personal and strategic network.	Has very good operational and personal network, combined with an excellent strategic network.
2.	Has an unhealthy lifestyle. Uses too much alcohol, caffeine or other drugs. Is a heavy smoker.	Does not do enough physical activity. Is overweight, or has high blood pressure. Gets insufficient sleep or rest.	Takes care of physical and mental health. Eats mostly healthy food, does sufficient physical activity, gets enough rest and sleep.	Has a good mental and physical condition.	Is mentally and physically in top condition.
3.	Maintains a negative, pessimistic outlook. Concentrates on negative only.	Has low self-esteem. Lacks trust in colleagues and co-workers.	Is aware of own worth and value, but also of own shortcomings and room for development. Remains in positive mood, despite setbacks.	Maintains an optimistic, positive outlook. Works on self-development.	Always looks at the bright side of life. Continuously works on self-improvement.
4.	Does not listen to what other people have to say. Is unaware of other people's feelings and emotions.	Is unable to express own feelings and views in a convincing way.	Is assertive, not passive or aggressive.	Listens to, understands, and integrates others' feelings and views in the bigger picture.	Is a 'giver' not a 'taker'.
5.	Works inefficiently or becomes overwhelmed with workload. Is not capable of adapting to high work pressure. Becomes stressed or panics when under pressure. Displays negative emotions to others inappropriately. Shows complacency.	Uses overtime as only strategy to cope with heavy workload or tight deadlines. Sometimes lacks planning and prioritising skills. Is overly perfectionist, indecisive, or impatient with others.	Generally copes with high levels of work and tight deadlines. Manages to get all his/her work done in time and to a good quality standard. Keeps cool under pressure, works more intensively and longer hours when pressure is on.	Combines good work-life balance with efficient and effective behaviour at work. Has strategies for coping with large volumes of work.	Manages own workload as well as the workload of others effectively and efficiently. Remains calm under pressure. Sees where corners can be cut to meet tight deadlines without sacrificing quality of work.

Resilience Indicators – continued

	UNSATISFACTORY	IMPROVEMENT NEEDED	MEETS EXPECTATIONS	EXCEEDS EXPECTATIONS	EXCEPTIONAL
anchor	1 - Extremely Weak 2 - Very Weak	3 - Weak 4 - Fair	5 - Satisfactory 6 - Good	7 - Strong 8 - Very Strong	9 - Excellent 10 - Outstanding
6.	Considers calmer periods as opportunities for complete inactivity, thus wasting time.	Limits himself to catching up on the backlog, deploys no extra activities otherwise.	Takes care of professional and personal development during the calmer periods at work. Expands own operational network.	Anticipates busy periods and prepares for them. Expands own personal and strategic networks.	Makes optimal use of calmer periods to further develop own performance. Prepares mentally and physically for busier periods to come.
7.	Regards unsuccessful endeavours as personal failures. Loses self-confidence and self-esteem after a failure or setback.	Responds defensively to criticism. Refuses to learn from failures and setbacks. Tends to blame the environment for own failures.	Responds confidently and non-defensively to criticism. Accepts that not everything in life works out fine. Acknowledges own mistakes, and learns from them. Moves on after setbacks and missed opportunities.	Considers failures and setbacks as learning opportunities. Turns setbacks and failures to his/her advantage.	Handles failures and interprets setbacks professionally, not personally. Anticipates failure and has a backup strategy. Has clear strategies for coping with failure.
8.	Is frustrated by the management, has little tendency to work with it constructively. Intolerant of ambiguity in work content or organisational situation. Externalises frustrations with management.	Does not always alert management to problems. Does not always take steps to establish with management the conditions for smooth working relations. Does not succeed in bringing sceptical superiors to his/her way of thinking.	Tolerates ambiguity in work content or organisational situation. Copes with demands by management and understands their role. Alerts management to problems. Has open and cooperative attitude towards management.	Actively seeks feedback from management and builds on it. Works autonomously but knows when to involve the management. Has gained the confidence of management and is a point of reference.	Understands and works with management, not against it. Actively manages expectations from management. Endeavours to become involved in decisions related to his/her work.

Resilience Indicators – continued

	UNSATISFACTORY	IMPROVEMENT NEEDED	MEETS EXPECTATIONS	EXCEEDS EXPECTATIONS	EXCEPTIONAL
anchor	1 - Extremely Weak 2 - Very Weak	3 - Weak 4 - Fair	5 - Satisfactory 6 - Good	7 - Strong 8 - Very Strong	9 - Excellent 10 - Outstanding
9	Resists organisational change, and sticks to old habits and traditional ways of working. Reacts negatively to change. Feels threatened by change or reorganisation.	Is suspicious of change and its implications. Has difficulty adapting to new working environments. Is discouraged by organisational change.	Adapts to new ways of working and broader organisational changes. Sees organisational change as part of life.	Sees change and reorganisation as an opportunity for improvement. Adjusts quickly to unexpected changes.	Embraces change. Proposes more efficient ways of doing things. Sees organisational change as a positive challenge.
10.	Lacks inner discipline. Shows over-indulgence.	Is sometimes caught up by excitement.	Is mindful. Focuses on task and is not distracted by things around. Manages to get rid of bad habits.	Keeps negative emotions under control at all time. Replaces bad habits by good ones.	Is able to control emotions, behaviour and desires in the face of external demands.

Leadership

Anchors

1. Explains ideas clearly, simplifies the complex.
2. Adapts communication to the level of the audience.
3. Communicates clearly and knowledgeably.
4. Shares information with others.
5. Seeks input from others.
6. Understands and supports organisational goals.
7. Helps others perform at their best.
8. Self-aware and open to feedback.
9. Leads by example.
10. Delegates effectively.

Indicators

	UNSATISFACTORY	IMPROVEMENT NEEDED	MEETS EXPECTATIONS	EXCEEDS EXPECTATIONS	EXCEPTIONAL
anchor	1 - Extremely Weak 2 - Very Weak	3 - Weak 4 - Fair	5 - Satisfactory 6 - Good	7 - Strong 8 - Very Strong	9 - Excellent 10 - Outstanding
1.	Has difficulty in finding the right words to express themself.	Does not always clearly structure their ideas; has difficulty in articulating thoughts and vision. Is hesitant and transmits uncertainty with body language or tone of voice.	Speaks and writes clearly, connects with their audience and gets messages across with relative ease. Engages spontaneously with their audience.	Explains vision and ideas clearly and succinctly. Strikes a good balance between detail and the need for clarity.	Explains even complex issues and ideas clearly and succinctly, simplifies the complex. Convinces sceptics and opponents of his/her points of view.
2.	Has difficulty tailoring communication to the needs of others; communicates 'too much,' 'too little,' or 'too late.'	Does not always keep the audience in mind.	Tailors information to audience and individual needs.	Effectively adjusts the level of detail and tone to the audience.	Effectively adapts communication to audience; effectively distinguishes between 'need to know' and 'nice to know'.
3.	Appears distracted or uninterested. Does not listen to what others say.	Interrupts others to express own point of view. Has difficulty getting to the point. Uses facts that are not always accurate or relevant.	Appears knowledgeable and enthusiastic. Actively listens to and synthesises perspectives of others.	Appears credible and reliable. Actively listens to and integrates diverse contributions.	Speaks with conviction and authority. Listens to, synthesises, and integrates others' ideas.
4.	Does not share information in a timely manner, creating problems for colleagues and stakeholders. Shies away from delivering tough messages.	Tends to 'hold on' to information; has difficulty distinguishing between critical and non-critical information.	Gives others the information they need in a timely manner.	Shares accurate, timely information with the right people in the right format.	Displays openness and transparency in sharing information with others. Is prepared to deliver tough messages when necessary.
5.	Avoids contact with co-workers and partners.	Keeps communication to a minimum; is reluctant to share thoughts and ideas.	Maintains an open and honest dialogue with co-workers and partners.	Encourages others to share ideas and integrates others' thoughts and opinions.	Consistently and effectively seeks and incorporates others' ideas to ensure optimal results.

Leadership Indicators – continued

	UNSATISFACTORY	IMPROVEMENT NEEDED	MEETS EXPECTATIONS	EXCEEDS EXPECTATIONS	EXCEPTIONAL
anchor	1 - Extremely Weak 2 - Very Weak	3 - Weak 4 - Fair	5 - Satisfactory 6 - Good	7 - Strong 8 - Very Strong	9 - Excellent 10 - Outstanding
6.	Resists change. Maintains focus on immediate, routine tasks. Work efforts do not align with unit and department goals.	Contributions and work efforts often do not reflect an understanding of unit and department goals.	Effectively aligns work efforts with organisational and department goals.	Understands and supports the need to align work with organisational initiatives and goals.	Encourages and leads changes that enhance organisational and workforce effectiveness.
7.	Hinders sharing of knowledge and/or expertise, focused largely on own development. Fails to spot or nurture future talent. Fails to create development opportunities for others.	Does not openly share expertise or information with others. Spots future talent but fails to nurture it.	Assists others in developing skills and knowledge. Helps people to resolve problems and overcome obstacles.	Consistently and actively assists others in expanding and developing skills and knowledge. Coaches and/or mentors others. Creates targeted development opportunities for others.	Inspires and helps others to evelop skills and competencies to perform at their best. Spots and nurtures potential future talent.
8.	Is not motivated to learn and grow, believes that others are responsible for their development.	Often resists to feedback on performance. Rarely asks for help or feedback.	Is self-aware and open to feedback from others. Displays integrity.	Very self-aware; asks others for feedback in an effort to improve skills and knowledge.	Demonstrates a high degree of self-awareness; asks others for feedback on performance; is a continuous learner. Is authentic in everything he/she does or says.
9.	Demotivates others. Betrays lack of conviction in chances of success.	Keeps too low a profile to make a leadership impact. Does not react when developments require assertive action. Is inconsistent in supporting staff to achieve defined goals.	Is enthusiastic about their work and transmits enthusiasm to others. Encourages and supports staff to achieve performance and development goals.	Sets a good example in terms of enthusiasm and commitment. Encourages and engages staff to make optimal use of skills and knowledge. Makes themself visible and accessible to colleagues.	Leads and motivates by example. Inspires staff to perform at their best. Shows drive and determination to succeed.

Leadership Indicators – continued

	UNSATISFACTORY	IMPROVEMENT NEEDED	MEETS EXPECTATIONS	EXCEEDS EXPECTATIONS	EXCEPTIONAL
anchor	1 - Extremely Weak 2 - Very Weak	3 - Weak 4 - Fair	5 - Satisfactory 6 - Good	7 - Strong 8 - Very Strong	9 - Excellent 10 - Outstanding
10	Does not delegate; does most of the work by themself. Assigns work inappropriately. Does not keep development and performance goals in mind. Has unrealistic expectations and perception of staff skills and knowledge.	Doesn't effectively match work assignments to staff talent and proficiencies. Does little to monitor team progress or provide follow-up.	Plans ahead and organises work. Thoughtfully delegates work to develop staff and achieve goals. Monitors team progress and provides follow-up.	Effectively links work assignments to achieve individual and unit performance goals.	Effectively delegates work to develop skills and knowledge. Ensures optimal outcomes, aligns work with individual, unit, and organisational goals.

Learning and Development

Anchors

1. Explains ideas clearly, simplifies the complex.
2. Actively developing and applying new knowledge, skills, and competencies.
3. Personal development.
4. Asking for advice and assistance.
5. Seeing own role within the organisation.
6. Seeing the "bigger picture".
7. Learning other languages.
8. Learning strategy.
9. Active listening.
10. Teaching others.

Indicators

	UNSATISFACTORY	IMPROVEMENT NEEDED	MEETS EXPECTATIONS	EXCEEDS EXPECTATIONS	EXCEPTIONAL
anchor	1 - Extremely Weak 2 - Very Weak	3 - Weak 4 - Fair	5 - Satisfactory 6 - Good	7 - Strong 8 - Very Strong	9 - Excellent 10 - Outstanding
1.	Has difficulty in finding the right words to express themself.	Does not always clearly structure ideas; has difficulty in articulating thoughts and vision.	Speaks and writes clearly, simplifies the complex.	Explains vision and ideas clearly and succinctly. Strikes a good balance between detail and the need for clarity.	Explains even complex issues and ideas clearly and succinctly, simplifies the complex.
2.	Allows knowledge levels to remain constant and/or outdated. Shows little interest in developing new skills or acquiring new knowledge.	Remains fixed in personal ways of working, does not try to develop. Takes a long time to learn new information.	Takes new information on board quickly. Learns from observation. Adapts to new ways of doing things.	Volunteers for new and challenging tasks. Is resourceful when it comes to familiarising themself with the latest developments in their field.	Takes active steps to improve own knowledge and development. Develops new skills on his/her own initiative.
3.	Stays in their comfort zone and settles for routine. Does little to overcome their weaknesses.	Sees personal development in exclusively professional terms. Does little to develop their strengths.	Knows own strengths and weaknesses. Identifies personal failings and tries to overcome them. Sets personal goals.	Sets themself inspiring challenges. Sets and achieves personal goals.	Works actively on developing personal strengths and overcoming their weaknesses. Improves knowledge and skills out of personal interest and natural curiosity.
4.	Does not take opportunities to ask for personal feedback from others. Fails to learn from mistakes, continues to make them. Does not accept constructive feedback.	Does not learn from experience. Avoids new challenges and learning opportunities. Makes limited use of the experience of colleagues.	Seeks personal feedback on performance from others. Learns from mistakes and avoids repeating them. Responds positively to negative feedback and learns from it.	Rethinks and adjusts their approach to take account of feedback received. Learns from input and suggestions from colleagues.	Actively seeks feedback from others to improve own performance. Pools knowledge and expertise.

Learning and Development Indicators – continued

	UNSATISFACTORY	IMPROVEMENT NEEDED	MEETS EXPECTATIONS	EXCEEDS EXPECTATIONS	EXCEPTIONAL
anchor	1 - Extremely Weak 2 - Very Weak	3 - Weak 4 - Fair	5 - Satisfactory 6 - Good	7 - Strong 8 - Very Strong	9 - Excellent 10 - Outstanding
5.	Focuses exclusively on own tasks and role. Has limited vision of developments elsewhere. Lacks understanding of how own work contributes to the objectives of the organisation.	Does not always respect the boundaries between his/her responsibilities and those of colleagues.	Knows what their department does and where it fits in. Understands the objectives of the organisation and contributes towards their achievement.	Takes initiatives to improve organisation-wide procedures and workflows.	Projects a positive image of their organisation to the outside world.
6.	Makes no effort to interact with other departments or organisations. Lacks vision of what happens upstream and downstream of own department.	Gives little thought to wider organisational objectives.	Understands how his/her department contributes to the achievement of wider organisational goals. Interacts extensively with other departments and organisations.	Uses knowledge of wider organisational processes to improve collaboration with other organisations.	Sees the 'bigger picture' and contributes actively. Is aware of the wider 'political' context, and his/her own contribution.
7.	Besides own mother tongue, is only a basic user (A1, A2) for one of the three working languages.	Besides own mother tongue, is only an independent user (B1, B2) for one of the three working languages.	Is a proficient user (C1) of at least three languages, including their mother tongue, one of the working languages, and another official EU language.	Is a proficient user (C1, C2) of the three working languages, or of more than three official EU languages.	Is a proficient user (C1, C2) of at least three official EU languages, and an independent user (B1, B2) of at least one non-EU language.
8.	Is not aware of their own learning style.	Does not apply their own preferred learning style systematically.	Knows and applies own preferred learning style.	Has a clear learning strategy, and applies it successfully.	Uses different learning styles in different circumstances

Learning and Development Indicators – continued

	UNSATISFACTORY	IMPROVEMENT NEEDED	MEETS EXPECTATIONS	EXCEEDS EXPECTATIONS	EXCEPTIONAL
anchor	1 - Extremely Weak 2 - Very Weak	3 - Weak 4 - Fair	5 - Satisfactory 6 - Good	7 - Strong 8 - Very Strong	9 - Excellent 10 - Outstanding
9.	Appears distracted or uninterested. Frequently interrupts others. Does not listen to what others say.	Interrupts others to express own point of view.	Listens to and learns from other people's ideas and contributions.	Actively listens to and learns from other people's ideas and contributions.	Listens to, synthesises, and integrates others' ideas into own understanding
10.	Keeps own knowledge and understanding to themself. Considers colleagues as competitors.	Teaches others only when explicitly asked to do so.	Considers teaching others as part of his/her job description.	Mentors or coaches others when asked to.	Actively mentors or coaches others. Sees coaching and mentoring as part of his/her job description.

Annex 2 Sample In-tray (E-tray)

Instructions

In the exercise below you are provided with a series of emails which relate to organising and preparing for a conference and working with others in their day-to-day work.

There are 16 situations which relate to the information provided in the emails.

For each situation you are given the choice of three possible action options. Your job is to decide how appropriate each action is as a response to the situation.

Totally disagree that the action is a good response to the situation	Mostly disagree that the action is a good response to the situation	Feel that the action has roughly equal good and poor elements in this situation	Mostly agree that the action is a good response to the situation	Totally agree that the action is a good response to the situation
- -	-	- / +	+	+ +

The actions can relate to different aspects of the situation and are not necessarily alternatives to each other, therefore you should rate each action according to its own merits.

Please note, for the purposes of completing this exercise you should assume that you are a fluent French speaker.

You have 50 minutes to complete this exercise.

Scoring

Each of your answers is scored on a sliding scale according to how closely it agrees with the correct answer as pre-determined by experts in this form of assessment. 4 points are awarded for a fully correct answer, with no points given for the least appropriate answer.

This can be seen in the marking key example below. In this example, the experts deemed the action option to be a very poor response (- -) to the situation, so you would get 4 marks for selecting it as a very poor (- -) response yourself. If you instead picked it as moderately poor (-), you would receive 3 points. If you picked it as neutral (- / +), you would get 2 points. If you picked it as moderately good (+), you would get 1 point. If you picked it as very good (+ +), you would get 0 points.

Action is a very poor response to the situation	Action is a moderately poor response to situation	Action is a neutral response to the situation	Action is a moderately good response to the situation	Action is a very good response to the situation
- -	-	- / +	+	+ +
CORRECT				
4	3	2	1	0

Each action option is also assigned to a specific competency. In this exercise there are 16 situations, with three action options for each, and therefore 48 answers to give. Four competencies are assessed and there are 12 answers associated with each competency. This means there is a maximum of 48 points per competency. You can thus work out your total score on all of the competencies by adding up the related responses. In the full marking key below, the following competencies are abbreviated as follows:

- Analysis and Problem Solving - APS
- Delivering Quality and Results - DQR
- Prioritising and Organising – P&O
- Working with Others - WWO

Emails

Email: 1

To: YOU
From: Tobias Fiser
Subject: Agricultural Markets Conference
Date: 1st February 20XX, 9:04

Hello,

I hope you enjoyed your two days away from the office and are happy to be back in the Unit.

To remind you, I'm away for the next few weeks (returning next Thursday 11th February) and need you to finalise the Agricultural Markets Conference that is running on the Monday and Tuesday after I return (15th – 16th February). As you know, this is being run by the Directorate-General but we are taking a key role in organising it this time and it's an important occasion for Wine and Spirits. Our superior Monique Meunier (as well as many of the other superiors in the Directorate General) will be keen that this goes well, as she is speaking there!

Here's the information about the conference so far:

The Agricultural Markets Conference is a two-day event run twice a year over two days. It allows experts both within the EU and externally to meet to discuss current policy, upcoming change, and latest research as it relates to agriculture across the EU.

Of particular importance to our specific Unit is of course the following:

- Ensuring EU wine producers are competitive (both within the EU and outside)
- Creating a transparent international marketplace to allow import and export to be as clear and efficient as possible
- Promoting new growth and production techniques while...
- ... Preserving important traditions, and preventing wine growers from being forced into new methodologies at the risk of damaging their product and/or the environment

Also, as you know Eric left last week, so here is an update on the team for your reference. I will be able to support when I'm back, and you will be working closely with other peers in our Unit: David Bland, Isabella Jensen and Elisabet Kivi. Our superior, Deputy Head of Unit Monique Meunier, is keen that this conference goes well so may be in touch about this. You may also be contacted by other Unit Heads particularly those who are involved in the conference, such as Rasmus Jokela and Lukas Bosman. They are keen that this goes well as it is an important event for the whole Directorate-General. A quick note: one of our speakers (Park Sung-Joon) has not yet confirmed. Can you contact Park to make sure he is attending please?

I'm going to pull together all of the information you should need to look after this in my absence – should take me about an hour to get this together.

Thanks,

Tobias Fiser

Administrator
Wines, spirits, horticultural products, specialised crops
Directorate-General for Agriculture and Rural Development

Email: 2

To: YOU
From: Isabella Jensen
Subject: David Bland
Date: 1st February 20XX, 10:15

Hi,

I've been having a lot of difficulty working with David recently. He is always criticising my ideas and making it difficult for me to share my thoughts. We were coming up with ideas on how the EU could help improve the exporting of spirits to Asia, and every time I offered a suggestion he would interrupt or tell me it was unworkable. Monique was there and didn't seem interested in the problem, or at least didn't do anything. I feel that a lot of my ideas, which I had spent time preparing, were overlooked. What should I do?

Issy

Email: 3

To: YOU
From: Tobias Fiser
Subject: Agricultural Markets Conference Briefing
Date: 1st February 20XX, 10:24

Hello,

Please find below an outline of the practicalities of the Agricultural Markets Conference, which you need to look after in my absence:

- The conference runs between Monday 15th February and Tuesday 16th February. It is run twice a year, with the previous one being in August last year.
- The venue is the Zwaan conference facilities – we have booked out most of their west wing for the days.
- Your main contact at the venue is Richard Laplace. He is looking after food, rooms, security, etc. We are providing most of the material.
- There are approximately 215 delegates, all booked in. About 65% of these work for the EU, 20% represent special interest groups (such as farmers) with the rest typically working for businesses that supply e.g. pesticides.
- Food is being provided a la carte by the venue; I have sorted this all out, but let Richard know if you have any concerns. All delegates are eating.
- You will need to finalise the material:
    - Pens and pads
    - USB sticks with presentation material (already prepared)
    - Timetables and conference information
    - The venue will provide flip charts, whiteboards, projectors, technology, etc.
    - Please be aware that we had complaints at the last conference about the unprofessional quality of the material – Elisabet can provide you more information about this if needed, as she was the person who sorted this last time.
- We will be making a press release next week, David Bland is looking after this as he is very experienced handling matters in relation to the media.

Hopefully this is enough, as mentioned I can help you out once I get back.

A quick aside... Monique noticed that Ludvig Blom is on the delegate list for the conference. Unfortunately he was banned from EU conference events after inappropriate behaviour at the last conference. Please can you ensure that he does not attend this.

Thanks,

Tobias Fiser

Administrator
Wines, spirits, horticultural products, specialised crops
Directorate-General for Agriculture and Rural Development

Email: 4

To: YOU
From: Elisabet Kivi
Subject: Mia Thompson
Date: 1st February 20XX, 12:40

Hello

Just had a note from Mia. She has become very ill and won't be able to attend any meetings for the next couple of months. She will recover, but please don't contact her with work-related questions as she needs to rest – her Deputy Head of Unit Simon Gruber is the best point of contact in her absence.

Thanks,

Elisabet

Email: 5

To: ALL
From: Monique Meunier
Subject: Agricultural Markets Conference Speakers
Date: 1st February 20XX, 15:07

Dear all,

I take great pleasure in confirming our final speaker list for the Agricultural Markets Conference in a fortnight. I've managed to get some great speakers both within and outside of the EU. Please find the list of main speakers below:

Speaker	Day	Topic
Hanne Smets	15th Feb AM	The Common Agricultural Policy: an update
Park Sung-Joon (external)	15th Feb PM 1	Asian Agriculture: an update
Monique Meunier	15th Feb PM 2	Vine rights: is limitation delivering
Clive Kubler (external)	16th Feb AM	Promoting International Cooperation across Agricultural Industries
Mia Thompson	16th Feb PM 1	Feed the future...sustainable models of agriculture in developing markets
Anna Balog	16th Feb PM 2	Cobweb theory: challenges for local food producers. An EU problem?

Of course, there will be plenty of other meetings, presentations and opportunities to network outside of these keynote speeches. I'm looking forward to my own presentation.

I expect high turnouts for each of these speakers. I understand that there are almost two hundred delegates at the conference and the room has been booked accordingly.

I look forward to seeing you all there, thank you for your hard work so far.

Best Regards,

Monique

Email: 6

To: YOU
From: Rasmus Jokela
Subject: Eastern Europe wine production report
Date: 1st February 20XX, 15:59

The report you sent me about changes in wine production was a fascinating read. Unfortunately, the tables are totally broken, so I can't read any of the data. I'm pretty good at working with computers, but I couldn't figure out how to fix this or recover the tables. This means I cannot share this with others. Did you check this before you sent it over?

I really need it by the end of today if at all possible.

Email: 7

To: YOU
From: Elisabet Kivi
Subject: Stationery Ordering Spreadsheet
Date: 1st February 20XX, 16:25

Hi,

I'm having difficulty with the spreadsheet you set up for our Directorate that lets us log what stationery we need. I know you were the one who created this, and I don't mean to cause offense, but it just doesn't work. I lost several of my most recent inputs and had to enter them again – I could have totally lost some important pens that I needed.
The system doesn't make sense to me and I think it has difficulty when more than one person is trying to place a request at once. I'd be much happier to return to what we were doing previously – emailing the relevant person each time we needed something new. Would you agree that the new system has been a bit of a letdown and we should return to the old way?

Thanks,

Elisabet

Email: 8

To: YOU
From: David Bland
Subject: Work Credit
Date: 2nd February 20XX, 8:51

I am really disappointed that for the recent Eastern European wine production report that is to be distributed across the Directorate, you took all the credit. I understand that you sent it across to Rasmus without mentioning all of the work I put in collating the data. I think this is unacceptable, as I worked very hard to help ensure your report was of a high standard.

Email: 9

To: YOU
From: Lotte Stevens
Subject: Printed Material and Branded Stationery
Date: 2nd February 20XX, 11:12

Hello,

I have just received an out of office for Tobias Fiser telling me to contact you. Tobias set up the following order last week:

- 300 pens
- 300 pads (branded)
- Printed timetables and delegate packs

He mentioned that this was needed for Monday 15th February to be delivered to the EU offices. However, he has not confirmed the details yet. Could you confirm and arrange for payment for this please?

Thanks,

Lotte

Account Manager
Brussels Business Services

Email: 10

To: YOU
From: Isabella Jensen
Subject: Technical difficulties
Date: 2nd February 20XX, 14:23

Just to let you know, I seem to have stopped receiving emails around lunchtime, so apologies if I'm not responding to anything important. Can you confirm whether you've received this email please? Can you call or talk to me if you have anything important to say today, to make sure that I get the message.

Issy

Email: 11

To: YOU
From: Elisabet Kivi
Subject: Presentation for Monique
Date: 2nd February 20XX, 14:52

Hi,

I'm trying to put together the slides for Monique's presentation at the conference. Unfortunately, I'm having a lot of difficulty – I don't understand a lot of the key points from the meeting I had with her, my notes don't make it clear what she really means. Would you have time this afternoon at 4pm to help me please, Monique really wants me to get this done today? I know you've worked on similar presentations with Monique in the past, I'm sure you will have some great insight into the parts that I don't understand.

Elisabet

Email: 12

To: YOU
From: Lukas Bosman
Subject: Translation Help Please!
Date: 2nd February 20XX, 15:45

Hello,

I'm wondering if you can help, as I know you're a fluent French speaker. I've been trying to communicate with someone from an important agricultural think tank in France. We have been funding them to advise us further in regards to our sustainable agriculture regulation, and this is going to tie into the conference in a few weeks. However, I think we're having trouble communicating – as you know my French is limited and I've not been able to communicate with them in Dutch or English.

This has become a real issue recently where they failed to pass on information to me in time for a critical deadline back here. Then of course I still need to get their lengthy report translated to understand it – it looks like it contradicts our understanding of regulation of international tax! Would you be able to read through the report and translate it? This needs to be this week or early next.

Thanks,

Lukas

Email: 13

To: YOU
From: Tobias Fiser
Subject: Database/Analysis system
Date: 2nd February 20XX, 19:43

Hello,

As you know, I'm away for a few weeks. For part of this I'm attending a conference that discusses database systems that specialise in tracking and analysing import/export information. I've been reading around a lot about one in particular, MoveBase, that I think sounds really promising. I think you should take a look at it too, and we can discuss my thoughts when I return. I think this could be an important upgrade for our Unit and our whole Directorate, and I'd like somebody to support me when I speak to the Director about it.

Thanks,

Tobias

Email: 14

To: YOU
From: Monique Meunier
Subject: Fire Alarm Test
Date: 3rd February 20XX, 8:32

Quick note to remind you that there will be a fire alarm test today at 4pm. This is just a test of the alarm itself, we will not need to leave the building.

Email: 15

To: YOU
From: David Bland
Subject: FW: Press Article
Date: 3rd February 20XX, 8:55

I need to bring something to your attention. The details in the following press article shouldn't be out with the press yet. I think perhaps somebody in our Directorate has been leaking details about the conference. I know you are both responsible for the conference and wondered what your thoughts are about this?

Agricultural Markets Conference – 15th-16th February
Published 3rd February

The European Union is holding its regular event, the Agricultural Markets Conference, in 2 weeks' time. Over 200 delegates are thought to be attending, including several from both inside and outside of the EU. Speakers from outside the EU include Park Sung-Joon, who will be talking about Asian Agriculture, and Clive Kubler who will be heading up a panel discussion about how the EU can support international trade (both inside and outside of the EU). It is also known that Hanne Smets is going to be making a major announcement related to the EU's Common Agricultural Policy.

Situations

Situation 1: One of the speakers at the Agricultural Markets Conference (Park Sung-Joon) has yet to confirm attendance, although your superior Monique thinks he has. How do you deal with this situation? Rate each response on a scale ranging from - - (totally disagree) to + + (totally agree).

Q No.	Action	- -	-	- /+	+	+ +
1	Contact Monique to let her know that Park has not yet confirmed but that you will update her when he has.					
2	Contact Park to introduce yourself and ask whether he can confirm that he will be speaking.					
3	Ask your peer Tobias why he's not been able to confirm this yet and whether he can do so.					

Situation 2: Your peer Elisabet Kivi has contacted you to let you know that Mia Thompson is unwell for the next two months. How do you deal with this situation? Rate each response on a scale ranging from - - (totally disagree) to + + (totally agree).

Q No.	Action	- -	-	- /+	+	+ +
1	Contact your superior Monique to try to determine a new speaker to replace Mia at the conference.					
2	Arrange for flowers to be sent to Mia while she recovers.					
3	Email the Deputy Head of Mia's Unit, Simon Gruber, asking him to replace Mia at the conference.					

Situation 3: Your peer David Bland has contacted you stating that somebody in your Directorate has leaked details about the Agricultural Markets Conference to the press, citing a recent newspaper article as evidence. How do you deal with this situation? Rate each response on a scale ranging from - - (totally disagree) to + + (totally agree).

Q No.	Action	- -	-	- /+	+	+ +
1	Approach those in the Directorate who may have had contact with the press and ask them if they leaked the information.					
2	Contact the paper and ask them not to report on the conference yet as you will be releasing details later.					
3	Ask David what he recommends in this situation and what points he is uncomfortable with the press knowing.					

Situation 4: In an email summarising the last Agricultural Markets Conference, your peer Tobias Fiser has mentioned that there were complaints about the unprofessional quality of the material. How do you deal with this situation? Rate each response on a scale ranging from - - (totally disagree) to + + (totally agree).

Q No.	Action	- -	-	- /+	+	+ +
1	Email your peer Elisabet and ask for further information about the feedback from last time and for her own insights.					
2	Email the current provider of material and ask them to hold off on delivery until you've established the issues.					
3	Cancel the current order for pens, pads and printing.					

Situation 5: Lotte Stevens, Account Manager at a printing and stationery company, has asked for sign off on an order to your peer Tobias Fiser proposed. How do you deal with this situation? Rate each response on a scale ranging from - - (totally disagree) to + + (totally agree).

Q No.	Action	- -	-	- /+	+	+ +
1	Give the go ahead to Tobias' order as it's important to get the material as soon as possible.					
2	Ask whether the order can be delivered prior to Monday 15th February so that you have it in time for the conference.					
3	Ask whether this can be delivered to the venue rather than the EU offices on 15th February.					

Situation 6: Your superior Monique Meunier has stated that the rooms at the Agricultural Markets Conference are "booked accordingly" for "almost two hundred delegates", but in another email Tobias mentioned that there are approximately 215 delegates. How do you deal with this situation? Rate each response on a scale ranging from - - (totally disagree) to + + (totally agree).

Q No.	Action	- -	-	- /+	+	+ +
1	Contact the event manager at the venue to ensure that the rooms are booked for enough delegates.					
2	Leave the situation as it is, as your superior's language was vague and she did not contradict that rooms had been booked for 215 delegates.					
3	Contact your peer Tobias Fiser to get his insight into whether the appropriate rooms have been booked.					

Situation 7: Your peer Tobias Fiser has informed you that, according to your superior Monique Meunier, somebody on the Agricultural Markets Conference delegate list called Ludvig Blome has been banned from EU conferences. How do you deal with this situation? Rate each response on a scale ranging from - - (totally disagree) to + + (totally agree).

Q No.	Action	- -	-	- /+	+	+ +
1	Write to Ludvig personally to inform him that unfortunately he cannot attend the upcoming conference.					
2	Check with Monique to confirm that Ludvig is banned.					
3	Try to find out more information about why Ludvig was banned by reviewing records from the last conference.					

Situation 8: Your peer Elisabet Kivi has asked for your help putting together some slides for a presentation your superior is giving at the Agricultural Markets Conference – she asked for your help yesterday, but you were out of the office. How do you deal with this situation? Rate each response on a scale ranging from - - (totally disagree) to + + (totally agree).

Q No.	Action	- -	-	- /+	+	+ +
1	Apologise for not getting back to her sooner and for not being able to help her.					
2	Ask Elisabet to send you the work that she has done so far so that you can finish putting the slides together for her.					
3	Meet with Elisabet to offer your support and work together on the slides if she still needs.					

Situation 9: Your peer Tobias has emailed you suggesting use of a specific piece of database software called MoveBase, which can be used for tracking and analysing import/export information. How do you deal with this situation? Rate each response on a scale ranging from - - (totally disagree) to + + (totally agree).

Q No.	Action	- -	-	- /+	+	+ +
1	When Tobias returns from his time away, agree to support him in presenting the idea to the Unit Director.					
2	Wait until Tobias returns and then ask him if he has any further insights into the database system.					
3	Perform your own review of this and similar systems while Tobias is away so that you can present your own viewpoint when he returns.					

Situation 10: Your peer David Bland has contacted you accusing you of taking credit for his work on a report that you sent to a superior, Rasmus Jokela. How do you deal with this situation? Rate each response on a scale ranging from - - (totally disagree) to + + (totally agree).

Q No.	Action	- -	-	- /+	+	+ +
1	Send an email to Rasmus immediately that explains the contribution that David made.					
2	Apologise and reassure David he will get due credit on future projects that you collaborate on.					
3	Respond making it clear that you didn't take specific credit and that output is always team-based so David should not worry.					

Situation 11: A superior Rasmus Jokela has emailed stating that the tables in a document you sent to him are unreadable and he cannot figure out how to fix this. How do you deal with this situation? Rate each response on a scale ranging from - - (totally disagree) to + + (totally agree).

Q No.	Action	- -	-	- /+	+	+ +
1	Ask Rasmus what software he is using to open the document and whether he's had similar issues before.					
2	Try to meet with Rasmus to explore the issue and check how the document appears on his computer.					
3	Check that the tables in the document are formatted correctly and then send it to Rasmus again.					

Situation 12: Your peer Elisabet Kivi has emailed you to raise concerns about a spreadsheet you set up that tracks stationery requirements throughout the Directorate, suggesting that you return a previous system as she does not like this one. How do you deal with this situation? Rate each response on a scale ranging from - - (totally disagree) to + + (totally agree).

Q No.	Action	- -	-	- /+	+	+ +
1	Speak to others who have been trying to use the new system, and request that they move back to the old system too to help make the use of the system consistent.					
2	Explain to Elisabet the benefits of your new system and why you implemented it, making it clear that she will get used to it if she uses it enough.					
3	Look for opportunities to gather input such as hers to try to understand where the new spreadsheet can be improved.					

Situation 13: One of your peers, Isabella Jensen, has emailed you stating that she is having difficulty working with David Bland as he constantly criticises her ideas and undermines her. How do you deal with this situation? Rate each response on a scale ranging from - - (totally disagree) to + + (totally agree).

Q No.	Action	- -	-	- /+	+	+ +
1	Advise Isabella to tell your superior Monique, so that she can resolve the issue through the proper channels.					
2	Meet with Isabella, offering to speak to David if she wishes.					
3	Approach David yourself and tell him his behaviour is upsetting Isabella.					

Situation 14: Your superior Monique Meunier has sent an email to let you know that there is a fire alarm test in the afternoon today. How do you deal with this situation? Rate each response on a scale ranging from - - (totally disagree) to + + (totally agree).

Q No.	Action	- -	-	- /+	+	+ +
1	Speak with other members of your Unit in person to make sure that they are aware of this.					
2	Email Monique thanking her for reminding you of this information.					
3	Set a reminder in your schedule of the upcoming fire alarm.					

Situation 15: Your peer Isabella Jensen emailed to tell you that she is not receiving emails. How do you deal with this situation? Rate each response on a scale ranging from - - (totally disagree) to + + (totally agree).

Q No.	Action	- -	-	- /+	+	+ +
1	As the issue was yesterday, assume that Isabella has resolved it by now and focus on other emails.					
2	Email the IT department on Isabella's behalf asking them to resolve her issue.					
3	Send her an email and then follow up by meeting with her in person to check the message got through.					

Situation 16: Your colleague Lukas Bosman is having difficulty working with a French-speaking think tank. He has asked for your help as he considers you a strong French speaker. How do you deal with this situation? Rate each response on a scale ranging from - - (totally disagree) to + + (totally agree).

Q No.	Action	- -	-	- /+	+	+ +
1	Ask Lukas how he came to be working with a French think tank when he doesn't speak French.					
2	Offer to translate the report for Lukas to make sure he understands it clearly.					
3	Offer to support Lukas by communicating directly with the think tank in future.					

Full Marking Key

Situation 1: (related emails: 1, 5)

Q No.	Competency	- -	-	- /+	+	+ +	Rationale
1	WWO	2	3	4	3	2	It will be useful for Monique to know this, so making contact with her is a good step. However, it will not resolve the main issue itself, the need to confirm the speaker.
2	DQR	0	1	2	3	4	This solution tackles the most important issue directly, the need to confirm the speaker – the event is only a few weeks away, and your peer Tobias has told you that you should contact Park directly.
3	P&O	4	3	2	1	0	Tobias is on leave, so this solution will not get an efficient response. Furthermore, you have been told to contact Park directly, so going back to Tobias is not likely to be as effective as making contact yourself.

Situation 2: (related emails: 1, 4, 5)

Q No.	Competency	- -	-	- /+	+	+ +	Rationale
1	APS	0	1	2	3	4	This is an appropriate situation to raise upwards as Monique is likely to have insight into a suitable replacement. Monique was responsible for finding the original set of speakers so is likely well-positioned to support with finding another.
2	WWO	1	2	3	4	3	While this doesn't resolve the immediate issue, it is a thoughtful response to Mia's illness and is likely to show sympathy and help you build the relationship with her.
3	WWO	3	4	3	2	1	This reaction may be inappropriate and not get the best results. Although it shows some initiative, Simon may not be an appropriate presenter or may not be comfortable being pressured into it. You should at least ask whether he wants to do this, but it would be recommended to check that this is acceptable before proceeding.

Situation 3: (Related emails: 1, 3, 15)

Q No.	Competency	- -	-	- /+	+	+ +	Rationale
1	WWO	3	4	3	2	1	This approach may help you figure out how the information has reached the paper. However, it does not deal with the issue itself. The tone of asking others if they leaked the information may also come across as negative and is unlikely to get cooperation.
2	DQR	2	3	4	3	2	This may well help you prevent future reoccurrence of similar stories until David's press release next week, but does not take action to correct the current issue. It does not draw on David's expertise and responsibility.
3	P&O	0	1	2	3	4	In this case, this is an appropriate opportunity to delegate the task back. You are told that David is looking after the press release next week, and so he is likely to have insight into the best way to present this to the press– for example, if there is anything it is important that they shouldn't know.

Situation 4: (related emails: 1, 3, 9)

Q No.	Competency	- -	-	- /+	+	+ +	Rationale
1	APS	1	2	3	4	3	Elisabet is likely to be a good source of information on what happened last time, who the provider was, what needed to be improved, etc. This makes this a good approach.
2	P&O	0	1	2	3	4	This is a strong response. It puts in place a temporary solution (not making the order) while you establish the facts about what happened last time. Should you find that the new provider is likely to be acceptable, you can then re-confirm the order.
3	APS	4	3	2	1	0	There is no information to suggest that the current provider is the same as at the last conference, so cancelling their order may be inappropriate. Indeed, Tobias is aware of the poor material from last time and has placed an order with one company, so this indicates that he may have already taken steps to ensure this is ok.

Situation 5: (related emails: 1, 3, 9)

Q No.	Competency	- -	-	- /+	+	+ +	Rationale
1	P&O	4	3	2	1	0	This is a poor solution, as you need to confirm whether the quality of material is acceptable. You also know that the delivery is scheduled for over a week away, indicating that you have time to ensure the final order is correct.
2	P&O	0	1	2	3	4	This approach will give you time to review the material to check that it is acceptable (and may even give you time to get it replaced if it isn't).
3	DQR	2	3	4	3	2	While this shows an understanding that the material is being delivered to the wrong place on the day, by instead getting it delivered earlier and to your offices it gives you more time to confirm that the material is acceptable.

Situation 6: (related emails: 1, 3, 5)

Q No.	Competency	- -	-	- /+	+	+ +	Rationale
1	DQR	0	1	2	3	4	This is an efficient way to get the most accurate information, to check to keep the issue under control.
2	DQR	4	3	2	1	0	You are responsible for making sure the conference runs smoothly, so it is your responsibility to follow up on possible issues like this. There is enough information to indicate this could be an issue, so overlooking it is a poor response.
3	P&O	3	4	3	2	1	While Tobias may have this information, he is currently out of the office for several weeks. You should think of someone better to contact.

Situation 7: (related emails: 1,3)

Q No.	Competency	- -	-	- /+	+	+ +	Rationale
1	DQR	2	3	4	3	2	While this shows a focus on responding to the task, this is a big step to take without confirming the details.
2	P&O	0	1	2	3	4	As your superior was the person who seems to have raised this issue, she is the best person to check with to ensure Ludvig needs to be uninvited. This is a good step to take before taking further action.
3	APS	4	3	2	1	0	This is an inefficient use of your time, as it is not your responsibility to understand why Ludvig is banned. You should seek to confirm that he should be banned and then take action.

Situation 8: (related emails: 1, 5, 11)

Q No.	Competency	- -	-	- /+	+	+ +	Rationale
1	P&O	3	4	3	2	1	While this shows recognition that Elisabet was looking for help yesterday, it assumes that the issue is no longer a problem. If she still needs support, this is a weak response. You should check assumptions like this before planning whether to help or not.
2	DQR	1	2	3	4	3	This approach shows a focus on getting the job done but overlooks the needs of your peer. It is likely to resolve the immediate issue but you could go even further in this situation to support Elisabet and so help her beyond the immediate task.
3	WWO	0	1	2	3	4	This solution is focused on supporting Elisabet and helping her overcome her difficulty. This will help her resolve both her immediate issue as well as support her in similar situations in the future.

Situation 9: (related emails: 13)

Q No.	Competency	- -	-	- /+	+	+ +	Rationale
1	WWO	2	3	4	3	2	This shows a desire to support your peer. It is somewhat hasty to be agreeing to support prior to Tobias' attendance at the conference, as he may come back with other ideas or information about what will work best.
2	APS	0	1	2	3	4	This approach shows an understanding that Tobias' email has come early in the process, and he may come back from his conference with different information or a different view.
3	P&O	3	4	3	2	1	This shows a desire to find more information to best understand the options, but you may benefit from waiting until Tobias returns to see what he has learned and whether MoveBase is an option worth pursuing.

Situation 10: (related email: 8)

Q No.	Competency	- -	-	- /+	+	+ +	Rationale
1	WWO	1	2	3	4	3	This approach may help pass on the credit where it's due but could come across as unnatural and only really tackles the immediate issue.
2	WWO	0	1	2	3	4	This shows a concern for the situation and a desire to rectify it in future.
3	APS	3	4	3	2	1	This is a defensive approach that may frustrate David further rather than helping resolve the issue.

Situation 11: (related email: 6)

Q No.	Competency	- -	-	- /+	+	+ +	Rationale
1	APS	1	2	3	4	3	Seeking out this information is likely to give you a better understanding of the situation and what may be going wrong.
2	WWO	0	1	2	3	4	By meeting with Rasmus directly you can tackle the issue together as well as help build your working relationship with him.
3	APS	4	3	2	1	0	This approach is unlikely to work: as the original document did not work properly there is little value in just re-sending it.

Situation 12: (related email: 7)

Q No.	Competency	- -	-	- /+	+	+ +	Rationale
1	APS	4	3	2	1	0	This solution does not show an appreciation that the new system could be better, and that you should seek to understand people's difficulties in more depth before abandoning the idea.
2	DQR	2	3	4	3	2	Explaining the benefits is a good way to try to win her over, but she might have insightful input into how to continue developing the spreadsheet. She may also become frustrated if you tell her what to do rather than discussing it.
3	APS	0	1	2	3	4	This helps gather more information to best understand why the system has been seemingly unsuccessful. This may help you resolve any difficulties people are having.

Situation 13: (related emails: 2, 8)

Q No.	Competency	- -	-	- /+	+	+ +	Rationale
1	APS	3	4	3	2	1	As Monique has shown little interest in the problem so far, you may be better off thinking about how you or Isabella can talk to David, rather than risk seeming like you are 'reporting him' to your superior.
2	WWO	0	1	2	3	4	This solution shows a willingness to tackle the issue head on, but also shows sensitivity to those involved.
3	DQR	2	3	4	3	2	Isabella has not asked you to talk to David directly, so may be upset if you approach him behind her back. A better solution would be to talk to her first, get a better understanding of the issue, and agree a way forward together.

Situation 14: (related emails: 10, 14)

Q No.	Competency	- -	-	- /+	+	+ +	Rationale
1	APS	0	1	2	3	4	While this idea may generally be unnecessary, in this case you know that at least one peer is not receiving emails. By informing her of this you can make sure she is aware. By speaking to others in your Unit you can make sure that even if the issue is broader your team will know.
2	WWO	2	3	4	3	2	This is a polite response but not particularly valuable to anyone.
3	P&O	4	3	2	1	0	There will be no need to take action as this is just a test of the alarm itself. You will be able to remember this by the afternoon, so setting a reminder is not likely to be of any use.

Situation 15: (Related emails: 10)

Q No.	Competency	- -	-	- /+	+	+ +	Rationale
1	DQR	4	3	2	1	0	This is dismissive of the problems a peer has. By speaking with her you can figure out whether the issue is still occurring and whether she needs any additional support (for example, sending emails on her behalf) at the moment.
2	P&O	2	3	4	3	2	This shows a focus on delivery but overlooks the fact that she may have already taken these steps. You would be better quickly checking the situation with her.
3	P&O	0	1	2	3	4	Although she may have resolved the issue by now, a quick email will not take long. You can then meet with her to discuss the situation and offer support.

Situation 16: (related emails: 12)

Q No.	Competency	- -	-	- /+	+	+ +	Rationale
1	DQR	4	3	2	1	0	This response shows no focus on resolving the issue to hand, rather it seeks to blame someone for the current situation.
2	DQR	2	3	4	3	2	This solution is acceptable. This may be too much of a commitment for you (Lukas said the report was lengthy) and there may be more appropriate people to take this task on (for example, there may be technical jargon that you are not aware of in French). You may benefit in this situation by checking whether this is appropriate.
3	WWO	0	1	2	3	4	This approach deals with Lukas' direct request and need. It is likely to help him deal with his problems, as you have the expertise he needs.

Annex 3 Sample Case Study

Candidate Brief

This case study exercise is based on the creation of the "High-Level Expert Group on Fake News" by the European Commission.

The task you are given, acting as a Commission official, by a fictitious head of unit, is entirely imaginary. However, it is intended as a simulation of the sort of assignment which an Administrator might face in real life.

"Fake news" – fabricated news stories with the deliberate aim of fooling readers – has become an increasingly visible global phenomenon. Viral fake news received more engagement from Facebook users than real news in the final three months of the US presidential election campaign in 2016. A growing number of EU citizens follow the news on social media. Six out of ten news items shared on social media have not been read by the user who shares them. And recent US research has shown that most young, digital-savvy school and college students have difficulties identifying fake news.

The role of the High-Level Expert Group on Fake News is to advise the Commission on scoping the phenomenon, defining the roles and responsibilities of relevant stakeholders, grasping the international dimension, taking stock of the positions at stake, and formulating recommendations. The intention is that, as far as possible, the High-Level Group should include several representatives of each field of expertise, be it academia or civil society delegate. The Commission aims at a balanced selection of experts.

For this exercise, you will take on the role of an Administrator working for the Commission Directorate-General DG CNCT (Communications Networks, Content and Technology).

It is important that you accept the scenario as it is presented to you. Although in real life you would have access to other sources of information and would be able to consult your colleagues, in this exercise **you are limited to the information contained in the documents provided**. You are, however, allowed to make logical assumptions where information is missing or incomplete.

You may rearrange the information in any order you wish and add remarks or make notes as necessary. However, remember that the assessors will base their evaluation exclusively on what you write. Therefore, be sure to explain the reasoning behind your ideas and write down all the information on which you wish to be evaluated.

The case study is designed to assess the following competencies: Analysis and Problem Solving, Communicating (Drafting Skills), Delivering Quality & Results, and Prioritising & Organising.

Specifically, it will be your task to:

- **Create an operational definition of the term "fake news", and how it affects democracy in general and the EU in particular**
- **Outline the mandate and a draft timetable for the High-Level Expert Group**

- **Clarify the criteria by which the Members of the High-Level Expert Group will be selected**

In total, you have 90 minutes for this case study. Please answer as precisely as you can and write as clearly and legibly as possible.

Please note: Today is 13 November 20XX.

BACKGROUND INFORMATION

From:	Catherine McDonagh
To:	<your name>
Date:	13/11/20XX
Subject:	High-Level Expert Group on Fake News
Importance:	High

Dear [your name]

The Commission launched today a public consultation on fake news and online disinformation and is setting up a High-Level Expert Group representing academics, online platforms, news media and civil society organisations. The work of the High-Level Expert Group (HLEG) as well as the results of the public consultation will contribute to the development of an EU-level strategy on how to tackle the spreading of fake news.

You have been appointed to be part of the secretariat of the High-Level Group. In this context you are asked to create a draft working paper in which you define the scope of what is 'fake news', the HLEG's mandate and objectives and a provisional timetable for them to present the results of their work in spring next year.

The HLEG will start its work in January, but before that we have to be clear by which criteria we will select and appoint the Members. Please let me know your ideas on this as well.

Our Commissioner can't wait to start working on this important issue, so I would like to have your document by tonight.

Catherine McDonagh,

Head of Unit

Source document: Fake News

Wikipedia

Fake news is a type of yellow journalism or propaganda that consists of deliberate misinformation or hoaxes spread via traditional print and broadcast news media or online social media. Fake news is written and published with the intent to mislead in order to damage an agency, entity, or person, and/or gain financially or politically, often with sensationalist, exaggerated, or patently false headlines that grab attention. Intentionally misleading and deceptive fake news is different from obvious satire or parody which is intended to humour rather than mislead its audience. Fake news often employs eye-catching headlines or entirely fabricated news stories to increase readership, online sharing and Internet click revenue. In the latter case, it is similar to sensational online "clickbait" headlines and relies on advertising revenue generated from this activity, regardless of the veracity of the published stories. Fake news also undermines serious media coverage and makes it more difficult for journalists to cover significant news stories.

Easy access to online advertisement revenue, increased political polarization, and the popularity of social media, primarily the Facebook News Feed, have all been implicated in the spread of fake news, which have come to provide competition for legitimate news stories. Hostile government actors have also been implicated in generating and propagating fake news, particularly during elections. An analysis by Buzzfeed found that the top 20 fake news stories about the 2016 U.S. presidential election received more engagement on Facebook than the top 20 news stories on the election from 19 major media outlets.

With the expansion of technology, the need for views and ratings has been increasingly higher. For media outlets, the ability to attract viewers to their websites is a necessity in order to please advertisers that pay for advertising on their websites. If publishing a story with false content will produce a big caption and attract viewers it may be worth producing in order to benefit advertisers and ratings.

Source document: 'Fake news' and the EU's response

European Parliamentary Research Service

Fake news – deliberately fabricated stories posing as journalism with the aim of manipulating readers – became an increasingly visible global phenomenon during last year's presidential election campaign in the United States, not least due to the growing use of social media as a source for news. Whereas recent research indicates that a majority of people have difficulties determining when news is fake, the EU's steps towards countering this growing information challenge are still tentative.

A global phenomenon with political impact

The phenomenon of 'fake news' is as old as the printing press. However, it gained momentum and global visibility during the final months of the 2016 US presidential election, when viral fake news across the political spectrum received more engagement on Facebook than real news. The Australian Macquarie Dictionary (AMD) – which chose 'fake news' as its word of the year for 2016 – defines it as 'disinformation and hoaxes published on websites for political purposes or to drive web traffic, the incorrect information being passed along by social media'. Explaining the choice, the AMD argued that the term 'captures an interesting evolution in the creation of deceptive content as a way of herding people in a specific direction'. Social media and their personalisation tools have accelerated the spread of 'fake news'. A growing number of EU citizens follow news on social media; six out of ten news items shared are passed on without being read first; and US research has shown that most young, digital-savvy school and college students have difficulties in identifying fake news.

Disinformation as an information warfare tool

Fake news headlines seem tailored to trick users into sharing the stories, making them spread fast and far amongst like-minded users. Sometimes the aim is simply to generate traffic ('clickbait'). However, when designed to deceive users for political purposes, it falls under 'disinformation': dissemination of deliberately false information. Disinformation is part of a strategic tool kit that non-state and state actors can use to undermine adversaries. Russia has been using information operations in its on-going hybrid war against Ukraine, and continues to apply it in its 'holistic' information warfare against the EU and the West. Fake news proliferation during the US presidential campaign was accompanied by selective leaks of emails from Democratic Party officials. A declassified US intelligence assessment said that Russia used professional 'trolls' (internet warriors) and Russian state broadcaster RT 'as part of its influence efforts'. In March 20XX, a cyber-security expert told a US Senate panel investigating President Donald Trump's alleged ties to Russia that the information measures had worked, because Trump and his team promoted narratives, including false ones, serving Russian interests. In the same hearing, the Senate Intelligence Committee's Mark Warner claimed that Russia paid thousands of people to create and pedal fake anti-Hillary Clinton news, targeting key swing states.

The Kremlin has acknowledged its information warfare capabilities ahead of key elections in Europe. So far, Russia has denied all allegations of interference in the US election. But on 22 February 20XX, Russian Defence Minister, Sergey Shoigu, announced that 'information operations forces have been established that are expected to be a far more effective tool than all we used before for counter-propaganda purposes', arguing that Russian 'propaganda needs to be clever, smart and efficient'. At the same time, Russia's foreign ministry itself began to publish 'materials that contain false information about Russia ' on its website. Security analysts say that Shoigu's announcement indicates that Russia can no longer deny propaganda activities. The most likely targets for Russian information operations are its immediate neighbours (Ukraine, Belarus, and the Baltic States), the western Balkans, and major EU countries holding elections in 20XX, in particular France and Germany). There is also concern that the 2019 European Parliament elections could be targeted. Pro-Kremlin information campaigns boost Moscow's narrative of a 'weak and morally decayed EU that is about to collapse'.

'Fake news' as a slur for unwelcome media reports: a 'post-truth' phenomenon?

The 'fake news' trend is seen as an element in the deeper democratic challenge of what is known as the 'post-truth' era. Post-truth – the Oxford Dictionaries' word of the year for 2016 – is defined as 'relating to or denoting circumstances in which objective facts are less influential in shaping public opinion than appeals to emotion and personal belief'. In a move that allegedly signified this 'new reality', President Trump's counsellor, Kellyanne Conway, used the notion of 'alternative facts' to describe claims made by White House press secretary, Sean Spicer, about the size of the crowds attending the inauguration ceremony, contradicting what he called 'shameful and wrong' mainstream media reports. The same day, Trump – talking to Central Intelligence Agency staff – called the media 'some of the most dishonest human beings on earth'. Trump has repeatedly described news (outlets) that he appears to dislike as 'fake news', 'dishonest', an 'enemy of the people' and 'the opposition'.

International media watchdogs warn against 'misleading the public'. Information freedom watchdogs, such as Reporters Without Borders, warned in March 20XX that Trump's statements could set a 'dangerous example for the world's press freedom predators' who see the notion of 'fake news' as justification to criminalise critical media. Also in March, the UN special rapporteur on freedom of opinion and expression, the OSCE representative on freedom of the media, and other international monitors of freedom of expression issued a joint declaration on 'fake news', disinformation and propaganda. They expressed alarm at 'instances in which public authorities denigrate, intimidate and threaten the media, including by stating that the media is "the opposition" or is "lying"', thus undermining public trust and confidence in journalism as a public watchdog, with the risk of misleading the public by 'blurring the lines between disinformation and media products containing independently verifiable facts'

Growing concern in Europe raises pressure on social media companies

In Europe, reflecting the increased concern over the 'fake news' phenomenon, the European Parliament's then-President, Martin Schulz, in December 2016 called for a European solution to the problem of fake news. Andrus Ansip, European Commission Vice-President in charge of the digital single market as well as digital economy and society, said in January 20XX he was 'worried' about fake news, 'especially after the elections in the United States'. He urged Facebook and other social media firms to boost their efforts to counter 'fake news', adding that self-regulatory measures in the sector could be complemented by 'some kind of clarification' from the EU. On 14 March, German Justice Minister, Heiko Maas, proposed imposing fines of up to €50 million on social media companies who fail to remove hate speech and 'fake news'. Also in March, Sweden announced plans to boost the resilience of its society ahead of the 2018 general election. Fact-checking websites are currently mushrooming across the world, among others the pan-European fact-checking coalition CrossCheck. Although social media platforms have resisted being labelled as publishers, Facebook announced a tool that enables users to 'flag' fake news reports for review by third-party fact-checkers from the International Fact Checking Network (IFCN). The initiative cooperates with media outlets in EU Member States and became operational on 22 March 20XX. There are also increasing calls, including from the Organisation for Economic Co-operation and Development, for children to be taught in schools how to spot fake news.

The European Council in 2015 asked the EU High Representative, Federica Mogherini, to submit an action plan on strategic communication to address Russia's ongoing disinformation campaigns. As a result, the EEAS's East StratCom task Force was set up in September 2015. Since then, the team – consisting of some ten people – has been working without its own budget, drawing on the existing EU strategic communication budget and staff from EU institutions and Member States. It relies heavily on volunteers to collect the disinformation stories (more than 2500 examples in 18 languages since 2015) it presents and explains in its weekly newsletters, as part of its efforts. The European Parliament, in its 23 November 2016 resolution on EU strategic communication to counteract propaganda, warned against Russian anti-EU propaganda, and called for reinforcement of the East StratCom task force, including through 'proper staffing and adequate budgetary resources'. A number of prominent European security experts, historians and lawmakers – including Members of the European Parliament – in an open letter of 21 March 20XX criticised Mogherini's alleged 'irresponsibly weak' stance on Russia's 'brutally aggressive disinformation campaign' (boosted by over € 1 billion annually by the Kremlin). The signatories called for a budget in single million euros for the East Stratcom task force, 'so it can start fulfilling its mandate.' They added that 'Europeans need to know by who and how they are being manipulated.'

Source document: How to Spot When News is Fake

Adapted from European Parliamentary Research Service Blog

- **1. Check the media outlet**

  Do you know it? Check the 'about' section. If the language there is overly dramatic, be sceptical. Who is behind it? Who is funding it? Double-check what other (trustworthy) sources say.

- **2. Check the author**

  Does this person even exist? A well-respected journalist always has a track record. If the author has made up his or her name, the rest is also likely to be fake.

- **3. Check the references**

  Does the author use reliable sources (for example, well-established and respected media outlets)? Are the quoted experts real specialists? If the story uses anonymous (or no) sources, it could be fake.

- **4. Think before you share**

  The headline might be catchy to generate clicks. It could be distortions of real or old events – or it could be satire. If an event is real, mainstream media will cover it. Compare and draw your own conclusions.

- **5. Join the myth-busters**

  Keep on top of the latest tricks used by those spreading fake news. * Report fake stories. Spread the word.

  * For example follow @EUvsDisinfo, @StopFakingNews, or @DFRLab.

Source document: The E.U. Agency Fighting Russia's Wildfire of Fake News with a Hosepipe

Time Magazine

In 2015, as Russia plunged millions of dollars into an escalating disinformation campaign against the West, the European Union's defense consisted of just one person.

A former journalist had been seconded from the Czech Republic to the E.U.'s newly-established East StratCom Task Force, and was working furiously to de-bunk the Kremlin-backed fake news that flooded people's inboxes, TV screens, and social media timelines. "[He was working] literally seven days a week," said an E.U. official involved in the bloc's strategic communications efforts, who asked for anonymity in order to speak freely. "He was going to an early grave if we didn't get some help."

Getting help proved tricky. Despite a clear, and explicitly stated, aim from Moscow to use disinformation as part of its foreign policy, the E.U. moved at its customary slow pace. "Some countries didn't really feel the threat," said the official, citing the usual divisions which plague a co-ordinated E.U. response. While places like the Baltic nations, Poland, and Scandinavia—having been victims of Russian disinformation for years—advocated a robust response, others including

Hungary and southern European nations which depend on Russian investment or energy were less enthusiastic.

Even Germany "wasn't particularly supportive", the official said: "They were not really convinced there was a problem."

The U.S. elections apparently helped change their minds, with Moscow accused of deploying hacking and other means of disinformation to sway the result of the 2016 Presidential election. In September, it emerged that 3,300 Russia-backed ads had appeared on Facebook during the 2016 election campaign.

Now East StratCom is enjoying a reversal of fortune. On a recent visit to their headquarters in a bright and modern building in the heart of the E.U. district, staffs were busy putting together their weekly newsletter. They have built a volunteer network of 500 NGOs, diplomats, think tanks and other media professionals who regularly send them examples of fake news. These are then debunked in the newsletter, on Facebook and Twitter.

The efforts come as a string of high-profile European elections has raised awareness of Russia's attempts to destabilize the democratic process. In the Netherlands, authorities reverted to counting ballots by hand to thwart any attempts at hacking in March elections. New French President Emmanuel Macron called Kremlin-funded media outlets RT and Sputnik "agents of influence" which spread rumours about him during the campaign. In Germany – which holds elections later this month — false reports on Russian media of a migrant raping a 13-year-old Russian-German girl brought thousands of people out into the street in protest, giving Berlin a wake-up call in the powers of propaganda.

But combating Russia's propaganda networks remains a "David and Goliath struggle", the E.U. official conceded. The Kremlin's efforts to destabilize the E.U. and promote pro-Russian policy are alleged to include outright hacking, backing for anti-E.U. political parties, heavily biased news reporting, and an army of Internet "trolls" who stalk social media with pro-Russian messages. East StratCom will have expanded to 14 employees by the end of this year, but only three of them are working full time on de-bunking disinformation. Their Twitter feed has around 27,000 followers — compared to 2.62 million for RT – while its Facebook page has just over 17,000 likes. Sputnik has over a million.

The E.U's leadership says there's only so much it can do, given the resources it is already pouring into multiples crises within Europe. Speaking to TIME in an interview in February, European Commission President Jean-Claude Juncker said he was "certain that the Russians are trying by all the means they have to have a propaganda influence on European and international affairs." But he added: "They have thousands of people telling stories which do not reflect reality. We have only a few people [rebutting these] because I don't want to engage a thousand new civil servants to react."

Maja Kocijančič, the spokesperson for E.U. foreign affairs, told TIME in July that East StratCom "is doing an excellent job operating within their current allocated resources".

But for some, those "allocated resources" border on the negligent. In an open letter published in March, more than 120 signatories from across government, media, security and civil society accused the E.U. of being "irresponsibly weak" on disinformation. The European Parliament, meanwhile, called on the E.U. to more than double the staff of East StratCom and give it a budget in the millions. The 28 E.U. governments declined to back that proposal, and the unit still does not have its own budget, relying on a small share of the E.U.'s existing strategic communications budget.

And the threat is far from over. As well as German elections on Sept.24, there are fears of Russian meddling in elections in Sweden in 2018, and in the European Parliament elections in 2019. "We are still reactive, not pro-active," said Petras Auštrevičius, a Lithuanian Member of the European Parliament and one of the signatories of the open letter. Auštrevičius advocates more radical measures to curb the influence of Russian media. "I do not exclude a cut-off of the broadcasters," he said. "If they are really hostile against us, against our values, we should not shy away from taking even more principled measures."

He also thinks a proposed German law which would fine social media platforms up to $50 million if they fail to promptly remove "illegal content" should be expanded throughout the E.U. Earlier this year, the E.U. commissioner for the digital economy, Andrus Ansip, told the *Financial Times* that while he would prefer social media sites to pursue self-regulatory measures, they could be complemented by "some kind of clarifications". He did not expand on what those might be, and replying to a question from TIME, his spokesperson once again stressed that "these media carry the main responsibility to act against fake news".

So for now, East StatCom remains on the front line. A recent edition of the newsletter took on an implausible story published on Russian and Lithuanian news websites about an American B-52 plane dropping a nuclear bomb on a Lithuanian town. "If a tree falls in the forest and there's nobody around to hear, does it make a sound?" it asks. "What about a nuclear bomb that falls over a Lithuanian town, and no one notices?"

But the question is — above the din of the Russian propaganda machine, can anyone hear the E.U.?

Source document: Fake news: What exactly is it – and can it really swing an election?

The Daily Telegraph

"Fake news" was not a term many people used 18 months ago, but it is now seen as one of the greatest threats to democracy, free debate and the Western order.

As well as being a favourite term of Donald Trump, it has been named the word of the year, raised tensions between nations, and may lead to regulation of social media. And yet, nobody can agree on what it is, how much of a problem it is, and what to do about it.

The origins of fake news

Governments and powerful individuals have used information as a weapon for millennia, to boost their support and quash dissidence.

Octavian famously used a campaign of disinformation to aid his victory over Marc Anthony in the final war of the Roman Republic. In its aftermath, he changed his name to Augustus, and dispatched a flattering and youthful image of himself throughout the Empire, maintaining its use in his old age.

In the 20th century, new forms of mass communication allowed propaganda's scale and persuasive power to grow, particularly during wartime and in fascist regimes.

This sort of propaganda was largely funded and controlled by governments, but the blatant bias it carried waned as the ideological struggles became less apparent. Added to that, as populations became more used to mass communication, they could more easily see through it.

Enter the Internet and social media

Before the internet, it was much more expensive to distribute information, building up trust took years, and there were much simpler definitions of what constituted news and media, making regulation or self-regulation easier.

But the rise of social media has broken down many of the boundaries that prevented fake news from spreading in democracies. In particular it has allowed anyone to create and disseminate information, especially those that have proven most adept at "gaming" how social networks operate.

Facebook and Twitter allowed people to exchange information on a much greater scale than ever before, while publishing platforms like WordPress allowed anyone to create a dynamic website with ease. In short, the barriers to creating fake news have been undone.

Russia, the US election and Trump

Hoaxes and falsehoods have been associated with the internet since its early days, but it is only in the last two years that organised, systematic misinformation campaigns, often linked to governments, have emerged, and their effect on democracy and society scrutinised.

Last year's US election has been seen as providing a fertile breeding ground for fake news. Some credit Donald Trump's anti-establishment rhetoric and distrust of the mainstream media. Others blame widening partisanship, which meant readers were more prone to believe and share stories that fit their beliefs.

But the rise of social media itself has also been seen as central. Sites like Facebook are accused of creating "filter bubbles", the phenomenon of showing people things that they like or tend to agree with, and hiding those that they don't.

Critics of Facebook and Twitter say the sites are purpose built for spreading misinformation, with the reach of a story dependent on its ability to go viral – something that often depends on sensationalism and emotional reactions more than truth itself.

Headlines such as "Pope backs Trump", "Hillary sold weapons to ISIS", "FBI Agent Suspected in Hillary Email Leaks Found Dead" went viral on Facebook in the run up to the election, garnering thousands of shares.

But fake news goes beyond the US. According to Freedom House, 30 governments identified this year pay "opinion shapers" to promote propaganda online.

What exactly is fake news?

One of the problems of actually doing anything about fake news is that it comes in multiple variants, from different actors and with different motives. These include but are not limited to:

- **Commercially-driven sensational content**: Stories that are not ideologically driven, but very often have absolutely no grounding in fact. Their key goal is to drive web traffic and, as a result, generate advertising income. Pop-up websites run by Macedonian teenagers fall into this category.
- **Nation state-sponsored misinformation:** The goal here isn't revenue, but influence. Outlets in Russia or elsewhere might produce content to swing public opinion, sow division or give the illusion of support for a particular candidate or idea, either domestically or abroad. Fabricated stories can often be mixed with true or sensationalised ones.
- **Highly-partisan news sites:** These can conflate fact and opinion, are nakedly supportive of one political viewpoint or party, and often position themselves as alternatives to the mainstream media.
- **Social media itself:** Swarms of Twitter bots posting doctored or misleading photos, adverts on Facebook paid for by Russian intelligence outfits, videos on YouTube claiming terrorist incidents are hoaxes. These are not links outside of social media but are part of the social networks themselves.
- **Satire or parody:** Light-hearted publications such as The Onion and Daily Mash have existed well before fake news was seen as a problem.

This is not to mention news stories from mainstream outlets that turn out to be hoaxes or mistakes, but had genuinely good intentions behind them when published.

And of course, there's Donald Trump, who constantly refers to outlets such as CNN and the New York Times as "fake news". His administration also coined the term "alternative facts" when presented with evidence of low turnout at Trump's inauguration.

These different definitions and motives make it incredibly difficult to effectively counter fake news. Some types, such as commercially driven fake websites, have been countered by cutting off advertising, but this does not affect misinformation campaigns, for example. Warnings on potential fake news stories have been introduced by Facebook, but this does little to combat content that exists on the site itself.

Has it had an influence?

It is hard to tell. Facebook's chief executive Mark Zuckerberg initially said the idea that misinformation on Facebook influenced the election was a "crazy idea", but has backtracked, saying he regrets the comments.

The sheer scale of Facebook and Twitter – 2bn and 330m users respectively – and the hours spent on them each week suggest many eyeballs have come into contact with fake news stories or misinformation campaigns.

According to a study from Stanford University, fake news websites received 159 million visits during the month of last year's US election, and other research has shown the most widely-shared news stories during the election were fake. The majority were also pro-Trump.

There is less evidence of fake news taking off in the UK during the Brexit vote or this year's general election, although there is evidence that bots have been used in both.

However, there is a difference between reach and influence. The latter is a very difficult thing to measure, and this has been true of media for years – how much does the media drive beliefs, and how much does it reflect beliefs?

One less measurable effect may have been that the sheer quantity of fake news stories may have reduced trust in mainstream media – if scepticism about what people read online increases, they may not know what to think. In these situations, people tend to stick to their prejudices.

Source document: European Commission Press Release

Brussels, 13 November 20XX

The Commission launched today a public consultation on fake news and online disinformation and set up a High-Level Expert Group representing academics, online platforms, news media and civil society organisations.

The work of the High-Level Expert Group as well as the results of the public consultation will contribute to the development of an EU-level strategy on how to tackle the spreading of fake news, to be presented in spring next year.

First Vice-President Frans **Timmermans** said: *"The freedom to receive and impart information and the pluralism of the media are enshrined in the EU's Charter of Fundamental Rights. We live in an era where the flow of information and misinformation has become almost overwhelming. That is why we need to give our citizens the tools to identify fake news, improve trust online, and manage the information they receive."*

Andrus **Ansip**, Vice-President for the Digital Single Market, added: *"We need to find a balanced approach between the freedom of expression, media pluralism and a citizen's right to access diverse and reliable information. All the relevant players like online platforms or news media should play a part in the solution."*

Mariya **Gabriel**, Commissioner responsible for Digital Economy and Society, stated: *"At the heart of my action lies the defence of citizens' right to quality information which is a cornerstone of our* *democracies. I want to have an open and broad discussion about fake news to address this complex phenomenon in order to overcome the challenges ahead of us."*

Public input expected until February

Citizens, social media platforms, news organisations (broadcasters, print media, news agencies, online media and fact-checkers), researchers and public authorities are all invited to share their views in the public consultation until mid-February. It will gather opinions on what actions could be taken at EU level to give citizens effective tools to identify reliable and verified information and adapt to the challenges of the digital age.

The contributions are expected in three main areas:

1. The **scope** of the problem, i.e. how fake news is perceived by citizens and stakeholders, how they are aware of online disinformation, or how they trust different media
2. Assessment of **measures already taken** by platforms, news media companies and civil society organisations to counter the spread of fake news online, as well as positions on the roles and responsibilities of the relevant stakeholders
3. **Possible future actions** to strengthen citizens access to reliable and verified information and prevent the spread of disinformation online

This consultation only addresses fake news and disinformation online when the content is not *per se* illegal and thus not covered by existing EU or national legislative and self-regulatory actions.

High-Level Expert Group opens for applications

The Commission is inviting experts to apply for the High-Level Group on fake news to advise the Commission on scoping the phenomenon, defining the roles and responsibilities of relevant stakeholders, grasping the international dimension, taking stock of the positions at stake, and formulating recommendations. As far as possible, the group should include several representatives of each field of expertise, be it academia or civil society delegate. The Commission aims at a balanced selection of the experts.

The call for application is open until mid-December. The High-Level Expert Group is expected to start in January 20XX+1 and will work over several months.

Background

Online platforms and other Internet services have provided new ways for people to connect, debate and to gather information. However, the spread of news intentionally misleading readers has become an increasing problem for the functioning of our democracies, affecting peoples' understanding of reality.

On 17 and 18 November last year, the Commission hosted its second Annual Colloquium on Fundamental Rights, on the topic of "Media Pluralism and Democracy". A Eurobarometer survey showed that European citizens are worried about the independence of the media, and levels of trust in media are low.

In his mission letter, President Jean-Claude **Juncker** tasked Commissioner for the Digital Economy and Society Mariya Gabriel to look into the challenges the online platforms create for our democracies with regard to the spread of fake information and initiate a reflection on what would be needed at EU level to protect our citizens.

In June 20XX, the European Parliament adopted a Resolution calling on the Commission to analyse in depth the current situation and legal framework with regard to fake news and to verify the possibility of legislative intervention to limit the dissemination and spreading of fake content. The Commission has confirmed that this is a priority and has included the initiative against fake news online in next year's Work Programme.

Sample Solution

NOTE TO THE FILE

1. INTRODUCTION

Fake news – fabricated news stories with the deliberate aim of fooling readers – has become an increasingly visible global phenomenon that poses a threat to democracy, in Europe and abroad.

On 13 November 20XX the Commission launched a public consultation on fake news and online disinformation and aims to set up a High-Level Expert (HLEG) Group representing academics, online platforms, news media and civil society organisations. The work of the High-Level Expert Group as well as the results of the public consultation will contribute to the development of an EU-level strategy on how to tackle the spreading of fake news and protect democracy.

The HLEG will start its work in January next year. The present note proposes an outline for the mandate of this group and the criteria by which its Members will be selected and appointed.

2. WHAT IS FAKE NEWS? AN OPERATIONAL DEFINITION

Fake news is a type of journalism that consists of deliberate misinformation spread via traditional print and broadcast news media or online social media. Fake news is written and published with the intent to mislead in order to damage an agency, entity, or person, and/or gain financially or politically.

Although not new, this phenomenon is often said to be more pervasive and impactful today than ever before because of the ease with which news can be posted and shared by anyone on social media, the velocity at which such news may spread online, and the global reach it might effortlessly attain.

3. HOW DOES FAKE NEWS AFFECT DEMOCRACY IN EUROPE?

The fake news trend is seen as an element in the deeper democratic challenge of what is known as the 'post-truth' era. Post-truth is defined as relating to or denoting circumstances in which objective facts are less influential in shaping public opinion than appeals to emotion and personal belief. Fake news attempts to manipulate public opinion and this is clearly against democratic values.

Easy access to online advertisement revenue, increased political polarization, and the popularity of social media, have all been implicated in the spread of fake news, which has come to provide competition for legitimate news stories. Hostile government actors have also been implicated in generating and propagating fake news, particularly during elections.

Furthermore, fake news is undermining the credibility of the legitimate press, an important cornerstone of the democracies of Europe.

An additional problem for Europe is that non-EU companies dominate the social media, which makes it even more difficult to prevent the spreading of fake news.

4. HIGH-LEVEL EXPERT GROUP

The High Level group will advise the Commission on scoping the phenomenon of fake news, defining the roles and responsibilities of relevant stakeholders, grasping the international dimension, taking stock of the positions at stake, and formulating recommendations. More specifically the HLEG will:

- Analyse in-depth the current situation and legal framework, as well as the potential political and social risks associated with the spread of disinformation online;
- Define the scope of the problem and explore legislative or non-legislative interventions to limit the dissemination of fake content;
- Define the roles and responsibilities of all relevant stakeholders with attention to the functioning of social networks and other online platforms, and the vulnerabilities of professional news media;
- Assess the effectiveness of the voluntary measures put in place so far by online platforms and news media organisations to counter fake news;
- Assess possible improvements to such existing voluntary measures;
- Sketch out the direction for developing quality journalism (data journalism, investigative journalism, etc.) and improving media literacy as complementary actions to promote trust in media and users' awareness;
- Identify guiding principles for possible self-regulation based on shared good practices and coordination of relevant policies and activities at EU and national levels.

5. SELECTION PROCEDURE

The Commission aims at a balanced selection of experts including several representatives of each field of expertise, be it representatives of civil society, social media platforms, news media organisations, journalists and academia.

Wherever possible, a balanced selection across the Member States will be sought, as well as a gender balance in accordance with the EU regulations.

All candidates must get the official support of their national government.

The composition of the HLEG will be published in the Official Journal of the EU.

6. CONCLUSIONS

The issue of fake news is high on the political agenda of the current Commission. The work of the High-Level Expert Group (HLEG) as well as the results of the public consultation will contribute to the development of an EU-level strategy on how to tackle the spreading of fake news.

Scoring Guide

For the sake of practice, only read this part after completing the exercise above.

Please find below a sample top-level scoring guide we created for this case study exercise; it is similar to the one EPSO is likely to use.

Analysis and Problem Solving

- Did the candidate provide a comprehensive presentation of the political, legal, economic, financial, technical or scientific issues?
- Did the candidate provide specific legal or technical references? (Research data, case-law, legislative instruments, historic facts, etc.)
- Did the candidate demonstrate an in-depth understanding of the background documents by providing examples, facts, names, data or other information?
- Did the candidate use their knowledge to interpret the charts, statistics, financial and economic data correctly?
- Did the candidate demonstrate a thorough understanding of the cross-references and draw the right conclusions from them?

Communicating

For this competency, the following would be indicators of a **positive response**:

- Writes clearly, precisely and fluently. Arguments remained consistent throughout. Response is well structured (e.g. sets out response under headings, includes summary at end).
- Uses the correct balance of detail and conciseness (e.g. paraphrases information in the brief rather than simply repeating it).
- Avoids jargon (or explains it if used).
- Communicates in a manner that captures the attention and interest of the audience (e.g. poses rhetorical questions, writes in a lively style).
- Can identify and convey the key points of an argument. Uses professional, relevant and high quality ideas to back up arguments (e.g. the key points are stressed in an introduction and then again in the conclusion).
- Tailors writing style so that it is appropriate to target audience (e.g. explains jargon, but not in a patronising manner; understands the priorities and perspective of the target audience and adapts the message accordingly).
- Uses an appropriate document format (email, note to the file, letter, press release).

The following would be indicators of a **poor response**:

- Writes unclearly, imprecisely or in a disjointed manner. Arguments are inconsistent at times.
- Response is poorly structured (e.g. response reads as a stream of consciousness, hard to follow. Recommendations contradict themselves at times).

- Is either overly detailed or overly brief in their communications (e.g. repeats large chunks of the background brief, or alternatively writes very little making it hard to follow what is being said).
- Uses jargon without explanation.
- Communicates in a manner that is dull, flat or uninteresting to read (e.g. simply lists facts in bullet point form throughout).
- Fails to identify or convey the key points of an argument (e.g. writes as if all aspects equally important).
- Adopts a writing style that is inappropriate to the target audience (e.g. too informal or too brief).
- Uses no formatting, just plain text.

Delivering Quality and Results

- Did the candidate answer all aspects of the questions?
- Did the candidate consider the wider EU context of the issues? (Considering an overall EU approach instead of national or regional one; implications for various Member States and neighbouring countries, long-term effects of a policy or initiative etc.).
- Did the candidate mention international examples, current events, place the information in a global context? (Linking current affairs to the facts of the file; mentioning international organisations' perspectives; diplomatic efforts, political events etc.).
- Did the candidate demonstrate a solid understanding of the field? (Confident use of terminology, concepts, ideas; reference to renowned achievers in the field etc.).
- Did the candidate refer to important facts, legislation, research or other information demonstrating their familiarity with the topic? (Mention of publications, public events, industry best practices and policies etc.).
- Did the candidate use their knowledge to interpret the charts, statistics, financial and economic data correctly?
- Did the candidate demonstrate a thorough understanding of the cross-references and draw the right conclusions from them?

Prioritising and Organising

For this competency, the following would be indicators of a **positive response**:

- Describes how they would conduct preparation in advance of implementing actions (e.g. who they would speak to, which stakeholders to consult, how they would identify the financial and human resources required).
- Prioritises tasks appropriately (e.g. distinguishes the important from the urgent).
- Sets realistic deadlines and milestones (e.g. not too far in the future, but not unrealistically short).

- Describes how progress would be monitored (e.g. through meetings, emails, project plans, milestones).
- Considers how they would respond to last minute changes (e.g. if resources become unavailable or cash-flow problems occur).
- Manages own workload effectively – i.e. completes a reasonable amount of work in the time available for the exercise.

The following would be indicators of a **poor response**:

- Advocates proceeding to action immediately before any further research is conducted (e.g. fails to identify possible risks or issues that need to be resolved before starting work, does not read relevant parts of the background materials).
- Makes incorrect prioritisation judgements (e.g. focuses on relatively unimportant issues to a disproportionate degree in their response while ignoring important issues).
- Sets overly ambitious or overly lengthy deadlines and milestones.
- Allows projects to proceed without outlining how they would be monitored (e.g. covers this at a very broad level, "we will keep an eye on things as they progress" or not at all).
- Has not allowed contingencies for changing circumstances.
- Works inefficiently or becomes overwhelmed with workload (e.g. finishes early and produces a small amount of work; or runs out of time and produces an unfinished response).

Annex 4 General Competency Based Interview Questions

There are lists with hundreds of competency based interview (GCBI) questions circulating on the internet. These lists were compiled by candidates who have passed this interview already, wanting to help other candidates in their preparation for this rather unusual kind of interview. However, despite the good intentions there are some fundamental problems with these lists:

- They are huge and overwhelming. Rather than helping they scare people away from a decent preparation.
- These lists can be very confusing, because the same – underlying – questions may come up multiple times, but formulated differently.
- Since the questions on these lists are the result of what people remember from their interview, they may be entirely wrong, because misunderstood in the first place.

Remember that the competency based interview is a *structured* interview, meaning that all the candidates, regardless of the competition, get the same type of questions, or they use the same pool of questions for all candidates. This does not mean that the questions will be formulated in exactly the same way – the interviewers have some leeway in this respect – but the behaviour in the "typical situations" they are looking for is the same.

EPSO competitions are very well and strictly organised, to make sure that all the candidates have a "level playing field" and to have an assessment that is as fair and objective as is humanly possible.

In the competency based interview, these principles are translated into a fixed set of "anchors", five per competency. For the GCBI, an anchor is a typical situation in which you may have demonstrated some behaviour in relation to that competency. Of course, every profession is different in terms of the situations one is confronted with, but the anchors are common denominators across all professions.

If you want to learn more about the general competencies – and probably get some inspiration to tailor your "best possible" answers, please refer to Annex 1.

When preparing for the competency based interview it is advised to find an example for each of the anchors as listed below. Apply the STAR model whenever possible.

Delivering Quality and Results

This competency could be described as "meeting, and exceeding, the expectations of your supervisors or stakeholders". It is not enough to produce results; they have to meet expectations.

1. **Dealing promptly with problems and requests.**

   Tell them about a situation where you took an initiative, that is where you did something that was not strictly part of your job description, but went beyond.

2. **Being proactive, finding more effective and efficient ways of working.**

   Tell them about a situation where you improved an existing work process, a procedure, or just the way things were done. For example automating part of a process or introducing new tools.

3. **Overcoming obstacles and delivering qualitative results.**

   Describe a situation where something unexpected happened, hindering your efforts to complete a task, and what you did to work around this problem.

4. **Delivering quality work on time.**

   Here you are supposed to come up with an example of where you managed to deliver good results on time, and what you did to make this happen. Sometimes, this question is asked the other way around; in other words, you missed a deadline. It is then important that you describe what you did to minimise the overrun.

   This is closely related to resilience and prioritising and organising.

5. **Working to a high standard of quality.**

   Tell them about a situation where your work exceeded the expectations of your supervisor/stakeholders, and how they expressed this fact.

Learning and Development

This competency is about your attitude towards – and how you go about learning – new (hard) skills and developing your soft skills.

1. **Developing new skills.**

   Tell them about a period in your life/career where you were actively acquiring new knowledge or knowhow (e.g. a professional skill, another language, using a new IT tool). Explain clearly how you did it, and the efforts this needed.

2. **Personal development.**

   Explain what you did to develop a "soft" skill like time-management, speaking in public, conflict management, or negotiating. It may be difficult to use the STAR model here, but don't worry: personal development is a life-long endeavour.

3. **Asking for advice.**

   Here they want to hear that you are open to feedback from your colleagues or supervisors, and that you adapt your behaviour accordingly. Be specific.

4. **Knowing the immediate working environment.**

   You have to demonstrate that you are aware of your immediate working environment, and that you know why your contribution matters. We suggest you start with the "mission statement" of the organisation (company, agency, DG...) and you gradually "zoom in" to your own position. No STAR answer!

5. **Seeing the "bigger picture".**

   Explain the business your organisation is in, and give an example where you needed assistance from people outside your own organisation/entity to do your own work. STAR could apply but not necessarily.

Resilience

Resilience is about how you cope with stress, and how you "bounce back" from adversity. Resilience is to be distinguished from "perseverance" (as it is often translated into Spanish or other Latin languages). As a candidate with a pilot's licence once explained, perseverance is being able to fly a plane for 10 hours without falling asleep, while resilience is knowing what to do when you realise you're out of fuel.

1. **Coping with a heavy workload and tight deadlines.**

   Describe a specific situation where you had a heavy workload and tight deadlines, and explain what you did to contain the stress involved (planning, prioritising, delegating and/or asking for help, renegotiating the expectations, doing overtime, etc.). Typical STAR answer expected here.

2. **Adjusting to peaks and troughs in workload.**

   Explain what you did during a calmer period at work (e.g. dealing with backlog, learning new skills, personal development, planning for the future). Be specific!

3. **Handling failures and setbacks.**

   Here you should tell the assessors about a big disappointment or a professional failure, how you coped with it and what you have learned from that situation. The assessors are not interested in how you got into that situation but in what you did to overcome the problems, mentally.

4. **Working with hierarchy.**

   This question is sometimes formulated as "having a conflict with your hierarchy" but what they want to hear is how you deal with situations where there is a difference of opinion between you and your supervisor or stakeholder. You have to demonstrate assertiveness.

5. **Facing changes.**

Change is one of the major stress generators, so they are interested in how you respond to changing circumstances in your work environment such as a new job, a new supervisor, moving to another country for your work, or new working methods.

Working with Others

This competency is about factoring in the human aspects in your working relations.

1. **Working cooperatively, reaching consensus.**

Tell them about a situation where you managed to find a consensus with some of your fellow workers in order to reach a common objective. Explain what you did to achieve the consensus.

2. **Developing working relationships.**

Give a specific example of how you welcomed a new colleague, or what you did to blend in to a new working environment. Show them how you reach out to people, and don't forget to tell about the human interactions (so not only professional relationships). Sometimes, the question is asked the other way around: what you did to blend in when you were the newcomer.

3. **Multicultural environment.**

Explain how you are aware of, and accepting of, cultural differences. Use a very specific example from your past (e.g. studying abroad, working in a non-EU country, etc.).

Avoid stereotypes. Show them that you do not judge other people based on your own cultural standards.

Possibly not a STAR answer.

4. **Working with other departments.**

Related to learning and development but focus on the human interactions here.

5. **Other points of view.**

Demonstrate how you try to understand the positions, and their reasons, of other people when solving problems, or getting some work done. You can "agree to disagree" but still work together. Empathy and sympathy are what is looked for here.

Leadership

For this competency, the assessors want to see how you behave as leader, finding the right balance between formal management and inspirational leadership.

1. **Leading and steering.**

   Here you can go both ways; either give an example of you taking the opportunity to "steer" other people (e.g. coordinating a team) or you "inspiring" other people (e.g. leading by example).

2. **Enthusiasm and commitment.**

   Here you would give an example of a situation of where you inspired other people by means of your own enthusiasm and commitment (leading by example).

3. **Motivational skills.**

   Tell them about a situation where you had to motivate other people to do something about which they were initially not very enthusiastic. Explain how you used "intrinsic motivation" (e.g. purpose, autonomy, and mastery) rather than the "carrot-and-stick" approach to get things done.

4. **Mentoring and coaching.**

   Give them a specific example of where you had the opportunity to coach or mentor a colleague, and tell them exactly how you did it. Be aware that "coaching" and "mentoring" are not the same, so put the emphasis of your actions accordingly.

5. **Coordination and monitoring.**

   This would typically be about a situation where you were formally in charge of a group or a team, and the things you did to coordinate and monitor their work.

Communicating

In EPSO, the communicating competency is split – equally – between written and oral communication. While the written part is typically assessed with a case study, oral communication can be assessed during the oral presentation and/or the competency based interview. If in your competition this is done during the competency based interview, there will be no questions on communicating, but instead the assessors will observe your behaviour during the entire interview. It is therefore important to deliver a clear, crisp, and comprehensive "self-presentation" and to use the STAR model wherever this is applicable. During the competency based interview, the assessors will pay particular attention to the following (positive) indicators:

1. Oral communication is clear and precise.
2. Handling questions confidently.

3. Simplifying complex subject matters.
4. Persuading, getting acceptance of proposals.
5. Adapting style to the audience.

Some tips for preparing

A good idea is to create an Excel spreadsheet with all the anchors relevant to the competencies that will be assessed in your GCBI (check your Notice of Competition for that).

Put the anchors in the first column.

In the second column, write down the keywords that will remind you of the Situation, Task, and trigger of the story you are going to tell them for each anchor.

In the third column, write down a list of keywords (10, 15, 20) reminding you of the Actions you're going to talk about.

In the last column, put another 2 or 3 keywords to remind you of the Results.

Don't write your stories in full and learn them by heart. If you do, and simply repeat them parrot fashion in your interview, your stories will sound artificial and fabricated, which is a negative indicator for (oral) communication.

To find inspiration, think of those periods in your career where you were highly motivated. People who are highly motivated tend to "behave" better than people who are not, and you will tell the story in a more enthusiastic way – which is in turn a positive indicator for (oral) communication.

If you're running out of inspiration, have a look at Annex 1, the right-hand side of the tables obviously. You may come across examples that you have experienced yourself.

Finally, make sure to have a backup for those situations that are either very old, not in direct connection with your work, or when "recycling" situations you may have already used in a previous question.

Annex 5 Sample Oral Presentation

ASSIGNMENT

IMPORTANT NOTICE:

This is a fictitious document produced solely for the purpose of this exercise. All references to existing states, international organisations, private companies, departments, their representatives etc. should be considered as mere examples. The views expressed do not represent the position of these bodies or persons. Participants are therefore advised to rely solely on the information provided and not on any prior expertise in the field when answering the questions.

For this exercise, you will take on the role of Administrator in the Unit B1 of the Directorate General Environment. The documentation you need is included in this booklet. It comprises a number of e-mails, newspaper articles, and other information that you will have to analyse and digest in order to be able to deal properly with the assignment given to you.

It is important that you accept the scenario as it is presented to you. Although in real life you would have access to other sources of information and would be able to consult your colleagues, in this exercise you are limited to the information contained in the documents provided. You are, however, allowed to make logical assumptions where information is missing or incomplete.

You may rearrange the information in any order you wish and add remarks or make notes as necessary.

This Oral Presentation is designed to assess the following competencies: Analysis & Problem Solving, Communicating (Oral communication), Delivering Quality & Results, and Resilience. No previous knowledge is required to carry out the assignment or to answer the questions.

Specifically your task(s) will be:

To present to your colleagues during your monthly unit meeting:

- **A brief description of what the shale gas fracking technology is about**
- **The main pros and cons of this technology**
- **The position taken by the European Commission with respect to this technology**

You have 30 minutes to analyse the information, note the most important findings, and prepare a presentation. You will then have 10 minutes to present your presentation. This will be followed by a 10-minute question and answer session, during which the assessors will ask you specific questions related to your presentation.

Please note:

Today is Wednesday, 15 September 201X

Last year was 201X-1, next year will be 201X+1

PLEASE DO NOT TURN THIS PAGE UNTIL YOU ARE ASKED TO DO SO

DOCUMENTS

Hydraulic fracturing or Fracking - from Wikipedia
Main technologies or sub-processes: fluid pressure
Inventor: Floyd Farris; J.B. Clark (Stanolind Oil and Gas Corporation)
Year of invention: 1947

Induced hydraulic fracturing (hydrofracturing, also commonly known as fracking or fraccing) is a mining technique in which a liquid (in most cases water) is mixed with sand and chemicals and the resultant mixture is injected at high pressure into a wellbore. This creates small fractures in the deep rock formations, typically less than 1mm wide, along which gas, petroleum and brine may migrate to the well. Hydraulic pressure is removed from the well, then small grains of proppant (sand or aluminium oxide) hold these fractures open once the rock achieves equilibrium.

The technique is very common in wells for shale gas, tight gas, tight oil, and coal seam gas and hard rock wells. This well stimulation is usually conducted once in the life of the well and greatly enhances fluid removal and well productivity, but there has been an increasing trend towards multiple hydraulic fracturing as production declines.

The first experimental use of hydraulic fracturing was in 1947, and the first commercially successful applications were in 1949. As of 2012, 2.5 million hydraulic fracturing jobs have been performed on oil and gas wells worldwide, more than one million of them in the United States.

Proponents of hydraulic fracturing point to the economic benefits from the vast amounts of formerly inaccessible hydrocarbons the process can extract. Opponents of hydraulic fracturing point to environmental risks, including contamination of ground water, depletion of fresh water, contamination of the air, noise pollution, the migration of gases and hydraulic fracturing chemicals to the surface, surface contamination from spills and flow-back, and the possible health effects of these. There are increases in seismic activity, mostly associated with deep injection disposal of flowback and produced brine from hydraulically fractured wells. For these reasons hydraulic fracturing has come under international scrutiny, with some countries protecting it, and others suspending or banning it. Some of those countries, including most notably the United Kingdom, have recently lifted their bans, choosing to focus on regulation instead of outright prohibition. The European Union is in the process of applying regulation to permit this to take place.

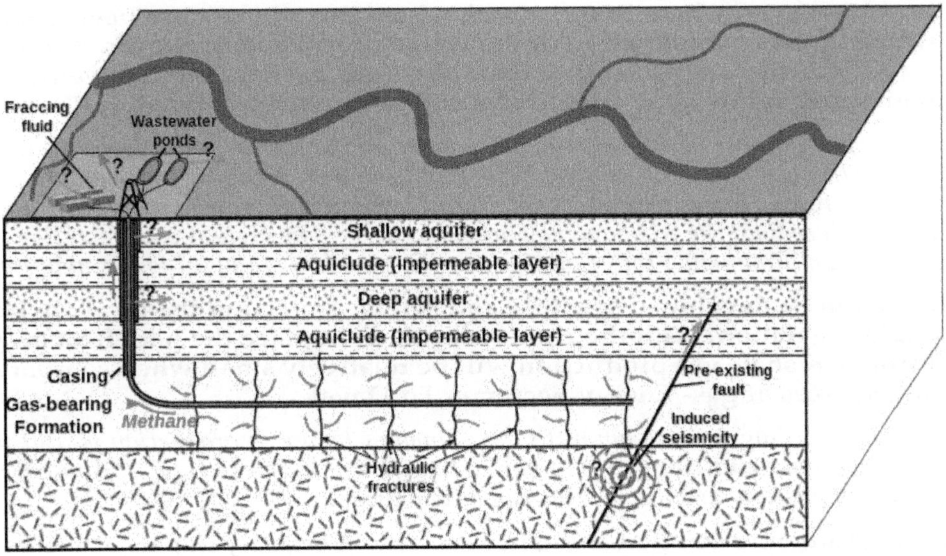

Pros and Cons of fracking

Source:
http://www.channel4.com/news/fracking-shale-gas-hydraulic-fracturing-truth-myth-facts-uk

Shale is important for our country. It could bring 74,000 jobs, over £3bn of investment, give us cheaper energy for the future, and increase our energy security- David Cameron

Truth or myth: The Institute of Directors claims that shale gas could create 74,000 jobs. Geologists, engineers, construction workers, business analysts, truck drivers and public relations staff are examples of the people needed by the industry as well as cement and steel manufacturers, equipment manufacturers, drilling services companies.

The US has clearly demonstrated fracking is dangerous, destructive and devastates communities. Despite regulation this will also be the case in the UK. Only one well has been drilled and fracked here and it caused earthquakes that damaged the well so gas and chemicals could leak out- Anti-fracking protester

Truth or myth: A government-commissioned report in 2013 found that drilling had caused tremors and that this was likely to happen again if fracking resumed. But it said that while "such an event would be strongly felt by people within a few kilometres from the epicentre and could cause some alarm", no structural damage was likely.

Latest estimates suggest that there's about 1,300 trillion cubic feet of shale gas lying underneath Britain at the moment – and that study only covers 11 counties. To put that in context, even if we extract just a tenth of that figure, that is still the equivalent of 51 years' gas supply- David Cameron

Truth or myth: Government projections only go up to 2030, when natural gas demand is estimated to amount to 78.8bn cubic meters, more than current levels. The BGS on the other hand hasn't estimated how long our shale gas reserves might last. The UK's extractable reserves are still an unknown.

The reality is that everywhere in the world, where this process has been put into use, it has resulted in the contamination of the water, of soil and of the air. When the governments and industry are promoting their shale gas agenda, they conveniently leave out the evidence that this is an abomination- Ex-oilfield executive Ian R Crane

Truth or myth: The number of official studies confirming the link between water contamination and fracking are limited. However, high levels of pollution were recently found in and around the Barnett Shale in Texas. Toxic substances, including arsenic, selenium and strontium, were all found at levels higher than the recommended levels in wells. The highest concentration of arsenic was 16 times the Environment Protection Agency (EPA) safety standard for drinking water.

UK shale gas can be developed sensibly and safely, protecting the local environment, with the right regulation. With the right safeguards in place the net effect on national emission from UK shale gas production will be relatively small when compared to the use of other sources of gas- Energy Secretary Ed Davey

Truth or myth: According to the Committee on Climate Change, if production is well regulated, shale gas can have lower emissions than imported liquefied natural gas (LNG). A recent report for the European Commission also reached the same conclusion.

There are large and uninhabited and desolate areas. Certainly in part of the north east, where there's plenty of room for fracking, well away from anybody's residence where we could conduct without any kind of threat to the rural environment- Lord Howell of Guildford

Truth or myth: It's difficult to say but a US report suggests that fracking could have an impact on habitat, water quality, water quantity, noise and air pollution. However, these studies are at an early stages.

If we don't back this technology, we will miss a massive opportunity to help families with their bills ... fracking has real potential to drive energy bills down- David Cameron

Truth or myth: A recent report commissioned by energy regulator Ofgem estimated that if shale gas production meets up to 21 per cent of demand then wholesale gas prices in the UK could be cut by between 2 per cent and 4 per cent between 2020 and 2034 from their current levels. However, a similar report by the Energy and Climate Change Committee suggested that, while UK shale gas production may help to secure energy supplies, this may not lead to cheaper energy bills.

Total, a French company who can't frack in their own country because the French government has stopped the French countryside being ripped up, have now turned their sights on the UK countryside, where the UK government seem happy to allow the industrialisation of our green and pleasant land- Greenpeace climate campaigner Lawrence Carter

Truth or myth: The French parliament voted to ban the controversial technique for extracting natural gas from shale rock deposits known as hydraulic fracturing, or fracking, in 2011. France's constitutional court upheld a ban in 2013. The court ruled that in imposing the ban, lawmakers were pursuing a legitimate goal in the general interest of protecting the environment and noted differences between geothermal and shale gas exploration techniques.

The US Perspective

Energy politics

Legislation and regulation on shale gas selected states

Basins | Current plays | Prospective plays

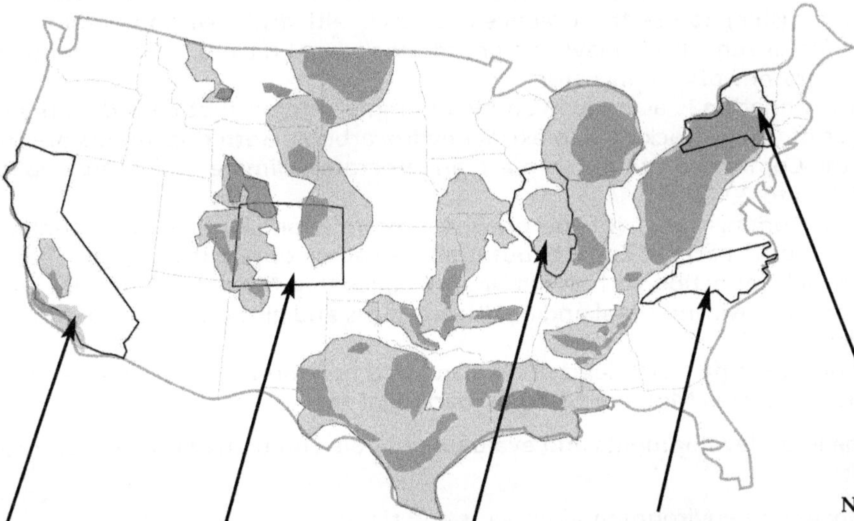

CALIFORNIA

SB 4, 2013 (enacted)
Creates a permitting system for fracking wells, requires ground water monitoring and ensures public transparency throughout the fracking process

COLORADO

The Air Quality Control Commission, a regulator, introduced rules in 2014 seeking to reduce the amount of methane and other volatile organic compounds released into the air at fracking wells

ILLINOIS

Hydraulic Fracturing Regulatory Act, 2013 (enacted)
Requires testing of water sources near fracking wells, disclosure of fracking chemicals, well location restrictions and public comment periods on drilling applications

NORTH CAROLINA

SB 786, 2014 (enacted)
Authorises state to begin issuing permits in 2015 for fracking. Allows oil and gas companies to withhold information on fracking chemicals that is confidential, although it must be provided to energy officials

NEW YORK

SB 4276 & AB 5974, AB 6365, AB 5378 (pending)
Would establish a five year moratorium on high volume fracking, prohibit drilling within 10 miles of New York City's water supply and require permits for water withdrawals of more than 5,000 gallons a day

Source: E1A; FT Research

EUROPEAN COMMISSION

PRESS RELEASE

Brussels, 22 January 2014

Environment: European Commission recommends minimum principles for shale gas

Today the European Commission adopted a Recommendation aiming to ensure that proper environmental and climate safeguards are in place for "fracking" – the high-volume hydraulic fracturing technique used notably in shale gas operations. The Recommendation should help all Member States wishing to use this practice address health and environmental risks and improve transparency for citizens. It also lays the ground for a level playing field for industry and establishes a clearer framework for investors.

The Recommendation is accompanied by a Communication that considers the opportunities and challenges of using "fracking", to extract hydrocarbons. Both documents are part of a wider initiative by the Commission to put in place an integrated climate and energy policy framework for the period up to 2030.

Environment Commissioner [of the previous Commission] Janez Potočnik said: "Shale gas is raising hopes in some parts of Europe, but is also a source of public concern. The Commission is responding to calls for action with minimum principles that Member States are invited to follow in order to address environmental and health concerns and give operators and investors the predictability they need."

Building on existing EU legislation and complementing it where necessary, the Recommendation invites Member States in particular to:

- **Plan ahead** of developments and evaluate possible cumulative effects before granting licences;
- **Carefully assess** environmental impacts and risks;
- Ensure that the **integrity** of the well is up to best practice standards;
- **Check the quality of the local water, air, soil** before operations start, in order to monitor any changes and deal with emerging risks;
- **Control air emissions**, including greenhouse gas emissions, by capturing the gases;
- **Inform the public** about chemicals used in individual wells, and
- Ensure that operators apply **best practices** throughout the project.

The Commission will continue facilitating the exchange of information with Member States, industry and civil society organisations on the environmental performance of shale gas projects.

Next steps

EU Member States are invited to apply the principles within six months and, from December 2014 onwards, inform the Commission each year about measures that they have put in place. The Commission will monitor the application of the Recommendation with a publicly available scoreboard that will compare the situation in different Member States. It will review the effectiveness of this approach in 18 months.

Background

Conventional natural gas is trapped in reservoirs underground. Shale gas is different – it too is a natural gas, but it is trapped inside rocks that have to be broken open ("fractured" or "fracked") to release the gas. In the EU there is limited experience to date of high-volume hydraulic fracturing on a large scale and at high intensity. The practice involves injecting high volumes of water, sand and chemicals into a borehole to crack the rock and facilitate gas extraction. So far experience in Europe has been focused essentially on low volume hydraulic fracturing in some conventional and tight gas reservoirs, mostly in vertical wells, constituting only a small part of past EU oil and gas operations. Drawing on the North American experience where the high volume hydraulic fracturing has been broadly used, operators are now testing further this practice in the EU.

The environmental impacts and risks need to be managed appropriately. As more wells need to be drilled over a wider area to obtain the same amount of gas as in conventional wells, the cumulative impacts need to be properly assessed and mitigated.

Most EU environmental legislation precedes the practice of high-volume hydraulic fracturing. For this reason certain environmental aspects are not comprehensively addressed in current EU legislation. This has led to public concern and calls for EU action.

Annex 6 Sample Group Exercise

ASSIGNMENT

IMPORTANT NOTICE:

This is a fictitious document produced solely for the purpose of this exercise. All references to existing states, international organisations, private companies, departments, their representatives etc. should be considered as mere examples. The views expressed do not represent the position of these bodies or persons. Participants are therefore advised to rely solely on the information provided and not on any prior expertise in the field when answering the questions.

Together with the other members of your group, you are all working in the European Commission's Secretariat General, which is a unique Directorate General that deals with, among other issues, horizontal questions of EU policy.

One of these issues is the "European Transparency Initiative" and the "Transparency Register", also often called "Lobby Register". The Transparency Register is currently being reviewed so that it can be improved, based on the experience since its creation. Your group is responsible for coming to a basic agreement on some key issues related to this review process.

You are asked to find an agreement among you, and make a recommendation on the following questions:

- **Is the EU Transparency Register working as it should, and if not, what are the major flaws?**
- **Should the Transparency Register be made mandatory, and if so, by when?**
- **Should the Council, national and regional lobbying be included and if so, how?**

The exercise is structured as follows:

- You will have 15 minutes to go through the information individually to prepare for the meeting. You are allowed to make notes on the documents.
- After this preparation, the group will have 50 minutes to conduct the meeting and work out a common solution.

You may make logical assumptions where you think the information is missing or incomplete. Please do not designate a formal chairman for this meeting.

Please note: Today is Monday, 5 December 20XX
Last year was 20XX-1, next year will be 20XX+1

DOCUMENTS FROM HERE TO PAGE 260 ARE FOR ALL CANDIDATES

Abbreviations

ALTER-EU	Alliance for Lobbying Transparency and Ethics Regulation
CEO	Corporate European Observatory
IIA	Interinstitutional Agreement
SEAP	Society of European Affairs Professionals

WIKIPEDIA
The Free Encyclopedia

Lobbying (also **lobby**) is the act of attempting to influence decisions made by officials in the government, most often legislators or members of regulatory agencies. Lobbying is done by many different types of people and organized groups, including individuals in the private sector, corporations, fellow legislators or government officials, or advocacy groups (interest groups). Lobbyists may be among a legislator's constituencies, meaning a voter or block of voters within his or her electoral district, or not; they may engage in lobbying as a business, or not. Professional lobbyists are people whose business is trying to influence legislation on behalf of a group or individual who hires them. Individuals and nonprofit organizations can also lobby as an act of volunteering or as a small part of their normal job (for instance, a CEO meeting with a representative about a project important to his/her company, or an activist meeting with his/her legislator in an unpaid capacity). Governments often define and regulate organized group lobbying that has become influential.

The ethics and morality of lobbying are dual-edged. Lobbying is often spoken of with contempt, when the implication is that people with inordinate socioeconomic power are corrupting the law (twisting it away from fairness) in order to serve their own conflict of interest. But another side of lobbying is making sure that others' interests are duly defended against others' corruption, or even simply making sure that minority interests are fairly defended against mere tyranny of the majority. For example, a medical association may lobby a legislature about increasing the restrictions in smoking prevention laws, and tobacco companies lobby to reduce them: the first regarding smoking as injurious to health and the second arguing it is part of the freedom of choice.

European Union

The more political influence the European Union ("EU") gains on a global level and the more policy areas it covers, the more interesting it becomes for lobbyists. With the Enlargement of the European Union in 2004, this development has taken a further step, bringing in not only a lot more players and stakeholders but a wide range of different political cultures and traditions, as well. According to Austrian Member of the European Parliament ("MEP") Hans-Peter Martin, the value of lobby invitations and offers each individual MEP receives can reach up to €10,000 per week.

In 2003 there were around 15,000 lobbyists (consultants, lawyers, associations, corporations, NGOs etc.) in Brussels seeking to influence the EU's legislation. Some 2,600 special interest groups had a permanent office in Brussels. Their distribution was roughly as follows: European trade federations (32%), consultants (20%), companies (13%), NGOs (11%), national associations (10%), regional representations (6%), international organizations (5%) and think tanks (1%), (Lehmann, 2003, pp iii).

The fragmented nature of the EU's institutional structure provides multiple channels through which organized interests may seek to influence policymaking. Lobbying takes place at the European level itself and within the existing national states. The most important institutional targets are the Commission, the Council, and the European Parliament. The Commission has a monopoly on the initiative in Community decision-making. Since it has the power to draft initiatives, it makes it ideally suited as an arena for interest representation.

There are three main channels of indirect lobbying of the Council. First, lobbying groups routinely lobby the national delegations in Brussels. The second indirect means of lobbying the Council is for interest groups to lobby members of the many Council-working groups. The third means of influencing the Council is directly via national governments. As a consequence of the co-decision procedures, the European Parliament attracts attention from lobbyists who target the rapporteur and the chairman of the committee. The rapporteurs are MEPs appointed by Committees to prepare the parliament's response to the Commission's proposal and to those measures taken by the Parliament itself.

Lobbying in Brussels was born only in the late 1970s. Up to that time, "diplomatic lobbying" at the highest levels remained the rule. There were few lobbyists involved in the system and except for some business associations, representative offices were rarely used. The event that sparked the explosion of lobbying was the first direct election of the European Parliament in 1979. Up until then, the Parliament consisted of a complex, and companies increasingly felt the need of an expert local presence to find out what was going on in Brussels. The foundation of lobbying was therefore the need to provide information. From that developed the need to influence the process actively and effectively. The next important step in lobbying development was the Single European Act of 1986, which both created the qualified majority vote for taking decisions in the Council of the European Union (the "Council") and enhanced the role of the Parliament, again making EU legislation more complex and lobbying further more important and attractive for stakeholders.

Library Briefing
Library of the European Parliament 02/03/2011

Establishing a common transparency register

Efforts to ensure proper transparency in EU policy-making are a relatively recent phenomenon. Whilst the European Parliament has had a register of lobbyists for more than 15 years, it publishes no detailed information on the registrants. In contrast, the Commission's register has been operational for little more than two years.

An EP report on the Commission's proposed voluntary register in 2008 called for a more comprehensive approach: a common, mandatory register of all three institutions – Commission, Council and Parliament. Following one of the report's recommendations, a joint Commission-EP high-level working party was established to negotiate the setting up of a joint register.

A number of issues have arisen, stemming both from consultation with various interest group representatives and following the Commission's one-year review of its own register. Mandatory registration has remained a contentious issue, whilst the Council has remained cautiously tight lipped as to its own participation.

In November 2010, the working party agreed a draft agreement for a common transparency register. If agreement is obtained from both institutions it is aimed to be operational by June 2011.

Background

Lobbying is a relatively new concept in EU policy-making and the EU has only recently begun regulating lobbyists' activities from the perspective of transparency.

According to Commissioner Siim Kallas, speaking in March 2005, "lobbyists' transparency is too deficient in comparison to the impact of their activities".

Specific concerns over lobbying in the EU have included suggestions of privileged access, the so-called 'revolving doors' phenomenon referring to the movement of personnel between roles as legislators or regulators and lobbies and of dubious methods and pretences of independence.

It was only in 2005 that the European Commission (EC) launched the European Transparency Initiative (ETI). It represented a review of the EC's overall policy to transparency. The establishment of a voluntary register of interest representatives was an integral part of this.

The Commission and EP registers

The European Parliament register

The EP register of lobbyists has been in existence since 1995. Rule 9(4) of the Rules of Procedure allows the Quaestors to grant access passes for a maximum of one year to persons who are required to adhere to the Code of Conduct and sign a publicly accessible register also now available on the EP website. In this context, the EP register, it has been argued, is a de facto mandatory register.

The Council of Europe, which in 2010 proposed its own European code of conduct, has described the formula, whereby only lobbyists' names and organisations are made public (although more detailed information is also collected by the EP), as "very soft, if not vague".

The Commission register

The Commission launched its voluntary register in June 2008 having adopted its Code of Conduct for interest representatives a month earlier. By 1 March 2011, 3663 organisations had registered.

Only entities engaged in lobbying activities are expected to register, individual citizens are not. Registrants fall into four categories:

- professional consultancies and law firms,
- in-house lobbyists and trade associations,
- NGOs,
- think tanks.

Financial disclosure differs for each category. Consultancies and law firms are expected to list the contributions of each of their clients, providing either an absolute figure in brackets of €50 000 or by percentage (of total revenue from lobbying) in 10% brackets. The other categories have less demanding requirements.

The Code of Conduct, based on existing professional codes as well as the EP's Code, contains seven rules. Failure to comply can result in either suspension or exclusion from the register.

Towards a common register

The Commission register is widely considered to be an important step towards greater transparency in EU policy-making. There has nevertheless remained a strong argument, put forward initially by the EP and several stakeholders in the 2007 consultation, for a common register of interest groups, a so called 'one-stop shop', covering the Commission, EP and Council.

The EP, in its 2008 report on the ETI, called for an inter-institutional agreement on a mandatory register of the three institutions including full disclosure, a common mechanism for expulsion and a common code of conduct. It proposed that a working group be set up to address this issue.

The high-level working party on a common transparency register

The joint EP-Commission working party, met for the first time in December 2008. In April 2009, it was agreed to open a new page on the Europa website with links to and information about the institutions' current registers. A draft text for a common code of conduct was also agreed along with a series of guidelines for the future register to be considered in the light of the Commission's review of its own register.

The working party resumed its discussions at the beginning of the new Commission's term of office, attempting to resolve a number of outstanding points.

Some major issues

A number of stakeholders and academics have expressed views on how and in which areas the new joint register could improve on the current Commission register. In a communication of October 2009, the Commission itself assessed the effectiveness of its register after one year of operation.

Voluntary or mandatory registration?

A survey undertaken in March 2010 by ALTER-EU, a coalition of civil society groups campaigning for greater transparency, found that only 112 of 286 consultancies providing lobbying services (39.2%) were listed on the Commission's register. According to ALTER–EU this was clear evidence that the voluntary system did not work and that "genuine transparency can only be secured when registration becomes de facto mandatory, by linking physical access to disclosure requirements".

Similarly, a study from Friends of the Earth Europe found that more EU-based companies were registered in the USA, where a mandatory system applies, than in the Commission register.

The Society of European Affairs Professionals (SEAP) supports a voluntary system. It argues that the register should not distance the institutions from citizens or lessen the transparency of policy-making to those not registered.

Regulating lobbying in the US

Lobbying was first regulated in the United States in 1946. The registration of lobbyists at the federal level is currently governed by the Lobbying Disclosure Act 2007 (LDA), and the Obama administration has applied tougher measures to itself. The LDA contains several important features:

- Mandatory registration.
- Separate registration required for each individual client.
- Quarterly report on the income received from clients, rounded to the nearest $10 000.
- Departing members of the Senate must wait two years before lobbying former colleagues. Former House Representatives must wait one year.
- Breach of the act carries a civil penalty of up to $200 000. A criminal penalty of up to five years in prison can also be imposed.

According to the Commission, as its register was still in an 'expansion phase' it was not possible to draw conclusions on the quantitative data. It nevertheless added that the voluntary approach was working, pointing to the steady increase in registrants, and should be maintained. The Commission has also questioned whether the EU treaties provide a sufficient legal base for a mandatory list.

Who should register?

The Commission has noted that most think tanks and law firms have remained outside its register. Think tanks have argued that they should not be considered lobbyists because they provide scientific and academic research and do not wish to be assimilated to specific interests. However, the Commission in its review argued that their contributions may be aimed at influencing decisions and cited networking opportunities promoted by think tanks as an advantage of membership.

Law firms have cited concerns over client confidentiality as the main reason for not registering. The Commission's code of conduct excludes legal advice to clients from the scope of eligible activities, and a further explanatory clarification was later added. However, these reassurances do not appear to have been sufficient and to date only 19 law firms have registered.

Will the Council join?

It has so far proved difficult to convince the Council to join negotiations on a common register. As far back as 2003, in an informal statement, it had indicated that contact with lobbyists and NGOs was handled by the Commission. More recently it has maintained that Member States (MS) are lobbied in national capitals rather than Brussels. Furthermore MS have expressed concerns as to how their Permanent Representations would be affected.

There are, however, indications that the Council's position may be changing, with recent press reports suggesting a more favourable attitude from some MS

In September 2010, EP Vice-President Diana Wallis and EC Vice-President Maros Šefčovič, co-chairs of the working party, sent a joint letter to the Presidency emphasising the role of both the European Council and Council of Ministers in improving transparency in EU governance. They expressed a desire for both institutions to join the common system.

In a draft response, expected to be approved by Coreper shortly, the Council expresses its interest in having a role in the exercise and in discussing the necessary arrangements. It asks for further details on the practicalities.

The draft agreement

A draft EP-EC agreement was adopted by the working party on 10 November 2010.

Registration remains voluntary although Wallis has indicated the ultimate goal is a mandatory register. Professional consultancies or law firms with turnover of more than €1 million will now only declare the value of their clients in brackets of €250 000 rather than €50 000 (and the option of declaring the amounts in percentage terms has been removed).

Penalties for breaching the Code of Conduct remain limited to suspension or expulsion from the register. In this respect, the EP remains entirely responsible for the issue and control of access cards to its premises. Passes will only be issued to individuals from organisations who have registered, although registration does not confer automatic entitlement to a card.

The agreement must now be approved by the two institutions. It is expected to be voted by AFCO in April, with a plenary vote in May. It is hoped to have the register operational by June 2011.

Initial reaction

ALTER-EU considers that the new register will bring several improvements such as a better incentive for registration and an improved complaints procedure, but still leaves fundamental flaws and loopholes.

It argues that most lobbyists will sign the register, because it is a precondition for an EP access pass. But it doubts whether enough pressure will be put on those who did not sign the Commission register, in particular law firms and think tanks. For this reason it calls for mandatory registration to be introduced by 2015.

ALTER-EU also calls for greater transparency on financial declarations and in particular the sources of funding. It recommends that clients' expenditure should be measured in bands of €10 000 to match the US system. It also calls for better safeguards against 'under-reporting' of lobbying spending.

SEAP has welcomed the retention of the voluntary system and the increased clarity, compared to the Commission's register, on who should register. It, however, warns against the potential danger of restricting access to the EP, and in particular to committees and other meetings whilst remote viewing, via web streaming, remains limited. It calls for access badges to be granted to all those in the register who request them, and for the limit of four badges per organisation to be increased.

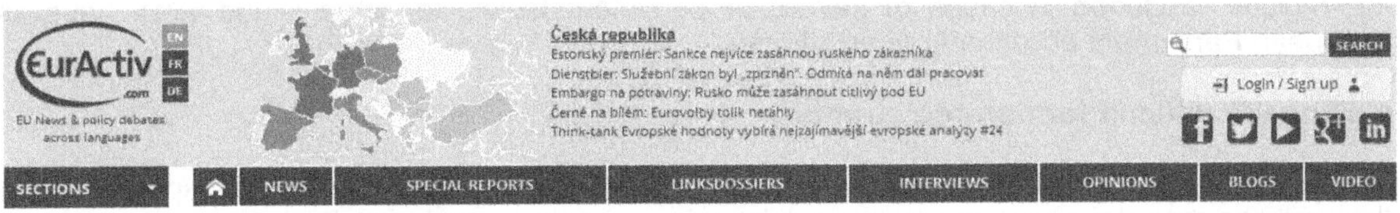

Council 'ready' to join EU transparency register

Published: 24/06/2011 - 08:31 | **Updated:** 24/06/2011 - 16:49

Openness in the EU institutions received a boost yesterday (23 June) after the Council of the European Union declared that it was "ready to consider" joining a new transparency register launched by the Commission and Parliament.

Yesterday, the Commission and the EU assembly launched a new online lobby registration scheme in a bid to improve the transparency of the EU decision-making process.

The launch represents the culmination of years of discussions between the two EU institutions on setting up a joint lobby register. Until now, lobbying activity has been subject to separate voluntary registers that apply only to the Commission and the Parliament.

"Today is a great day for the transparency of policymaking in Europe," said European Commission Vice-President Maroš Šefčovič after signing the agreement that launched the new 'transparency register' along with European Parliament President Jerzy Buzek.

Registration voluntary

Registration in the joint system is voluntary, but all lobbyists who wish to enter the Parliament's premises will have to register, giving them a strong incentive to do so.

Signatories will have to reveal the number of staff involved in advocacy and the main legislative proposals they have covered, as well as the amount of EU funding they have received.

Individuals are not expected to register unless they are self-employed individuals working under contract to represent their clients.

"All organisations, whether trade and professional associations, NGOs, think-tanks or others who have nothing to hide will be in the register and will provide the public and the [EU] institutions with information about their work," Šefčovič said.

By signing up to the joint register, organisations commit to a Common Code of Conduct to ensure that individuals always identify themselves by name and declare which entity they are working for. Signatories must pledge not to obtain information dishonestly.

A joint secretariat will be established to deal with complaints. If a complaint is upheld, the registrant concerned will be asked to conform to the rules or correct any false or misleading information in the register.

If an entity is found to have violated the Code of Conduct, it can be temporarily suspended from the register, excluded in cases of severe or persistent failure to comply, and even have its European Parliament access cards withdrawn.

Making life difficult for non-registrants

"All those who are not in the register will have to be asked why they can't be transparent – and they will see their daily work made more difficult by not being registered, in particular through the requirements of the European Parliament," said Šefčovič.

The Slovak commissioner also expressed his delight with the Council's decision to explore how it could take part in the scheme.

The Council said it was "ready to consider having a role in the register" and was looking forward to discussing "the possible modalities with the two other institutions".

The institution, which represents governments, has long been reluctant to participate in inter-institutional discussions on setting up a joint lobby registration scheme. Many of its employees are seconded from national posts at home, making their inclusion in an EU register more difficult.

"The Council considers that transparency should guide relations with interest representatives and that the register provides a useful basis on which to build and interact with them in an open, inclusive and consistent fashion," read a statement from the institution.

The new register replaces the Commission's own system for lobby registration, which has been in place since 2008 and features over 4,000 signatories. More than 1,700 organisations are accredited as interest groups in the Parliament.

Those registrants will gradually be transferred to the new system over the next twelve months.

The names of individuals will not be included, but the register will give details of the number of persons involved in lobbying activities as well as the amount of EU resources signatories have received.

Financial disclosure required

The scope of the register "covers all activities [...] carried out with the objective of directly or indirectly influencing the formulation or implementation of policy and the decision-making processes of the EU institutions, irrespective of the channel or medium of communication used," reads the text of the joint agreement on establishing a transparency register.

Such activities include outsourcing, media, contracts with professional intermediaries, think-tanks, platforms, forums, campaigns and grassroots initiatives, the document states.

Among the activities covered are contacting MEPs, officials or other staff of the EU institutions, circulating letters, information material or position papers, and organising social events or conferences, "invitations to which have been sent to Members, officials or other staff of the EU institutions".

"All organisations and self-employed individuals - irrespective of their legal status - engaged in activities falling within the scope of the register are expected to register," the document states.

The rules governing financial disclosure will be similar to those used by the Commission for its current lobby register.

Transparency groups want improvements

Transparency campaigners, meanwhile, warned that the new register would only be effective if it is used properly.

"The new register will be a test of the commitment of all parties involved in lobbying to greater openness," said Jana Mittermaier, head of the Brussels office at Transparency International, calling on officials and registrants to use the system "in the spirit of the Code of Conduct that accompanies it".

Indeed, the Alliance for Lobbying Transparency and Ethics Regulation (ALTER-EU), another campaign group, called for the scheme to be improved at the earliest opportunity.

Mandatory registration should remain the long-term goal of the Commission and Parliament. Preparations for a transition, at least by 2015, should start now, the campaign group demanded.

ALTER-EU wants the names of lobbyists who are found to have breached the rules to be published and thinks that the period of transition to the new scheme should be just three months rather than a year.

Mandatory lobby register requires EU treaty change

14.12.13 @ 08:08 By Nikolaj Nielsen

BRUSSELS - A treaty change or a unanimous decision from member states is needed to make the EU-joint transparency register mandatory.

"To get a legal base, we need a treaty change," German centre-right MEP Rainer Wieland, told this website on Friday (13 December).

"And we expect the commission to come up with a proposal for a legal base," added Wieland, who heads the parliament's working group on the joint transparency register.

A review of the register on Thursday recommends the European Commission come forward with a proposal to adapt the EU Treaty to make it compulsory.

The idea still has to get screened and approved by the parliament's constitutional affairs committee before a formal proposal is put forward to the commission.

Should the treaty change idea fall apart then the commission needs to put together another proposal by 2016, which would require unanimity among EU member states.

Wieland said this is the least favourable of the two options because it would exclude the parliament from having any influence.

"It is also possible the commission does not want to come with a proposal because it is out of any reach to get a decision of the council," he said.

If no decision is made, then the transparency register will come up for review again in 2017.

Parliament sources say European commissioner for inter-institutional affairs Maros Sefcovic wants to keep the register voluntary in order to attract more entries.

The commission's official line is that making the register mandatory would be too difficult.

"It would raise a great number of complex legal issues, in particular with regard to the scope of the register, and compliance with other articles of the treaties," it said in a statement.

The two sides came together to review the register and instead put forward some 30 recommendations to improve it.

One idea is to expand the scope to include all lobbying activities no matter where they take place geographically.

Another is to make a distinction between for profit and non-profit agencies.

Both the MEPs and the commission agree incentives need to be put in place to encourage more people to register.

The working group wants to shut out the exceptions to a rule that requires registration to access parliament buildings.

"These incentives include facilitating access to EP premises, the possibility to be consulted by the commission as experts or be heard at EP committee hearings," notes the working group.

But Olivier Hoedeman at the Brussels-based Corporate Europe Observatory described the recommendations as "incredibly vague."

He noted the commission meets with major corporations that are not in the registry like US investment bank Goldman Sachs.

The commission, for its part, estimates up to 75 percent of all relevant business-related entities and around 60 percent of NGOs operating in Brussels have registered.

Nearly 6,000 organisations are currently in the register, although pro-transparency groups say numerous entries are either out of date and contain errors.

Registrants are required to update the data once a year and on issues they lobbied on in the previous year.

Legal notice Contact ()

europa.eu **Transparency Register**

Search

EUROPA Transparency Register Code of Conduct

Code of Conduct

In their relations with the EU institutions and their Members, officials and other staff, registrants shall:

a. always identify themselves by name and by the entity or entities they work for or represent; declare the interests, objectives or aims promoted and, where applicable, specify the clients or members whom they represent;

b. not obtain or try to obtain information, or any decision, dishonestly, or by use of undue pressure or inappropriate behaviour;

c. not claim any formal relationship with the EU or any of its institutions in their dealings with third parties, nor misrepresent the effect of registration in such a way as to mislead third parties or officials or other staff of the EU;

d. ensure that, to the best of their knowledge, information which they provide upon registration and subsequently in the framework of their activities within the scope of the register is complete, up-to-date and not misleading;

e. not sell to third parties copies of documents obtained from any EU institution;

f. not induce Members of the EU institutions, officials or other staff of the EU, or assistants or trainees of those Members, to contravene the rules and standards of behaviour applicable to them;

g. if employing former officials or other staff of the EU or assistants or trainees of Members of the EU institutions, respect the obligation of such employees to abide by the rules and confidentiality requirements which apply to them;

h. observe any rules laid down on the rights and responsibilities of former Members of the European Parliament and the European Commission;

i. inform whomever they represent of their obligations towards the EU institutions;

Individuals representing or working for entities which have registered with the European Parliament with a view to being issued with a personal, non-transferable badge affording access to the European Parliament's premises shall:

j. comply strictly with the provisions of Rule 9 of, and Annex X and the second paragraph of Article 2 of Annex I to, the European Parliament's Rules of Procedure;

k. satisfy themselves that any assistance provided in the context of Article 2 of Annex I to the European Parliament's Rules of Procedure is declared in the appropriate register;

l. in order to avoid possible conflicts of interest, obtain the prior consent of the Member or Members of the European Parliament concerned as regards any contractual relationship with or employment of a Member's assistant, and subsequently declare this in the register.

(from The record of a Captive Commission - The 'black book' on the corporate agenda of the Barroso II Commission)

Conclusions

As we have demonstrated in this report, the Commission has eagerly pursued a corporate agenda in all the areas investigated. Whether it is economic policy, financial regulation, agriculture, trade, or environmental policies, including climate change, the Commission has by and large pushed for policies in sync with the interests of big business. It seems the Commission has been convinced that such policies are generally synonymous with those of society at large, which is certainly not the case. There is constant struggle and debate within society over all the issues investigated here, and the fact that a powerful body of the European Union consistently follows the agenda of those with the money in a myopic manner is one explanation for a strongly growing critical attitude to the EU.

It can be argued that the developments analysed have always been present, and the work done by Corporate Europe Observatory since 1997 certainly bears witness to that fact. However, the Barroso II Commission seems to be a watershed in the history of the European Union. Its five years or so in office have been marked by economic and financial crisis, and for that reason we have seen a noticeable further concentration of power in the hands of the Commission, and the Commission pursuing a corporate agenda even more vigorously than in the past – and in many respects with more success.

That development can be viewed as a mere consequence of the combined personal qualities and political viewpoints of this particular Commission. That certainly is an important factor, but there's much more to the problem. First, there is one of the main missions of the Commission, namely to expand the EUs and its own competence by deepening economic integration. Second, there are the main pillars of European cooperation and the foundational elements of the EU Treaty; namely the economic freedoms, which are becoming vehicles for corporate interests. Third, there is the structure of the Commission itself – its independence, and all the highly developed channels that can be used by corporate lobbyists which are – as in the case of the advisory groups – put at their disposal. Fourth, there is the lack of accountability to the public at large, which makes it infinitely more difficult for public interest groups to have a say. The European Commission, in far too many cases, has proven to be de facto unaccountable not just to the public but to the European Parliament as well.

While overwhelming, these are not problems that are impossible to address. Indeed, they have to be solved somehow if European cooperation is to have a future. But it will not be easy. The first steps would certainly be to have the Commission adopt strict rules on lobbying and lobbyists, including a mandatory register, a code of conduct, effective rules on revolving doors including a long "cooling-off" period, and a new culture in its advisory structure, with corporate dominated expert groups made a thing of the past. Despite the obvious need for such rules, however, the Commission is fighting tooth and nail to avoid any real reform. This makes it all the more clear that it is unlikely the Commission will reform itself. There is a need for a broader political effort to mend things at the top of the European Union. One such effort should include a full stop for further competences to the European Commission, a deepening of democratic transparency for the Commission, and indeed a roll back of its powers. As it stands, the Commission is a disgrace to democratic traditions in Europe.

THIS DOCUMENT IS FOR CANDIDATE 1 ONLY

Contact Events RSS feed

ALTER-EU Europe's campaign for lobbying transparency

Home

Greater lobbying transparency

The European Parliament and European Commission launched the so-called "Transparency Register", the new joint Commission and Parliament register of interest representatives in the EU in 2011. As the new register brought a number of improvements, ALTER-EU welcomed it, although it stressed from the outset that several fundamental flaws remain. These should be fixed as soon as possible.

Crucial improvements include:

- Mandatory registration should remain the long-term goal of the Commission and Parliament. A Commission proposal for a mandatory register covering all EU institutions should be introduced by the end of 2015. In the short term, the Commission and Parliament must act with determination to make registration an obligation for all actors involved in EU lobbying (including law firms and think tanks) and to improve the reliability of the information disclosed.
- Full transparency regarding the size of lobbying consultancies' clients in ranges of 10,000 euro;
- Safeguards against under-reporting, including: regular checks on registrations and meaningful enforcement of the rules to prevent under-reporting.
- Clearer guidance on disclosure requirements is needed (depending on what is released) so that there's a greater level of transparency on funding sources of all registrants;
- Publication of the names of lobbyists that have been found to be in breach of the rules.

Why lobbying transparency matters

Between 25,000 and 30,000 professional lobbyists currently roam the corridors of the EU institutions, a large majority representing business interests. Without rules on transparency and ethics for lobbying, the influence of corporate lobbyists on EU policy-making has largely remained out of public sight. The influence granted to corporate lobbyists in EU decision-making raises serious concerns over the impartiality of EU decision-making and its democratic principle.

50 per cent or more of our laws come from Brussels and it is vital that these decisions work in the interests of people and environment, and not just big business. Yet some of the most important people making decisions about how our lives are governed are too-cosy with big business. In recent years, a number of Commissioners, MEPs and top officials have walked through the 'revolving door' meaning that they have left their EU jobs and instead started working for big business. When this happens, big business gains inside-knowledge, vital contacts, and above all, powerful influence. This helps to make Brussels even more business-dominated and remote from citizens' concerns and the public interest. With the European Parliamentary elections and a change in the Commission fast approaching, the EU revolving door is likely to start spinning again.

ALTER-EU demands the following:

• A revised Code of Conduct for Commissioners to include a three year cooling-off period for Commissioners taking lobby jobs (or any other job which provokes the risk of a conflict of interest) and a revamped Commission ethics committee

• Further changes to the EU's Staff Regulations to better regulate the revolving door to include a two year cooling off period for officials

THIS DOCUMENT IS FOR CANDIDATE 2 ONLY

seap
society of european affairs professionals

Background

A joint European Parliament and European Commission Transparency Register was launched on 23 June 2011. It has been the subject of annual reports. The joint secretariat has issued guidelines and since the start of 2013 an inter-institutional high-level working group has been conducting a review. SEAP has participated in three rounds of consultations with other stakeholders during this review phase. This paper consolidates certain views of SEAP expressed in those consultations and proposes some practical steps to make the Register more effective. SEAP is committed to the highest standards in public affairs. It promotes self-regulation; promotes transparency and openness in EU decision-making; acts as the voice of the profession to the EU institutions; provides a forum for public affairs professionals to meet; and ultimately contributes to the making of EU law and policy that is fit for purpose. SEAP's Code sets out the ethical standards that SEAP members must observe when making representations to the EU institutions. Each SEAP member must endorse the Code and participate in training on the Code.

SEAP's high-level position on the Register

1. **A Register for all three Institutions**. A number of Member States are actively considering their own national registers of lobbyists. The definitions and rules are often different leading to compliance issues.

There is an immediate need for harmonisation. SEAP urges renewed efforts to include the Council in the Joint Register as a first step towards better harmonisation.

2. **Voluntary**. A 2013 study by Aberdeen Business School suggests that the voluntary Register has been a success with the majority of organisations active in Brussels now registered. While SEAP supports the introduction of more incentives to encourage those organisations that have not yet registered to do so, it is important that any reform does not have the effect of distancing the EU Institutions from EU citizens and businesses.

A proportionate approach is needed which does not prevent organisations from making contact with MEPs or Commission officials.

3. **Supporting ethical behaviour**. The Register's code correctly is about transparency not conduct. Promoting the highest standards of conduct is the role of SEAP and the few other organisations that are ethical code holders with complaint procedures to uphold those ethics. The Register should explicitly support these code holders.

Add a named check box for Registrants to show adherence to codes of behaviour, such as SEAP's.

SEAP's suggestions to improve the incentives to register

Currently there are two incentives to register:

a) it is the right thing to do;

b) there is an option to be notified about Commission consultations.

While SEAP strongly believes that the first of these is paramount we suggest a number of simple additional incentives that could be introduced immediately.

1. **A challenge question**. While the Register should not be a barrier to democratic discussion, it would be good practice to ask if organisations are registered.

Every MEP and Commission official seeing a lobbyist should ask the question; "Are you Registered?"

And if the answer if no then ask; "Why not"?

The meeting may continue regardless of the answer but the official or MEP may like to pass on to the Register Secretariat from time to time common reasons why certain organisations are not registered.

2. **Officials and MEPs attending third party conferences**.

While leaving it to individual discretion, the default should be officials and MEPs only attend conferences organised by those on the Register (or those ineligible for the Register).

3. **Holding an event in the European Parliament buildings**

This should be reserved only for those on the Register (or those ineligible for the Register).

4. **Participation in Commission Expert and Consultative Groups**

This should be reserved only for those on the Register (or those ineligible for the Register).

THIS DOCUMENT IS FOR CANDIDATE 3 ONLY

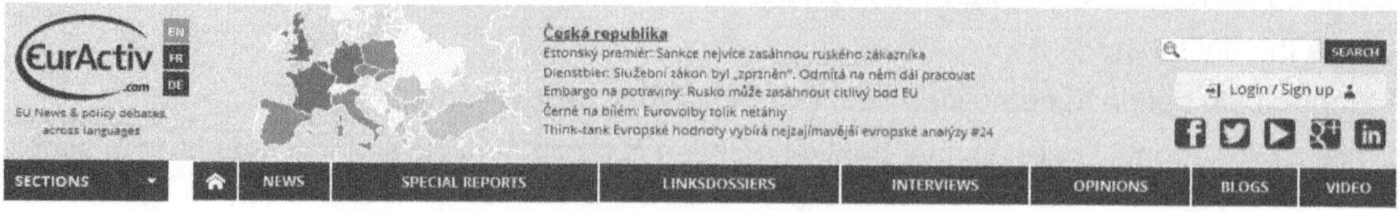

Brussels defends track record on lobbying transparency

The European Commission has defended its track record on corporate lobbying and transparency, after accusations it used the financial crisis to increase its powers while pursuing a big business agenda.

A report by watchdog Corporate Europe Observatory severely criticised the EU's executive for its closeness to corporates.

"On top of this, the Commission has fought tooth and nail to avoid effective regulation of lobbyists, including by opposing a mandatory register [of lobbyists]," the report said.

Kenneth Haar, co-author of the report, said, "The Barroso II Commission is the European Commission at its worst. With the crisis, it has managed to expand its competence, and has used its new powers to impose policies that fit neatly with the interests of big business."

The current transparency register of lobbyists is voluntary. 450 out of the 750 groups lobbying the EU on finance and banking reform are not on the current register, the report said.

The disclosure requirements are also too limited, the report said, before praising MEPs for making registration a pre-condition for lobbyists to be given entry badges to the European Parliament. The European Parliament has called on the Commission to make the register mandatory by 2017.

Commission denounces 'campaign-driven' report

The Commission, which described the report as "campaign-driven" and guilty of distorting "some obvious facts," blamed a lack of support from member states for the failure to create a mandatory register. There is a basis in EU treaties to create such a register but it would require the unanimous support of member states in the Council of Ministers, it said.

"At present, the Commission and Parliament still try to convince the Council to join them even in the voluntary register. There is however no majority in the Council for this at present," said Antony Gravili, the spokesman for Commissioner Maroš Šefčovič, in charge of EU Inter-institutional relations.

A mandatory approach could narrow the very broad scope of the current Transparency Register, which would not cover the organisations already included in the current voluntary approach. "Mandatory does not mean better," he said.

He said the current register included more than 6,500 organisations and about 25,000 individuals, a success. An estimated 75% of all relevant business-related organisations and about 60% of NGOs operating in Brussels have registered, he added.

THIS DOCUMENT IS FOR CANDIDATE 4 ONLY

Transparency Register

europa.eu

EUROPA Transparency Register Code of Conduct

New measures to encourage lobbyists to sign the EU Transparency Register

AFCO Press release - Institutions – 18-03-2014 - 12:37

Measures to encourage lobbyists working with the EU to sign the EU's public "Transparency Register" were backed by the Constitutional Affairs Committee on Tuesday. MEPs reiterated their demand that the register be made compulsory and meanwhile approved new provisions to push interest groups to make their relations with the EU more transparent.

Roberto Gualtieri (S&D, IT), MEP in charge for the update of the Register, said: "The approval of this report, which endorses an agreement reached by Parliament and the European Commission, is an important step towards greater transparency of the EU institutions. We insist on our request for a mandatory register for all organizations engaged in EU policy-making and call on the Commission to take all necessary steps for this purpose. Parliament pledges to adapt its internal provisions in order to guarantee incentives for the registered organizations. "

The decision was approved unanimously.

So far an estimated 75% of all relevant business-related organisations and approximately 60% of NGOs operating in Brussels have signed the Register. The committee reiterated its demand that signing the register be made compulsory and asked the European Commission to table a proposal, by the end of 2016, to this end.

Incentive measures

The committee backed the introduction of incentive measures that would link the registration to:

- further facilitation of access to Parliament's premises and help in contacting MEPs,
- easier authorisation to organise or co-host events on its premises,
- facilitated transmission of information, including through specific mailing lists,
- participation as speakers in committee hearings,
- better chances of getting patronage by the institution for events,

The committee also encouraged the Commission to adopt similar measures.

Clearer definitions

The committee called for a more detailed definition of the notion of "inappropriate behaviour", as defined in the Code of Conduct attached to the Register, and asked for full disclosure of the identity of all clients represented by each registered organisation.

Background

The current Register was set up jointly by the Parliament and the Commission in 2011. Parliament has always wanted the register to become compulsory, but it has proven difficult to find a suitable legal basis for this in the EU Treaty.

Next steps

These measures will be implemented internally by the Parliament. MEPs also asked for an evaluation of the Register before the end of 2017.

THIS DOCUMENT IS FOR CANDIDATE 5 ONLY

COUNCIL OF
THE EUROPEAN UNION

Brussels, 25 November 2013

16711/13

INST 631
POLGEN 234
INF 210
AG 10

NOTE

from:	General Secretariat of the Council
to:	Delegations
No. prev. doc.:	14983/13 INST 539 POLGEN 194 INF 176 AG 9
Subject:	Report of the GSC on the review process of the Transparency Register - meetings of the Working Group on 6 and 13 November 2013

1. The sixth and seventh meetings of the high level working group on the revision of the Transparency Register took place on 6 and 13 November 2013.

2. The meeting held on 6 November focussed essentially on the legal framework of the **Transparency Register**. The Working Group had invited four experts1 to set out their views on this issue at a public hearing.

While one of the experts suggested that Article 298 TFEU, which provides for the adoption of

regulations aiming at ensuring an open, efficient and independent European administration, could possibly serve as a legal basis for creating a legally binding register system, it was concluded at the meeting by other experts and, subsequently, by the legal service of the European Parliament and the Commission that the only appropriate legal basis for introducing such a legally binding system would be Article 352 TFEU2 in view of the need to cover the legislative process. Both legal services underlined also the procedural difficulties (unanimity in the Council and consent of the European Parliament) entailed by this legal basis.

3. At the meeting of 13 November, the Working Group **continued the debate on the legal framework of the Transparency Register** in the light of the conclusions reached at the previous meeting, discussing in particular the modalities and procedure related to the legal basis for introducing a mandatory register system. Several members of the Working Group took the view that the move towards a mandatory regime should be taken into consideration and a number of prerequisites would need to be met before this could happen. During the discussion, the need for a clear definition of the scope and consequences of any compulsory scheme was stressed, and it was recalled that the existing joint transparency register had the widest embrace in the world in terms of scope, even with its present voluntary registration basis.

4. The Working Group then proceeded to an exchange of views on an **indicative list of measures and elements of suggested improvements to take into account in the review of the Transparency Register**. The indicative list included both a series of modifications on which consensus had emerged during the previous discussions in the Group and a number of additional measures, which were examined.

5. Among the suggested **modifications of direct interest to the Council**, the indicative list of measures, on which an agreement has been reached, included the **exemption of Member States' governments**, third countries governments as well as intergovernmental public organisations and **their diplomatic missions from the scope of the register**. The same applied to activities directed at **Member States national structures**, including their **Permanent Representations** in Brussels.

6. As regards the **sub-national entities**, it is suggested that **Regions should not be expected to register**, although the possibility to register should remain open for those who wish to do so on a voluntary basis. All other sub-national entities (including cities) or any mixed entity should be expected to register when engaged in activities falling under the scope of the register directed at the EU institutions.

7. Among the measures discussed is notably the inclusion of a possible additional provision in the Interinstitutional Agreement (IIA) to the effect that each institution, party to the agreement, will recommend incentives to encourage registration of interest representatives, as far as is possible within its own powers of organisation, using internal rules or administrative codes, which should possibly be amended to attain that end after the adoption of the new IIA. The Working Group will resume its deliberations at a meeting to be held on 3 December in Brussels. An additional meeting has been scheduled for 12 December in Strasbourg.

THIS DOCUMENT IS FOR CANDIDATE 6 ONLY

Ombudsman calls on Member States to back EU Transparency Register

Press release no. 11/2014 - 16 April 2014

Author: Cathy Yeulet

The European Ombudsman, **Emily O'Reilly**, has called on the Council of the European Union to participate in the Transparency Register of EU interest representatives. She also encouraged the European Commission to follow the European Parliament's (EP) example of introducing much stronger incentives for lobbyists to register. This follows yesterday's vote on a revised Transparency Register in the EP.

Emily O'Reilly commented: "Lobbying plays an important role in functioning democracies. However, ordinary citizens who take an interest in these matters will continue to be baffled as to why the EU does not support, more directly, their right to know which interests are lobbying the EU institutions and for which purposes. As the current voluntary register does not fulfil this role sufficiently, it should be given teeth. For example, the Commission could instruct its officials not to discuss policy with unregistered lobbyists. Furthermore, to be effective, the Council should participate in the register as it is one of the key decision-making institutions in the EU. These steps could be taken now, without waiting for the register to become mandatory."

Much stronger incentives needed for lobbyists to register

The Transparency Register is jointly run by the EP and the Commission. It contains around 6,500 organisations. However, many lobbyists do not find it worth their while to register.

In its report, the EP calls for incentive measures to encourage lobbyists to sign the register, including, for example, restricting access to EP premises for non-registered organisations. Parliament also asks the Commission to adopt similar measures.

The Ombudsman regularly deals with complaints about the Transparency Register, e.g. about allegedly inaccurate information given on the register. In that context, she called on the Commission to improve the monitoring and comparability of data in the register. She also recommended that the Commission systematically inform lobbyists and other interest representatives it meets about its intention to release their names, should requests for public access be made about their lobbying activities.

The European Ombudsman investigates complaints about maladministration in the EU institutions and bodies. Any EU citizen, resident, or an enterprise or association in a Member State, can lodge a complaint with the Ombudsman. The Ombudsman offers a fast, flexible, and free means of solving problems with the EU administration. For more information: www.ombudsman.europa.eu

Annex 7 Sample Motivational Interview Questions

This quiz is intended to test your knowledge of the EU. The questions are along the lines of those you can expect in the motivational interview – so the more questions you can confidently answer the higher your chances of doing well in that interview.

The motivational interview is for AD5 generalists only. However, it is always a good idea to know a lot about your employer and your working environment; this will boost your understand ing of your work, enhance your motivation and in the end make you a better employee. This is certainly true for EU officials.

1. Why do you want to work for the EU?
2. How has the EU benefitted you as a citizen?
3. What are the EU fundamental values as defined in the Treaty of Lisbon? Explain your understanding of each one of these values.
4. What are the citizen's fundamental rights as laid out in the Charter of Fundamental rights?
5. What are the four freedoms of the European Union as set out in the treaty of Rome?
6. What changes did the Lisbon Treaty bring to the functioning of the EU?
7. Explain: acquis communautaire.
8. Explain: co-decision procedure.
9. Name all the current Member States of the EU.
10. What is the difference between "official" and "working" languages?
11. What is the difference between a directive and a regulation?
12. Describe the democratic legitimacy of the EU and its institutions. What is the so-called democratic deficit and how could it be addressed?
13. What is the European Semester and which policy areas are affected by it?
14. What is the difference between the European Single Market and the European Free Trade Association?
15. What is the difference between the European Single Market and the Eurozone?
16. What is the "Schengen area"?
17. What do you know about the New Pact on Migration and Asylum that was presented by the European Commission in September 2020?
18. What is the role of Free Trade Agreements and name at least 5 countries with which the EU has such an agreement.

19. What is the current status of TTIP? And the trade agreement with China?
20. What do you imagine your role to be after a few years working for the EU?
21. What are the advantages and disadvantages of working for the EU?
22. Name the most important EU institutions and what their role is.
23. Explain: right of initiative. Which institutions have that right?
24. Explain: European Citizen's Initiative.
25. EU budget: where does the money come from?
26. Who decides on the EU budget? How?
27. What is the role of the European Central Bank?
28. What is the role of the Court of Auditors?
29. What is the role of the Court of Justice of the EU?
30. What is the role of the European Ombudsman?
31. What is the difference between an Agency, a Delegation, and a Mission?
32. What are – in your opinion – the three main challenges of the EU today? Why?
33. What are the priorities of the Von der Leyen Commission and how far are these different from the Juncker Commission?
34. Explain: "Green Deal".
35. What are the policy areas over which the EU assumes exclusive competence?
36. What are the conditions for membership of the EU?
37. Summarise in outline the history of the EU including the main treaties and the successive enlargements.
38. What are the convergence criteria for joining the eurozone?
39. What are the main features of EU competition law? How are they enforced?
40. Explain: GDPR.
41. How does the EU fight organised crime and human trafficking?
42. What does the term "subsidiarity" mean? Which are the areas where the EU alone can pass laws, and where the role of the Member States is limited to applying the law?
43. What is the difference between the European Investment Bank (EIB) and the European Central Bank (ECB)?
44. What is "intellectual property" (IP) and why is it important to protect it? How is this enforced in the EU?
45. What do you know about the Digital Services Act package?
46. Explain the final version of the Brexit deal.
47. Explain the compromise that was reached on the "rule of law mechanism" in the Multiannual Financial Framework.
48. Do you think the EU is a sustainable model in a changing world?
49. What has been the EU's role in combatting climate change? Is it enough?
50. Overall what is the biggest threat facing the EU? And the biggest opportunity?

Annex 8 Sample Competency Passports

1. Competency Passport for AD Generalist

This report is based on the assessment centre for AD competitions. It consists of the following elements:

- A general description of the competency framework
- A global overview of the different strengths and weaknesses of the participant
- A description per competency of the main findings
- The scoring method

The report is based on data gathered through a range of exercises:

- A case study in the chosen field
- A group exercise
- A structured interview
- An oral presentation

The Competency Framework

General competencies measured during the assessment.

Analysis and Problem Solving
Identify the critical facts in complex issues and develop creative and practical solutions
Communication
Communicate clearly and precisely both orally and in writing
Delivering Quality and Results
Take personal responsibility and initiative for delivering work to a high standard of quality within set procedures
Learning and Development
Develop and improve personal skills and knowledge of the organisation and its environment
Prioritising and Organising
Prioritise the most important tasks, work flexibly and organise own workload efficiently

Resilience
Remain effective under a heavy workload, handle organisational frustrations positively and adapt to a changing work environment
Working with Others
Work co-operatively with others in teams and across organisational boundaries and respect differences between people
Leadership
Manage, develop and motivate people to achieve results

Field-specific competencies are also measured in during the assessment centre.

Competency Overview

The chart below positions every general competency against the average score, providing a quick overview of strengths and weaknesses of the participant.

The chart gives the competency profile of the participant, without reflecting details and nuances. The next section of the report gives a more detailed view on the results obtained for each competency.

The specific competency is not scored in this chart, but is mentioned below, as well as the total score.

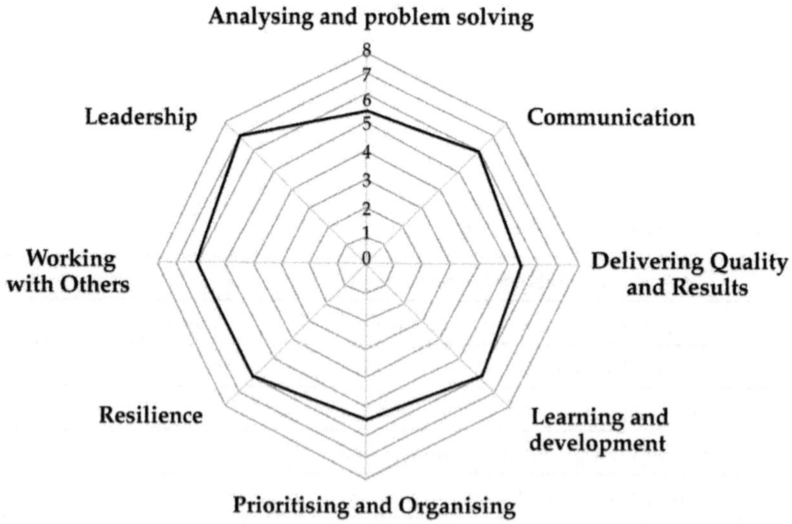

Key

1 Extremely weak
2 Very weak
3 Weak
4 Fair
5 Satsifactory
6 Good
7 Strong
8 Very strong
9 Excellent
10 Outstanding

Scoring Method

Calculation of overall score

The method for calculating your overall score is specified in the Notice of Competition. This is:

General competencies

General Competencies	Score	Passmark
Sum of all scores on the general competencies	47.5/80	50/80

Score: 47.5 out of a total of 80 points for all general competencies (maximum of 10 points per competency)

Pass mark: minimum of 3 points per competency and an aggregate of 50 points for all general competencies

Weighting: 75 % of the overall score

Specific Competencies

Specific Competency	Score	Passmark
Job Specific Knowledge	12/20	10
Sum of all scores on the specific competencies	12/20	N/A

Weighting: 25 % of the overall score

Overall score

Applying this method, your total score is thus calculated as (total points for specific competencies) x weighting applicable + (total points for general competencies) x weighting applicable

	Score	Score/100	Weight in the total score
General competencies	47.5/80	59.38/100	75%
Specific competencies	12/20	60/100	25%

Total weighted score: **59.53/100**

Analysis and Problem Solving	
Competency score	5.5/10
Comments: The candidate describes the problems in detail but lacks time to present the solutions. He draws information from various sources and subjects it to critical analysis. The candidate has a good grasp of the complexity of the background infomation, but should adopt a less descriptive and more analytical approach to tasks.	
Communication	
Competency score	6/10
Comments: The candidate delivers the oral presentation confidently and makes good use of visual aids. He engages relatively well with the audience. His writing style is reasonably well structured but could be more precise.	

Delivering Quality and Results	
Competency score	5.5/10
Comments: The candidate addresses the main issues but misses the opportunity to add further value by developing relevant points more fully. He should try harder to convert understanding of issues into clear recommendations for action. He anticipates potential problems and provides justification for the proposed solutions, but should make a greater effort to achieve consistent quality throughout all parts of the assignment.	
Learning and Development	
Competency score	6/10
Comments: The candidate reacts positively in situations where he realises that he lacks skills and takes steps to gain proficiency in new areas of competence. As a participant in a group discussion, the candidate listens actively and uses information to improve his own understanding. However, he could obtain a clearer insight by asking more questions.	

Prioritising and Organising	
Competency score	5.5/10
Comments: Working on a dossier as part of a team, the candidate takes control of the discussion at several points, ensures that the main issues are prioritised and is focused on maintaining the debate within the time limit. He identifies a few of the key issues but does, however, omit others. He could improve his output by bringing more of the available information into play and by looking at the situation from different angles.	
Resilience	
Competency score	6/10
Comments: The candidate copes with high workloads and competing claims on his time by remaining focused. He makes good use of slack periods to organise additional resources, such a reports and research, in preparation for future tasks. In high-pressure situations such as speaking in public, he handles tough questions well and recovers from poor time allocation in his presentation. He should develop his ability to use a limited amount of preparation time to the best effect.	

Working with Others	
Competency score	6/10
Comments: He takes initiatives to improve communication and cooperation within teams and strives to resolve conflicts in a harmonious manner. When discussing a subject with other people, the candidate intervenes to the maximum possible, often clarifying points to the group and seeking consensus. However, he should make a greater effort to find common ground between his own position and other views around the table.	
Leadership	
Competency score	7/10
Comments: The candidate sees how different people with different skills can contribute to an end result and keeps everybody on board and committed. Working on a dossier as part of a team, he clearly wants to take leadership of the debate and keeps the group focused.	

Job Specific Knowledge	
Score	12/20
Comments: The candidate demonstrates good job specific knowledge but could apply it in greater depth.	

2. Competency Passport for AD Translator

This report is based on the assessment centre for AD competitions. It consists of the following elements:

- A general description of the competency framework
- A global overview of the different strengths and weaknesses of the participant
- A description per competency of the main findings
- The scoring method

The report is based on data gathered through a range of exercises

- Translation test from language 2 to language 1
- Translation test from language 3 to language 1
- A group exercise
- A structured interview
- An oral presentation

The Competency Framework

General competencies measured during the assessment.

Analysis and Problem Solving
Identify the critical facts in complex issues and develop creative and practical solutions
Communication
Communicate clearly and precisely both orally and in writing
Delivering Quality and Results
Take personal responsibility and initiative for delivering work to a high standard of quality within set procedures
Learning and Development
Develop and improve personal skills and knowledge of the organisation and its environment
Prioritising and Organising
Prioritise the most important tasks, work flexibly and organise own workload efficiently
Resilience
Remain effective under a heavy workload, handle organisational frustrations positively and adapt to a changing work environment
Working with Others
Work co-operatively with others in teams and across organisational boundaries and respect differences between people
Leadership
Manage, develop and motivate people to achieve results

Field-specific competencies are also measured during the assessment.

Competency Overview

The chart below positions every general competency against the average score, providing a quick overview of strengths and weaknesses of the participant.

The chart gives the competency profile of the participant, without reflecting details and nuances. The next section of the report gives a more detailed view on the results obtained for each competency.

The specific competency is not scored in this chart, but is mentioned below, as well as the total score.

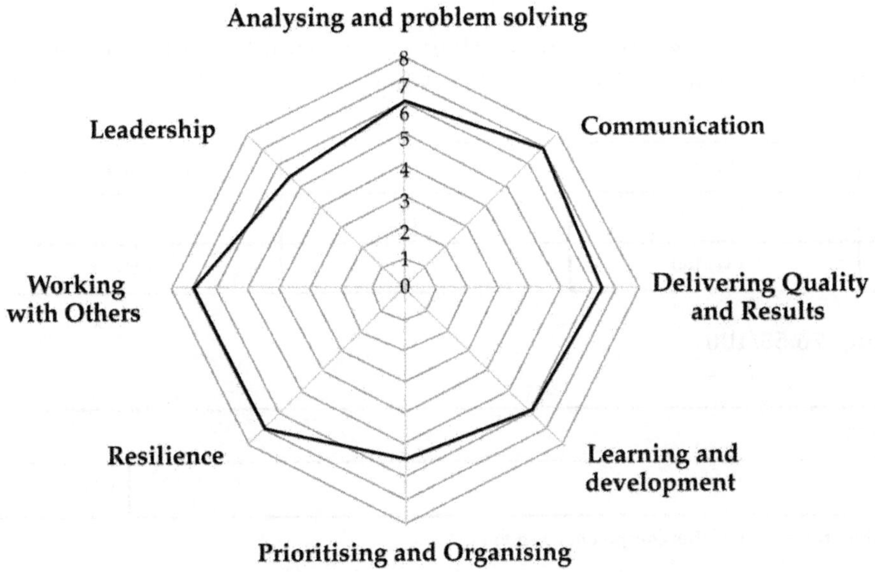

Key

1 Extremely weak
2 Very weak
3 Weak
4 Fair
5 Satsifactory
6 Good
7 Strong
8 Very strong
9 Excellent
10 Outstanding

Scoring Method

Calculation of overall score

The method for calculating your overall score is specified in the Notice of Competition. This is:

General competencies

General Competencies	Score	Passmark
Sum of all scores on the general competencies	50.5/80	40/80

Score: 50.5 out of a total of 80 points for all general competencies (maximum of 10 points per competency)

Pass mark: minimum of 3 points per competency and an aggregate of 40 points for all general competencies

Weighting: 35 % of the overall score

Specific Competencies

Specific Competency	Score	Passmark
Translation test: L2 to L1	61/80	40
Translation test: L2 to L1	73/80	40
Sum of all scores on the specific competencies	134/160	N/A

Weighting: 65 % of the overall score

Overall score

Applying this method, your total score is thus calculated as (total points for specific competencies) x weighting applicable + (total points for general competencies) x weighting applicable

	Score	Score/100	Weight in the total score
General competencies	50.5/80	63.13/100	35%
Specific competencies	134/160	83.75/100	65%

Total weighted score: **76.53/100**

Analysis and Problem Solving	
Competency score	6/10
Comments: In this competition, the rating of this competency is good **Strengths observed** Being able to think about the practical consequences of recommendations/proposals Making feasible proposals that go beyond the obvious **Observed opportunities for development** Analysing and linking complex information provided by others Exploring several courses of action as part of a group discussion	
Communication	
Competency score	7/10
Comments: In this competition, the rating of this competency is strong **Strengths observed** Speaking clearly and precisely Delivering a captivating and engaging presentation **Observed opportunities for development** Adjusting style and content to the audience or the interlocutor	

Delivering Quality and Results	
Competency score	6.5/10
Comments: In this competition, the rating of this competency is good **Strengths observed** Dealing promptly and personally with problems **Observed opportunities for development** Overcoming obstacles and constraints effectively and creatively	
Learning and Development	
Competency score	6/10
Comments: In this competition, the rating of this competency is good **Strengths observed** Actively developing and implementing new skills and making concrete efforts to improve knowledge and competencies **Observed opportunities for development** Understanding the wider context of a simulated situation Giving attention to all participants in a group	

Prioritising and Organising	
Competency score	5.5/10
Comments: In this competition, the rating of this competency is satisfactory **Observed opportunities for development** Being flexible when faced with new aspects arising with information from coworkers Addressing all relevant issues appropriately **Weak points observed – to improve** Optimising the available time by structuring the debate towards getting results within the deadline	
Resilience	
Competency score	7/10
Comments: In this competition, the rating of this competency is strong **Strengths observed** Seeing organisational changes and new approaches as a positive challenge Staying focused and keeping a calm posture **Observed opportunities for development** Working autonomously whilst knowing when to involve the hierarchy	

Working with Others	
Competency score	7/10
Comments: In this competition, the rating of this competency is strong **Strengths observed** Mastering of intercultural skills Encouraging and facilitating communication between people **Observed opportunities for development** Interacting constructively and in a friendly way but actively with others	

Leadership	
Competency score	5.5/10
Comments: In this competition, the rating of this competency is satisfactory **Observed opportunities for development** Coordinating the allocation and delegation of tasks in a group Keeping the group focused on desired results **Weak points observed – to improve** Being a role model to motivate team members Organising the follow-up within a group	

Translation test1: L2 to L1	
Score	61/80
Comments: In this translation test, the rating of the candidate's performance is 'strong'	

Translation test2: L3 to L1	
Score	73/80
Comments: In this translation test, the rating of the candidate's performance is 'excellent'	

3. Competency Passport for Assistants

This report is based on the assessment evaluation for assistants (AST3):

- A general description of the competency framework
- A global overview of the different strengths and weaknesses of the participant
- A description per competency of the main findings
- The scoring method

The report is based on data gathered through a range of exercises:

- An in-tray exercise
- A structured interview
- A case study in the chosen field
- A group exercise

The Competency Framework

General competencies measured during the assessment.

Analysis and Problem Solving
Identify the critical facts in complex issues and develop creative and practical solutions
Communication
Communicate clearly and precisely both orally and in writing
Delivering Quality and Results
Take personal responsibility and initiative for delivering work to a high standard of quality within set procedures
Learning and Development
Develop and improve personal skills and knowledge of the organisation and its environment
Prioritising and Organising
Prioritise the most important tasks, work flexibly and organise own workload efficiently
Resilience
Remain effective under a heavy workload, handle organisational frustrations positively and adapt to a changing work environment
Working with Others
Work co-operatively with others in teams and across organisational boundaries and respect differences between people

Field-specific competencies are measured during the assessment centre.

Competency Overview

The chart below positions every general competency against the average score, providing a quick overview of strengths and weaknesses of the participant.

The chart gives the competency profile of the participant, without reflecting details and nuances. The next section of the report gives a more detailed view on the results obtained for each competency.

The field-specific competency is not scored in this chart, but is mentioned below, as well as the total score.

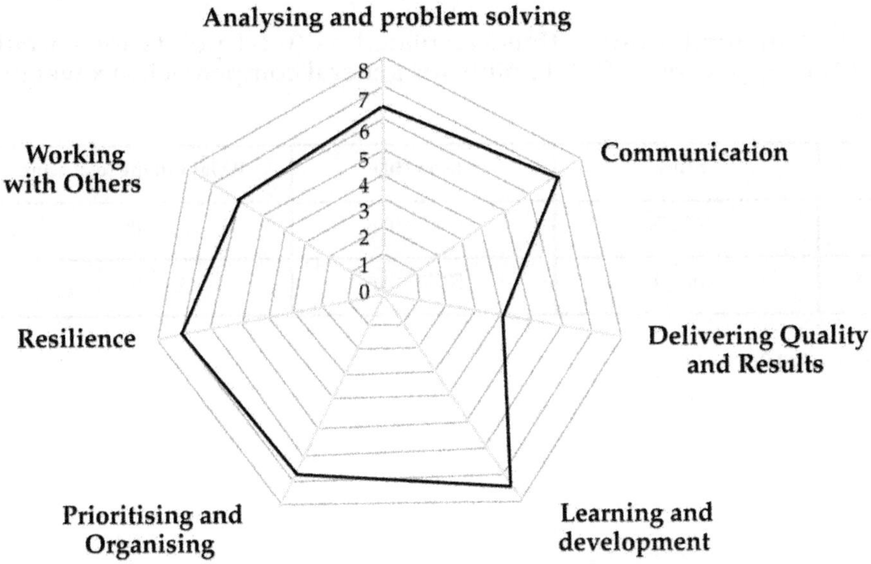

Key

1 Extremely weak
2 Very weak
3 Weak
4 Fair
5 Satsifactory
6 Good
7 Strong
8 Very strong
9 Excellent
10 Outstanding

Scoring Method

Calculation of overall score

The method for calculating your overall score is specified in the Notice of Competition. This is:

General competencies

General Competencies	Score	Passmark
Sum of all scores on the general competencies	44.5/70	35/70

Score: 44.5 out of a total of 70 points for all general competencies (maximum of 10 points per competency)

Pass mark: minimum of 3 points per competency and an aggregate of 35 points for all general competencies

Weighting: 70 % of the overall score

Specific Competencies

Specific Competency	Score	Passmark
Job Specific Knowledge	16/30	15
Sum of all scores on the specific competencies	16/30	N/A

Weighting: 30 % of the overall score

Overall score

Applying this method, your total score is thus calculated as (total points for specific competencies) x weighting applicable + (total points for general competencies) x weighting applicable

	Score	Score/100	Weight in the total score
General competencies	44.5/70	63.57/100	70%
Specific competencies	16/30	53.33/100	30%

Total weighted score: **60.5/100**

Analysis and Problem Solving	
Competency score	6.5/10
Comments: In this competition, the rating of this competency is good **Strengths observed** Showing willingness to explore data from different sources **Observed opportunities for development** Critically evaluating proposed solutions and examing their implications **Weak points – to improve** Adopting a creative approach in the search for solutions	

Communication	
Competency score	7/10
Comments: In this competition, the rating of this competency is strong **Strengths observed** Answering questions confidently Speaking clearly and precisely **Observed opportunities for development** Organising and structuring ideas in order to help the reader follow the reasoning	

Delivering Quality and Results	
Competency score	4/10
Comments: In this competition, the rating of this competency is fair **Observed opportunities for development** Producing a high standard of work by choosing the actions that ensure qualitative results from a list of proposed actions Developing concrete recommendations to achieve qualitative results **Weak points observed – to improve** Exploring resources with set procedures to deliver results fully in line with the expectations Proposing detailed solutions and ensuring they withstand close scrutiny	
Learning and Development	
Competency score	7.5/10
Comments: In this competition, the rating of this competency is strong **Strengths observed** Actively developing and using new skills and knowledge Understanding personal contribution to team objectives and looking beyond own role	

Prioritising and Organising	
Competency score	6.5/10
Comments: In this competition, the rating of this competency is good **Observed opportunities for development** Identifying priorities and adapting routines accordingly Adjusting approach to the demand of the task **Weak points observed – to improve** Understanding the urgency level of different tasks	
Resilience	
Competency score	7/10
Comments: In this competition, the rating of this competency is strong **Strengths observed** Seeing organisational changes and new approaches as a positive challenge Continuing to perform in a stressful situation during an observed collective task	

Working with Others	
Competency score	6/10
Comments: In this competition, the rating of this competency is good **Strengths observed** Understanding the need to pay attention to other people's input and points of view **Observed opportunities for development** Interacting with all members of a group Striving for consensus	

Job Specific Knowledge	
Score	16/30
Comments: The candidate demonstrates sufficient job specific knowledge.	

Annex 9 Frequently Asked Questions

Below is a compilation of questions we frequently get during classroom training sessions and in personal coaching. Many of the questions are also tackled in different ways elsewhere in this book but we've listed them here in a separate annex to make your life easier.

What is an open competition?

The EU institutions select candidates for permanent contracts through open competitions. These are tests and assessment exercises designed to measure your professional skills and a number of core competencies. In view of the very large number of applicants, this is the fairest and most transparent selection procedure. This means that spontaneous applications cannot be taken into account.

How long does a complete competition normally take?

EPSO works to a yearly planning cycle and the internal target is to manage a complete competition (from the publication of the Notice of Competition to the publication of the Reserve List) in one year. At the beginning of a calendar year they indeed publish a provisional agenda, listing the competitions they intend to organise, but in practice competitions commonly take more than a year. Take for example the 2018 AD5 graduate competition. It opened in March 2018 and the Assessment Centre took place in February to March 2019. If you take into account that it takes at least a couple of months to then establish the Reserve List, it is clear that the real duration of that competition will be more than a year. As it happens, this is by far the biggest competition EPSO organises – in terms of number of candidates, complexity and size of the Reserve List – and of course, the bigger the competition the longer it takes. But we think that one year is a bit optimistic.

What is the difference between "hard" and "soft" skills?

For the learning and development competency in the GCBI we frequently get asked about the difference between "hard" and "soft" skills.

In essence, hard skills are teachable abilities or skills that are easy to quantify. Examples of hard skills include a degree or certificate, speaking a foreign language, machine operation, computer programming, and so on. Soft skills, on the other hand, are open to opinion and judgement, skills that are much harder to quantify. Also known as "people skills" or "interpersonal skills," soft skills concern the way you relate to and interact with other people, to the way you behave.

Hard skills are learned at school and university, from study and practice. There are usually specified levels of proficiency and a direct path to how to excel with each hard skill. For example, accounting is a hard skill. You can take basic accounting and advanced accounting courses. You can then work to get experience and take an exam and be certified as a professional accountant, and so on.

In contrast, there is no simple path to develop soft skills. Most soft skills have to be learned on the job, often by trial and error. There are many books and guides on soft skills, but they only take you so far, because there aren't any easy step-by-step instructions on how to master a soft skill. Soft skills are not easily measured; it takes a difficult assessment process, managed and done by professional evaluators and even then the results only serve to compare people, they are not absolute.

In EPSO, your "field competencies" are hard skills, and all the "general competencies" are soft skills.

Is my age important?

The honest answer to this is: "it depends".

First of all, you should know that there is no age limit in the admission criteria in any of the competitions (including CAST) organised by EPSO, and it would even be illegal for them to use your age as a measure to score you. However, there is an implicit lower limit in the diploma and professional experience requirements (unless you are a child prodigy of course) and another – more explicit – upper limit at the pensionable age for EU officials; even though you could participate in a competition, you will never be hired when you have already reached the pensionable age.

In terms of how your age could influence your scores in the Assessment Centre there is a distinction to be made between those competitions that do not require any previous professional experience, and those that have a minimum professional experience requirement. A typical example of the first category would be the AD5 generalist (so-called graduate) competitions, as opposed to the (AST or AD) Specialist competitions for the second category.

For those competitions where no professional experience is required, it is the intention to recruit people who are still young enough to be "malleable" into good all-round EU officials. So, in theory, the younger you are, the better. However, it is obvious that people fresh from education and without much real life experience will find it harder to demonstrate their "general competencies" in the Assessment Centre. Since the exercises typically simulate a work environment, those with little job experience will find it harder to understand what is expected in terms of behaviour at work. The effect of all this is that the average age at recruitment of AD5 generalists (in the Commission) is around 34.

For the Specialist competitions there is a completely different picture. Usually, the pre-selection of Specialists is done with a so-called talent screener. The main parameter in the talent screener is the length of your (relevant) experience, which ensures that only very experienced people are invited to the Assessment Centre. Usually, it is not enough to have the minimum required experience; other candidates with (much) more experience than you will make it. This is of course a major source of frustration for younger professionals. Once in the Assessment Centre, the experience factor kicks in again, resulting in older candidates on the Reserve List. We have no statistics about this, but our guess is that the average age of successful Specialists must be in their 40s and certainly much older than for generalists. For the institutions, this has a tremendous advantage in that Specialists can be "operational from day one". One drawback is of course that older people are less inclined to follow the whims of management and politicians; they can be more difficult to handle…

Can I choose the language of my Assessment Centre, and when do I have to do that?

Most candidates choose their mother tongue as the first language, and this is perfectly possible as long as it is an official EU language. The consequence of this choice is that you will have to take the pre-selection tests in that language. You might think that this is an advantage, but it isn't necessarily. The thing is that most of the CBTs are originally drafted in English (or French) and are then translated later on into the other official languages. Despite the quality control it could therefore happen that the translated version is not perfect when it comes to conveying the intended messages or options.

The e-tray and the Assessment Centre are in your second language. Even though there is no formal testing of your command of the second language (linguists excepted of course), it goes without saying that the command of your second language will influence your scores for the various exercises (oral and written). It is therefore important at the very outset in applying for a competition that you make the right choice for your second language. By far the greatest number of candidates take the Assessment Centre tests in English but there is no different treatment – or assessment – for candidates who take their Assessment Centre in another second language.

In conclusion, if you have a very good command of English on top of your mother tongue, it might be advisable to take English as your language 1, and your mother tongue as language 2, provided of course it is one of the three (i.e. adding French or German) – or possibly five (adding Spanish or Italian) – languages in which the Assessment Centre will be organised.

Is it an advantage or a disadvantage if I am invited early in the Assessment Centre campaign?

Some candidates complain because they are amongst the first invited to the Assessment Centre. They say that this is a disadvantage because they don't have as much time to prepare for the AC as those who are called later. We don't believe that's true.

First of all, the planning of when the AC will take place is publicly announced well in advance. Second, you will get the letter giving the results of the pre-selection tests (CBTs, e-tray, talent screener) right after the closure of these tests. At that moment you will know whether or not you will be invited to the Assessment Centre, though you don't yet know the exact date. So you will at a minimum have the time to prepare until the earliest starting date of the AC campaign, and that should be at least three weeks in advance. In our opinion, this is enough to fine-tune your preparation. Don't believe that having a couple of weeks more time will fundamentally improve your behaviour in the AC. Changing your behaviour – who you are – fundamentally takes time, a lot of time, years perhaps. Brushing it up with some targeted training, or reading this book, doesn't. And no training in the world can turn a Fiat cinquecento into a Porsche, not even if you spend years on it.

In fact, having too much time to prepare for an AC can even be a disadvantage for some people. The longer the wait, the more nervous and confused they may get, and some will simply put off preparing until the last minute anyway. We need a bit of time pressure to get us going.

EPSO takes all the necessary measures and precautions to make sure that every candidate gets the same fair and objective treatment in the competitions, and we believe that they are doing a good job on that.

Who are the assessors?

In every Selection Board there are two kinds of assessors: permanent and non-permanent. Let's start with the largest group, the non-permanent members.

The non-permanent members are EU officials, working for one of the institutions, and they are specialists in the field of the competition. They also have a sufficiently high seniority, at least one level above the grade of the competition. Non-permanent members have been asked by their institution to represent either the administration or the staff representatives (the trade unions) on the Selection Board for that competition. This participation is always on a voluntary basis, as it would be a very bad idea to have disgruntled employees on a jury. So, non-permanent members have their regular job in the institutions, and they work for EPSO whenever this is required for their competition (typically 1 or 2 days per week during an AC campaign).

Once accepted onto a jury, its members have to be trained in the EPSO Assessment Centre methodology and the various exercises that will be conducted in their AC. Members of a jury also have to sign a declaration in which they promise not to reveal the internal proceedings, or to breach the privacy rights of the candidates. They also cannot have been a trainer, or a coach, for EPSO Assessment Centres and they are not allowed to be such until one year after the end of their mandate on the jury. Finally, if a member of a Selection Board detects a potential conflict of interest with one of the participants, he or she will have to withdraw from the assessment of that candidate.

The permanent members are EU officials too, but they have been seconded to EPSO for a period of two years, which can be extended. They work in EPSO on a full-time basis. Rather than being a specialist in any field they are HR people, usually with a lot of experience in selecting and recruiting staff. The group of permanent members working for EPSO make sure that every Selection Board contains at least a few permanent members to form the "backbone" of the jury and to help the non-permanent members do a good job.

Will the topics of the various exercises (e-tray, case study, oral presentation, group exercise) be related to the field of the competition?

We already mentioned that most of the members (the non-permanent members) of specialist Selection Boards are themselves specialists in the field of the competition. Also, it is the jury who bears the final responsibility on the content of all the exercises in the AC. It is therefore not surprising that the topics of the e-tray, case study, oral presentation, and group exercise will most likely be related to the field of the competition. And this makes sense, because the purpose of these exercises is to assess your general competencies, and these will be easier to observe in a simulation of a familiar environment for both the candidates and the assessors.

Will I be assessed on my command of the language used in the Assessment Centre?

The short answer to this is "No". Apart for those competitions where the command of one or more languages is part of the professional competencies (translators, interpreters, lawyer-linguists) there are no exercises in the AC where this is explicitly tested, or scored. But it must be clear that if you have a poor command of language 2 this will negatively affect your communicating competency.

What is a "structured" interview?

A structured interview is an interview with a fixed duration (typically 30, 40, or 50 minutes) and a fixed number of predefined questions. In a structured interview, all the candidates get the same questions, or at least questions about the same subjects or situations. Both the general competency based interview and the field interview in EPSO are structured interviews.

In comparison with non-structured interviews, the structured ones have the big advantage that they are more objective, and that the candidates are compared on well-defined criteria. The interviewers have little or no leeway to direct the candidate in one or another direction. This does not prevent them from asking follow-up questions but these are intended to help the candidate, not to influence their answers, or to test their resilience, for example.

I have little or no professional experience, so how can I tell them about my behaviour as a professional in the general competency based interview?

For those competitions where no professional experience is required (AD5 generalists, for example) you can use examples of your behaviour from your academic career, social activities, volunteering, or even your private family life.

I have never been in charge of other people, so how can I tell them about my leadership competency?

The leadership competency is not so much about your experience in leading or steering people but more about how you influence, motivate, and inspire other people. If you really have no experience in a professional setting you should still be able to find examples from other areas of your life, such as a project at school, youth camp, sports club, volunteering and the like.

Is the score of my talent screener used to calculate my score at the Assessment Centre?

No. The talent screener (TS) is just a pre-selection tool; consider it as an "alternative CV" for the use of the jury to filter out those candidates with the highest potential. The real assessment of your professional competencies is done in the Assessment Centre (field interview, specific exercises).

Once you are invited to the Assessment Centre we advise you to have a closer look at the scores of your TS, and try to understand why they are what they are. Especially when the score for a particular question is lower than what you had expected, you should try to think of a better way of explaining your educational or professional experience during the field interview. And since the field interview is a structured interview you should prepare an answer for all the questions, even the ones where you said "No" in the TS, or received a very low score.

This said, do not forget that the interviewers in the field interview will have your TS (and all the other information you gave during the application process) at their disposal, so that they can cross-check what you say during the interview with what you have written in the TS. But they will not base their scores in the interview on the scores from the TS.

I just had my Assessment Centre, how long will it take before I know the results?

In order to be able to calculate your score for the AC the jury needs to have both the (partial) scores of the written part (in most cases the case study) and the oral part of the AC. Typically, the written part takes place before the oral, and – this is important – it is a different group of people doing the scoring, which means that both processes can run in parallel, simultaneously. In any case, the (preliminary) reserve list can only be established once all the candidates have done their AC. On their website EPSO announces the period during which the AC takes place, so you can easily find out when exactly they can – theoretically – start working on the reserve list. Then add 2-3 months to the publication in the Official Journal and you will have an idea of when the results will be made public.

You will, however, probably be informed earlier, because you have the right to remove your name from the public list (maybe because you don't want your current employer to know) and of course they have to give the rejected candidates the opportunity to file a complaint or a request for review.

Once the AC is finished, the jury still has to write the competency passports for all the candidates who took part in the AC, even those who won't end up on the reserve list. This is a rather tedious job, because the observations they made during the various tests may be contradictory, so the texts have to be consolidated in order to have a coherent match with the scores (i.e. the average of the scores obtained for the various tests). This of course takes some time, and explains the relatively long waiting time.

What is a competency passport?

A competency passport is a written report of how you were perceived during the Assessment Centre. It typically includes your scores (for all the competencies, including those in the field), the totals, and whether you made the pass marks or not. It will normally NOT contain how you performed as compared with the other candidates in your AC; this information will be sent to you in a separate letter.

Besides the scores, the jury will also give you some textual information about the positive indicators they have observed for the various competencies and, if applicable, where they think there is room for improvement from your side.

You should not consider the competency passport an absolute and definitive judgement; it is only a snapshot of how you were perceived by that specific jury on that given day in the AC. Remember that it was a competition, trying to identify the best candidates from a group of already very good candidates. If you are not on the reserve list it does not mean that you are a bad candidate: others were simply (considered by the jury to be) better.

The competency passport is a tool for your personal development, a tool to help you better understand your strengths and weaker points. Consider it as a token of appreciation from the jury, and EPSO, for all the efforts you have made to go through this gruelling procedure.

You can of course put your competency passport in an annex to your CV or motivation letter when you apply for another job, even outside the EU administration. It is definitely worth more than an endless list of recommendations from previous employers, as it is obvious that you would never put a negative reference in your CV. EPSO, on the other hand, is considered as an objective third party, and this means a lot.

I am on a reserve list, what's next?

Being on a reserve list is not the end of the story. Instead another, very different, type of competition starts, which is much like a real job hunt in the private sector.

The first thing to do is to update your CV on the EPSO portal, and keep it up-to-date as you go along. Besides your competency passport, potential recruiters will inevitably first have a look at your CV before they decide to ask you for a job interview.

Once you are on a reserve list you will get access to the internally published vacancies via your EPSO account. You should proactively consult these lists, and not just wait for a recruiter to call you or send you an email.

In any case, it is definitely worth being proactive and contact heads of unit in areas you are targeting for employment. They may have a vacancy that was not published yet.

What is the validity period of a reserve list?

Apart from the AD5 generalist competition, most competitions are organised on an ad hoc basis, meaning only when a real need has been identified. This means that for most competitions the validity period will extend over several years (3-4). In contrast, AD5 generalist reserve lists are initially only valid for just one year, since there's a competition every year. However, in practice, because of the needs of the institutions, the validity of reserve lists is frequently extended, and EPSO will publish this information in the Official Journal.

How "real" is the Assessment Centre? Can assessors truly evaluate you in a single day?

The Assessment Centre method is "as good as it gets" in terms of selecting candidates for posts and roles in large organisations like the EU. It is a good trade-off between selecting the "best possible" candidates and giving everybody a fair chance to compete, for a reasonable cost. Of course, the selection process in EPSO is not perfect, but no other method is. Assessment Centres are considered to be "best practice" in the field of corporate recruiting and selection.

Am I being evaluated while at EPSO's premises other than during the exercises?

No. You are only "observed" during the formal parts of the AC, in other words while doing the various exercises. This means that you have a perfect – and totally legitimate

– opportunity to get to know the other candidates, and socialise with them. This is a particularly interesting opportunity to prepare – for example – for the group exercise.

There are no cameras to observe your behaviour outside the exercise rooms, and even the exercises – or interviews – are not recorded; the only records that will remain in your file are the notes and observations made by the assessors. This does not mean of course that you can be rude or impolite towards others taking part.

How can the assessors ensure that they are not biased when evaluating me?

Before they are admitted to a jury, all members have to sign a declaration in which they pledge to keep the confidentiality of the proceedings and that they will withdraw from the observation of those candidates where there might be a potential conflict of interest (for example, because a candidate has worked for them or is a relative).

It is also the case that, for example for the GCBI, the interviewers are not allowed to consult the application form, CV, or results from previous tests (case study, talent screener) before they start the interview. The reason for this is to avoid personal biases during the interview.

Of course, the assessors are only human beings, with their own flaws and prejudices. To balance out personal biases it is therefore a standard procedure to have every competency – for all the candidates – assessed by (at least) four people. Therefore the score that will appear on your competency passport is effectively the result of observation by (at least) four different individuals, thus creating a "level playing field" for all the candidates.

The president of the competition and the permanent members will do everything that is humanly possible to guarantee fair treatment for everybody, but – if you doubt this happened in your case – you can always file a complaint or launch an appeal procedure. This is your legal right, and nobody can blame you for doing so.

If I speak a lot or I'm very shy, does it impact my score?

There is no objective reason why shy – or introverted – people should be scored differently than outspoken – or extraverted – individuals. Both personality traits have their place in every organisation or even in every position within an organisation.

Of course being shy or tacit is not the same as being non-assertive. Assertiveness is an aspect of resilience; good employees – and officials – stand up for their ideas and values and defend these in dealing with colleagues, supervisors and stakeholders. Being assertive is a matter of self-respect and respect for others.

Should I "be myself", or should I try to act in the way that is "expected" of me?

The best advice we can give here is to be yourself as much as you can. Do not try to play a role or fool the assessors into a different perception of who you really are. It is in nobody's interest, not even yours, because you might end up in a job for which you are not suited and you will be unhappy as a result.

What happens if there are only a few candidates who speak the same language as I do? Is there any interpretation during the AC?

We have indeed heard of group exercises with interpretation, but this is for sure a very exceptional situation. You will normally be in a group where everybody has the same "language 2" and participating in the same competition.

Is there a clock in the room for the oral presentation and the group exercise?

Yes, indeed more than one. The funny thing here is that these clocks are not necessarily perfectly synchronised, so if you pick a clock, stick to it, and avoid being confused.

Is there a clock in the room during the interviews?

Yes, there are clocks in the room, but we would advise you to let the interviewers take care of the time management. For the GCBI, when preparing, make sure you can answer the questions in less than 90 seconds. For the field interview, since you cannot anticipate the follow-up questions, just try to remember as many details as possible of your past career and don't worry about the timing at all.

What if the assessors ask me a question I really have no answer for?

In our experience this is rather exceptional, especially when you are well prepared for the Assessment Centre (i.e. the GCBI). Have a look at Annex 4 of this book, and make sure that you have an answer in mind for all the anchors. You will normally not be short of answers during the interview.

It could happen that you didn't really understand the question you were asked (in other words, you couldn't establish the link between the question and the anchors in Annex 4). In this case, don't be afraid to ask the assessors to reformulate the question. This will give you some more reflection time, and it will probably trigger the properly prepared answer in your mind.

Should I try to mingle or network with other candidates during the day?

Yes, as much as you can. This will make you feel more at ease, because after all you are all in the same boat and it can be a relief to share your worries with others. What is more, mingling with the other candidates for your group exercise will also give you the opportunity to get on the same page as to how to behave during that exercise, and to coordinate the group effort.

We even advise to have lunch together. This will make you feel more at ease during the group exercise and behave more like a group of colleagues (knowing each other) rather than some strangers you only met when entering the meeting room.

Are travel costs reimbursed?

EPSO does not contribute to any travel expenses incurred by your participation in any computer-based tests or preliminary/intermediate tests (i.e. multiple choice question tests, e-tray exercise and translation tests).

Candidates invited to the case study or to a written test in the field having an address of residence in a country outside the EU are entitled to claim a contribution towards their travel expenses if these tests are part of the Assessment Centre (please refer to your Notice of Competition).

When you participate to the Assessment Centre tests you may, if you are eligible, request a contribution for your travel expenses, but not a reimbursement of all expenses actually incurred. In addition, as regards subsistence costs, a contribution is foreseen only if the various tests at the Assessment Centre take place over two consecutive days or are separated by a maximum of three days. You will not receive any contribution to your accommodation costs for the night before or the night after the Assessment Centre.

As a general rule, the address of residence indicated in your EPSO account will be used as the basis for the calculation.

Annex 10 Glossary

People within the EU institutions and in the media dealing with EU affairs often use "Eurojargon" words and expressions that they alone understand. In the field of EU careers, it can be very confusing to the general public, which is why the following "plain language guide" was created.

Please note: this glossary does not include purely technical or legal terms, or jargon used in only one language. Neither is it legally binding and it is purely for information purposes.

Abstract Reasoning

One of the tests in the pre-selection phase of the EPSO exams (or for Specialists, it may be required in the Assessment Centre itself). Using a series of images, this test requires candidates to identify which one should be next in the row, based on an inherent logic between the presented images. Generally, there are 10 abstract reasoning questions in a competition, and the allocated time is 10 minutes.

Accuracy Test

One of the tests in the pre-selection phase of the Assistant exams for EU careers. This test requires candidates to identify, based on a table and various icons, mistakes, errors, typos or other "inaccuracies" in a control line under heavy time-pressure. The more inaccuracies that can be identified during the allocated 6 minutes, the higher score the candidate gets.

Administrators (AD)

European permanent officials selected by the European Personnel Selection Office (EPSO) are categorised into Administrator (AD) and Assistant (AST) groups. Administrators must have a college or university degree issued on the basis of at least 3 years of studies, and they must have passed a selection competition to be given an open-ended permanent contract.

Admission Test – see *Pre-selection tests*

Age Limit

There is no age limit to apply for EU careers and jobs; however, the maximum age is determined by the retirement limits provided by the Staff Regulations of EU officials, which is 65 years (or in some special cases and on an individual basis, even before that).

The minimum age is not determined either given the fact that to meet the formal criteria, candidates are certain to be at least 18 years old.

Analysis and Problem Solving

This competency is one of the 7+1 that EPSO evaluates in candidates via the Assessment Centre tests. To achieve a good score in this competency, candidates must demonstrate they can quickly understand complex files (e.g. in the case study), are able to propose viable solutions and practical approaches to the matters outlined therein, and be able to separate key elements and information from irrelevant data.

Assessment Centre

A common method of personnel selection in the public and private sector that has proven to be one of the best ways to find suitable employees for a given position. EPSO introduced Assessment Centres (ACs) in 2010 as part of the reformed EU recruitment system so that candidates are evaluated on the basis of their competencies instead of solely on the basis of their specific knowledge. Assessment Centres are used for all profiles including Administrators, Assistants, Linguists and Specialists on all levels: entry level, head of unit and even directors or director-generals. The Assessment Centre is usually held in Brussels (travel and accommodation costs are reimbursed) where a number of trained assessors, who are usually seconded EU officials from various directorates and EU institutions, evaluate candidates in the different exercises during a full day. The tests depend on the given competition one is sitting, nevertheless they generally include a structured interview, a group exercise, an oral presentation (AD only), a case study and in some cases, a professional skills test or translation. For those Specialist exams where the number of applicants has not reached a certain threshold (e.g. 600 applicants), the psychometric tests comprising abstract, verbal and numerical reasoning tests are held as part of the Assessment Centre instead of being held a few weeks or months earlier.

Assistants (AST)

European permanent officials selected by the European Personnel Selection Office (EPSO) are categorised into Administrator (AD) and Assistant (AST) groups. Within the career grading structure (and pay scales) there is overlap between AD and AST positions. Assistants must have a high school or vocational school qualification and may or may not possess professional experience.

For AST3, however, professional experience or higher-level qualifications are required as there are AST3 positions covering financial management, project management, communication or other related issues. AST-SC (SC standing for Secretary) is a sub-category for more basic office jobs.

Case Study

One of the exercises in the EPSO Assessment Centre for Administrators, Specialists and some Assistants is to complete a complex case study task. Candidates are given a comprehensive background file, which they need to quickly read through and answer 3-4 open-ended questions.

The answers need to be written on paper, or more recently, on a computer screen, and reflect the candidate's understanding of the data, issues at stake, ideas and positions that are outlined in the background file.

One of the competencies being assessed in the case study is their domain-specific knowledge (which can be demonstrated by adding many references to EU institutions, procedures, technical terms, industry jargon, expressions and concepts that reflect the candidate's knowledge of his or her field), along with the analysis and problem solving, prioritising and organising skills.

Communication skills are also assessed, given the written expression nature of the exercise.

CAST Permanent

CAST stands for Contract Agents for Specific Tasks. Contract Agents (sometimes called Contractual Agents) are recruited to do manual or administrative support service tasks or to provide additional capacity in specialised fields where an insufficient number of officials with the required skills are available.

Permanent means that there is no deadline to apply to a CAST profile, it is an open-ended selection method where candidates keep their successful results for a pre-determined period of time.

Communicating

One of the 7+1 competencies that are measured and evaluated in EU competition candidates via the Assessment Centre's various exercises such as the oral presentation, the case study and the structured interview.

Competencies

The generic name for the 7+1 skills and abilities that are measured throughout the EPSO Assessment Centre's various tests, such as the group exercise, case study and others. Competencies can be defined as "groupings of related behaviours, traits and motivations that each predict successful performance in a particular aspect of a role". Competencies in an EU context are the following: analysis and problem solving, communicating, delivering quality and results, learning and development, prioritising and organising, resilience, and working with others. Administrators are evaluated on one more competency, namely that of leadership (making 7 + 1).

Competency Based Interview

This is referred to by EPSO as the general competency based interview, to distinguish it from the interview in the field. It is sometimes still referred to as the structured interview, though this is confusing as the interview in the field is also a structured interview. It is not to be confused with a classic job interview in which there is no formal structure. In the GCBI candidates are asked questions about past situations in their life to demonstrate to which level they possess (or do not possess) a given competency from the 7+1 competencies identified by EPSO, usually focusing on resilience, leadership, working with others, learning and development (sometimes also delivering quality and results and communication).

Assessors tell candidates which competency is being tested so they can adapt their answers accordingly. Given that the style and type of questions that are asked are relatively known, it is possible to prepare very well for this exam.

Computer Based Tests (CBT)

Since 2010, EPSO has been administering all pre-selection tests on a computer in order to enhance the reliability, efficiency and accuracy of the exams. This also ensures that candidates are assessed on an equal and non-discriminatory basis and there is no national, gender or other bias in the selection methods. For generalist competitions (Administrators, Assistants, Linguists) EPSO uses computer-based tests for the case study exercise and/or for the professional skills tests as well, and pre-selection tests are required for most Specialist competitions too.

The downside of computer based tests is that candidates cannot highlight, circle or mark parts of the question, though for numerical reasoning tests an on-screen and a physical calculator is offered.

Competency Passport

A written document that EPSO issues after the selection procedure is finished. It includes a full evaluation of the candidate's competencies based on the matrix EPSO has created. For successful candidates, it becomes part of their EU official personal profile so that future training needs can be planned accordingly. For unsuccessful candidates, it serves as a benchmark report so they can draw individual conclusions and improve where needed.

Computer Literacy Test

This test is part of the Assistant (usually AST-SC, secretary) exam in which candidates are asked questions on their knowledge of Microsoft Office software. This generally includes Excel, Word and PowerPoint, along with other computer skills such as online awareness, internet security basics, e-mail rules and Outlook literacy, keyboard shortcuts and similar items.

Contract Agents (CA)

Contract Agents are recruited in order to reinforce capacities both in specific areas of expertise and in support functions and to work in areas where a long term requirement has not yet been defined. To some degree contract agents have come to be used to substitute for permanent officials.

Contract staff positions are available for a wide range of jobs, requiring different levels of qualifications. They are divided into four function groups:

- I. manual and administrative support-service tasks
- II. clerical or secretarial tasks, office management and other equivalent tasks
- III. executive tasks, drafting, accountancy and other equivalent technical tasks
- IV. administrative, advisory, linguistic and equivalent technical tasks.

Minimum qualifications required for the engagement of Contract Agents are as follows:

(a) in function group I: successful completion of compulsory education.

(b) in function group II:

- a post-secondary education attested by a diploma, or
- a secondary education attested by a diploma giving access to post-secondary education, and appropriate professional experience of three years. The secondary education diploma giving access to post-secondary education may be replaced by a certificate of adequate professional training of not less than three years on condition that there was no similar professional training giving access to higher education at the time it was issued or,
- successful completion of intermediate education plus two years relevant supplementary specialised training plus five years' appropriate professional experience.

(c) in function group III:

- a post-secondary education attested by a diploma, or
- a secondary education attested by a diploma giving access to post-secondary education and appropriate professional experience of three years.

(d) in function group IV: completed university studies of at least three years attested by a diploma and appropriate professional experience of at least one year.

Only diplomas and certificates that have been awarded in EEA Member countries or that are the subject of equivalence certificates issued by the authorities in the said Member countries shall be taken into consideration.

Contract Agents are employed for a fixed maximum period of 6 years, often with a shorter initial but renewable contract of 6 to 12 months, depending on the type of job. In some Agencies, Offices Representations and Delegations the contract can lead to an indefinite contract.

Delivering Quality and Results

One of the competencies EPSO evaluates in the Assessment Centre. It is mostly in the case study, e-tray exercise or the oral presentation that this competency is tested: candidates must demonstrate that they are not only able to identify a problem or analyse a complex file but can also come up with actionable, specific proposals or plans as a result of their exercise.

E-tray Exercise (or In-tray Exercise)

The electronic, computerised version of the in-tray exercise simulates a work environment on a computer where e-mails need to be read, sorted and responded to in a timely manner. This test is used for Assistant (AST) exams in the Assessment Centre phase. For the first time, in 2015 EPSO also introduced the e-tray as an "intermediate test" stage between pre-selection and the Assessment Centre in the generalist Administrator competition.

EPSO and EU Institutions

The European Personnel Selection Office (EPSO) is the centralised selection (but not recruiting) arm of all EU institutions and bodies such as the European Commission, the European Parliament, the Council of Ministers, the European Court of Auditors, the European Ombudsman, the European Economic and Social Committee, the Committee of the Regions, and the European Court of Justice. As a general rule, it does not run selection procedures for EU agencies located in the various Member States (though there are exceptions from time to time), nor is it involved with selection for the European Central Bank or the European Investment Bank.

Field Interview

The field interview, or interview in the field, is only used for Specialist competitions. It is used to assess candidates' specific competencies in their field of expertise and validates and explores the information already given in the talent screener. As with the competency based interview, this is a structured interview in that it follows a set pattern and the same questions are asked of all the candidates.

General competency based interview – see *Competency based interview*

Group Exercise

The group exercise is one of the tasks in the Assessment Centre that is compulsory in all profiles. This means that groups of (typically 6) candidates are required to take part in a simulation based on a background file that all of them must read and then try to come to a conclusion on within 50 or so minutes.

Assessors are not part of the group exercise and they only observe the individual behaviours, leadership, analytical and communication skills of each participant.

Intermediate test – see *E-tray Exercise*

Internal Competition

Occasionally EPSO and EU institutions may announce internal competitions in which only existing Administrators, Assistants and temporary agents (but not contract agents) who are already working in an EU institution can take part.

The goal is to help in the career mobility of those who may be eligible for higher positions, or temporary agents who wish to obtain a permanent employment contract. These exams follow the same rules as any other set by EPSO and the Staff Regulations.

In-tray Exercise – see *E-tray Exercise*

Language Requirements

Citizenship and languages are disconnected and they are not linked in any way, except for enlargement-related exams where specific citizenship and language rules may apply. In some other cases the competition's specific language profile automatically determines the required first language (e.g. compulsory French as the first language for translator exams in the French language), but this is independent of citizenship (for EU citizens). In other instances candidates are free to choose their first language (Language 1) as long as it is an official EU language.

The second language (Language 2) is a candidate's first foreign language and it is the language in which the Assessment Centre takes place. Exceptions are for some Linguist exams (and sometimes for certain Assistant exams) where the second language is usually specified along with the third language (if required at all).

Laureates

The term laureates refers to those candidates who have been placed on a reserve list as a result of their success in an EPSO competition and now are "recruitable" by any EU institution until the end of the validity period of the reserve list.

Lawyer-linguists

Lawyer-linguists are always Administrator (AD) level officials and may be recruited at a higher level (AD7 instead of AD5) to attract more candidates, with the condition being that they must stay in their position for at least 3 or more years without being able to transfer to other EU institutions or positions. A law degree is required, along with knowledge of at least two or three languages at a very high level so that they can carry out translations and revisions from multiple source languages. Lawyer-linguists generally work for the Council of Ministers, the European Court of Justice or the European Parliament, though some other institutions may employ a few of them as well.

Leadership

Leadership is one of the competencies that is assessed by EPSO, but only for Administrator (AD) roles and not for Assistants. Leadership does not mean a managerial skill but rather the ability to deliver results, be proactive, mobilise a team or co-workers behind a specific goal, and make sure there is no deviation from plans without prior consent. A certain level of social adaptability is also needed.

Learning and Development

This competency is one of the 7+1 that assessors evaluate candidates on in the Assessment Centre. To achieve a good score in this competency, candidates must demonstrate they are able and willing to learn new topics, issues and subjects, and provide examples from their career or personal experience of situations where they faced a challenge created by an unfamiliar issue and they mastered the issue, succeeded and developed personally.

Linguists

Linguist is the common name for translators and interpreters; however, lawyer-linguists are considered as Specialists given their required degree in law. Linguist exams are announced each year in June or July for different language combinations, but the exam they need to pass is by and large the same as for any other Administrator profile. Linguists are always AD level officials once recruited and they can move to other non-linguistic positions after the initial 2-3 years.

National Quota

In the EU institutions, there is no national quota for Member State citizens; however, there is a requirement in the Staff Regulations providing that a "proportional representation" is required.

This means that each Directorate General has benchmark figures on the nationality of its staff and aims to recruit new officials in a way that meets this requirement.

Notice of Competition (NoC)

Every EU competition starts with a Notice of Competition, which is the official and authentic document in which the details and conditions of the exam are provided.

The NoC is published in the Official Journal of the EU (also online) and it provides the number of people EPSO plans to place on the reserve lists, the language requirements, the degree/school certificate or other qualification requirements and many other details.

Numerical Reasoning

One of the tests in the pre-selection phase of the EU exams (or for Specialists, it may be required in the Assessment Centre itself). Using a table with semi-complex data and multiple cells, it requires basic calculation (adding, subtracting, multiplying, dividing), occasionally also percentage calculation. Generally, there are 10 numerical reasoning questions in a competition, and the allocated time is 20 minutes.

Official Journal (OJ)

Published by the EU's Publication Office in Luxembourg, it is the authentic document in which all administrative and legislative documents are published every weekday. In the EU career context, the Notice of Competition is also published in the Official Journal given its legal nature.

Open Competition

Every EU competition that EPSO publishes on its external website is by default open to anyone who meets the formal criteria (including EU officials who may wish to apply to jump to a higher grade, or temporary agents who wish to "finalise" their contract). EPSO also occasionally organises internal competitions (see entry above).

Oral Presentation

One of the exercises in the EPSO Assessment Centre for generalist Administrators is to make a presentation of up to 10 minutes based on a background file, and then be ready to answer questions for another 8-10 minutes.

Specialists are not usually required to do this exercise given their relatively different profile. In most exams, it measures such competencies as resilience, communication, analysis and problem solving, and delivering quality and results.

Pre-selection Tests

Pre-selection tests refer to the exams that EU career competition participants are required to sit to be considered for the Assessment Centre. For most exams, pre-selection tests are required given the large number of applicants. However, when the number of applicants (mostly for Specialist exams) is lower than approximately 600, or alternatively 8 times the number of people EPSO intends to invite to the Assessment Centre, EPSO does not require these tests to be taken, though there is still a pre-screening in the form of a so-called talent screener.

Typically, the pre-selection tests include abstract, verbal and numerical reasoning tests and a situational judgment test, and for Assistants, there are extra tests such as accuracy and precision, and prioritising and organising. The language of the pre-selection tests is Language 1, except for the situational judgment test (used only selectively in Administrator competitions), which is usually conducted in Language 2.

Reasonable accommodation(s)

In providing reasonable accommodation(s) EPSO aims at ensuring that candidates with disabilities and specific needs can fully express their competencies and compete on equal basis with other candidates. Providing reasonable accommodation(s) is a way to remove potential obstacles presented by individual's disability or medical condition, without modifying the nature or level of the qualification that is being assessed.

Recruitment

Recruitment is the final phase of the selection procedure and it is NOT handled by EPSO (they only deal with the selection of potential new officials – they don't themselves recruit). It is up to the specific Directorate General or EU institution to decide whom they wish to invite for a final interview from among those who have been placed on a reserve list.

Recruitment happens after candidates face a "classic" free-form interview (as opposed to a "structured" interview, see below) in which they are asked questions on their knowledge in the specific field, motivation and personal profile. A medical examination is required and if all goes well, a job offer is extended to the candidate who then becomes an EU official, with a 9-month probation period.

Reimbursement of Costs

In order to provide equal chances for all EU citizens, EPSO reimburses travel and hotel costs for those who need to travel to Brussels to the Assessment Centre. The reimbursement may take a few weeks but it is a right that all candidates have once they are invited to the Assessment Centre.

For the pre-selection exams, no reimbursement is possible (even if a candidate has to travel to another country where an exam centre is located; though each EU Member State has at least one exam centre, the above situation may happen in other parts of the world).

Remote online testing

Remote online testing allows candidates to sit the tests at home, in the office etc. without needing to travel to an EPSO testing centre. Remote testing takes place via online video-conferencing. All technical details are provided in due time, including instructions on how to test the connection before the actual day of testing. Candidates must check their EPSO account at least twice a week.

Reserve List

After passing all stages of an EPSO competition, successful candidates (also called "laureates") are placed on a so-called reserve list.

This list is published in the Official Journal of the EU and everyone on it can be recruited by any EU institution for a permanent post. Each reserve list has a validity of 1-3 years, depending on the competition and also on when the next competition in the same field is due to be published.

The validity can be extended in the event that there are still candidates on the list, based on the decision of EPSO.

Resilience

One of the 7+1 competencies that are measured and evaluated in EU competition candidates via the Assessment Centre.

Resilience refers to the "ability to cope under pressure" and "maintain an effective performance under heavy workload". It can also refer to the ability to handle "organisational or administrative stress".

The most common exercises in which this competency is tested are the oral presentation and the structured interview. The most important aspect of resilience in the structured interview is when stress management or the efficient handling of a frustration can be demonstrated by reference to a specific, unexpected event instead of talking in general terms about a prolonged period of heavy workload.

Scientist and Scientific Jobs

EPSO from time to time publishes open competitions for scientists and scientific jobs as Specialist exams. These always include a "talent screener" in which candidates are required to state their professional background and prove their profile's relevance to the job. Other than that, candidates are still required to go through an Assessment Centre and in most cases they also need to take abstract, verbal and numerical reasoning tests.

The most likely place of employment is in DG Research of the European Commission, or the Joint Research Centre of the Commission, which has offices in several EU countries.

Selection Board

A Selection Board is an independent body set up for each competition that EPSO announces and administers. Legally speaking, each Selection Board acts on its own and it is responsible for the proper management and supervision of a given competition.

The Selection Board can also check the pre-selection tests that candidates are required to sit, and in most cases it is the Selection Board members who act as assessors during the Assessment Centre.

It is also the Selection Boards who decide on the eligibility of candidates' work experience and qualifications. Some members are from EPSO and others are EU officials who volunteer to become members of a Selection Board. There is usually a staff representative and/or a trade union member in each board, along with an administrative assistant from EPSO who is formally speaking not part of the board.

Situational Competency Based Interview (SCBI)

The SCBI tests a number of general competencies by asking candidates how they would react in a specific situation. It consists of a one-to-one meeting with a trained interviewer who provides additional information during the interview, according to a semi-structured script. Approximately two to three weeks before the SCBI testing period, candidates receive a written assignment and background information to help them prepare. In the assignment, candidates will be asked to replace a colleague and assume responsibility for various tasks and situations to be discussed during the interview. Additional situations, not based on the assignment, will also be included. Candidates are allowed to consult the written assignment and background information during the interview.

Specialists

In EPSO competitions, we can distinguish between generalists, specialists and linguists, though in administrative terms there is no such distinction at the time of recruitment or employment.

Competitions that are not scheduled on a regular annual basis and require specific experience in a particular field are considered specialist exams. As explained in Chapter 8 such competitions have recently come to dominate.

For Specialists there is always a talent screener in which work experience, academic qualifications and other factors are carefully checked to make sure that only candidates with a fully relevant profile are allowed to take part in the Assessment Centre. The Assessment Centre involves a mix of testing of general and specific competencies.

Staff Regulations

EU officials, temporary agents and contract agents are bound by the Staff Regulations – the official "labour code" setting out the rules of their employment, obligations, rights, pension, salary and any other matter concerning their relation with the EU institution or body they are working for.

The reason for the Staff Regulations' existence is the independence these "agents" or "servants" enjoy from any governmental or other entity: they are not bound by the labour laws of any EU Member State given their only affiliation is to the EU institution that employs them.

Structured Interview

Both the general competency based interview (for all) and the field interview (just for specialists) are, strictly speaking, structured interviews as they both follow a scenario and questions that are chosen from a list of pre-selected questions in an organised manner. However, the term "structured interview" is sometimes used as shorthand specifically for the competency based interview.

Talent Screener

The talent screener is an online system in which candidates provide self-declared answers regarding their work experience, specific skills or knowledge (e.g. work experience in the field of environmental impact assessment etc.), which is then evaluated individually for each candidate by the Selection Board of the given EU exam.

Translators

This is one of the profiles in the Administrator (AD) open competitions, though in some cases Assistant (AST) or contract agent (CAST) exams may have translation-related profiles announced as well. Translators are usually required to have a degree but there is no obligation to have this in translation or language studies, so as to ensure that candidates with a broad range of profiles are eligible. All EU institutions employ translators, and many work in Luxembourg for the European Parliament or the Council of Ministers in Brussels.

Verbal Reasoning

One of the tests in the pre-selection phase of the EU exams (for Specialists, it may be required in the Assessment Centre itself). Using a short paragraph of text on virtually any topic, candidates are required to choose from 4 or 5 answer options the one that fully matches the statements in the original text.

There is always only one correct answer because other options may contain insufficient information or false statements. EPSO allows candidates to sit the verbal reasoning tests in their Language 1.

Working with Others

One of the 7+1 competencies that are measured and evaluated in EPSO competition candidates via the Assessment Centre's various exercises such as the oral presentation, the case study and the group exercise. This competency requires candidates to demonstrate understanding of their team members, cooperation with colleagues and a generally positive attitude when tension arises within a group. It is best tested in the group exercise and the structured interview.